Dealing with Drug Abuse

Dealing with
Drug Abuse

A Report to the Ford Foundation

FOREWORD BY MCGEORGE BUNDY

THE DRUG ABUSE SURVEY PROJECT

Patricia M. Wald, Co-chairman

Peter Barton Hutt, Co-chairman

James V. DeLong, Executive Director

Edgar May   Annette Abrams

Peter A. Wilson   Peter B. Goldberg

John F. Holahan   Paul A. Henningsen

Andrew T. Weil, M.D.

PRAEGER PUBLISHERS
New York • Washington • London

PRAEGER PUBLISHERS
111 Fourth Avenue, New York, N.Y. 10003, U.S.A.
5, Cromwell Place, London SW7 2JL, England

Published in the United States of America in 1972
by Praeger Publishers, Inc.

Library of Congress Catalog Card Number: 77-189472

Printed in the United States of America

Contents

v

Foreword

by McGeorge Bundy

This report grew out of an effort by the Ford Foundation to understand the massive and complex problem of drug abuse in the United States and to determine the most effective ways in which the Foundation might contribute to efforts to deal with the problem.

Like many institutions working in such fields as education and poverty, we encountered the growing blight of drug abuse increasingly in the 1960's. The Foundation made a number of grants to projects that dealt with drug abuse as an aspect of a larger problem, as in work with high school students, faculty, and parents to understand and overcome the alienation of youth. As drug abuse increased, however, the Foundation considered whether it might undertake a larger program. The study that led to this report, undertaken in mid-1970, was the first step in that consideration.

The second important step was to join with three other foundations that have shared our concern with drug abuse—the Carnegie Corporation, the Commonwealth Fund, and the Henry J. Kaiser Family Foundation—in financing one of the principal recommendations of the report, namely, the establishment of an independent national Drug Abuse Council. The four foundations have now committed substantial funds for the first several years of the Council's work.

The functions of the Drug Abuse Council will include

- Analysis of the development and results of public policies in the drug-abuse field
- Dissemination to the public of accurate data on the causes, extent, and treatment of drug abuse

- Promotion of needed research
- Synthesis and distribution of available information in research and treatment
- Evaluation of treatment and education programs

Details of the Council's composition and plans are expected to be announced shortly after this manuscript goes to press.

The report leading to the establishment of the Council—the work of an outstanding independent task force of lawyers, scientists, and other investigators—identified four major problem areas in the drug-abuse field: heroin addiction in urban ghettoes; drug experimentation by the young; overuse of legal stimulants and tranquilizers; and the use of drugs to control deviant behavior, especially among children.

The task-force report was intended principally for the Ford Foundation's guidance. Yet, the scope and quality of the work were such that the Foundation shared the first draft, in December, 1970, with legal, scientific, and governmental authorities active in efforts to control and prevent drug abuse. The reaction to the report was strongly affirmative. The report was praised for its thorough, clear, and sober analysis, and a number of authorities urged the Foundation to make it available to a wider audience. Accordingly, the Foundation asked the staff of the developing Drug Abuse Council to bring up to date those sections dealing with aspects of the problem in which there had been substantial change since the first draft was prepared. We believe that this revised, expanded, and updated report is both a forerunner and the first product of the Drug Abuse Council. As such, we believe it is a promising harbinger of other contributions the Council may make, both in understanding this spreading danger to American society and in helping to curb it.

We hope that the report will be useful to the public at large as well as to specialists, for the drug-abuse problem is so broad and complex that effective efforts to overcome it will demand the understanding and support of as many Americans as possible.

Preface

In April, 1970, the Ford Foundation asked us to undertake a broad survey of the drug-abuse problem in this country and to report back by the end of the year on what activities private foundations might usefully undertake in this field. During May to December, 1970, we had the opportunity to review the drug-abuse field, both through a study of the literature and through extensive interviews. The report was completed by December 1, 1970, and submitted to several foundations for their consideration.

We did not anticipate making any startling new discoveries in this field, and, in fact, we have made none. We cannot say that there is a magic solution to the problem of drug abuse. Rapid or remarkable results in this area cannot be promised. Alleviation of local and national drug-abuse problems will come, in our judgment, through a slow and painful process of social change and accommodation. Insofar as our report can help to establish the mechanisms by which such change and accommodation may begin, and even be accelerated, it will have more than served its intended purpose.

The report is reproduced here without change. Although we have added occasional footnotes to indicate significant developments since December, 1970, we have concluded that any attempt to take note of every factual change would be both futile and unnecessary. Suffice it to say that developments during the past year have only underscored the thrust of the original report.

Appendixes to the main report were developed largely by the project staff both during 1970 and after the report itself was completed and submitted to the foundations, in order to record some of the more detailed information gathered in the course of the survey. These staff papers may be considered current as of about September, 1971. Although they do not always represent a consensus of the project participants, they do make a useful contribution to knowledge and discussion in the field.

It is not possible to name all of those to whom we are indebted for assistance with the survey and the report. We spoke to hundreds of people throughout the country, all of whom generously provided time and material. The trustees, officers, and staff of the Ford Foundation provided complete freedom for this inquiry, together with ample financial support. We are especially indebted to Mitchell Sviridoff and Thomas Wright for their personal involvement. The Carnegie Corporation, the Commonwealth Fund, and the Kaiser Foundation have been most encouraging in their consideration of the report, as have numerous other foundations and organizations.

We could not have undertaken the work involved in this survey or completed the report without the strong support of James V. DeLong, the only professional staff member who worked on the project from beginning to end. His tenacity in ferreting out the types of elusive facts on which any useful report must inevitably rely, and his detailed and repeated review of the work product have won him the respect of the entire drug-abuse field. We would also like to give special thanks to Peter Wilson, who was with the project during the first hectic period.

Substantial support in the form of time and resources was freely donated by the Washington law firm of Covington & Burling. We also wish to thank the support staff—Meg Gleason, Jacqueline Volpe, Angela Corley, Joan Henderson, Janine Yunker, and Lilly Smith—for their skill and patience in finding and keeping track of material and in preparing and revising endless drafts.

Finally, we are gratified by the announcement that the Drug Abuse Council proposed in the report has been established and is beginning operations. We wish its new President, Thomas E. Bryant, M.D., and the Chairman of its Board, Bethuel M. Webster, success in bringing this new venture to fruition.

PATRICIA M. WALD
PETER BARTON HUTT
Co-chairmen

Washington, D.C.
December, 1971

Dealing with Drug Abuse

The Drug Abuse Survey Project: Summary of Findings, Conclusions, and Recommendations

by Patricia M. Wald and Peter Barton Hutt

The Present Problem and Efforts to Control It • A More Promising Approach to Drug Abuse • The Drug Abuse Council

This report, which summarizes the results of the Drug Abuse Survey Project, is based upon extensive reading and numerous interviews with workers in the field throughout the country.

Part I describes the present drug-abuse problem in this country and what is currently being done to control it. Part II summarizes the project's views on a more promising approach to drug-abuse problems. Part III sets forth the project's recommendations for private foundation activity in this field.

Two preliminary observations are essential to this discussion. First, in many aspects of this field, important basic facts have not yet been determined and perhaps cannot be determined in the near future; conclusions, therefore, depend on fragmentary information and primarily on judgment. Because of the emotional and moral attitudes involved in drug issues, conclusions differ widely among individuals and are strongly and deeply held. Secondly, even where facts exist, experts in the field often disagree on their meaning and significance. We have found few areas in which there is not widespread disagreement.

As a result, in arriving at the project's conclusions and recommendations, we have relied strongly on the judgment of the Co-chairmen and the Executive Director. It should be understood that at least one recognized expert could readily be found to challenge, perhaps vehemently, virtually any statement we make or might make. It appears that there can be no such thing as consensus or a noncontroversial report on drug abuse.

THE PRESENT PROBLEM AND EFFORTS TO CONTROL IT

THE NATURE AND EXTENT OF DRUG ABUSE

Staff Report 1 describes the characteristics of the most common drugs of abuse. For purposes of this report, such socially accepted and legal drugs as alcohol and nicotine have been excluded, and "drug abuse" has been limited primarily to heroin, marijuana, stimulant and depressant drugs, and hallucinogens.

The effects of a drug, the pattern of drug use, the prognosis for the user, and the bases of social concern all vary widely depending on the drug used, the age and class of the user, and the circumstances. No categorization, therefore, is totally satisfactory. The four core problems, however, have been broadly delineated by many commentators as: (1) the use of heroin in urban poverty areas, (2) experimentation with a wide variety of drugs by the young, (3) the use of drugs by middle-aged and older persons as a form of quasi-self-medication, and (4) the use of drugs as a behavior-control device.

Heroin in Urban Poverty Areas. According to our best estimates, there were, as of November, 1970, approximately 150,000 to 250,000 active heroin addicts in the United States.[1] (Some estimates run as high as 300,000 heroin addicts in New York City and 600,000 nationally, but these figures have little support.) The addicts are heavily concentrated in the poorest areas of large metropolitan areas. Probably half live in New York, and 60 to 70 per cent of them are black, Puerto Rican, or Mexican-American. Almost 85 per cent are male.

These figures represent people who use heroin on a daily basis, injecting a dose every six to eight hours as the effect of the previous dose wears off. They may spend anywhere from $10 to $100 per day on heroin, depending on their dosage and tolerance, their economic ability to sustain the habit, the purity of the drug bought, and the price level of the city in which they live.

There is an additional, though unknown, population that uses heroin only occasionally, either alone or as part of a pattern of multiple drug use. The size of this group is a matter of conjecture and debate. Some experts believe that repetitive use of heroin leads inexorably to addiction, whereas others believe that there is a substantial number of intermittent users who do not become addicted.

It is not possible to resolve this issue definitively. It seems probable, however, that a large number of persons have experimented with heroin a few times without becoming addicted. Heroin is easily available in the slum areas of most major cities. Although a large habit is expensive, a single dose is cheap ($1 or less for a capsule containing about 1 mg. of heroin in Washington, D.C.), and the unit of sale in many places is so small that a neophyte can take it without much fear of an overdose. It seems likely that a large percentage of the young black males in any large urban lower-class area have tried heroin. The majority who have experimented with it have not become addicted. And, although the potency of heroin makes it difficult to believe that large numbers of intermittent users never become addicted, this possibility cannot be ruled out on the basis of present information.

Although heroin is a primary drug for the addict, multiple drug use is exceedingly common. According to some studies, between 40 and 60 per cent of the addicts use one of the amphetamines or barbiturates as a secondary drug on a regular basis. Cocaine, a strong nonaddictive stimulant, is also used widely.

The tremendous wave of concern about heroin that has swept the country appears to be caused primarily by the fear of crime associated with addiction. Heroin itself does not cause criminal behavior in any physiological or psychological sense, but the need to maintain an expensive habit often does. A heroin addict will do almost anything to obtain money to buy the drug. There is virtually no way in which a poor, black, unskilled youth can earn legally the $30 per day that is required for the average habit. To maintain his addiction, he can deal in drugs, engage in consensual crime, or steal. It is reasonable to estimate that addicts steal between $1 billion and $2 billion in merchandise per year. Estimates of thefts in New York City alone range from a low of $.25 billion to a high of $1.9 billion. There is some evidence that up to 50 per cent of property crimes in the major metropolitan areas with a serious heroin addiction problem are committed by addicts. On the other hand, there is evidence that most addicts engaged in crime before they became addicted. Addiction, therefore, cannot necessarily be regarded as the cause of a criminal life-style, although it unquestionably intensifies criminal activity.

A secondary cause of the current concern about heroin is the fear that it has, or will, spread throughout society. While heroin is undoubtedly now available in the suburbs, there is little evidence that it represents a substantial problem there. It remains largely a lower-class drug.

A third cause commonly cited for the concern about heroin is fear of the effects of the drug on the user. Actually, there is no proof that heroin itself causes any organic damage to the body or brain similar, for example, to the extensive damage caused by alcohol. Death through overdose has been attributed by medical experts to the fact that heroin is a powerful nervous-system suppressant that may cause respiration to cease when the dosage exceeds the individual's tolerance, or to the fact that some individuals may experience a severe allergic reaction to heroin.

It seems possible that many addicts would function normally if given a steady supply of good-quality drugs. The real harm to users is that they presently tend to become social dropouts, in that the illegal status of the drug causes them to spend all their time obtaining and using it. There seems little doubt that, if it were not for the fear of crime and the spread of heroin to the suburbs, most of society would not be seriously worried about heroin addiction.

Youthful Drug Experimentation.   Within the last five years there has been a substantial increase in the use of illicit nonopiate drugs by the young, particularly among middle-class college and high school students and young military personnel. The prevalent drugs of abuse for this group are marijuana (and, to some extent, the more potent cannabis product, hashish), oral amphetamines and barbiturates, LSD, and other hallucinogens. During 1971 the use of heroin by GI's in Vietnam became, for the first time, a matter of grave public concern.

As of November, 1971, the best estimates are that 15 million people in this country have experimented with marijuana. Possibly 30 per cent of these go on to become occasional users, and 5 per cent become frequent users. While these estimates are very uncertain, survey research supports the conclusion that marijuana use has spread fantastically in the last few years. One survey of 200 colleges found that 47 per cent of those interviewed had smoked it— 34 per cent occasionally and 13 per cent frequently. There are major differences among colleges, of course. Other surveys found that 70 per cent of the student body at one medical school were current users of marijuana, as compared with 44 per cent and 5 per cent at two other medical schools. Extrapolating from available statistics, it is likely that 20 per cent of all Americans between the ages of 15 and 35 have used marijuana at least once —a crime for which they could have been imprisoned by the federal government for up to ten years.[2]

There is currently little evidence that marijuana causes physical harm. The federal government is now engaged in a crash research program to find out the short- and long-term effects of marijuana. Critics of this research program argue that it is intended simply to justify current federal policy and is not a sound independent scientific investigation. Even persons who are sympathetic to marijuana use will be surprised, however, if it is discovered that marijuana use in large amounts over a long period of time is totally harmless. The real issue over marijuana appears to be not whether it causes mild physical damage but whether its use has already spread so widely that, as is true of alcohol, the social costs of efforts to prohibit it exceed the physical costs that would be incurred by eliminating criminal penalties for, or even legalizing, its use.[3]

Experimentation with oral amphetamines and barbiturate drugs, all of which have recognized medical uses and are therefore often easily obtainable, is probably second only to the use of marijuana. Some 18 per cent of the students in the 200-campus survey had tried amphetamines, and 15 per cent had tried barbiturates, but only 2 per cent and 1 per cent, respectively, had used them frequently. There are no more reliable estimates available.

A quite dangerous pattern of middle-class youthful amphetamine drug use is the injectible methamphetamine ("speed") culture. Intravenous injections of methamphetamine usually take the form of continuous use of massive doses for several days. Users may become psychotic while under its influence, and it is probably the drug most likely to lead directly to violence. There is some evidence that it causes serious organic damage. Speed also tends to make the user lose interest in food, sleep, and hygiene. Because of these extreme effects, a speed "run" is hard to sustain over any length of time, and the end of a period of heavy speed use—the "crash"—produces serious depression. Users have learned over time that they can make the crash smoother by taking barbiturates or heroin. Reports from San Francisco, the first city to have a sizable speed culture, are that heroin is becoming the drug of choice for a large proportion of former speed users because it is a more pleasant "down" than the barbiturates.

The use of LSD originally peaked in about 1967, declined briefly, and then started to increase again as the early reports about genetic damage caused by the drug were discredited and as use spread downward into the high schools. The survey that found marijuana use among 47 per cent of college students on 200 campuses found that 11 per cent had used LSD, but only 1 per cent used it frequently. The National Institute of Mental Health had earlier reported surveys showing a 2 to 9 per cent range of LSD use among college students, with an over-all average of 5 per cent. While a ratio of one LSD experimenter to every five triers of marijuana seems too high for the population at large, or even for most colleges and high schools, it does illustrate a higher rate of current usage than has been suspected.

There is general agreement that LSD is a powerful drug that should be used with care. In clinical use, severe reactions are rare. One study found that 25,000 administrations of LSD or mescaline to 5,000 people resulted in serious complications in only 0.08 per cent of experimental subjects and 0.34 per cent of subjects who were undergoing therapy. There is no scientific certainty concerning other types of reaction that have been alleged, but not proved, to result from LSD use, such as flashbacks and birth defects. The long-term effects are not known.

Youthful experimentation may also involve heroin, especially in the ghetto. A recent survey of juvenile addicts in Washington, D.C., showed that over half started directly by mainlining heroin rather than first using other drugs. Among middle-class youth, however, experimentation with marijuana predominates, and heroin is probably the least used drug.

Youthful middle-class experimentation with heroin as part of a pattern of multidrug use does appear to be increasing. This phenomenon is too new, and information is too fragmentary, to judge whether it represents the beginnings of significant growth in middle-class addiction. Preliminary reports indicate that people who become involved with heroin in this non-ghetto context have less tendency toward heavy involvement.

The extent of penetration of drugs other than marijuana is difficult to assess. Considerably fewer young people seem to have tried oral doses of amphetamines and barbiturates than have tried marijuana, but more appear to have tried them than have tried LSD. The number of young people who become heavily involved with amphetamines (especially injectible methamphetamine) and barbiturates is unknown but is probably of about the same magnitude as those heavily involved with LSD.

Society's current concern about youthful drug experimentation is often attributed to the possible detrimental effect on the health of drug users. Certainly, concern about the potential harm from heroin experimentation in the ghetto is far more justified than concern about marijuana experimentation in the suburbs. It is our judgment, however, that physical harm is actually only a partial cause of this public concern. There are, after all, up to 9 million alcoholics, whose alcohol abuse affects a total of well over 30 million people in this country, a far larger number than are affected by drug abuse; yet, this enormous health problem has created relatively little public concern.

Rather, the principal force behind the present public concern about youthful middle-class experimentation seems to relate to differences in perceptions and life-styles between older and younger generations. Older persons tend to accept the use of drugs only for therapeutic purposes. They do not regard alcohol and nicotine as "drugs" and believe that the substances can be prop-

erly used for social and personal pleasure. But the older generation regards the use of drugs, such as marijuana and LSD, for
social and personal pleasure as symptomatic of disrespect for law
and authority and as an attempt to escape responsibility. In contrast, many in the younger generation tend to regard the use of
drugs for social and personal pleasure as entirely proper. Use of
such drugs as marijuana and LSD is therefore viewed by them as
an opportunity for enhancement of personal experience, an act of
social custom within a peer group, or a mark of youthful rebellion
and independence similar to smoking weeds or sipping beer
behind the barn fifty years ago.

   Drug Use among the Middle-aged and Elderly.   Millions of people use psychoactive drugs as a way of coping with the tensions
and problems of everyday living. Current estimates are vague, but
in a 1967 survey 25 per cent of all persons over 18 reported use
of a psychoactive drug during the preceding year. The number of
persons reporting use of a tranquilizer at some time in their lives
rose from 7 per cent in 1957 to 27 per cent in 1967. American
industry apparently produces about 4 billion dosage units of barbiturates (not including other major and minor tranquilizers) and
8 billion dosage units of amphetamines each year. It is charged
that half of these are diverted to the illegal market at some point,
and an unknown proportion of the rest are prescribed carelessly.
Some of these drugs are used by heroin addicts and youthful experimenters. Most are not so used, however, and the problem
of self-prescribed use of these drugs is one that pervades all
strata of society. (In addition, about 10 per cent of the 80 million
people who use alcohol have a serious problem of dependence.)

   The National Institute of Mental Health (NIMH) is now conducting a series of comprehensive drug-use surveys, which should
provide an accurate picture of the extent of middle-age and
elderly drug abuse with legal as well as illegal drugs. The project
includes research into the frequency and situational aspects of
this problem.

   Why certain persons become dependent on these drugs is not
clear. As in the case of heroin addiction, there is considerable debate as to what physiological and psychological factors are involved.

The personal costs of this type of drug abuse can be very high. Of all the potential drugs of abuse, alcohol is one of the most damaging, since even relatively light consumption clearly causes some damage to such organs as the brain and liver, and heavy consumption causes serious damage and sometimes death. Barbiturates cause damage very similar to that caused by alcohol, and, in the formal literature, these two drugs are regarded as essentially additive and interchangeable in chronic intoxication. With barbiturates, as well as alcohol, there is a serious risk of lethal overdose. The personal costs of steady amphetamine use are not clear. Experts believe that large doses entail a high risk of organic damage. There appears to be no clear evidence concerning smaller doses.

The social costs of alcoholism are now fairly well known and need not be detailed here, but the social costs of the abuse of barbiturates and amphetamines are still largely unknown. The social benefits attributable to these drugs are equally uncertain. There is clearly a widely felt need for the particular effects of the various drugs. It is far from clear that elimination of this form of drug abuse would result in net benefits to the society, because one cannot be sure that other possible responses to life situations would be less harmful. It is possible that reducing the use of tranquilizers would result in a rise of the violent crime rate, or in the divorce rate, or in child beating. It almost certainly would require greater institutionalization of persons with borderline emotional problems.

Drugs in Behavior Control. A fourth emerging problem is the overprescription of drugs to control the behavior of captive populations, such as overactive school children and nursing-home residents, where other, nondrug methods of control should properly be used instead. Recent information has revealed significant use of amphetamines to calm down behavior in the classrooms of urban public schools. At the other end of the age spectrum, tranquilizers are reportedly being used far too extensively on elderly patients in nursing homes to keep them from clamoring for the attention of overworked attendants.

These drugs are properly used, within limits of sound medical practice approved by the Food and Drug Administration, for hyperkinetic children and elderly patients with emotional problems. There is a serious danger, however, that they may be used as a simple method of managing school children, institutionalized patients, and correctional inmates as a substitute for a competent staff and the other resources needed in dealing with those not able to care for themselves. And, as the range of behavior-controlling drugs becomes wider, we can anticipate even greater problems in their use in unwarranted situations.

BASIC RESEARCH ON DRUG ABUSE

Existing Research. Most of the basic research now being done on drugs of abuse is conducted by the NIMH Addiction Research Center (ARC) at Lexington, Kentucky, or conducted or financed by grant or contract through the NIMH Division of Narcotic Addiction and Drug Abuse and the NIMH Division of Psychopharmacology.

ARC is an interdisciplinary group doing basic research on the physiological effects of a number of drugs of abuse, and one of the very few to our knowledge that has recently conducted any research with heroin. Its 1970 budget is about $.8 million. Its principal functions are research on the abuse potential of drugs and on opiate antagonists. ARC would need far more personnel, ranging from senior research scientists to technicians and paraprofessionals, and far more funds if it were to expand its activities broadly to include basic research on the cause and nature of all drug abuse and drug dependence.

NIMH funds for intramural and extramural research relating to drug abuse have increased threefold in five years.[4] The figures below include research in pharmacology, sociology, psychology,

Year	Budget Authority ($ 000,000)
1966	6.4
1967	10.6
1968	13.3
1969	14.1
1970	16.3
1971	18.3
TOTAL:	$79.0

and many other areas. They also apparently include at least some of the research on psychoactive drugs sponsored by the NIMH Division of Psychopharmacology, which is interested primarily in the use of drugs in the treatment of mental disorders.

The research funds are dispersed among the various drugs of abuse, not concentrated on one or two. For 1970, the only year for which we now have information, the division by drugs was as follows:

Drugs	Allocation ($ 000,000)
Opiates	3.8
Marijuana	2.3
Hallucinogens	1.8
Barbiturates	5.3
Amphetamines	2.8
Other	.3
TOTAL:	$16.3

NIMH is unable to provide either a dollar breakdown on the types of research represented (pharmacology, sociology, etc.) or a breakdown by drug for previous years. In 1970, $1.3 million of the money spent on marijuana research was dispersed through special contracts. ARC received $.8 million of the money designated for opiate research to operate its program. An undeterminable amount is spent by the Division of Psychopharmacology and other parts of NIMH.[5] The balance of research expenditures represents about 50 grants to specific individuals and institutions given on application.

The allocation of grant resources is determined primarily by an advisory committee of physical and social scientists that reviews all applications for funding and assigns them a priority ranking on the basis of scientific merit. While NIMH administrators have some authority to overrule the committee (they can fund a low-priority project instead of a high-priority one, but they cannot fund a project if the committee refuses to assign it any priority at all), we have been informed that this happens rarely.

We have also been informed that little or no effort is made to create a *program* of research. Applications are reviewed in a vacuum. Consideration is not given to the importance or relevance of the research to policy issues or to major scientific and medical questions, or to alternative uses of the research budget. The results of prior projects are reportedly not made available to the committee for its consideration in reviewing current grant applications. No significant effort is made to encourage grant applications in areas of particular interest to scientists, physicians, and the government.

The Justice Department's Bureau of Narcotics and Dangerous Drugs (BNDD) has engaged in some research in the past and still has some ongoing efforts on the abuse potential of drugs, the sociology of drug use, the characteristics of dealers, and the market structure of the drug traffic. The decision has recently been made, however, that BNDD's research role is to be limited to subjects related to law enforcement.

A major problem with basic research conducted or funded by the federal government is that it is necessarily limited by governmental policy. Thus, as might be expected, there are large gaps in our basic knowledge about drugs of abuse. In particular, basic experimentation with the effects of heroin on chronic heroin addicts has been virtually ignored in view of the strong federal policy against any such research. Until very recently, federal policy also virtually precluded marijuana research in humans. Federal regulations single out LSD and a handful of other hallucinogens, from among all known drugs, as requiring specific Food and Drug Administration (FDA) approval of an Investigational New Drug Plan (rather than just filing the plan, as is true for all other drugs) before clinical investigation may begin. Under the 1970 federal drug-abuse law, research with heroin, marijuana, and LSD may be conducted only after the Secretary of HEW has approved the researcher and the protocol. In short, current governmental policy is a critical factor in determining the type of research that may be done under federal auspices or approval.

Other possible sources of funding for basic research on drugs of abuse are the states, the universities, and the pharmaceutical industry. Thus far, the states have concentrated on applied research, primarily in the area of treatment. The universities appear to have no significant source of funds for basic research other than the federal government. And the pharmaceutical industry concentrates primarily on product-oriented applied research. As a practical matter, therefore, most basic research depends on federal funds.

The pharmaceutical industry's research efforts are not only product-oriented but, indeed, have the goals of increasing the number of psychoactive drugs, enhancing their effect, or improving their activity in some other fashion. From the standpoint of drug abuse, the pharmaceutical industry is working night and day to create products that will intensify the problem. Many of these drugs, of course, have enormous medical value that far outweighs their abuse potential.

The Need for Additional Basic Research. It is apparent that there is a serious lack of basic information about how drugs of abuse work and their long-term effects on the body. Many examples could be given, but a few will make the point:

Since World War II, there have been over 3,000 technical papers on LSD. But scientists still do not know why LSD causes a psychoactive effect, or whether it is toxic, or whether it causes birth defects, or whether the widely reported "flashback" effect is real or imagined and, if real, has an organic basis. In short, many of the most important questions remain unanswered.

Morphine was first isolated in the early 1800's, and heroin was synthesized in the late 1800's. Among the things we still do not know about these drugs are the mechanisms by which tolerance develops, or whether an addict can be stabilized on a given dose, or whether the drugs cause any organic damage, or the mechanism by which they alleviate pain, or even whether withdrawal can be psychologically as well as physically induced.

While it is common knowledge that many drug users, including those on methadone, use combinations of drugs, little is known about the effects of these combinations. For example, mixtures of heroin and cocaine, or of amphetamines and barbiturates, are often taken, but we do not know how they interact.

We have been unable to discern agreement among researchers on what is and is not known, or on the priority needs for research, with respect to the drugs of abuse.

Basic research questions concerning psychoactive drugs can be divided roughly into two groups: (1) toxicological and pharmacological effects, and (2) psychological and perceptual effects.

Scientists probably know most about the toxicology (organic damage done to the human body) of drugs of abuse, yet even here there are many unanswered questions. It is known, for example, that excessive use of alcohol and barbiturates causes extreme damage to the brain and liver. It is suspected that amphetamines in massive doses also cause organic damage, but scientists are not yet sure. There is insufficient toxicological information on the opiates (e.g., heroin, morphine), the cannabinols (e.g., marijuana, hashish), and the hallucinogens (e.g., LSD, mescaline), the three categories of drugs with which the country is most concerned.

The organic damage caused by drugs is, of course, only one aspect of the more general study of pharmacological effects—that is, on what cells does a drug operate, how does it operate, what metabolites are triggered, and so forth. Nor are such questions unique to drugs of abuse. There appears to be no general theory of drug action based on the chemical structure of drugs into which discrete studies of the pharmacology of the drugs of abuse can be fitted. And there is a question whether psychoactive drugs do or do not represent a separate class of pharmacological compounds that can be studied at a theoretical level, independent of the study of pharmacology generally.

Basic pharmacological research would undoubtedly provide useful knowledge for basic researchers, from which they may some day construct a general theory of psychoactive drug action. The central-nervous-system effect of drugs is, however, a particularly difficult area of study. Many of the drugs with which we are concerned have effects that are apparently quite subtle and difficult to delineate. Some of the major tranquilizers, which exert immensely potent effects on the brain, have been studied intensively by NIMH for almost twenty years, and we still do not really know how they work. It is uncertain whether more could be learned faster by studying LSD, marijuana, or even heroin. In short, the road to a general understanding of the pharmacological effects of psychoactive drugs is difficult, and basic research in this area is not guaranteed to be productive.

Brain functioning is, of course, one of the current frontiers of science, and the complexities of studying the central nervous system make it likely that this area will remain a frontier for years, if not decades. Although drugs are simply one type of instrument for the study of the broader questions, the drugs of abuse may be a particularly interesting input because they clearly have large effects on the brain.

There is a great deal of work to be done here, and much of it will be important. As the pharmacologists study the physiological correlates of drugs and the psychopharmacologists and experimental psychologists study the psychic correlates, at some point in time linkages will be made leading to a unified view of the entire process.

The second category of potential research concerns the general interaction between drug taking and psychological and perceptual awareness. Such psychological variables as anxiety levels, attitudes toward self, perceptions, attention span, and mental ability are all affected by drug taking. Conversely, pre-existing states of mind and attitude have a significant impact on whether an individual will seek drugs in the first place and on the actual effects of a drug once it is taken.

Historically, because drug abuse has been looked at primarily from the standpoint of deviant behavior, the study of its psychological and perceptual effects has been placed largely under the heading of psychopathology. Interest in the role of external stimuli, of which drugs are but one example, in altering the individual's perception and awareness of his surroundings has increased in recent years. There is, for example, greater scientific interest in the subjective experiences and descriptions, rather than simply objective phenomena, connected with drug taking. As with basic pharmacology, there is much important information yet to be obtained in this developing area, all of which is fundamental to a better understanding of human functioning; but the progress of such research will likely be slow and uncertain.

This area of interest, also, is not discrete. There are clearly physical correlates for different states of perception and awareness, although the links have yet to be forged.

DRUG EDUCATION AND PREVENTION

There is substantial uncertainty and confusion in the area of drug education and prevention. Although nearly all workers in the field believe strongly that sensitive and accurate drug-education programs can play an important role in preventing harmful drug experiences among youth, there is no real evidence that such educational efforts are successful. Educators are cautious about new programs because of concern in some quarters that too much discussion about drugs of abuse could glamorize them and lead to experimentation. There is also increasing concern about the use of ex-addicts in schools. Although they are popular with students for "telling it like it is," there is justifiable fear that providing them with an aura of prestige may lead significant numbers of students to believe that they can and should try drugs themselves.

Past efforts have generally been of the "scare" type, emphasizing the moral and physical degradation of drug abuse and generously sprinkled with blatant misinformation, especially about marijuana. In schools, such lectures are usually delivered by gym teachers or visiting law-enforcement officials. Their aim has been one-dimensional—to stop young people from trying any illegal drugs.

It is now widely recognized that drug education, to succeed with increasingly sophisticated young audiences, must be accurate, factual, and consistent with the listener's own experiences or observations. Although a truly candid educational program may reduce involvement with the more dangerous drugs, such as heroin, it may also increase experimentation with the less dangerous drugs, such as marijuana, and many educators are reluctant to be drawn into an approach with such potentially controversial consequences. The federal government spent $3.5 million during the summer of 1970 in an attempt to train 350 schoolteachers, administrators, and student leaders to conduct workshops in their home communities dispensing information about drugs. The ability to withstand attitudinal confrontations of skeptical students was stressed. We have no indication whether this program was successful.

Virtually none of the myriad drug-education programs swamping the market from private companies, civic organizations, and even the government itself has been evaluated. The only detailed evaluation we have seen, involving a model-education program in a high school, showed that students improved not only in their factual knowledge but in their cautionary attitude toward drug use. That evaluation showed that the students liked the personal accounts of ex-addicts best but chose doctors to tell the facts. The students wanted more emphasis on the particular drugs in common use in their school and an approach that took the drugs up one by one rather than all grouped together.

The current emphasis among educators is on a continuous spectrum of education about drugs generally (legal and illegal), from kindergarten through high school, and on the integration of drug education into other social-problems curricula, which would include alcohol, smoking, sex, family living, and so forth. Dr. Norman Zinberg of Harvard has been evaluating such an experimental course for senior and junior high schools outside of Boston and expects to produce an effective and exportable curriculum. Dr. William Soskin in California has a different kind of program, for which school credit is given, that creates a third force besides family and school in the youth's life—a primary group with which he shares experiences all week, including a heavy emphasis on inner exploration.

One intrinsic problem with any kind of school-based education is that a large portion of serious student drug users have already rejected school. The motivational exploration that educators stress can be carried on only in a spirit of trust, and too many schools still require teachers and counselors to report all known or suspected users to the police. Only a few schools have had the courage to experiment with the designation of one or more teachers or counselors as official confidants to whom students can turn for help without fear of exposure. Few schools have close working alliances with treatment resources to which they can refer students. Parental permission for such treatment poses another legal obstacle to such desirable arrangements. It is doubtful that the federal government's crash summer teacher-training program can surmount these basic problems without a more fundamental change in community attitudes.

The National Coordinating Council on Drug Abuse Education and Information, composed of nearly one hundred government and private agency members, has recently entered the drug-education field.[6] It conducts evaluations of the explosion of anti-drug films and literature and stresses rational, coordinated efforts by city leaders to explore the basis and true extent of a community's drug problems and how the community can best utilize its resources for dealing with them. NCC's approach is that drug education should not aim at suppression of all illicit drug use but should teach children to make rational decisions based on reliable information about which drugs they will use and how much they will use them.

It can reasonably be expected that more federal money will be channeled to the states and cities for drug education, with little direction on how it should be spent. There are only the most primitive notions of how to determine whether a drug-education program has been successful. Even the goals of such programs are hotly contested. And there is little emphasis on evaluation techniques by the federal government.

At least in the immediate future, most schools will probably be unable to alter their basic authoritarian structure to the kind of open-minded approach to drug education that will help early experimenters or drug-prone students. The mere presentation of basic facts, even if honestly set forth, can be expected to have limited value in stopping the spread of youthful experimentation, and a law-enforcement orientation that requires school personnel to report all users will totally undermine education efforts.

It is probably also true that adults, more than school children, need accurate drug information to counter long-held myths. An appalling number of well-educated parents, as well as their children, still fail to understand the real differences among drugs of abuse. This misunderstanding is perpetuated in the 1970 federal drug-abuse law, which provides a one-year maximum prison sentence for possession of any illegal drug, regardless of whether it is quite dangerous (like heroin) or less harmful (like marijuana).

TREATMENT

With respect to treatment, two basic problems exist. First, relatively few drug-dependent persons are currently in treatment programs, largely because the programs do not have sufficient facilities or staff. Second, existing treatment for drug abuse and drug dependence has not produced impressive results (except for some methadone programs), and, even if all drug abusers and drug-dependent persons had treatment available to them, the outcome would be uncertain.

There are three general types of treatment modalities for users of drugs other than heroin. In many urban centers where drug use flourishes, crisis clinics have been set up to offer immediate emergency services to drug users and other troubled youths. They are typically staffed by youths under volunteer professional direction. They give out drug information, analyze street samples, "talk down" people with bad reactions, and see that those in genuine medical danger get to hospitals. Some also refer persons to long-term treatment programs or themselves offer individual or group therapy to drug users. San Francisco's Haight-Ashbury Free Medical Clinic is the best-known example of such clinics now found in many cities.

Therapeutic communities, which operate on the basic assumption that a character defect causes drug use, treat all drug users with encounter-group therapy or a more gentle form of "rap session" therapy.

Users of speed and LSD, and even heavy marijuana users, may well have underlying psychiatric problems. The only treatment available for them thus far is the kind of individual or group therapy used with other mental-health patients. Its success remains largely unevaluated.

Because heroin is regarded as the most serious drug threat to society, there has been a much more concentrated effort at treatment for heroin addicts. In New York City, where probably 50 to 60 per cent of the nation's heroin addicts reside, an estimated 10 per cent are in some form of treatment. Washington, D.C., has perhaps 15 per cent of its estimated 15,000 addicts under treatment. As of October, 1970, there were about fifty methadone projects throughout the United States serving a total of about 9,000–10,000 persons.[7] Nationally, it is safe to say that well over 90 per cent of all heroin addicts are not in any treatment program at all.

The two main treatment modalities for heroin addicts are (1) abstinence, bolstered by outpatient or inpatient group therapy, and (2) methadone maintenance, with or without supportive services. (A possible third approach is longer-term "detoxification" with methadone, which is given in decreasing dosages until the subject is entirely drug-free.) In New York City, nearly 4,000 heroin users are currently in fifty residential therapeutic communities, and 5,000–7,000 are reportedly on methadone. In Washington and Chicago, about half of all persons in treatment programs are on methadone and half on abstinence programs. There were, until recently, only a handful of addicts on methadone in California because of a legal restriction on its use outside institutions. Some legal restrictions still exist today. Many other large cities still have no methadone program at all.

Most methadone programs have long waiting lists. Almost all treatment programs have selective admission criteria and thus are probably skimming off the cream of the addict population. They do not appear to handle the most criminally active and hard-core addicts.

As compared to abstinence, methadone is clearly showing better results. Depending upon the degree of prescreening and the amount of supportive services built into the program, between 45 and 80 per cent of those admitted to methadone programs are successfully treated, as measured by continuation in the program, decreased arrests, job stability, and other social indicators. Experimentation is being tried in a few places with "barebones" methadone (without supportive services) to see what portion of the addict population can make it on the substitute drug alone, without concomitant social-adjustment help. The most promising approach we have seen is putting both methadone and nondrug treatment programs under the same administrative roof. From a research standpoint, this permits accumulation of a body of data from which a typology may be developed to show which kind of addict succeeds in which kind of program. There is some concern, however, that a multimodality program, combining maintenance and abstinence alternatives, may confuse patients and reduce the effectiveness of both approaches.

The more comprehensive the methadone program, and the more complete the data collection and evaluation, the more costly the program will be and the fewer patients it will be able to serve. Costs per patient per year may vary from a high of over $2,000 for a full service program to a low of $500 for a "bare-bones" program.

Methadone has thus far been used primarily with older addicts who have volunteered for treatment. Except in Washington, the average age of persons in methadone programs has been over thirty, close to the age when statistics indicate that a sizable portion of both addicts and criminals tend to "mature out" of their deviance. Whether methadone will do as well with an involuntary population of younger age remains to be seen.

There is a sizable problem of methadone acceptance, especially in the black community, because of opposition from groups who view it as a crutch indistinguishable from heroin and a source of white enslavement of blacks. Detoxification from methadone maintenance is being tried with a small number of patients. If this proves successful, the cloud of lifelong dependence now hanging over methadone will be removed and methadone should prove more acceptable among blacks.

Another problem is the possibility of "leakage" in the control system. Diversion of methadone poses a danger, as is indicated by the death of several non-opiate users who had not built up a tolerance and who ingested large doses. On the other hand, methadone appears to be safe for use by addicts in controlled maintenance programs.

Although all available evidence indicates that methadone is a safe and effective method of treatment, the federal government has nevertheless concluded, apparently for policy reasons, to inhibit its use by giving it only investigational status. This raises costs and staff requirements and limits the number of addicts who can be treated. It is unclear what additional information, if any, would persuade the Food and Drug Administration to alter this decision.[8]

Until methadone leaves the research context in which it now legally resides, its potential parameters will remain unclear. And just how much federal money will be available in the future to encourage methadone or multimodality programs in all major cities is unknown.

Some work is also being done on the nonnarcotic antagonists, primarily cyclazocine and naloxone, which block the euphoric effect of heroin. Several hundred people have now used these antagonist drugs. The chief problems in their use have been the short duration of action of both drugs—four to eight hours for naloxone, about the same as heroin, and 22 to 26 hours for cyclazocine, about the same as methadone—and, until recently, unpleasant side effects from cyclazocine. Work has been undertaken on longer-acting antagonists and on an implant that could discharge the drugs over a period of weeks. The antagonists, however, apparently do not satisfy the drug craving as methadone is said to do and have not proved as popular with addicts.

Other, more conventional methods of treating heroin addiction appear to have a substantially lower success rate than methadone, although comparison is difficult because of the differences in the types of drug users treated, the criteria for success, the statistics kept, and so forth.

Therapeutic communities like Daytop Village, Odyssey House, and Phoenix House purport to have up to a 75 per cent success rate with those who stay in the program, but they do not include in their figures the large number of addicts (estimated as high as 50 per cent) who drop out within the first month or two. Dr. Jerome Jaffee's work in Chicago, which to our knowledge constitutes one of the few attempts to compare the effectiveness of methadone and therapeutic communities with the same population, shows a startlingly greater success with methadone than with the therapeutic community. Of the 2,500 addicts who have been treated in the New York City Addiction Services Agency's Phoenix

Houses since 1967, only 130 have graduated back into community life (and 90 per cent of these work in addiction programs). An inpatient in such a facility costs $3,000 to $5,000 per year compared to a cost of $500 to $2,000 for a methadone patient, but methadone may require a longer, or even a permanent, period of treatment. It seems highly unlikely, in any event, that there could ever be a sufficient number of residential therapeutic communities to have a major impact on the problem.

Black community organizations, such as Colonel Hassan's Blackman's Development Fund and the Bonabond Agency in Washington, also claim a special ability to keep black addicts off heroin by abstinence therapy following detoxification with methadone and appeal to racial pride. But thus far their claims of success have received no objective evaluation.

NIMH is still committed to comprehensive community mental-health centers as the answer to the drug-treatment problem, but recent federal legislation for the first time permits support of drug-treatment programs unaffiliated with these centers. We have been able to find only a few examples of success with the community-mental-health-center approach and an equal number of outright failures. The successful community-mental-health-center, drug-treatment programs would appear to be just as successful if they were not affiliated with the centers, and even in theory there is reason to question the inclusion of drug treatment under the umbrella of the centers. In any event, we are unable to find statistics on the effectiveness of this approach.

Virtually everyone agrees that individual psychiatric therapy not only is impractical because of the large number of addicts but generally produces poor results with addicts.

There is one method of treatment that has not been attempted in this country since the Bureau of Narcotics, with the support of the American Medical Association, stamped it out in the early 1920's—heroin maintenance. At one time, there were some forty heroin-maintenance clinics in several areas of the country, unfortunately under rather loose procedures. The Bureau succeeded in banning them by 1923 and has since done everything possible to discredit this method of treatment. The suggestion by a prestigious joint American Bar Association–American Medical Association

Committee in the late 1950's that experimentation with a heroin clinic program again be undertaken was met with a vicious attack by the Bureau of Narcotics. During the past five years, the Bureau of Narcotics (now the Bureau of Narcotics and Dangerous Drugs) and NIMH have argued that the British system of narcotics maintenance has utterly failed and could not reasonably be considered for use in this country. (Staff Paper 7 of this report, prepared for the Project after an extensive on-site inspection and investigation, concludes that the British system of narcotics maintenance appears to have succeeded in containing the narcotics problem there.)

One outstanding deficiency in the treatment field involves evaluation. Several treatment programs, mostly methadone-maintenance programs, have data-collection and evaluation components. The Dole-Nyswander program in New York has been intensively evaluated by a prestigious medical committee, and indeed the evaluation of methadone in various programs throughout the country has now reached the point where there can no longer be serious question about the general usefulness of this treatment approach. The vast majority of the treatment programs, however, and particularly the non-methadone programs, have relatively narrow or quite inadequate data-collection and evaluation components, or no such components whatever. Moreover, data collection and evaluation are not standardized, with the result that comparison of programs or techniques for different patients, taking into account the many possible variables, is simply not possible at this time.

The Illinois Drug Abuse Rehabilitation Program, under Dr. Jerome Jaffe, has an unusually sophisticated system of data collection and analysis combined with a multimodality treatment program, thus permitting direct comparison of the effectiveness of different techniques. Similar programs with useful research components include the Washington, D.C., Narcotics Treatment Agency, under Dr. Robert Dupont, and the Connecticut Mental Health Center in New Haven, under Dr. Herbert Kleber. But no such program has the funds or time to standardize data collection for all other programs or to persuade others to adopt a uniform system, much less to attempt to standardize and persuade others to adopt uniform evaluation criteria.

Without sufficient detailed data collected on a standardized basis by a substantial number of different projects, there can be no satisfactory comparative evaluation of various treatment approaches for different types of drug users. Largely unsubstantiated and disputed claims of success and failure will continue to dominate the field until adequate evaluation is accomplished.

A second deficiency apparent throughout the country is the lack of enough trained administrators to run treatment programs. The few outstanding treatment projects emphasize the need for scholar-administrators with a medical and drug-abuse background but also with management skills. The most able project directors do not fall into the typical civil-servant mold but, rather, are men willing to take gambles and basically to let themselves be "burned out" in a few years. How to create a reserve of people equipped with this unique combination of talents and how to provide incentives for them to enter the field are critical questions in the future of treatment.

LAW ENFORCEMENT

Law enforcement has, of course, been the primary means by which society has attempted to control drug abuse in the past and at present appears to represent the principal effort for the future also. Arrests for drug offenses have increased dramatically during the past few years, from 31,752 in 1960 to 134,006 in 1968 and over 230,000 in 1969. Such arrests of persons under eighteen rose from 1,688 in 1960 to 33,091 in 1968 and over 57,000 in 1969.

There is, however, an acknowledged lack of direction and of trained manpower in state and city efforts, which results in scant disruption of illicit traffic above the street level. Most arrests are of users. The principal sellers arrested are amateurish young soft-drug peddlers and addict street dealers. Studies show that almost all heroin addicts get arrested at least once every two years of active addiction and spend an average of 15 per cent of their addicted life in jail. In New York City in June, 1970, there were 4,000 drug arrests compared with 1,800 in June, 1969. About 60 to 70 per cent of those arrests involved heroin. In Washington, D.C., arrests doubled in the first six months of 1970 and now run about four hundred per month; over 50 per cent involved heroin. California reportedly made 150,000 drug arrests for use and possession in 1969, a 300-per-cent increase over 1967, and it is unclear whether all of these are reflected in the national statistics.

BNDD has recently announced that it will provide no more than consultative services to local police in use, possession or small trafficking cases, and it is increasingly shifting its resources to the apprehension of large traffickers. In 1969, its agents made or instigated 4,000 arrests; for 1971, this figure is expected to fall to about 1,875. Basically, however, the criminal-law approach appears to have had little impact on the growth of the problem, as is demonstrated by the fact that illegal drug use, by everyone's calculation, is increasing and shows no signs of leveling off.

The federal government formerly took the position that illegal drugs that are imported, such as heroin and marijuana, could be stopped at the border if sufficient resources were allocated to this effort. In spite of recent large increases in budget and manpower, however, no significant impact has been made. Border seizures of heroin amounted to less than 5 per cent of the estimated imports in 1970. Indeed, the price of heroin has been falling steadily and the quality increasing, which indicates a failure to stem the supply. There is strong evidence that Operation Intercept, the attempt to impede the flow of marijuana from Mexico into the United States, has resulted in significant substitution of other drugs for marijuana.

The illegality of heroin is, of course, the sole reason for its high cost in this country. In England, the pharmacy cost of heroin is $.04 per grain (60 mg.), or $.00067 per mg. In the United States, the recent street price is $30-$90 per grain, or $.50-$1.50 per mg., depending on the time and place of sale and the quantity and quality of the drug.

As a result of the failure to stop heroin at the border, recent federal government policy has concentrated on cooperation with foreign governments, primarily Turkey, to reduce their opium production. Since it is estimated that the United States requires only 50,000 to 60,000 pounds of opium each year for illicit heroin use, since this amount is about 1.5 per cent of the total world production of opium, and since the entire U.S. demand could probably be met by cultivation of about five square miles of opium,[9] and since opium could readily be grown in other parts of the world, a program based upon suppression of opium production seems no more likely to succeed than the program based upon prevention of importation.

Finally, the initial hypothesis that drugs were not interchangeable—that, for example, a heroin addict would not be likely to switch to a different drug (e.g., the barbiturates or amphetamines) if heroin were unavailable—does not appear to be true. There is evidence that users will freely substitute even less potent drugs if their drug of choice is not immediately available. There is a far greater pattern of multiple drug use than was previously thought to exist. Suppression of one drug for a period of time, whether long or short, appears, therefore, to have a limited effect on drug abuse generally.

The law-enforcement approach to drug-abuse problems has been ameliorated by legislation permitting civil commitment in lieu of criminal punishment. Under present legislation, however, such treatment is largely illusory, since it is almost wholly institutionalized and often results in greater punishment than would be imposed by a criminal sentence. It is doubtful that institutionalization under these programs has been markedly more successful in rehabilitation than criminal sentencing.

New York, California, and the federal government have civil-commitment treatment programs that take a relatively restricted class of criminal defendants in lieu of prosecution or sentencing (as well as persons committed voluntarily or by relatives and others). The New York and California civil-commitment programs have proved very expensive—$4,000 to $5,000 per patient per year for care and treatment in New York, and a total of $12,000 for all costs. About $250 million was spent by New York State in 1967–70, the major share for capital construction and custodial salaries. Only one out of five patients successfully survives the parole period in the California program, and less than 25 per cent the New York program. The federal Narcotic Addict Rehabilitation Act (NARA) program currently has under 1,000 persons in an outpatient status and 800 in an inpatient status. Many addicts are ineligible for treatment because of the restrictive admission criteria contained in the Act, and almost half of the cases referred for evaluation are rejected because they are found "not likely to be rehabilitated." In general, civil commitment programs have suffered from cumbersome legal machinery, restrictive admission requirements, inflexible terms of inpatient residence, expensive security consciousness, lack of dynamic programs, and active resentment among inmates because of the prisonlike climate and poor treatment efforts.

Juvenile courts appear to offer one of the most flexible ways of channeling youthful users into early treatment, yet they are rarely used for this purpose. Almost all addicts are arrested first while in their teens. Most juvenile courts already have the power to divert drug users rapidly to a treatment agency, even without a formal finding of law violation, and they can keep all records confidential. Speedy urinalysis and a closer working relationship between juvenile courts and community treatment programs might have an impact on the problem. Ordinary juvenile institutions are less useful. They are experiencing an increasing problem with contraband drugs (we have been told that many youths get their first drug experiences there), and few, if any, have drug education or therapy programs, or indeed any urinalysis surveillance, after inmates leave the institution.

The federal government (as well as local and state police agencies) has been severely criticized for devoting its law-enforcement efforts to drug users and addict pushers and failing to prosecute large drug wholesalers. In New York and Washington, and probably elsewhere as well, grassroots organizations claim to know the identity of the larger wholesalers and in some instances state that they have turned information over to law-enforcement officials without results.

The short working life of undercover agents, the large amounts of cash necessary to make substantial "buys," and the structure of the heroin market, which is designed to insulate higher figures from contact with the drug, are the reasons most commonly cited by law-enforcement and community officials for the paucity of results in disrupting the heroin traffic. But the factor more commonly cited by ghetto groups, and increasingly also by such respected citizens as former Chief Justice Earl Warren, is corruption of narcotics agents. More than thirty federal agents were reportedly indicted on bribery and narcotics-sale charges during

1969 and 1970. The view is endemic in ghetto areas—and apparently it is justified at least in part—that the federal, state, and local police are not doing their job, and that they should be able to arrest more dealers and distributors than they do. Although it may be partly a question of better training, direction at the top, and placement of a higher priority in the area, there may also be widespread corruption involving pay-offs at the lower levels between police and pushers.

Both previous and present federal drug statutes make possession of an illegal drug of abuse a crime. When the Drug Abuse Control Amendments of 1965 were enacted to cover nonopiate drugs, possession for personal use was not made a crime, but this was changed in 1968 because of the LSD scare. The legislation enacted by Congress in 1970 to recodify and modernize all the federal drug-abuse laws continues the policy of making possession a criminal offense, with a one-year maximum sentence for possession of any illegal drug and twice this term for second and subsequent offenses. Neither prior law nor new legislation provides that an addict is not criminally liable for possession of a drug to support his habit. Test cases are being litigated to develop this defense as a matter of constitutional or common law, and the staff of the National Commission on Reform of Federal Criminal Laws has proposed that this should in any event be a statutory defense. Congressional support for such a defense would, however, appear difficult to obtain.

Regardless of judicial or legislative reform, it appears that the law-enforcement process will remain a significant, and probably by far the most important, intake unit for drug-dependent people for many years to come. At present only a few, crude attempts are being made to utilize this intake path to channeling addicts into useful treatment programs outside the civil commitment procedures.

Drug users are generally processed as ordinary criminals, and, conversely, a large percentage of ordinary criminals, when tested by urinalysis, are found to be drug users. Urinalysis tests in the criminal courts and detention facilities of major urban centers show that one-third to one-half of all criminal defendants, including juveniles, are currently using drugs, and some estimate that

80 per cent of the serious property crime in Washington, D.C., is committed by drug users. The likelihood that a criminally processed drug user will be given any specific treatment during his incarceration is slight. But even more basic, attempts at treatment programs in the prison setting have been markedly unsuccessful. Indeed, there is evidence that many nonusers or experimenters are first introduced to drug use or have their habits reinforced while in prison. One survey showed that 90 to 95 per cent of the heroin addicts who leave prison without treatment follow-up lapse almost immediately into drug use. Many of the major urban areas now have parole programs that test for drug use through urinalysis, and a few offer parolees methadone, group-therapy, and/or halfway-house programs. Nonmethadone programs with probationers and parolees, however, have not proved very successful. The majority of such probationers and parolees have had to be returned to prisons or court for drug violations.

LEADERSHIP

It is our belief that a major reason for the confusion and division within the drug-abuse field and the country in general is the lack of effective leadership, on both a governmental and a nongovernmental level. Effective leadership, by our definition, includes such functions as keeping the country informed about drug abuse and the latest drug research and arranging an open climate for medical and social research and for reasonable experimentation with different models of control. Effective leadership should, further, avoid eliciting emotional public reaction to isolated incidents and attempt to remove the drug problem from national politics.

Within the federal government, there are three organizations substantially concerned with drug abuse: BNDD, NIMH, and the Department of Defense.[10]

BNDD has for years pursued a national approach to drug abuse characterized by suppression of illegal drugs and the enforcement of criminal penalties for drug abusers. Although Bureau officials now emphasize the need for rehabilitation, the basic policy position of BNDD has not been significantly altered. The legislation recodifying federal drug-abuse laws, drafted by BNDD and passed

by Congress in October, 1970, represents little change in fundamental narcotics policy and only reinforces and codifies existing
law (except for some modification of penalties). The reason for
the recodification, indeed, was not a desire for reform but a need
to repair legislative provisions voided by the Supreme Court on
constitutional grounds.

The new law still includes marijuana and heroin in the same
classification, provides a uniform penalty for possession of any
illegal drug, and contains such harsh sanctions as a thirty-year
maximum prison sentence for an eighteen-year-old with a prior
offense who sells marijuana to a twenty-year-old friend if there
is any profit involved in the transaction. Any change in the basic
BNDD approach of penalizing drug abuse seems highly unlikely
in the near future.

During the past two crucial years of public-policy development, NIMH has been singularly impotent as an independent
voice in policy decisions and has seemingly been forced to
accede to the BNDD approach of relying almost exclusively
upon law enforcement. There is no reason to believe that NIMH
will be given substantially more leeway in putting forward
policy alternatives in the immediate future. Although there are
a number of NIMH personnel working on drug abuse who do
favor a more flexible and health-oriented approach toward drug
users and who would promote such an approach if allowed and
encouraged to do so, a significant change in federal policy is
required before they can be expected to speak out publicly on
these matters.

Until mid-1970, the Department of Defense denied that there
was any drug-abuse problem at all in the military. It has now
admitted that drug abuse does indeed exist in the armed services
and is initiating a program for treating users as an alternative
to punishment and dishonorable discharge.

Legislation has been introduced in the U.S. Senate to liberalize
treatment under the Narcotic Addict Rehabilitation Act, to revi-
talize the narcotics work of NIMH, and to authorize a far more
comprehensive health, welfare, and rehabilitation approach to
the problems of drug abuse by the federal government. But even
if such legislation is enacted, the present administration's em-

phasis on the law-enforcement approach could undermine its effective implementation.

The state government picture varies, of course, from state to state. Suffice it to say that, thus far, few states have refused to follow the lead of BNDD with respect to narcotics policy and that of the U.S. Congress with respect to narcotics legislation. As an example of the current climate, the August, 1970, Conference of Uniform State Law Commissioners approved a draft of a uniform state drug-abuse law, prepared by a BNDD attorney, with the understanding that it could be revised before final publication to reflect any appropriate changes in light of federal legislation then pending in Congress. An earlier draft, based upon what BNDD had hoped to have passed by Congress, was enacted by two states before the final version was available.

The nongovernmental organizations interested in the field of drug abuse have not exerted significant leadership during the past two years. During this critical time of public-policy determination, professional, medical, and scientific organizations such as the American Bar Association, the American Medical Association, the American Public Health Association, and the National Academy of Sciences–National Research Council have spoken out only on specific issues of interest to them and only on isolated occasions. Because all these organizations deal only tangentially with drug abuse and must rely for their efforts primarily on busy professionals who have full-time jobs outside the organization, none of them could be expected to exert the effective leadership that is needed in this field.

There is no national voluntary citizens' organization in the field of drug abuse comparable to the National Council of Alcoholism (NCA), and NCA has recently decided that it will enter this field only to consider problems in which drug abuse and alcoholism interact. Both the North American Association of Alcoholism Programs and the National Association of State Mental Health Program Directors, which are organizations representing state tax-supported agencies, also deal only tangentially with drug abuse and have made no serious effort to become concerned with the field in detail.

Largely because of this void, a paper organization, the Committee for Effective Drug Abuse Legislation, was created to represent the medical-scientific viewpoint before Congress during the hearings on the new drug-abuse legislation. Since this organization has been concerned almost exclusively with the freedom to conduct research and is poorly funded, it has had to ignore many other important public-policy issues.

Another new organization is the previously mentioned National Coordinating Council on Drug Abuse Education and Information, created in 1969 to bring together virtually all national organizations, from the drug industry to consumer groups, and from the PTA to the National Student Association, for the purpose of developing an effective drug-abuse education program. Although the Coordinating Council is financed to a significant extent by the federal government and has governmental representatives on its board of directors, it has shown independence and a reasoned approach to education and community planning in the drug field. The Coordinating Council's achievements are largely the work of a very few people, however, and, because of its precarious financial underpinnings, it is uncertain how long and how vigorously it can continue its efforts.

A MORE PROMISING APPROACH TO DRUG ABUSE

The foregoing summary discloses a lack of leadership in the field of drug abuse, a law-enforcement approach that is often ineffective and even harmful, and a country deeply and even bitterly divided over the proper approach to drug abuse. We believe that an effective attack on drug abuse can be launched only in a climate of reason and tolerance, allowing us to discern the real evils of drug abuse while rejecting policies based on confusion, misinformation, and emotion.

Before we can begin to cope adequately with drug-abuse problems, therefore, we must begin to refine and clarify our thinking about them. The world is full of drugs, large numbers of which are psychoactive. The majority of adult Americans take alcohol as a tension reliever or to facilitate social intercourse, and the use of nonprescription and prescription drugs for similar purposes is endemic. The availability and variety of these drugs will probably not only continue but increase.

Many of the drugs used have profound therapeutic benefits that allow people to offset physical or mental pathology and function more normally. Few of us would be willing to forego these therapeutic benefits, and no one perceives the use of drugs to achieve normal functioning as abuse. An increasingly large number of people, however, are not willing to limit their drug taking to medically supervised attempts to offset pathology. Some engage in self-medication with drugs they have become acquainted with through legitimate medical use. This pattern often occurs in the case of tranquilizers. Some wish to escape an unwelcome reality with heroin or barbiturates. Others desire the very acute functioning associated with the amphetamines. Still others, especially the young, seek the pleasurable effects of hallucinogens or marijuana.

The basic philosophy underlying our present drug-control laws is that all of these self-induced effects are to be shunned, or at least are not to be sought through drugs other than alcohol. This is a decision based partly on the fear of actual physical damage caused by the drugs, but primarily on the belief that drugs damage society because they contribute to crime and alienation.

It seems inevitable to us that all segments of society will continue to be exposed to a myriad of drugs in the future, and that society must learn to cope with these chemicals as part of everyday life. It is not possible at present to foresee exactly how the necessary adjustments in social attitudes and policies will be made.

We do feel, however, that current national policy—which singles out particular drugs and makes their possession or use a crime—should be changed for very important empirical reasons. We believe that the individual and social harm caused by imposing criminal sanctions on drug users far outstrips the benefits of this approach. Handling drug users as criminals has created widespread disrespect for the drug laws, has resulted in selective enforcement, has possibly done more to encourage than to discourage illegal drug use, has undercut *bona fide* efforts to explain the important differences among various drugs in the physical and mental damage they cause, and has deterred drug abusers from seeking necessary help. We feel that, as a first step in bringing the problem back into perspective, criminal penalties for possession of illegal drugs for personal use only should be abandoned in many jurisdictions. If this were done, drug users— but not drug traffickers—could then be handled on a public-health and social-welfare basis. Like the Canadian LeDain Commission on Non-Medical Use of Drugs, which in its April, 1970, Interim Report recommended retention of only a perfunctory $100 fine for illegal possession of drugs as an interim measure pending issuance of its final report, we have seen no evidence that eliminating the criminal penalties for possession of illegal drugs for personal use would materially impede the effectiveness of law-enforcement efforts against trafficking or remove an incentive for drug users to seek treatment or have other unfortunate consequences.

This conclusion in no way depends on a belief that chemicals should be freely used to induce pleasure. Nor do we believe that it is necessary to await final resolution of the currently popular debate about whether alcohol or marijuana is the more dangerous drug, a debate that has succeeded only in provoking further generational confrontation about hypocrisy, permissiveness, and life styles. Most of those who advocate a public-health approach disapprove strongly of the unsupervised use of dangerous drugs, especially by young people. Our conclusion is based, rather, on a recognition that our present methods of handling the drug abuser are at best ineffective and at worst counterproductive, and that other approaches must be tried. Eliminating criminal penalties for possession for personal use would neither legalize a particular drug nor permit its use. Law-enforcement efforts would, and in our opinion should, continue, but they would be directed at illegal distribution. And illegal drugs would remain subject to confiscation wherever found.

If the confrontation over the role of the criminal law in enforcing private moral judgments or choices of drugs were eliminated, the country might be able to unite behind an intensified approach to research, prevention, treatment, and law enforcement directed against the upper echelons of the illegal drug traffic. Restrictions on scientific research inquiries into particular drugs might then be lifted and substantial public and private funds more easily directed toward the understanding of how drugs work on the mind and body and what effects, both short and long term, they produce. Education of young people against the reckless use of powerful substances that affect the mind could proceed in a free and open climate more calculated to influence their behavior.

As research discloses more about specific drugs, some might eventually become candidates for limited legalization, in the pattern now used for alcohol. In other cases, disclosure of severe or permanent damage to the mind or body would require that distribution controls remain under criminal penalty. With such potentially harmful drugs, the user who refuses to accept treatment, and who can be shown to constitute a danger to others, might be committed civilly for appropriate treatment.

Voluntary treatment for harmful effects of drugs could similarly be made more flexible and accessible under such a system. Restrictions against any experimentation with heroin maintenance and unjustified limitations on the use of methadone maintenance could be reviewed and possibly removed. More public funds would be devoted to current treatment efforts and to searching out new treatment methods, to permit adequate handling of all voluntary and involuntary patients.

Finally, law enforcement could continue to act as an intake unit for treatment programs for those drug abusers accused of minor trafficking or other crimes. Where the drug taking results in dangerous antisocial acts, it is not unjust to require the offender to undergo treatment as a condition of liberty or even to offer it to him within the confines of the institution. But law enforcement's main focus would be directed at illegal drug wholesalers. In this endeavor, it would have the wholehearted backing of vast numbers of Americans, young and old alike.

THE DRUG ABUSE COUNCIL

In the previous section, we outlined an alternative approach to drug abuse that we believe is more promising than the present national approach. Private foundations do not have the means fully to implement such an alternative approach, nor could they legally do all that would be required to bring it about. A foundation cannot, for example, properly engage in efforts to change legislation. On the other hand, pursuit of the public welfare is a well-recognized task of all private foundations, and an important aspect of the approach described above involves education, research, and related activities that have long concerned private foundations. The basic goal might be summarized as one intended to make national drug-abuse policy responsive to facts rather than emotion. This is clearly an area where foundations could properly play a very large role.

Our primary recommendation is that an independent, nonprofit Drug Abuse Council be established to fill the leadership void that now exists in all areas of the drug-abuse field. This would preferably be undertaken as a joint project by a number of private foundations and organizations. The Council would strive to become a vitally needed center of excellence for drug-abuse information, basic research, education, and prevention, evaluation of treatment and education programs, and related activities.

The federal government is not equipped to perform this function. Its activities in the drug-abuse field are fairly narrowly circumscribed by political necessities, it relies largely on recruitment of civil-service personnel even at the top leadership levels, and its financial commitments are short term and subject to the vagaries of Congressional and administration decisions. Federal activities in the drug-abuse field tend to be *ad hoc* reactions to current crises, such as the 1970 crash drug-education program in response to the well-publicized death of a twelve-year-old heroin addict, rather than well-considered, long-term programs.

Assuming that drug abuse will exist for years to come, and that the country's policies should be grounded on fact and reason rather than on emotion and politics, a long-range investment in education, research, and treatment is necessary. The Drug Abuse Council would be a long-term (ten years at a minimum) effort to obtain the factual information needed to provide a basis for sound policy and to disseminate to the public and to persons in key policy positions the best knowledge available in the field and the best analysis of this knowledge as it pertains to current programs.

The Council would have a board of 10 to 15 trustees. Working under the board's direction would be an interdisciplinary staff responsible for performing the Council's daily work, headed by a full-time president. The president would be a member of the Board of Trustees, but not its chairman.

The majority of the Board of Trustees should be professionals knowledgeable in the field of drug abuse. A few might be prestigious figures in the national scene, but persons who would commit themselves to a heavy working schedule consisting at a minimum of one formal meeting a month and substantial contact with the staff between meetings.

The Board of Trustees should include representatives of medicine, psychiatry, pharmacology, education, community leadership, law, and sociology. Board members would be appropriately compensated for their time and efforts. The chairman of the board should probably be located in, or accessible to, the city where the Council's headquarters are located—preferably Washington, D.C.—and he should be appropriately compensated for his additional work.

The president would initially work out with the board the direction for the Council's first efforts. He would then recruit his staff and proceed to implement those directives by drawing up a detailed set of proposals for Council action.

The initial core of the Council staff might consist of a medically trained person (probably a psychiatrist), a basic researcher in the biochemical field, a social scientist, a lawyer, and an editor-writer schooled in simplifying technical writing. This small nucleus could, of course, be expanded as the Council's president and board define priorities and activities.

It is obvious that the president must be a key personality, with proved administrative ability, and soundly grounded in the drug-abuse field, its politics, personalities, and peculiar history. He would be responsible for proposing projects to the board, arranging for their financing or administration, preparing draft reports for board consideration, and so forth. Successful implementation of the Council's objectives would depend to a degree on the president's capabilities.

The relationship of the staff to the Board of Trustees also deserves comment. Basically, there seem to be three types of staff-board working relationships. First, a board of trustees may operate as a figurehead, exercising minimal influence over the activities of the staff. Secondly, it may have broad policy- and priority-setting powers but leave most operating decisions to the working group. This requires a far greater commitment of time by the members of the board than the first relationship. Finally, the board may directly run the organization through a staff having little or no independent decision-making capabilities. In essence, this third type of relationship would require the melding of the board of trustees with the working group.

In the case of the Council, it appears that the most productive staff-board relationship would be the second type—a Board of Trustees with policy authority over the working group but not actively involved in the actual day-to-day operations of the group. Such a board would have an important role. Because of the controversial nature of the drug field, board members must be prepared personally to back Council projects and policy statements and to withstand the inevitable attacks almost from the day they convene. If the Council's pronouncements and work are to carry weight in professional and governmental circles and among the general public, the board must stand solidly behind them.

Once under way, the Council should explore the potential for action in many different areas. The following representative list, which reflects areas of current immediate concern, is not intended to exhaust the possibilities. Additional matters will be uncovered, and priorities will change, as developments occur in the field that cannot be predicted at this time.

Finally, it should be noted that the Council may carry out its objectives either by persuading others to undertake and finance the work or by underwriting the work itself. Whenever possible, the Council should encourage federal, state, and local governments to increase their roles in drug-abuse programs. In this respect, the Council should act as a watchdog, to make certain that public agencies fulfill their intended responsibilities. In many instances, however, private action, either funded or undertaken directly by the Council, will also be necessary and appropriate.

SPONSORSHIP OF BASIC RESEARCH

Although not nearly enough is known about the effects of drugs on the mind and body, the investment of new research funds must be carefully directed toward specific objectives, rather than merely toward supplementing federal funds. Some knowledgeable people are dubious about what could be accomplished by the contribution of a few million dollars in private research funds. Nevertheless, we believe that there are finite areas of basic research that the Council could profitably explore.

Encouragement of Interdisciplinary Research. Universities, where most basic research is done, tend to be structured along departmental lines. The incentive structures for researchers and, even more important, for graduate students tend to force the researcher to stay within his area and not become part of an inter-disciplinary group. The Council might usefully promote centers of interdisciplinarianism in this field.

There are cogent reasons for encouraging interdisciplinary research. The question of why the same amount of drug ingested by the same person produces dramatically different effects in different settings puzzles scientists and must be studied outside the laboratory as well as within, by psychologists and social scientists as well as by pharmacologists. Many of the basic pharmacological studies on the effects of heroin or methadone should be attached to treatment programs, so that the subjects could be studied and tested in the environment and under the conditions in which they become and remain drug-dependent. Some of the most creative hypotheses for basic research come from the cross-fertilization of different disciplines thinking about the same problem from different approaches. This is the kind of innovative exposure that the federal government's research program, based on the funding of finite projects to explore already articulated hypotheses, does not at present have the capacity to encourage.

One way of supporting this type of work would be to establish a new in-house center for the scientific study of drug abuse on an interdisciplinary basis. Another would be to put money into the best existing university centers, on the condition that they make some effort to study drugs of abuse in the context of their over-all work.

Of these two courses, the second seems preferable. A number

of first-class researchers in a relevant field may not regard drug abuse as their primary area of interest or as an area on which they would wish to concentrate their full time, and in any event they might not wish to move. The best researchers in the field might be more willing to study drug abuse, either separately or along with other matters of interest to them scientifically, if permitted to remain at their present location. To a large extent, this means funding interdisciplinary efforts in universities, because that is where the best researchers are currently found.

In addition to multidisciplinary research in universities, it might also be productive to fund a narcotics-research section in an existing institution or simply to fund individual projects wherever the best researchers exist. Finally, the Council might wish to participate in an ongoing treatment program for the unique information that the program might provide with a reasonable additional investment in a research component. Such questions as why heroin addicts stabilize at different levels of methadone dosage and whether long-term tissue changes are caused by a variety of drugs are often researched best with a large treatment population at hand. Each of these possibilities must be explored in greater detail by the Council staff before final recommendations can be made.

Detection of Drugs in the Body. Pharmacologists have informed us that the basic problem of drug detection in the body—where drugs go, how long they stay, what metabolites they produce, and what happens to them—is not being studied in the way present methodology would permit if research funds were available to perfect it. The technology of drug detection is an area that is very important to research but is not a high-priority item for any single researcher or university because the benefits are largely external to any particular project. This type of technological development would be of value to all researchers working in basic pharmacology. It would also enable the accurate identification of drugs in cases of acute toxic reaction and thus the development of better methods of treating or preventing such toxic reaction.

Research in this area could also be directed toward development of more accurate, rapid, and inexpensive equipment for a variety of purposes. Of particular importance for both law-enforcement and treatment programs is the chemical analysis of urine specimens to detect heroin and other illegal drugs. Urinalysis is used in broad surveillance programs in determining whether bail should be set for criminals, in probation and parole surveillance, in methadone-maintenance programs, and indeed in virtually all types of drug-treatment programs. It is essential to any evaluation of the success of these programs. Yet, in many burgeoning methadone programs, such as that in Minneapolis, no prompt and cheap urine testing is available, and samples must be mailed hundreds of miles for analysis.

There is substantial doubt whether surveillance programs are in all instances lawful, and even whether their use is productive or counterproductive with respect to treatment results. It will be some time before final answers can be obtained to these questions. Meanwhile, it is clear that urinalysis surveillance is increasing and will continue to increase (particularly if it is made mandatory for all methadone programs, as has been proposed). The problem is that urinalysis detection techniques can be costly, inaccurate, and very time-consuming. They may therefore limit the number of patients who can be admitted to treatment programs because of the cost involved in continuous urinalysis surveillance, wrong decisions may be made because of the erroneous results obtained, and persons may be deprived of liberty, placed under suspicion, or not given adequate treatment for long periods of time while awaiting results.

BNDD and a few private companies reportedly are interested in improving technology and methodology in this area, and there are some indications of progress. One company has apparently produced a marketable electronic device that would improve the speed and reliability of urinalysis but not reduce the cost. We have been assured that the technology for cheaper, reliable urinalysis is available but requires an initial investment to produce the models. Reducing the cost per unit from $1 to $2 to $.50 or less could mean a savings of $.25 million for large-scale projects and more for a city offering centralized urinalysis for all its programs. Hopefully, the Council could persuade the federal government to make the initial investment of a few hundred thousand dollars to conduct this work, if the need is not otherwise met in the near future.

Interaction of Different Drugs Taken in Combination. Large numbers of drug abusers use several drugs, some legal and some illegal, together or in substitution for another. The net effect of their interaction may be quite different from that of either one used alone. (There is some indication, for example, that heavy barbiturate use may neutralize the effect of birth-control pills used simultaneously.) Research on drug interaction could lead to knowledge that might prevent toxic fatalities.

Research with Heroin and Heroin Maintenance. We are unaware of any significant experimentation with heroin in this country, either in animals or in humans. Such research would be potentially very valuable in determining such questions as how an addict stabilizes on any given dose of heroin, how well he functions in society when consistently maintained on his drug, how wide a range of variation in dosage can be given without withdrawal, whether some people can use heroin indefinitely without becoming addicted, and how long a person must use a given dosage of heroin in order to become addicted. The usage patterns of different types of heroin addict also remain a mystery and have important research implications for treatment and education. Research on such issues as these might well have to combine field investigation and medical diagnosis.

One of the first problems the Council would face if it decided such research was desirable would be obtaining the necessary federal and state government permission, setting up the research in a way that would satisfy medical ethics, and justifying the need for the work to the public.

Miscellaneous. Another vital area not now being adequately researched is the effect of drugs, including marijuana and methadone, taken by pregnant women on the behavior and physical characteristics of the child.

A high-priority question is whether there is either an inborn physiological predilection to opiate addiction (as Dr. Dole suggests) or a drug-induced physiological readdiction vulnerability (as Dr. Martin suggests) or a learned response to external stimuli (as Dr. Wickler suggests) or none of these. Although we are not certain how this can be made the subject of a directed research project, it is a question of the greatest importance to the direction of treatment efforts, drug education, and even legal responsibility for addictive behavior. An attempt should be made to devise a series of experiments to advance this kind of research.

FUNDING PROGRAMS RELATING TO TREATMENT AND RESEARCH WITH RESPECT TO TREATMENT

We recommend that the Council should not, as a general rule, fund ongoing treatment programs, except insofar as they make possible unique research efforts not otherwise available. The Council's efforts in this area should instead be directed primarily toward providing the public climate necessary to assure appropriate public financing of any drug-abuse or drug-dependence treatment programs that are found worthy of support. As a practical matter, Council funds could not begin to match the amount of funding available from federal and state sources, if those sources could be persuaded to allocate appropriate amounts for treatment.

The failure of the Council to support ongoing treatment programs will undoubtedly subject it to criticism from community-action leaders. We feel, however, that the Council should have the more fundamental role of generating public support for drug-abuse programs and supporting and conducting research and evaluation that will begin to establish criteria by which the effectiveness of these programs can be measured. The Council should, further, disseminate information throughout the country with respect to programs that have proved to be worthwhile and that, therefore, will have a broad and long-range national impact.

The Council should, however, be on the lookout for truly experimental and research-oriented treatment programs that, absent nongovernmental support, will not be undertaken. Areas that deserve careful consideration include the following:

Basic Field Work in Programs for Juveniles and Hard-core Addicts. The populations least successfully treated are juvenile drug abusers and hard-core addicts for whom all known treatment methods have repeatedly failed. In our present state of almost total ignorance as to what kind of prevention or treatment programs will work with these populations, it may be necessary to send people out into the field to study the problem for six months to a year and then to come back and design operational program models. There is to our knowledge no present source of funding for any such basic field approach in new prevention or treatment techniques. Prototype projects designed to test specific hypotheses resulting from such field investigations might then be recommended for operation by federal, state, or local governments.

Heroin Maintenance. A related area that definitely seems worth exploring would be an experiment with heroin maintenance. A detailed study of heroin maintenance in the United States before it was stamped out by the Bureau of Narcotics and of the heroin-maintenance techniques that have been utilized in England should undoubtedly precede initiation of such experimentation in this country.

Research with respect to heroin maintenance—its possible use as a bait to get young addicts into other forms of treatment, its possible use as long-term maintenance for addicts who have repeatedly failed with other treatment methods, and other potential uses—might be a high-priority item for the Council.

As already noted, a substantial driving force behind the present public concern about heroin addiction is the fear of drug-related crime. Assuming that not all addicts can be rehabilitated, and indeed that the addiction problem will remain at least as great for some years to come, the hypothesis that drug addiction leads to crime and that a major portion of our crime wave is attributable to the high price of heroin must be put to the test. Such a controlled experiment could determine whether, using a heroin-maintenance system, crime is indeed reduced. The superiority of methadone over heroin, or vice versa, in maintenance programs could also be explored for the first time.

Management Assistance to Ongoing Programs. The Council might also consider providing ongoing or nascent treatment programs with desperately needed managerial assistance. A team of management consultants who could look at local programs and persuade their administrators to adopt proven techniques and perhaps to create a data-acquisition and digestion system where appropriate would be a major contribution to good treatment. The few successful project administrators we have seen are working full time in their own projects and cannot spend the necessary months advising other projects. Many methadone programs are subject to justified criticism, and a resultant loss of money, because of sloppy or uninformed management practices or failure to keep and record their data accurately. The kind of service we propose could reduce such needless problems.

Regional Networks. Finally, the Council might work with states and cities to help treatment centers from regional networks to share knowledge and experience, and even to cross-refer patients for specialized attention. This kind of regional network could also make cross-comparisons of variable techniques easier and allow interchange of personnel and pooling of funds for urinalysis, data collection, and training programs for personnel.

EVALUATION OF TREATMENT APPROACHES

Several different treatment approaches are in use today. There is also massive distrust among these programs, misinformation as to what is and is not being done, and a lack of any reliable means to separate truth from fiction. Evaluation approaches and criteria for the various programs are not standardized, and basic data often are not kept. Even when it exists, useful material is often not organized or published. It is therefore virtually impossible at this time to compare the effectiveness of any one approach with any other, or to study the effectiveness of a given approach for different types of patients. Because of lack of evaluative data, we do not know, for example, whether and to what degree the concurrent use of social services increases the effectiveness of methadone, or the per diem cost of patient treatment under different programs correlated with the rate of rehabilitation, or the dropout rate under various treatment programs, or the type of person (age, pattern of drug use, race, economic background) who volunteers for and is best handled under various treatment programs. There is a great need for an impartial body to attempt standardization of evaluation criteria and techniques nationally and to disseminate the results of objective evaluation of ongoing programs in order to promote the most useful components of these approaches and discourage ineffective and unproductive efforts.

One approach that the Council might consider in attacking the information gap is to develop a uniform data-processing system for drug-abuse projects and to provide several of the programs with the necessary software and consultative services to install such a system. Local treatment programs must participate actively in working out a good data-evaluation system if they are to be persuaded to cooperate. The results of the data collection might be fed to a central receiving station where Council experts could analyze it and interpret its meaning to the individual programs as well as to other interested parties.

The decision as to what criteria should be used to evaluate any treatment program, however, involves not merely data analysis but basic value judgments based on experience. The Council should be involved in setting these criteria. Major methadone programs, for example, have been attacked because some of the participants continue to use drugs intermittently. This raises the question of whether eschewing all illegal drugs should be the sole or even the primary goal for a treatment program, or whether enhanced social functioning and cessation of antisocial acts, such as stealing, are sufficient criteria for success. If the Council could contribute toward formulating uniform criteria that reflect a realistic and flexible perspective on what treatment programs can be expected to accomplish and in what period of time, and on the immediate and long-term nature of some of the goals of treatment, it would be doing a tremendously worthwhile job.

INFORMATION DISSEMINATION

Technical Information. Technical personnel in the field, researchers, treatment project personnel, and educators need a comprehensive and accessible service that they can tap for complete, accurate, and up-to-date information on specific aspects of drug abuse, such as treatment projects, ongoing or past research, model school curricula, or film listings. There are at present several fragmented attempts to provide this kind of informational coverage. On request, NIMH will supply, through its National Clearinghouse for Drug Abuse Information, selected material on drug-abuse problems. Within about six months, it is hoped that the Clearinghouse will be able to provide a computer printout of abstracts of all publications on any subject requested, concentrating on publications appearing within the last decade, and without evaluation of content. Because the NIMH Clearinghouse is a government service, it feels that it cannot exercise any discrimination in the articles it abstracts, and hence it often abstracts worthless material or several virtually identical publications of the same author in different periodicals. NIMH also sends periodically, to certain persons, the protocols of research grants in progress. The National Coordinating Council on Drug Abuse Education and Information is planning a looseleaf service to include information on treatment projects, legislation, films, and what is known about the nature and effect of individual drugs of abuse, but is not sure how complete it can be because of budget problems.

Ideally, there should be one comprehensive index and digest of all this material, perhaps in several looseleaf volumes, and preferably one that is not prepared by the federal government. It should encompass virtually all information pertinent to the field, including a reasonably selective cross-indexed review or abstract of past and present books, articles, reports, and scientific papers, reprints from nineteenth- and early twentieth-century literature on experiences with drug abuse that are otherwise not generally available, descriptions of current treatment and research projects, public-opinion polls and drug surveys, evaluated lists of educational materials, digests of laws, court decisions, and legislative proposals, and other material. The compilation of such a digest and its periodic updating would be an enormous undertaking, and one that might be best accomplished by subsidizing another organization to do the actual work. The relationship between the Council and the editorial board of such a publication would have to be resolved.

Another important way of disseminating and highlighting the best of current research findings is through a technical journal, circulated largely to physicians, scientists, and other specialists in the field. The Institute for the Study of Drug Addiction, in New York, currently publishes the *International Journal of the Addictions*, which covers both alcoholism and drug abuse. We have found this journal a very useful source of basic information. The publishers state that the very limited number of papers and abstracts, and the very small circulation, are due to a lack of funds.

There seems to be no reason to set up a second journal of this type. Subject to further exploration of this matter, we believe that the Council should give serious consideration to working with the Institute for the Study of Drug Addiction to expand the articles and abstracts in their journal in order to cover the field adequately (excluding alcoholism, which is covered well enough in a separate journal), to make the journal a monthly publication, and to increase its circulation. This would provide the field with the detailed results of all significant research on a current basis.

School Drug-Education Programs. The role of the Council in the race to the schoolhouse must be approached with care. The consensus is that private and public organizations are now generating too many drug-education programs without sufficient knowledge of basic educational techniques, pretesting, or evaluation of results.

There are not enough professional educators sufficiently schooled in drug abuse to teach teachers about drugs. Very often we have found that those who teach counselors and others responsible for drug education in the schools have themselves had no training except for a few lectures. It may be that the Council can affect this vacuum through support of university interdisciplinary research that can train a cadre of experts to teach the teachers in the universities and surrounding communities.

Another contribution of the Council might be to help subsidize the evaluation of drug films, literature, and curricula offered to the schools. It might also design or commission methods of evaluation by which school programs would be able to assess their own results.

Perhaps the most critical problem of most school drug-education programs is their passivity. The Council might support and disseminate information about some less traditional approaches, such as active engagement using drugs in behavior experiments with animals, discussion of nondrug inducement of altered states of consciousness, or extended discussions of values and what youngsters hope to get out of drugs. These represent a few of the more promising (but scarce) approaches we have encountered.

The attraction of television for the young child makes it a logical educational device on drugs. Consideration should be given to working with a group skilled in educational motivational techniques, such as Children's Television Workshop, on films for use in elementary school or over national television.

General Public Information. Perhaps the single most important service of the Council would be to act as an independent source of relevant information for the public about drug-abuse problems. There is a need for a new and wholly independent perspective on such fundamental issues as the nature and scope of the drug problem, the effects of present law-enforcement policies at all levels, the real dangers of youthful marijuana use, the treatment or recovery potential of different kinds of drug abusers, how much crime can really be accounted for by drug abusers, how the English system of heroin maintenance works and with what results, the federal government's activity in terms of dollars, and the allocation of those dollars among enforcement, treatment, research, and education, the foreign experience with marijuana users, and how a school—or a parent—should best react to the presence of drugs.

These are the issues that are troubling Americans. Two New York State public-opinion surveys showed that drug use was considered a major neighborhood problem by 23 per cent of those interviewed, surpassed only by burglary, vandalism, and unsafe streets. A *New York Times* survey of 463 New York voters, reported on October 4, 1970, placed drugs as the fourth most prominent problem facing the nation and the foremost problem facing the voter's immediate community. At present, the public receives its information on these matters primarily from government sources.

Many methods must be used to inform the public of key developments in the field and explore key policy issues in drug-abuse control. The Council could commission its own public-opinion surveys on key issues to guide the direction of its information efforts. State-of-the-art papers might be published, containing accurate but readable technical material on the nature and effects of drugs. Accounts of comparative experiences of different jurisdictions with varying law-enforcement, treatment, and education approaches could be prepared and disseminated.

Whether such material is widely read will depend in large part on its readability and press coverage. The Council will need a good editor, with a sound basic understanding of the sciences and able to write simply but accurately. It will also need a library capacity to collect and analyze information of all kinds;

it may in time want to become a national information center, publishing attractively packaged periodicals for the lay audience containing such analyses. It may use radio and TV for forums in which outstanding experts in the field can discuss key concepts and thus dispel some of the myths that abound. Different media, of course, would be targeted to different audiences—parents, youths, inner-city residents, and the suburban middle class.

Consultative Services for Key Officials and Organizations. The Council might wish to provide counseling services on a selective basis for key figures and organizations in the drug-abuse field, such as major professional organizations and leagues of city or state officials. Such persons might wish to utilize the expertise of Council staff in many areas before undertaking major policy commitments or advising their members. Meetings and symposia could be designed by the Council staff to facilitate communication between key professionals and policy-making officials and to disseminate its own findings.

LAW-ENFORCEMENT EFFORTS

Basic law enforcement is, of course, a federal, state, and local governmental function, and we would recommend that the Council not enter this field in any substantial way.

Although the federal government is now engaged in international negotiations to reduce the supply of opium and its foreign manufacture into heroin, as well as to increase border surveillance to reduce its importation, we cannot be optimistic about their efforts. Previous attempts by the United States to stop foreign cultivation and manufacture have proved frustratingly unsuccessful, and the number of world sources of opium and the ease with which foreign production quotas can be circumvented give no cause for belief that future efforts will be any more successful. There is also a widely held belief among experts in the drug field that, if any one drug of abuse were eliminated, a new one would almost certainly be available to displace it. Thus, even assuming that all heroin and marijuana were stopped at the border, marijuana could be grown in this country, synthetic hallucinogens (probably more toxic) could readily displace marijuana, and synthetic opiates and other drugs could readily be available for use in place of heroin. Although better border control or reduction of supply might tighten the market somewhat, thus forcing the price up, it seems unlikely that it would have a substantial long-range impact on the underlying causes and effects of drug abuse, or even on its prevalence. In sum, this appears to be an area of limited potential, wishful thinking to the contrary, and one in which the federal government is already investing heavily.

We do recommend, however, that some exploration be made into the reasons that law-enforcement officials at present seem unable to prosecute more of the high-volume drug pushers once the drugs get into the country, even though they profess to know who the pushers are, where they engage in their operations, and a great deal of other information about them. Prosecution of important nonaddict drug pushers can have a temporary effect on total drug availability at the street level and force some addicts into treatment. It would, in addition, have a substantial psychological effect in many ghetto communities, where it is often thought that the police purposely do not prosecute drug pushers because they have made deals with the illicit trader or because they wish minority groups to remain enslaved to drugs. We believe that exerting pressure on the commercial sellers of illegal drugs is a desirable objective and should be done in the most efficient way possible. For that reason, we recommend the exploration with federal and local authorities of ways to increase arrests at the top levels of the drug traffic. If the Council enters this area at all, it should work closely with the staff of the Police Foundation to encourage innovative strategies by state or local police departments. The active utilization of antidrug community groups to help in policing and exerting formal sanctions in their own neighborhoods against pushers is one area of potential.

The Council might also want to study the effect of various laws and law-enforcement policies on the actual use of drugs and the treatment of drug abusers. This area is badly in need of careful study. The results of such a study might then become the subject of a "white paper" by the Council for consideration by local officials, budgetmakers, and the public at large. It might also help to create a more open climate for experimentation in different control strategies. The current push from the federal government is for all the states to commit themselves legislatively to a single model of law enforcement. It would seem, however, that states should be as laboratories to try out different approaches and to evaluate the results stemming from those variations.

There also appears to be a real need for educational programs specifically aimed at law-enforcement and court personnel, who will probably continue to be the largest intake process for illegal drug users. Although BNDD runs a law-enforcement training program for state and local police officers with respect to narcotics laws, it does not appear to emphasize the medical and social aspects of drug abuse, its causes and effects, the community resources that can be utilized in combating it from a public-health and social standpoint rather than from a law-enforcement standpoint, the importance of not ruining the lives of young children as a result of unfortunate experimentation with drug abuse, and similar aspects of this problem. The Council might fruitfully direct its efforts to helping police and court personnel, both juvenile and adults, to develop informal mechanisms for rapidly screening and diverting serious drug users into treatment programs in lieu of legal processing. Conferences might be sponsored for law-enforcement and judicial personnel to focus on the best of these diversion programs. An effective juvenile-court treatment project along these lines is, in our opinion, one of the greatest unmet needs in the entire field.

Finally, many improvements in the present law-enforcement approach toward drug abuse may have to come from the courts. There will be increasing attacks upon the irrationality of present drug laws, centering upon the right to privacy involved in the personal use of drugs, and the extension of the ruling in *Robinson* v. *California* that a person may not be criminally punished for addiction to include possession, use, and presence in illegal establishments or association with other addicts. The question of the right to treatment for an addict can be expected to be raised not only in civil commitment programs, where treatment is minimal, but also in communities without methadone programs, or where methadone dispensation is severely restricted by law, or even ultimately where doctors are not allowed to prescribe it for addict patients.

In the juvenile field, a long-standing and perhaps legally vulnerable impediment to treatment is the legal requirement for paternal permission. Addicts can also be expected to raise their eligibility for welfare as "disabled persons" or as "medically needy" under Medicaid laws. Treatment programs all over the country have encountered difficulties in locating facilities in high-addiction areas because of outmoded zoning laws. The right of "gatekeepers," such as teachers and nurses, to withhold from law-enforcement authorities confidential information received from students may have to be tested in the courts. Limitations of treatment programs to selected kinds of addicts will probably also be legally attacked. The adjustment of our now-primitive body of drug-abuse laws to new medical developments in research and treatment may well have to come about through a series of court cases as well as, and even in the absence of, legislative changes. The Council staff should keep abreast of such legal developments and, where appropriate, lend financial assistance to legal groups seeking such adjustments. The D.C. Lawyers Committee project on training a corps of addict specialists and the comments filed on the methadone regulations by the Center for Law and Social Policy are examples of such worthy efforts.

THE LEADERSHIP ROLE

We have suggested that the most critical reason for establishing a Drug Abuse Council is to create independent leadership in the field. That leadership must inevitably be earned through professional and public credibility, and through excellence of staff and product. The Council must lead in formulating and disseminating sound ways of thinking and acting toward drug use. It must, in short, become a center for policy study in the drug field, to which researchers, legislators, educators, policy-making officials, and the lay public will turn for nonpartisan analysis and information.

This role can be accomplished primarily by using the best thinkers in many different fields to find out what is actually happening to drug users—not just the young experimenters or mainliners, but the older pill-takers as well—why they are taking drugs, and what other ways can be found to satisfy their underlying urges and needs. The "drug-abuse problem" needs to be perceived in a less rigid and emotional way by the public at large. The nation has to understand how our present system of drug controls really operates, and with what consequences to what people. It must be given a realistic notion, rather than palliatives, of what we can expect to accomplish through education, treatment, and law enforcement, and what part of the problem must be approached in even more complex and subtle ways.

At the same time, there must be a sense of urgency about the Council's work. As soon as it is organized, the Council must consider such matters of immediate importance as

- The work of the Commission on Marijuana and Drug Abuse established under the 1970 federal drug-abuse law
- The authority of the Secretary of HEW to authorize researchers to protect the privacy of research subjects under the 1970 federal law
- The obligation of the Secretary of HEW under the 1970 federal law to report to Congress on the proper methods of medical treatment of narcotic addiction
- The authority of the Department of Justice to establish quotas for drugs, like heroin, that have no accepted medical use but are needed for research purposes
- The proposed new International Protocol on Psychotropic Substances being considered by the U.N. Commission on Narcotic Drugs
- Implementation of the proposed new methadone regulations
- The proposals to conform state law to the 1970 federal law and the proposed new Uniform State Act
- The proposed new federal Rules of Evidence that affect the confidentiality of the doctor-patient relationship

Of equal importance, priorities must be established with respect to the broad work of the Council and work begun on its long-range objectives. The projects that should be given prompt consideration include the following:

Information

- Analysis of the 1970 federal drug-abuse law for youth, researchers, physicians, and others

- A publication on the nature and extent of drug abuse in the United States today—what drugs are being used, by whom, the number of users, the relative harm of various drugs, what happens to users, the impact of drug use on crime, and so forth
- Evaluation of the English system of narcotic dispensation—how it works, the problems it has encountered, and whether it has controlled the spread of opiate addiction—perhaps coupled with an evaluation of U.S. clinics of the 1920's
- An evaluative synthesis of information about the effects of marijuana, with an explanation for the layman of the implications (or lack thereof) of animal experiments
- Examination of the legal alternatives to current policy regarding marijuana, how they would work in operation, and their implications
- An explanation of appropriate criteria for judging a treatment program (especially methadone), analyzing such factors as the expectation that many patients will continue to use drugs, and the importance of recognizing the value of different types and degrees of success
- A review of the experiences of secondary schools with handling drugs—including the use of confidentiality guarantees, the designation of one or a few teachers as confidential advisers, expulsion or suspension, liaison with community treatment programs, and relations with law-enforcement officials
- Analysis of the legitimate expectations of curtailing the supply of drugs through border surveillance, Turkish crop subsidies, and similar techniques
- An examination of the amount of federal resources (and those of a few major states) being spent on the drug problem and their allocation

Research and Field Investigation

- Careful study of the reasons young people use drugs, what they want to get out of them, and how many have left drugs and are trying for the same effects in other ways

- A field study of peer pressure as a factor in youthful drug experimentation
- Categorization and review of the major characteristics of the drug-education programs in operation—how many have been evaluated, with what results, and how the children and teachers feel about them
- A study of the optimal role of the pharmaceutical industry in the prevention of abuse—including consideration of proper production quotas for particular drugs, diversion into illegal channels, needed research on abuse potential, and legitimate advertising to the public and to doctors
- A state-of-the-art conference on current research on the nature of heroin addiction—including the meaning of animal and human research, hypotheses being worked on, important issues, and productive lines of inquiry
- A study of the effects of heroin on users, in conjunction with a treatment experiment, to learn such basic facts as immediate effects on users, how to stabilize on heroin, the feasibility of simultaneous use of methadone and heroin, and whether a heroin user can function normally
- Analysis of the substitution of different drugs with different effects for the original drug of choice

Treatment

- A synthesis of what is and is not known about the treatment of juvenile users of the various drugs—including hypotheses on how to treat this key group and the treatment resources a community should have for experimenters and chronic users, for hard and soft drugs, and for older and younger juveniles
- A paper on the state of treatment generally, pulling together the record of methadone, antagonists, therapeutic communities, and community mental-health centers, with evaluations where they exist, and consideration of such issues as public or private facilities, professional or indigenous staff, outpatient or inpatient, and voluntary or compulsory treatment
- A study of the employment of ex-addicts in treatment—the kinds of jobs available, the legal and community barriers, what job-training programs work for this group, and whether

persons on heroin or methadone can do everything normal
people can

- Assemble management consultants and material for data-processing systems for fledgling treatment programs.

Law Enforcement

- Monitor how the new 1970 federal drug-abuse law works in a few major jurisdictions—how it is enforced, against whom, the penalties given out, and what happens to the classification sections
- Compare the experience in states with high (e.g., Missouri) and low (e.g., Nebraska) marijuana penalties to see the effect, if any, over a period of time on drug use, attitudes toward drugs, and drug education
- An analysis of the difficulties facing law-enforcement officials in the enforcement of drug laws against wholesale and retail traffickers

It is not possible to lay down a step-by-step program for changing the present climate surrounding drug abuse in the country. How to get the country to focus on the real evils of drug abuse and to attack them rationally without contributing to the creation of even greater ones is a monumental task. Hopefully, the Council will not be alone in working toward such an end and will be able to enlist the support of state and city governments, such branches of the federal government as NIMH, and other private and professional organizations. Hopefully, too, much of its work will affect the related problem of alcoholism and will help to end the fragmented approach toward different kinds of drug-taking. The pace of the work and the priorities must obviously be decided by the Council board and staff itself, guided by a realistic notion of the magnitude of the tasks facing them and the opportunity to do something constructive about them.

CONCLUSION

It is of fundamental importance that man has and will inevitably continue to have potentially dangerous drugs at his disposal, which he may either use properly or abuse, and that neither the availability of these drugs nor the temptation to abuse them can be eliminated. Therefore, the fundamental objective of a modern drug-abuse program must be to help the public learn to understand these drugs and how to cope with their use in the context of everyday life. An approach emphasizing suppression of all drugs or repression of all drug users will only contribute to national problems.

There is an urgent need for effective nongovernmental leadership toward a more reasoned approach to drug abuse in this country. A void exists that we believe can be filled by the creation of a new Drug Abuse Council. In our best judgment, the Council could successfully exert this leadership and could have a substantial and beneficial impact on drug abuse in this country.

NOTES

1. Evidence obtained during 1971 indicates that the number of active heroin addicts as of December, 1971, was probably between 250,000 and 300,000.

2. The Comprehensive Drug Abuse Prevention and Control Act of 1970 reduced these penalties to imprisonment for up to one year for a first offense and two years for each subsequent offense.

3. The 1970 Act established a Commission on Marijuana and Drug Abuse to review existing laws and policy and recommend necessary legislation and administrative action.

4. See Staff Paper 5 for the most recent figures.

5. This information has become available and is presented in Staff Paper 5.

6. In 1971 this organization changed its name to the National Coordinating Council on Drug Use Education.

7. By December, 1971, there were over 300 methadone projects and a large number of persons receiving methadone by prescription outside of these projects. An estimated 50,000 patients are now using this drug for maintenance. See Staff Paper 3.

8. In November, 1971, the Food and Drug Administration announced its intention to propose broader approval of methadone under a closely controlled distribution system.

9. These estimates are based on an addict population of about 100,000. During 1971, official estimates of the number of addicts were raised. It is now estimated that 100,000 to 120,000 pounds of opium are needed annually to supply the U.S. market.

10. In June, 1971, the President proposed a Special Action Office for Drug Abuse Prevention to coordinate federal drug-abuse efforts in treatment, education, and research. Regulation and law enforcement, and military and veterans' problems are not included.

The Drugs and Their Effects

by James V. DeLong

A Primer on Psychopharmacology • Drugs of Abuse

A PRIMER ON PSYCHOPHARMACOLOGY

Psychopharmacology, as the term is used here, refers to the study of the interactions of drugs with the central nervous system (CNS), including physical, behavioral, and subjective effects. The term is not always used so broadly; we have chosen a comprehensive definition because this brief paper is neither detailed enough nor sophisticated enough to require the fine divisions implied by more exact categorization into such subspecialties as neurophysiology, neurochemistry, neuropharmacology, psychopharmacology, neuropsychology, and so forth.

As will become obvious, there are many areas in which basic knowledge about the mechanisms of action of psychoactive drugs does not exist. Our purpose here is to describe for laymen the framework within which such knowledge must be sought, and the difficulties involved.*

---

* Since this paper was written by a layman for laymen, technical terms and discussion have been avoided as much as possible. In most cases where extended discussion would have to be highly technical, the conclusions of

The Nervous System[1]

The nervous system is composed of millions of nerve cells (neurons) that are by no means homogeneous in structure. Some are very long, even up to several feet; some are bushy, with many fibers reaching out to connect with other nerves; some are small and simple. The cells do not interlock with each other at the ends, where the impulse is transmitted from one to another. There are, instead, microscopic gaps, called *synapses*, between them, which must be bridged by the impulse.

There are several ways to categorize the parts of the nervous system, each useful for different purposes. One division is between the CNS—the brain and spinal cord—and the peripheral nervous system, which is everything else. The peripheral system is composed of nerve fibers extending out from cell bodies contained within the CNS and, to some extent, of cell bodies clumped outside of it but, of course, still connected. While the peripheral system has groups of fibers (nerves) and groups of cell bodies (ganglia), it is simple compared to the CNS, which consists of millions of tightly packed neurons, fiber groups (tracts), and clumps of cell bodies (nuclei) with billions of synapses.

The psychoactive component of the effect of drugs is due to their effects on the CNS rather than on the peripheral system, and it is the CNS with which we are concerned. The peripheral system is relevant only insofar as research into the mechanisms of peripheral action casts light on the workings of the CNS.

Another way of dividing the nervous system is by function. The *somatic* system includes both the central and the peripheral neurons that convey impulses from the sense organs, organize them in the brain, and deliver motor impulses to the skeletal muscles. The *autonomic* system governs the smooth muscles of the intestines, urogenital tract, and blood vessels; the heart muscles; and the endocrine glands. In short, the somatic system

experts on the present state of knowledge are set forth with a citation to the discussion leading to these conclusions. Drs. Avram Goldstein, Norman Zinberg, Andrew Weil, Frederick DiCarlo, and Alan Green all read earlier drafts of this paper. They prevented some embarrassing errors, but they are not to blame for any that remain.

controls the body's response to the external environment; the autonomic system governs the internal environment.

The autonomic system is further subdivided into two parts. The *sympathetic* system generally mobilizes bodily resources for action—it constricts visceral blood vessels so that more blood is directed to muscles and brain, accelerates the heart beat, inhibits intestinal and gastric activity, widens the pupils of the eye, and secretes adrenalin. The *parasympathetic* system is the antagonist of these effects. It acts to conserve bodily resources, usually by having effects that are the reverse of those of the sympathetic system. The parasympathetic system is more specific than the sympathetic, however. While the latter tends to act diffusely, causing all the effects at once, the parasympathetic system can act independently on different organs.

The differentiation between autonomic and somatic systems is clearest at the periphery of the nervous system. As one traces the systems toward the CNS, the distinction becomes more vague. In the main trunks of peripheral nerves, for example, the fibers of the different systems are bound together and can be separated only by tracing them to their terminations or on the basis of some differences in fiber types. Within the CNS centers, division of functions is always a matter of degree rather than of complete specialization. While some centers are concerned primarily with somatic or with autonomic functions, the two are always closely coordinated, and the separation is not complete.

The CNS itself is not, of course, a random melange of heterogeneous neurons. There are many different and identifiable parts to it—medulla, pons, cerebellum, midbrain, reticular formation, thalamus, optic tract, cerebral hemispheres, basal ganglia, and so forth. For some of these, the functions are fairly well established; for others, they are not. To try to describe these would be far beyond the scope of this appendix. For our purposes, it is enough to state the following propositions:

- There is much specialization within the CNS, in that a particular part will have a specific and identifiable function. (For example, the thalamus is a relay station, with impulses arriving from lower centers and being passed on to higher ones;

the hypothalamus has the primary control over autonomic functions; the cerebral cortex contains the more complex psychological functions; and so on.)

- Each part consists of packed nerve cells with many connections to each other and to different parts of the brain.
- Many, if not all, functions involve more than one CNS center.
- It is easier to study motor or sensory functions, where CNS activity can be correlated with an output, than to study pure cognitive functions, where it cannot.

PROBLEMS IN STUDYING THE CNS

The study of the CNS is extraordinarily difficult. As Kenneth Moore states, "The human brain contains a complex of millions of nerve cells that are anatomically independent but functionally interconnected. An impulse starting in one neuron can propagate throughout the nervous system over a variety of pathways. The route taken is determined by the inborn organization of the brain and by ongoing events that, because of neural plasticity, can establish new circuits."[2] Obviously, the number of permutations possible in such a system would make study difficult, even if no other problems existed. Moore, however, goes on to list some of the major impediments to research on the CNS:

- Many ideas about neural functioning derive from study of the peripheral system, where most synapses are well defined in that only one synapse exists at a particular point. In the CNS, the cell bodies are covered with synapses. They are also closely packed among other cells (the glia), which may perform some neural functions even though they are not neurons.
- In each peripheral synapse only one chemical transmitter is thought to act. Each CNS nerve cell may be affected by several different transmitters. [Transmitters are discussed on pp. 67–68.]
- Neural reactions occur in milliseconds and are hard to find and measure.
- The biochemical processes involved in peripheral systems

can be studied in test tubes (*in vitro*) where tissue slices can be made to react. This is not true for studies of the brain, because brain neurons *in vitro* are in a resting state, disconnected from the other neurons that ordinarily determine their activities. While artificial stimulation can be applied, there is no way of knowing whether this corresponds to actions in the body. In particular, it is difficult to relate any *in vitro* reactions to such higher functions as thought or emotion.

- Because the different units of the CNS have different functions and anatomies, the biochemical reactions of any particular part are probably not the same as those of any other part.

- There is a unique blood-brain barrier between the blood and the brain that makes chemical manipulation of the CNS via injection into the bloodstream more difficult than is manipulation of other tissues. [The capillaries in the brain are somewhat less permeable than the capillaries elsewhere in the body.]

- The synapses are so densely packed that chemical manipulation by administration directly to the brain is much more difficult.

- Some brain structures are not accessible in a live subject because they are surrounded by other structures. If it is not useful to study them *in vitro*, and one cannot study them *in situ*, it is rather difficult to study them at all.

- When experiments are carried out in a live subject it is often necessary to stop a chemical reaction quickly so as to preserve the tissue at a particular point in the process. This is usually done by rapid excision and immersion in a low-temperature liquid. Since the entire CNS is surrounded by bone, it is difficult to perform this operation quickly enough. Some chemicals present *in vivo* may never be identified because they are destroyed too quickly.[3]

This represents a formidable list of difficulties. And, since psychoactive drugs are usually fairly specific to the CNS—in that they affect the CNS without having much effect on other body systems—it is easy to see why knowledge of their sites and mechanisms of action is less than complete, despite intensive study during the past several decades.

THEORIES OF PSYCHOACTIVE DRUGS

The present theory about the manner in which psychoactive drugs operate is that they affect the transmission of the nerve impulses across the synapses. This hypothesis is based upon more general theories concerning the chemical nature of this transmission. Researchers know that in a peripheral system certain chemical substances (acetylcholine in the somatic system and norepinephrine in the autonomic) are associated with the stimulation of nerve impulses. These substances can also be found in the CNS and appear to be correlated with activity levels there.

Because nerve impulses are thought to be electrical in nature, the theory of their effect is as follows: A nerve impulse that reaches the synapse of a particular neuron stimulates the release of a particular transmitter substance. This substance affects the receptors of the adjoining nerve cell (the postsynaptic neuron), changes its electrical potential, and triggers an impulse within it. Most of the transmitter substance is taken back into the neuron from which it came, although some of it is destroyed by enzymes or diffused by the blood. The postsynaptic nerve then returns to its original state.

Psychoactive drugs may affect this sequence by stimulating or inhibiting the production of the transmitter substance, by causing its release from storage, by affecting the process by which it is taken back into the neuron, or by stimulating or inhibiting its destruction. These processes have an effect on the level and type of activity in the CNS and a consequent effect on the perceptions and activities of the body.

Beyond this, it is difficult to say anything with much certainty. Some psychoactive drugs are associated with increased CNS levels of particular substances that are thought to be transmitters, but the causation is not firmly established. Mandell and Spooner have pointed out that the evidence for transmitter theory is in many ways startlingly indirect.[4] Their final comment is: "Even on a neurochemical level, we must talk about empirical correlates of behavioral states. Rigorous establishment of the transmitter or modulator role of brain substances appears to remain for the future."

The strongest evidence that a particular substance has trans-

mitter functions concerns *acetlycholine* (ACh). Neurons sensitive
to this substance are distributed throughout the brain, so that it
can have excitatory or inhibiting functions, depending on the
region. ACh is difficult to study, because it does not pass the
blood-brain barrier easily and is destroyed rapidly after artificial
administration. Its effects on certain cells in the spinal cord have
been studied, but not much is known about effects at other synapses in the CNS. There is also fairly good evidence that two
catecholamines—norepinephrine (NE) and *dopamine* (D)—perform transmitter functions. Again, however, much of what is
thought about their action is derived from research with the
peripheral system, and conclusions must be approached warily.
NE and D, together with their degrading enzymes, are also
located in various regions of the brain.[5]

Some researchers believe that 5-hydroxytryptamine (5-HT),
often called *serotonin,* is also a transmitter, but the evidence is
not as strong as for the substances already discussed. As Moore
states, "Despite years of active investigation, the functional significance of this amine remains obscure."[6] The substance may
excite, depress, or have no effect on neurons, but the reasons for
the differences are not known. It has no functions in the peripheral system and is thus even more difficult to study than the other
possibilities.

A number of other substances may be transmitters, but the
evidence is ambiguous. For example, the brain contains a relatively high concentration of free amino acids, some of which may
have transmitter functions. And there are a number of other
possibilities, such as histamine, substance P, prostaglandins, and
ergothioneine.

MECHANISMS OF DRUG ACTION

Even if the transmitter theory were certain and a connection
between transmitters and psychoactive drugs proved, there would
be the problem of understanding the mechanisms by which the
drugs affect the transmitters. This problem relates to the more
general pharmacological question of the manner in which drugs
affect cells and to the basic pharmacological concept of receptor
sites:

. . . most drugs are thought to produce their effects by combining
with enzymes, cell membranes, or other specialized functional
components of cells. Drug-cell interaction is presumed to alter the
function of the cell component and thereby initiate the series of
biochemical and physiological changes that are characteristic of the
drug. . . .
  The cell component directly involved in the initial action of the
drug is usually termed . . . its *receptor.*[7]

In its simplest form, the receptor-site theory is that, at the
basic site of action of any drug, there are cells or cell surfaces
that form molecular bonds with the drug molecules. Current
theory is that these sites are stereospecific—it is not only the
chemical composition of the drug that determines whether the
receptor can bond with it but its three-dimensional geometric
shape as well. A cell surface might have, for example, three or
four different points of contact where different molecular bonds
could be formed. A drug molecule must have a geometric shape
that allows proper subgroups of the molecule to come in contact
with these points for the formation of a firm bond.
  This theory of stereospecificity explains why drugs that are
diverse in chemical structure may have similar effects (e.g.,
morphine, methadone, and meperidine). Even though chemical
structures are different, geometric structures can be similar. In
contrast, variations of the same substance with similar chemical
structures but different geometric structures may not have similar
effects.[8]
  The classic assumptions of receptor-site theory are: (1) One
molecule of drug combines with one receptor site, (2) a negligible fraction of the total drug is combined, and (3) the response
of the body to the drug is directly related to the proportion of
available receptor sites that are occupied.
  The interaction between drugs and cells is governed by the law
of mass action. The molecules of a drug are constantly associat-
ing with and dissociating from receptor sites. At some point, for
any given drug concentration, an equilibrium is reached where
association and dissociation balance. The drug-receptor interaction, therefore, is dynamic, not static. Since most drug-to-
receptor bonds are thought to be relatively weak ionic bonds

that are readily reversible, this concept of dynamic interaction becomes important in understanding the process of antagonistic effects, blockade, and reversibility of drug action. All are based on theories about differences in the strength of bonds formed by different drugs and on competition for receptor sites.

Since these basic assumptions do not, however, explain all the observed phenomena of drug action in many cases, including the action of narcotic analgesics, various departures from the basic occupancy assumption have been suggested. The most important are (1) that not only occupation of the receptor sites matters but also the intrinsic "efficacy" of the drug; (2) that it is not the occupancy of the site that matters but the act of occupying, and that drug effect depends on the relative rates of association and dissociation, and (3) that there are spare receptors that may be occupied, although at a lower level of efficiency, when the primary receptors are already occupied. These explain some of the otherwise unexplained phenomena, but they leave other, different mysteries of their own.[9] Nor are these questions likely to be settled soon.

There are two ways to gain information about a receptor. The first and only really satisfactory approach is to identify and isolate it. Then the investigation can follow established biochemical and physicochemical procedures. Sequence analysis can establish the primary structure of the macromolecules. Techniques like x-ray crystallography, high-resolution electron micrography, spectrophotometry, and analytical ultracentrifugation can yield data from which the secondary and tertiary structure may be deduced.

In the case of proteins, recent years have seen the elucidation of complete primary structures at an ever-increasing rate. . . .

The second way of obtaining information about receptors is indirect. It has dominated pharmacologic research in the past. The approach is to draw inferences about a receptor from the biologic end results caused by drugs. A powerful tool employed toward this end has been the study of structure-activity relationships (abbreviated SAR). A suitable biologic effect of a drug is chosen for study. A prototype drug, which elicits the characteristic effect, is then modified systematically in its molecular structure. Substituents are added or subtracted at various positions and in different steric configurations. A series of such chemically related drugs is known as congeneric series. By testing the members of a series and observing how biologic potency is affected by each molecular modification, one may ultimately draw conclusions about the precise mode of combination of a drug with its receptor surface.[10]

Unfortunately, the study of psychoactive drugs belongs in the second category. No one has found the receptor sites or knows which cells might be involved. Concerning narcotic analgesics, Goldstein says, "It must be remembered . . . that the receptor, whose structural features are inferred from the SAR studies . . . , is entirely hypothetical."[11]

Finally, theories of action at the receptor site say nothing about the biochemical events in the CNS that constitute the eventual product of the interaction of the drug and the receptor site. "Investigations of the mechanism of tolerance and of the mechanism of narcotic action have been hampered by the same difficulty—that the biochemical alterations produced by the drug in the whole brain are unlikely to have much to do with the specific biochemical changes that are responsible for the drug effects at the sites of drug action."[12]

Jaffe makes a similar point. After reviewing the various theories and experiments on the effect of opiates on cerebral neural action, cerebral metabolism, and neurotransmitters, he says:

> . . . Unfortunately, knowledge of the functional role of the several postulated neurohumoral transmitter agents in the CNS is still so limited and controversial that the demonstration of an effect of morphine on them has not yet contributed significantly to an understanding of either the neurophysiological and behavioral effects of the drug or its mechanism of action.[13]

DRUGS OF ABUSE

OPIATES

The Drugs.[14]   Opium is a natural substance derived from one variety of the poppy plant. It contains over twenty different alkaloids with varying properties, constituting 25 per cent of opium

by weight. A few of these—primarily morphine and codeine—
are medically useful.

In discussing opiate abuse, the specific drugs of concern are
the following:

- *Morphine* is a natural alkaloid constituting 10 per cent by
  weight of the raw opium.
- *Heroin.* Because heroin is produced by chemical treatment of
  morphine with acetic acid, the technical name for it is diacetyl-
  morphine. In terms of analgesic effect, heroin is a little over
  three times as potent as morphine—for example, it takes three
  milligrams of heroin to produce the same analgesic effect as
  10 milligrams of morphine.

  Although heroin is the principal opiate of abuse in the
  United States, most research has been done with the more
  readily available morphine. In the opinion of experts, such
  research is applicable to heroin if the dosage difference is
  considered, because heroin rapidly breaks down into morphine
  in the body. Thus, its subsequent pharmacological action is
  the same.
- *Methadone* is a synthetic opiate of approximately the same
  strength as morphine.
- *Meperidine* is another synthetic opiate that is about 10 to
  20 per cent as potent as morphine. It is better known under
  its trade name, Demerol.

While all four drugs are analgesic, euphorigenic, and in many
ways fungible, there are some differences among them, particularly
in maximal effect and duration of action. Throughout this paper,
morphine is the primary subject. Important differences in the
characteristics of the other opiates are discussed where relevant.

Because of lack of information, two topics are not discussed.
First, it should not be assumed that the effects and characteristics
of raw opium are the same as those of morphine. It has been suggested that the mixture of many different alkaloids in opium may
have substantially modifying effects on the action of any individual alkaloid, such as morphine.[15] This is unproved; but—since the
medical use of crude opium ended in the Western world soon

after 1850—there are no data either way. Secondly, it is possible to produce drugs from crude opium that are stronger than morphine. For example, some derivatives of thebaine, a nonanalgesic opium alkaloid, may be one thousand times more potent.[16] The effects of such superpotent opiates have not been studied and might differ qualitatively from those of morphine.

Medical Uses. In the late nineteenth century, opium and morphine were sometimes referred to by physicians as "GOM," "God's Own Medicine." They were used for asthma, dysentery, alcoholism, and a wide variety of other diseases—including the simple cough.[17] In fact, the opiates are effective cough suppressants, constipants, and tranquilizers, and, in an era lacking other drugs, their heavy use was natural.

Today, however, since there are drugs without the addictive potential of opiates that are equally, or nearly as, effective for most of these purposes, the medical use of opiates has become less common. Yet, the opiates are still the most effective pain-killing drugs known to medicine, and large quantities of morphine and meperidine are used as such every year. Although there is a continuing search for equally effective nonaddictive pain relievers, none has been found, and it may be that none will be. For a time, some of the narcotic antagonists were believed to have the desired properties; more recently, pentazocine was thought promising. But the latest evidence indicates that the analgesic qualities of these drugs are due to properties that also cause addiction.

Physical Effects and Toxicity. The exact method by which morphine blocks pain is unclear. It does not appear to block the transmission of the pain impulse through the nerves (as do local anesthetics), because sensation and feeling are not affected. For example, someone heavily dosed with morphine will still be able to feel a touch or other relatively slight sensations. In addition, experiments have shown that a patient, even after being given morphine as a pain reliever, can accurately determine the amount of pain he would be suffering without the drug. What seems to change is the relationship of the subject to the pain. Although he feels the pain and can tell how great it would be without the drug, he is not "bothered" by it. For these reasons, it is thought that the drug acts in the part of the brain that interprets the nerve message.[18]

For a nontolerant individual, morphine is highly toxic. A dose of 100 to 200 mg. would be sufficient to cause a fatal respiratory depression. This, like the analgesic effect, is a consequence of the effects of the drug on the CNS rather than on other parts of the nervous system—morphine reduces the responsiveness of brain-stem respiratory centers to concentrations of carbon dioxide.[19]

Tolerance to the respiratory effect increases rapidly, and no researcher has yet found an absolute limit to the quantity of morphine that can be taken by a tolerant individual without causing death. Some persons have been known to take as much as four grams of morphine without adverse effect.[20]

No one has discovered long-term organic damage caused by morphine. In autopsy, neither gross nor microscopic examination of tissues shows evidence of such effects.[21] Various studies have followed the medical history of addicts over a substantial period of time, and, according to one of the studies, "while there is ample evidence that the aberrant way of life followed by most heroin abusers has both acute and chronic medical consequences . . . there is insufficient scientific basis for maintaining that long-term use of opiates—in and of itself—is related to any major medical condition."[22]

Addicts do, however, suffer from a variety of conditions ancillary to their general life-style and frequently die of viral hepatitis, bacterial infections, or other diseases. The death rate of the addict population is not known, but it is usually estimated as about 1.5 per cent to 2 per cent per year.[23] Malaria used to be common among addicts, until dope sellers began using quinine to cut heroin. Other deaths are often attributed to an overdose of heroin sufficient to cause respiratory depression. The possibility of an overdose is always present, because the quality of street heroin so varies that an addict may not know how much pure heroin he is getting in any purchase or even how much he is used to taking.

Nevertheless, several experts have stated that overdose and disease do not explan all addict deaths.[24] In many cases, the dead addict did not receive more heroin than he was used to or should have been able to take, given his pre-existing level of tolerance. It is possible that some people have a special sensitivity to heroin that takes the form of an idiosyncratic response to a single dose or that is analogous to an allergic reaction triggered by repeated use. However, there are no reports in medical annals of persons having this reaction after receiving morphine in a medical setting. Since morphine is used extensively in medicine, it would be expected that such a serious effect would have been observed by this time. But there are also some reports of an unusually high death rate in England, where addicts receive pure heroin. The English data on this are incomplete, however, and the causative factors have not been adequately analyzed.

Morphine does cause some physical effects, of uncertain significance. There are changes in excretion of epinephrine and norepinephrine. Rapid-eye-movement (REM) sleep is depressed. Stabilized addicts become hypochondriacal, apathetic, and bored with other people and have fitful sleep.[25] Whether these responses signify permanent change or damage, however, is not clear.

In all animal species, including man, morphine has an excitatory effect as well as an analgesic one. This pattern is not unique to morphine; it is also true, for example, of barbiturates and alcohol. The reasons are not well understood. The effect could be due to be a difference in the speed with which the drug affects different CNS centers, with certain inhibiting centers being affected first. Or some CNS centers excited by the drug may react first, with the response subsequently suppressed by later-reacting centers. Various animal species, however, react to morphine in different fashions. The predominant effects in monkeys, dogs, rabbits, and rats, as well as in man, are sedative, while in horses, cats, and mice they are excitatory.

Man is considerably more sensitive to the effects of morphine than are most other animals. For example, the effective analgesic dose for a man is about 0.2 mg. of morphine per kilogram of body weight. In a dog it is at least ten times as high.[26] This raises a number of questions about the meaning of animal experiments—specifically, about the relative importance of direct physical (as opposed to psychological or psychoactive) consequences of taking the drug.

The opiates vary in several ways affecting consumer preferences, abuse potential, and the ability of an addict to stabilize his

dosage and lead a relatively normal existence. The major elements
of variance are as follows:

- *Peak effect.* This is usually calculated as the maximum analgesic effect that can be obtained from a given dose of the
  drug as measured by the ability to relieve pain. Sometimes
  euphoric effect is measured directly through the observation
  of physical correlates of drug taking or through verbal responses to tests designed to determine the degree of euphoria.
  It is generally assumed, although not indisputably proved,
  that the peak of analgesic effect and the peak of euphoric
  effect are the same.
- *Duration of action.* This is a more diffuse concept, because it
  could mean the duration of relief of a given amount of pain
  or the duration of the peak effect. Generally, as used in the
  sources, it seems to mean the length of time after administration before the drug user begins to feel withdrawal symptoms. Sometimes, however, the phrase "duration of analgesic
  action" is used. The exact meaning of this term is not clear,
  since it would seem to depend on the level of pain to be
  relieved. Empirically, it seems to be about the same as the
  generally accepted "duration of action" to withdrawal.
- *Method of administration.* All opiates can be taken orally,
  subcutaneously (by injection under the skin), intravenously
  (by injection into the vein), intramuscularly (by injection
  into the muscle), or through the nasal passages. The effects
  will differ somewhat, depending on the method used. In addition, the effect of different methods of administration varies
  with the drugs. For example, when taken orally, methadone
  retains its efficacy more than morphine.
- *Potency and power.* The power of a drug is defined by the
  upper limit of the absolute effects it can produce. The potency
  of a drug relates to the dosage that is necessary to produce a
  given effect. Thus, heroin is not more powerful than morphine,
  because both can produce the same effects; but it is more
  potent, because it produces equivalent effects at lower doses.
    Viewed narrowly, potency might seem of little significance
  medically, because one could always give more of the less

potent drug. Few drugs, however, are so specific that they have only one effect, and the differences in potency may not be uniform for all effects. For example, morphine is an analgesic producing a side effect of nausea. Heroin is a more potent analgesic, but this does not mean, necessarily, that it would be more potent in causing nausea.

As stated above, potency of an opiate is measured in terms of analgesic effects, and this is thought—and only thought— to equal euphoric effect. But, given the lack of knowledge about the mechanisms by which opiates work, it is not impossible that the various drugs affect different CNS centers in various ways, and that therefore qualitative variations occur in psychoactive experiences. Also, superpotent opiates, such as the thebaine derivatives, might have distinct effects that have not shown up in comparisons of existing drugs.

Although the basic facts about the opiates are not entirely clear, the following facts are known: [27]

- *Morphine*, taken subcutaneously, has its peak effect in one-half to one hour. Its duration of analgesic action is four to six hours, and the decline from the peak is rapid. When it is taken intravenously, the peak effect is reached sooner and is somewhat greater. Morphine is effective when taken orally, but the peak effect is much lower—perhaps only 20 per cent to 30 per cent of the subcutaneous peak. The duration of action of oral morphine is at least twelve hours and may be as long as twenty-four.
- *Heroin* is generally thought to act about the same as morphine. Some animal experiments, however, indicate that heroin crosses the blood-brain barrier more quickly than morphine. If this is true for humans, its peak would come more rapidly than the morphine peak. Addicts sometimes cannot distinguish between heroin and morphine when they are injected subcutaneously; most are able to do so, however, when the drugs are taken intravenously.
- *Methadone*, taken subcutaneously, has a peak effect in three hours and a duration of analgesic action of about twelve

hours. When methadone is taken orally, the peak is about 70 per cent as great and occurs after four hours. Duration of action after oral administration is around twenty-four hours, and the decline from the peak is slow. Intravenously injected methadone peaks almost immediately, and the duration of action is lessened accordingly.

- Subcutaneous *meperidine* has a duration of analgesic action of only two to four hours, and the peak is reached in less than an hour. With oral administration, the peak is about 50 per cent as high. Intravenous administration lessens the time needed to reach the peak effect. Addicted medical personnel, who have ready access to meperidine, tend to prefer that drug to the other opiates, possibly because of its fast action and relatively high potency when taken orally.

- The dosages of the different drugs required to produce the same peak effect when administered subcutaneously are: morphine—10 mg.; heroin—3 mg.; methadone—10 mg.; and meperidine—80 to 100 mg.

Addiction.   Three aspects of opiate use are particularly important to an understanding of addiction and its consequences: (1) the nature of the euphoric psychoactive effect; (2) the development of tolerance to the drugs; and (3) the development of physical dependence, with physical withdrawal symptoms, when the drug is removed.

Psychoactive Effects. Opiates cause a mental clouding characterized by drowsiness, an inability to concentrate, lethargy, and reduced visual acuity. As was mentioned before, stabilized addicts may be hypochondriacal, withdrawn, bored with other people, and less motivated. Opiates, however, do not cause slurred speech or significant motor incoordination.[28] In some persons, they produce a very pleasant euphoria, but this reaction is not universal. Many people find that dysphoria, consisting of mild anxiety and fear, results instead and may be accompanied by such unpleasant effects as nausea and vomiting. Dysphoria is extremely common at first use, even among those who eventually become addicted; indeed, to attain euphoric effects at first may be an atypical response. In some subjects, the initial response is a desire to engage in increased activity.[29]

Goldstein states:

> It is well known . . . that most people react with extreme displeasure to an initial dose of an opiate narcotic, both nausea and dysphoria being common responses. It was once supposed that administration of opiates in legitimate medical practice might "create" addicts. There is no valid evidence of this claim, although it is true that the incidence of addiction is high in the health professions, where there is easy access to addicting drugs. It is quite obvious, however, that of the many millions of patients who receive morphine, an insignificantly small fraction ever seek to take the drug again. Likewise, in the population as a whole, very few of those who could obtain morphine or heroin illegally, if they wished, become addicts.[30]

Despite this, people start taking opiates because they like or expect to like the effect. It is not known whether those who become addicts have a different response to the initial use, experiencing some atypical internal metabolic change, or whether they simply have more persistence.

For those who find that they have an affinity for the drug, the euphoric effect is very powerful, although its exact nature is almost indescribable. This effect can be divided into two parts. The first part is the "rush"—the initial impact of the drug on the nervous system. This appears to occur only when the drug is taken intravenously, and not when it is taken orally or subcutaneously. Sexual images are frequently used to describe this effect: "It was like a huge orgasm"; "It was like coming from every pore." The second part is the follow-up sensation of being "high." Describing this is more difficult, however, for there is no common experience from which a pattern can be drawn. Basically, the effect appears to be that of an emotional analgesic, suppressing anxiety and care, although the analgesia is not a mere deading of emotion. On the contrary, it can be a profoundly heightened sense of well-being. Whether everyone who persisted in opiate use would attain this euphoric state, or whether such a state is a selective reaction based on psychological factors, remains an unanswered question. There is no model of the addict personality as such that satisfactorily distinguishes between users and nonusers; nor is the psychic explanation the only one available. Some researchers believe that opiate addiction has a physiological basis, and that the attempt to find psychological variables is therefore pointless. The varying theories on this subject are discussed in the last part of this section.

Tolerance. A person can become accustomed to a drug's effects and thus require steadily larger doses to produce a constant effect. This phenómenon is common with many drugs in pharmacology, not just drugs of abuse. Tolerance is not the same as physical dependence and often occurs without it. It is an important aspect of opiate addiction, because the addict's need to take steadily larger doses to achieve a euphoric effect elevates the cost of his habit, causing increased criminal activity and presumably increasing any long-term toxic effects that may exist.

Tolerance does not always develop uniformly to all aspects of a drug's action. For example, while tolerance in time develops to the sedative effects of barbiturates, the amount needed for a lethal dose remains constant. On the other hand, tolerance seems to develop to all the major effects of narcotics. It "is characterized by a shortened duration and decreased intensity of the analgesic, sedative, and other CNS depressant effects as well as by a marked elevation in the average lethal dose."[31] As observed in the section on toxicity, limits on tolerance have not yet been determined.

Tolerance takes two forms. First, the body to some extent may increase its ability to metabolize or excrete the drug. While this has not been shown to be directly the case for the opiates, it has been shown that brain morphine levels become lower in tolerant than in nontolerant animals eight hours after drug administration. Secondly, constant brain levels of morphine will produce less effect in tolerant than in nontolerant animals, indicating that there must be some form of adaptation within the CNS at the cellular level. These two forms of tolerance are called "drug disposition" and "metabolic tolerance," respectively. Several theories have been developed to explain them—they are too complex to discuss here—only to come to the same conclusion, namely, that "the precise mechanisms underlying these two forms of tolerance to narcotics are not known."[32]

In a study of drug addiction as a social problem, an important issue is the speed with which tolerance develops. If, for example, tolerance develops rapidly, then whenever an addict increases his dose for a few days—or possibly even for a day—he will become tolerant to the increased dose and must therefore maintain at least that level of habit from then on to avoid withdrawal symptoms. Experimental evidence indicates that tolerance does develop rapidly. Human subjects have been brought to a level of 500 mg. of morphine within ten days. Tolerance to morphine begins with the first dose administered and builds rapidly; tolerance to heroin lags for a few days, then follows the same course. In animal experiments, it has been found that a dog, when given morphine continuously for eight hours, will begin to recover from behavioral depression by the end of that time, indicating a rapid development of tolerance to a given concentration of morphine in the body.[33]

It is not clear whether tolerance increases arithmetically or geometrically. For example, although a nonaddict might find 100 mg. of morphine fatal, none of the sources indicates whether a dose of 200 mg. would be fatal to an addict who was already taking 100 mg. per day, or whether a dose of 600 mg. would be fatal to an addict on 500 mg.

Another important question is how long tolerance lasts after an individual has been abstinent for a time. Generally, it is believed that tolerance disappears when the drug taking stops. There are numerous street stories to the effect that addicts will voluntarily detoxify themselves to the point where their habit becomes such as to be economically supportable. Yet, in one classic experiment rats were found to retain substantial tolerance to morphine for almost a year after the last administration of the drug.[34]

The final important aspect of tolerance is the phenomenon of cross-tolerance between drugs. Morphine, heroin, methadone, and meperidine are at least partial substitutes for one another, and tolerance to one confers tolerance to equipotent doses of the others.

Physical Dependence and Withdrawal. The term "physical

dependence" or "physical addiction" means that an organism requires a drug for "normal" physical functioning. Abstinence will result in physical symptoms of varying types and severity until the body adapts to the new state. The term "addiction," however, is eschewed by experts in the drug-abuse field. Since drug abuse is dependent on an intermixture of physical and psychic variables, and since drugs of abuse are often used in such low doses that the degree of actual physical addiction is questionable, experts feel that it is more correct to use the terminology "drug dependence of the morphine type" or "drug dependence of the barbiturate type."[35] Even the withdrawal symptoms developed by abstinent users may be psychogenic in origin. In addition, users of drugs that are not powerfully addictive physically (e.g., tobacco) sometimes have a more difficult time in abstaining from use than do users of addictive drugs. For these reasons, it makes some sense to blur the distinction between physical and psychological dependence when discussing drug abuse as a social problem.

This should not induce the belief, however, that there is no such thing as physical addiction or physical dependence. Clearly, an opiate user becomes physically dependent in the sense that abstinence will cause severe and well-documented physical symptoms. These include restlessness and drug craving, followed by yawning, lacrimation, runny nose, perspiration, fever, chills, vomiting, panting respiration, loss of appetite, insomnia, hypertension, general aches and pains, and loss of weight. The intensity can be "nearly unbearable" if the dosage is high enough.[36]

Several researchers have commented that withdrawal from opiates—as well as from barbiturates and other hypnotics—is characterized by *rebound hyperexcitability*; that is, during withdrawal, the physiological systems that were depressed by the drug are in a state of increased excitability. It is not clear, however, whether all withdrawal symptoms are rebound effects, or whether this is a general rule applicable to other drugs as well.[37]

Withdrawal from the various opiates has been studied scientifically. As a general rule, the intensity and duration of the withdrawal symptoms are related to the intensity and duration of the drug's action. Thus, morphine withdrawal starts within a few hours (four to ten, depending on the user's tolerance level), peaks rapidly (around the second day of abstinence), then declines sharply. Most of the obvious symptoms disappear within seven to ten days. Meperidine withdrawal reaches its peak in about twelve hours and lasts only four or five days. In some ways, however, its peak intensity is greater than that of morphine withdrawal. Withdrawal from methadone follows a slower course. No symptoms appear until about the third day. After this, they increase steadily until between the sixth and the ninth day, when they peak at a level less than two-thirds as intense as the peak for morphine withdrawal. Thereafter, they decline slowly, not disappearing until after about two weeks. The maximum intensity of methadone withdrawal is always tolerable, but its duration may be the factor that causes some addicts to regard the withdrawal from methadone as nastier than the withdrawal from morphine.[38]

The disappearance of the gross symptoms does not mean, however, that the withdrawal is complete. Increasingly, researchers are finding some effects that persist for many weeks longer, and empirical observations show that the relapse vulnerability is greatest immediately after withdrawal. Dr. William Martin divides the abstinence syndrome into *early* and *protracted* abstinence. In human experiments, subjects were stabilized on 240 mg. of morphine, then withdrawn slowly over a period of three weeks. They showed the general withdrawal symptoms discussed above, although in milder degree than occurs after sudden withdrawal. The symptoms persisted to some extent for six to nine weeks. After this, the protracted abstinence syndrome emerged, characterized by minor physical differences that persisted through the twenty-sixth week of withdrawal. The clinical significance of this is not clear, for it has not been proved that protracted abstinence contributes to readdiction. But careful experiments with rats have shown that postaddict rats have a greater liking for narcotics than do rats that have never been addicted. This preference lasts four to six months after withdrawal.[39]

While no limit on the development of tolerance to opiates has been found, there does seem to be a limit on the degree of physical dependence that can be developed, as measured by the intensity of the withdrawal symptoms. For morphine, this maximum is reached at dosages of around 400–500 mg. per day; higher doses do not result in more intense withdrawal symptoms.[40]

This points up the fact that tolerance to, and physical dependence on, a drug are not the same thing. The body can even develop a tolerance to drugs on which it does not become physically dependent. But tolerance is always present when physical dependence develops.

In the case of the opiates, the speed with which physical dependence develops seems to lag only slightly behind the speed of the development of tolerance. A patient receiving therapeutic doses of morphine for a week or two will not have recognizable withdrawal symptoms spontaneously after discontinuance, but these can be precipitated by an antagonist after only two or three days on morphine. By similar means, withdrawal has been caused in a dog after an eight-hour infusion of morphine. Goldstein believes that physical dependence is probably initiated with the first dose of the drug.[41] At that stage, of course, withdrawal would be so mild as to be unnoticeable, but it seems possible that a single dose could create a craving for the drug, even though the physical genesis of this feeling would be unknown to the user.

As might be expected, there are no definitive explanations for the phenomenon of physical dependence. Its existence is simply defined by the presence or absence of withdrawal symptoms. Jaffe states:

> At present no single model is able to account for all the complex phenomena that are seen with the many classes of drugs producing tolerance and physical dependence. It is likely that multiple mechanisms are involved, and that each model may reflect a facet of the truth. For the present the most heuristic models are the best ones.[42]

Goldstein also observes that, although "the mechanism of the development of tolerance and physical dependence is still unknown, . . . there has been no dearth of theoretical speculation."[43] It appears that dependence is due to "drug-induced alterations at the cellular level, with the most prominent changes occurring in the CNS . . . these changes are not limited to any one part of the CNS but occur throughout the entire neuraxis."[44]

The sources are silent, however, on two important questions about physical dependence and tolerance. The first of these concerns stabilization dosages. It is well known, for example, that an addict can be stabilized on a drug, since taking a given amount will result in neither withdrawal nor euphoria. But there is little information on how much latitude there is in the stabilization dose. That is, if a morphine addict is used to 100 mg., can he take anywhere between 90 and 100 mg. without becoming aware of the difference; or is his tolerance of deviation from his normal dose less than this? Also, are there variations between the opiates, depending on peak intensity and duration of action? Generally, experts believe that it is harder to stabilize on such short-acting drugs as morphine and heroin than on methadone. The short, sharp peak and rapid decay characteristic of the morphine effect may mean that a dose insufficient to produce euphoria soon results in bodily concentrations too low to prevent withdrawal.

Another important question is whether the euphoric effect disappears at high levels of opiate tolerance. That is, will an addict who is used to 500 mg. of morphine achieve euphoria if he takes 550 or 600 mg.? The fact that the severity of withdrawal levels off at around this dose might indicate an upper limit on the ability to obtain a euphoric effect. None of the sources found, however, presents evidence to support either possibility.

Finally, it is well known that physical dependence on a given opiate can be satisfied by any other opiate. This is the phenomenon of cross-dependence, described by Jaffe as follows:

> Cross-dependence may be partial or complete, and the degree is more closely related to pharmacological effects than to chemical similarities. A broad-spectrum drug such as methadone, which depresses the entire range of functions that are similarly affected by morphine, can completely substitute for morphine or meperidine. However, meperidine, which has a narrower spectrum with less autonomic and sedative effects, does not entirely prevent the autonomic manifestations of withdrawal from morphine.
>
> In general, any potent narcotic analgesic, regardless of chemical class, will show cross-dependence with other narcotic analgesics. . . .[45]

METHADONE MAINTENANCE

A successful method of treating heroin addicts is to maintain them on daily doses of methadone. More detail about the programs using this technique is contained in Staff Paper 3.

The pharmacological basis of methadone maintenance has been covered in preceding sections, albeit implicitly. The significant characteristics are as follows:

- Methadone is a synthetic opiate. Its administration to a heroin addict will either prevent the withdrawal symptoms caused by abstinence from heroin or end them if they have already developed.
- Methadone and the other opiates exhibit cross-tolerance. A person tolerant to one of them is tolerant to equipotent doses of another.
- The action of oral methadone lasts about twenty-four hours. A methadone program can administer the drug once a day, rather than three or four times, as would be necessary if morphine or heroin were used.
- High doses of methadone (e.g., about 80 mg. or more) will prevent withdrawal, block the euphoric effect from an injection of heroin, and prevent the "drug hunger" (defined by Dr. Jerome Jaffe as "a felt sense of physical abnormality") felt by addicts who have become abstinent.
- Lower doses of methadone (e.g., 50 mg.) will prevent withdrawal and the drug hunger. They will not block the euphoric effect of an injection of heroin, although presumably some minimum quantity of heroin is required. The success rate for programs using low doses is approximately the same as the rate for those using high doses for addicts in treatment six months. Experts believe that blocking the euphoria is not so important as preventing the drug hunger.
- No significantly harmful side effects of methadone have been discovered.

The effects of methadone on the heroin addict have been described diagrammatically by Dr. Vincent Dole.[46]

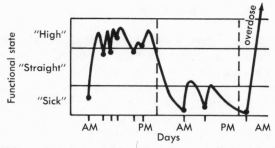

Fig. 1. Diagrammatic summary of the functional state of a typical "main-line" heroin user. *Arrow* shows the repetitive injection of heroin in uncertain dose, usually 10 to 30 mg but sometimes much more. Note that the addict is hardly ever in a state of normal function ("straight").

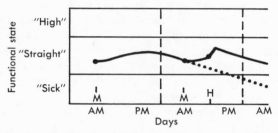

Fig. 2. Stabilization of the patient in a state of normal function by blockade treatment. A single, daily, oral dose of methadone prevents him from feeling symptoms of abstinence ("sick") or euphoria ("high"), even if he takes a shot of heroin. *Dotted line* indicates the course if methadone is omitted.

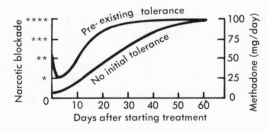

Fig. 3. The induction of narcotic tolerance by the gradual increase of methadone dosage. Two typical patients are shown: one starting with tolerance (from previous use of heroin) and the other with little or no tolerance (e.g., recently in hospital or jail). The right-hand ordinate shows the total daily dose of methadone (given in divided portions during the first months); the left-hand ordinate indicates the degree of narcotic blockade on an arbitrary scale (0 to ****).

Some important questions about the nature of methadone treatment remain unanswered. Because methadone and heroin can be substituted for each other in so many ways, it would seem logical that their effects would be cumulative, and that the addict on methadone would be able to achieve the euphoric state with a smaller dose of heroin than he normally used. Certainly, other drugs, such as alcohol and the barbiturates, have cumulative effects. Yet, many of the discussions about methadone treatment evidently assume, with actually saying so, that their effects are not cumulative.

The explanation may lie in the pharmacological principle that the body's response to many drugs is logarithmic, not linear. That is, as the dosage is increased, steadily larger incremental doses are required to produce a constant increment of response. Heroin and methadone may be cumulative in their effects, but the administration of methadone elevates the recipient to a point on the dose-response curve where only very large additional amounts of heroin have discernible impact.[47]

In this context, it is important to remember the suggestion made earlier that there may be a limit of 120–150 mg. per day of heroin (the equivalent of 400–500 mg. of morphine) above which additional amounts of the drug have no euphoric effect. If this limit is roughly true, even with substantial individual variations, then many methadone programs may simply boost the addict to the point where he cannot attain euphoria. Either he reaches this limit, which would be true at about 180 mg. per day of methadone, or he reaches a dosage that leaves too small a margin between his tolerance level and this limit for a euphoric dose. Lower doses (e.g., 50 mg.) would not approach the euphoric limit, but they might shift an addict to a point on the dose-response curve where the heroin dose he is used to taking would not have any euphoric effect.

Physiological Factors Underlying Addiction. It is commonly assumed that the causes of addiction are psychological, and that there is no inherent physical predisposition to addiction. There is, however, no experimental evidence that would rule out the possibility that drug addiction, or at least vulnerability to drug addiction, has a physiological basis. As Goldstein says:

Certainly socioenvironmental reasons can be found, *ex post facto*, to explain each case of addiction to heroin, the barbiturates, or alcohol, or of habituation to lysergic acid diethylamide [LSD], marijuana, nicotine, or amphetamine. But most people afflicted by the same adverse environmental circumstances do not seek escape through drug abuse. Despite the present paucity of evidence, therefore, the possibility should be entertained that the characteristic effects of psychotropic drugs upon mood, which underlie the development of drug abuse, may be at least in part genetically determined.

Investigation in this field has not yet transcended the difficulties of designing experiments free of self-selection or other kinds of bias, and of working out methods suitable for quantitation of subjective responses. It has been found, for example, that housewives who drink large amounts of coffee responded entirely differently to a test dose of caffeine in a placebo-controlled experiment than did housewives who never drink coffee. The coffee drinkers felt more alert and had a sense of well-being after caffeine, as compared with placebo. The non-drinkers obtained significantly fewer effects of this kind; on the other hand, caffeine made them feel nervous and "jittery." But it is not known if the group habituated to coffee would have reacted in the same way at an earlier age, before their first exposure to caffeine. Large individual differences are observed in the sensitivity of people to the sleep-disturbing actions of caffeine, but again it is not clear whether or not these are innate differences, independent of any prior exposure to caffeine. One investigation on the coffee drinking and smoking habits of monozygotic and dizygotic twins suggests that these two kinds of drug-seeking behavior are subject to genetic influences.[48]

Dole has suggested that an addict may have an underlying neurological vulnerability to addiction that is triggered by opiate use.[49] More recently, he has indicated that opiate use may induce a metabolic change that will cause the body to crave opiates thereafter.[50] But he is not optimistic about the potential of research on the question, given the present lack of testable hypotheses that might explain it.[51]

Another theory concerning physiological propensity to addiction is more complex. Martin has suggested that an addict has a particular physiological vulnerability to stress either before he takes his first narcotic drug or after he starts taking it. In Martin's view, this vulnerability is not lost after withdrawal from the drug, and stress situations will trigger a physiological reaction that results in a craving for the drug. Martin believes that there is some experimental evidence for this view and is more optimistic than Dole about possible research.[52]

THE HALLUCINOGENS

The Drugs.[53]

- *LSD* (*lysergic acid diethylamide*) is a synthetic drug discovered in 1938. It is closely related to the ergot family, and ergotamine tartate, used in treatment of migraine headaches, can be used as raw material in the manufacture of LSD.
- *Mescaline*, an alkaloid of the peyote cactus, was isolated in 1896. It is about .025 per cent as potent as LSD in producing an altered state of consciousness. But it is probably just as powerful.
- *Psilocybin* and *psilocin* are the active alkaloids of the Mexican magic mushroom and are about 1 per cent as potent as LSD.
- *DOM* (also called STP) and *MDA* are other hallucinogens chemically related to both mescaline and amphetamine.
- *DMT* (dimethyl tryptamine) is a short-acting hallucinogen.

Medical Uses.[54] Although there are no recognized medical uses for the hallucinogens at present, some of them have been, and are being, used experimentally for a variety of research and therapeutic purposes. LSD and mescaline, for instance, have been used for research on mental illness and in psychotherapy. Since certain effects of these drugs mimic the symptoms of schizophrenia in some ways, it has long been thought that study of these effects will yield insights into the nature and causes of psychotic states. A few experiments have been conducted in which terminal-cancer patients are given LSD in order to make the "waiting for death" period more meaningful. Through the LSD experience, the patient learns to live in the "here and now," taking each day as it comes rather than dwelling on his past. Alcoholics and drug addicts have also been given LSD as part of more comprehensive courses of treatment.

Physical Effects and Toxicity. LSD is effective when taken orally, which is the usual method of administration. Some users claim to have taken it nasally or by injection and state that injected LSD produces a powerful rush. It produces some somatic effects that are sympathomimetic, such as pupillary dilation, increased blood pressure, tremor, nausea, muscular weakness, and increased body temperature, but these effects are usually minor. The major effects are almost entirely on the CNS.[55]

The effective dosage is quite small. Perceptual changes, the most dramatic result, can be produced by as little as 25 μg. (micrograms). (1 gram = 1,000 milligrams = 1,000,000 micrograms.)[56] The standard dose taken by LSD users is probably around 200 μg., although the variability of street drugs makes it difficult to be accurate.

Although no human deaths as a result of the pharmacological action of LSD have been reported, animal deaths due to respiratory failure have occurred in response to massive doses. At present, it is not clear whether there is a fatal dose for humans, but it is clear that the ratio of the lethal dose (if there is one) to the therapeutic dose is very high. It is difficult to determine the significance of animal experiments for humans, because different species have markedly different reactions. Some animals, for example, have been found to be resistant to LSD; mice, in particular, detoxify the drug quickly, and the half-life (the period within which half the drug is metabolized) in a mouse is only seven minutes. In a human, the half-life is approximately three to three-and-a-half hours; the total duration of action of the drug is about twelve hours.[57]

Despite claims to the contrary, there is no reliable evidence that LSD causes birth defects. The early studies on this have been discredited, and no definitive work has been done since.[58] One exhaustive study concluded that pure LSD, in moderate doses, "does not produce chromosome damage detectable by available methods."[59] This problem is difficult to study, because that part of the population that uses LSD heavily is also likely to be malnourished, careless about hygiene and prenatal care, and prone to a variety of physical problems. Since LSD seems to be a relatively specific drug, in that it acts primarily on the CNS and has few peripheral effects, it is not particularly logical to expect that it will produce birth defects. It would be more sensible to study the large number of legal drugs that have massive effects on various body systems, because they would be more likely to affect the reproductive system as well. The stress on birth defects as a possible result of LSD appears to be motivated more by the desire to prevent its use than by the desire to prevent birth defects.

Psychoactive Effects.[60] The hallucinogens do not produce hallucinations in the classic sense—it is rare for a user to see things that are not there. Rather, perception is altered: Afterimages are prolonged and overlap with present perceptions; objects seem to move in a wavelike fashion or melt; and sensory impressions become overwhelming. Synesthesia—a state where colors are "heard" and sound is "seen"—is common.

Perhaps more important to the user than these perceptual effects are the subjective effects. Time may seem to pass very slowly; self-boundaries appear to disintegrate; and the user soon comes to feel a sense of oneness with the universe. There may also be a sense of unusual clarity, and one's thoughts may begin to assume extraordinary importance. Moods may change radically, from gaiety to depression, from elation to fear, or vice versa.

Many users attach great meaning to their experiences. Some regard the use of LSD as a form of psychotherapy, since they believe it increases one's self-knowledge and self-awareness, largely through the recall of old and hitherto buried memories. Others may go further and emphasize the mystical and religious aspects of their drug-induced feelings.

Some of the possible, long-term psychological reactions were examined in an experiment in which LSD was administered to previously naive subjects. The subjects were given a number of psychological tests—before taking LSD, immediately after the experience, and six months later.[61] All changes were quite small; the main findings indicated a negative correlation between the use of LSD, on the one hand, and aggression, competition, and preference for structure and conformity, on the other. Rather, a positive correlation with an increase in aesthetic appreciation was found. One result of the experiment was proved particularly illuminating: Fifty-nine per cent of the subjects who had been given 200 mg. of LSD thought that the drug had had lasting effects on their personality, even though the tests "provided only minimal supportive evidence."[62] In the control groups, none of those given 25 mg. of LSD, and 13 per cent of those given 20 mg. of amphetamine, had similar feelings about the experience. While other researchers have found a negative correlation between chronic LSD use and aggression and competition,[63] there is a self-selected quality to the voluntary chronic user that did not exist in the above experiment.

The major short-term risk of taking LSD is the "bad trip," a term used to describe several different types of adverse experiences. A mild adverse reaction can mean only that the images and feelings during the experience were unpleasant. At the other extreme, a serious panic reaction, accompanied by immense anxiety and fear, may occur. Bad trips are probably common, but most of them do not reach the severe level.

Under clinical conditions, serious adverse reactions appear to be rare. In one study, for instance, it was found that 25,000 administrations of LSD to 5,000 people in clinical settings had resulted in only 0.08 per cent serious reactions in experimental subjects and 0.34 per cent in subjects undergoing therapy. "Serious" was defined as causing either suicide or a suicide attempt or a psychotic break lasting more than forty-eight hours.[64]

Of course, most LSD use does not take place under clinical conditions; some observers believe that such use may therefore result in higher percentages of adverse effects, for several reasons. To begin with, putative LSD may be heavily adulterated with substances ranging from strychnine to methamphetamine. Also, use of LSD has been an illegal and deviant activity; this may make users anxious and more susceptible to bad reactions. It is also possible that a higher proportion of street users have psychological factors impelling them toward deviant behavior than would be true of an experimental population. Age differences may also be an important factor in adverse reactions (a theory in the field is that young users are more likely to lack the experience and identity that enable a more mature person to handle the powerful impact of the drug).

One could, of course, argue the precise opposite on almost

every point made in the last paragraph. For example, street users may seek out warm and supportive settings that reduce the incidence of bad reactions as compared with the clinical setting. LSD use may be deviant in the context of the larger culture but not in the subculture within which most users live. Older people, generally more rigid in their attitudes, may resist the drug effect and panic, while younger people, being more flexible, may accept the drug experience more easily. Contact with a subculture in which LSD is common may reduce fear of the drug, regardless of age, more than will clinical reassurances.

At present, there is no rational way to choose between these arguments. It should be emphasized that reports of large numbers of serious adverse reactions among street users have not been documented. What evidence there is consists mostly of anecdotes.

Chlorpromazine, a powerful tranquilizer used in the treatment of psychiatric illness, will counter the physical effects of LSD almost immediately. If, however, the LSD user is having a panic reaction, it may continue in spite of the chlorpromazine. Physicians familiar with this phenomenon believe that chemotherapy may prolong panic because of the anxiety its administration arouses in the patient. "Talking the patient down" in a calm manner is the preferred treatment.[65]

There are some long-term risks associated with LSD use. In some individuals, prolonged negative effects are associated with use of hallucinogens; cases of serious depression, paranoid behavior, and prolonged psychotic episodes have been documented. Whether the hallucinogens cause these effects is not clear. LSD may serve only to precipitate them in someone who is about to have such a problem anyway. The frequency of such effects is not known.

Another possible long-term effect of the hallucinogens is the flashback—a recurrence of some aspect of the drug experience vhen the subject is not under the influence of the drug. The flash-ack encompasses a wide range of possible LSD-like perceptual or subjective effects of varying degrees of severity and duration, lasting from a few minutes to several hours and occurring with indeterminate frequency. The user is not affected between experiences. Causation has not been definitely proved, however, and it could be that a controlled experiment would find similar experiences in a non-LSD-using population.[66]

The most common type of flashback recorded is the recurrence of perceptual distortion; the rarest is the recurrence of altered physical sensation; and the most dangerous is the recurrence of disturbing emotion and panic. (This may be hard to distinguish from the depressive reaction or schizophrenic episodes discussed above.) The last two types of flashbacks are more likely to occur after a bad trip than after a good one.

Assuming that flashbacks are caused by LSD, the mechanism responsible is a mystery. The theory that LSD persists in the nervous system is not compatible with its known short life, and the theory of a persistent, undiscovered metabolite is incompatible with the wide variations in onset and duration. Nevertheless, there is no lack of other theories, ranging from semipermanent changes in the optic pathways, to learned responses to stress, to dissociative reactions. Generally, it is probably psychological rather than chemical, but, given the lack of knowledge about the relationship between psychological and chemical events, this conclusion does not tell very much.[67]

There is no information on the incidence of flashbacks, the extent to which they occur after only one LSD experience, or the relative frequency of the different types.

The effects of the other hallucinogens are similar to those of LSD. Mescaline, which lasts as long and has about the same effects, although it is less potent, seems to be the user's drug of choice. It is unclear whether this preference is due to the publicity regarding possible birth defects caused by LSD or to some subtle difference in effect. It may just as well be due to the belief of many users that natural substances are superior to synthetics, a factor that may also account for the preference for the mushroom hallucinogens. This question has not been studied clinically, and it is difficult to know the effects of natural hallucinogens, since they are rarely available. Most street mescaline is either LSD or LSD plus speed or some other adulterant.

DOM (STP), MDA, and some other drugs are a cross between hallucinogens and amphetamines. The duration of action of DOM is sixteen to twenty-four hours, and rough observations indicate that the incidence of panic reactions and flashbacks has been higher than that associated with LSD. The physiological effects (rapid heart rate, dry mouth, dilated pupils) are also more pronounced. It is possible that, when the drug first appeared, users were more prone to panic, because they were not prepared for the long duration and greater physical reaction.[68] Jaffe states that low doses of DOM give some of the subjective effects of LSD without the perceptual or hallucinogenic effects, although the drug has typical psychedelic action at higher doses.[69]

According to some sources, MDA causes an LSD-type reaction for the first six to eight hours, but it also has amphetaminelike effects that persist for a longer time. Other reports are that MDA is *sui generis,* with LSD-like subjective feelings but without the perceptual distortion of LSD or depersonalization.[70]

DMT is a hallucinogen whose effects last only forty-five minutes to an hour. It is sometimes called "the businessman's lunch."

Tolerance.   Tolerance to the hallucinogens develops rapidly. If taken daily for three or four days, LSD will cease to have any substantial effect.[71] The tolerance does not appear to be so closely tied to the dosage as in the case with other drugs to which tolerance develops—that is, it seems that one cannot achieve the desired effect simply by increasing the dose. The sources, however, are ambivalent on this. Sensitivity returns after a few days of abstinence.

There is cross-tolerance among LSD, mescaline, and psilocybin but not between any of these and the amphetamines.[72] There is no information on DOM, MDA, or DMT on this point.

Physical Dependence and Withdrawal.   Hallucinogens such as LSD and mescaline do not produce physical dependence, and there are no withdrawal symptoms after discontinuation.[73] Again, there appears to be little information on DOM, MDA, or DMT; at least, there are no reports of dependence or withdrawal. They are likely to be about the same as LSD.

Mechanisms of Action.   A number of CNS effects of LSD are known; the manner in which LSD causes these effects, however, is still not known. LSD and the other hallucinogens interfere with the production and action of serotonin (also called 5-HT or

5-hydroxytryptamine) in the brain. This is an important body substance with significant effects on many organ systems. But, since the functions of serotonin in the CNS are not known, this does not represent substantial progress in understanding LSD.[74]

CANNABIS[75]

The Drugs. *Cannabis sativa*, the hemp plant, grows almost everywhere in the world. It flourishes in hot, dry climates, and it is generally believed that plants produced in such regions have the most pronounced psychoactive effects. *Marijuana* consists of the chopped leaves and stems of the cannabis plant. It is usually smoked, but it can be taken orally. *Hashish* is formed of resin scraped from the flowering top of the cannabis plant. It, too, can be smoked or eaten, and it is thought to be about five to eight times as potent as marijuana. Some experts believe there are qualitative differences in effect as well as simple differences in potency. *Kif, bhang,* and *ganja* are other preparations of cannabis used in various parts of the world. Their potency lies between that of marijuana and that of hashish.

The most important psychoactive ingredient of cannabis is known to be delta-9-tetrahydrocannabinol (THC), but the possibility of additional ingredients exercising some effect has not been precluded.

Cannabis is a difficult drug to classify. Although it is often referred to as a mild hallucinogen, it does not have many of the effects associated with hallucinogens, and probably has a different mechanism of action altogether. It also has some sedative effects but lacks many of the other characteristics of the sedative hypnotics. With good reason, therefore, it is usually classified as unique.[76]

Medical Uses. There is no accepted medical use for *cannabis* in the United States. In the past, especially during the late nineteenth century, it was quite popular among European and American doctors, who prescribed it for a variety of ailments ranging from menstrual cramps to migraine headaches. It was thus used generally as a mild anodyne (pain killer) or tranquilizer—but it may have more specific effects as well.[77]

By the early twentieth century, the use of *cannabis* for medical purposes had declined, largely because of inconsistency in the potency of the drug. Since *cannabis* was cultivated in many places with wide variations in climatic and soil conditions, no physician could be sure of potency of any given batch. This made it difficult to predict results. It also inhibited research, since non-replication of scientific findings might invariably have been due to differences in the drugs used.

Another problem was that there was no satisfactory way to administer the drug for medical purposes. Smoking is not a medically acceptable method, because the doctor cannot know how much of the drug is being inhaled and absorbed. Oral administration is possible, but effects are delayed. Moreover, since neither the plant material nor the resin is soluble in water, injection is difficult. Thus, as other drugs became available—particularly the barbiturate sedative hypnotics, which began appearing on the market in 1903—*cannabis* was replaced.

Almost no research has been done on the drug since the late nineteenth century, and government policies made such research impossible from 1937 to about 1968. Whether *cannabis* has unique medical uses or is in some ways superior to common tranquilizers now in use is therefore an open question. A revival of interest is now taking place, however, in the medical community. For example, several doctors are using *cannabis* to treat migraine headaches, and some research is being done into its effectiveness as a treatment for epilepsy. Certain variants of THC may lower the blood pressure of hypertensive people.[78]

The isolation and synthesis of THC—achieved in the early 1960's—has promoted such research by making consistency in dosage conceivable for the first time. In addition, NIMH has a project under way to cultivate *cannabis* in Mississippi, with the objective of providing drugs of constant quality to researchers. But there are still problems: For example, there is some evidence that THC is subject to oxidation, and that the potency of *cannabis* may therefore change over a period of time that varies with storage methods. Also, THC is expensive to synthesize and remains in short supply. Recent work has developed at least one water-soluble derivative of THC with a pharmacological profile similar to that of the original drugs. This should aid research further.

Physical Effects and Toxicity. The immediate physical effects of *cannabis* on man are mild. Heart rate is increased moderately. There is a dilation of the conjunctival blood vessels (i.e., a reddening of the eyes) and sometimes an increase in heart rate. There appear to be no changes in respiratory rate, pupil size, or blood-sugar level. After a single inhaled dose, measurable physical effects reach a maximum within half an hour and diminish three to five hours later.[79] When *cannabis* is eaten, the effects are delayed for several hours, and symptoms may persist for up to twenty-four hours.

As discussed in the next section, subjective effects of high doses of the cannabinols may be similar to those of LSD. This has led some to classify them as mild hallucinogens. Physical effects are not the same, however, because *cannabis* does not have the stimulating effects of LSD and has sedative properties that LSD lacks. There is no cross-tolerance between the cannabinols and the hallucinogens.[80]

At present, there is no reliable evidence of organic damage, and the most that can be said against *cannabis* is that the effects of long-term or heavy use have not been ascertained. To be sure, heavy, long-term smokers of *cannabis* develop bronchial disorders, but these seem no different from the difficulties experienced by heavy smokers of tobacco. Reports of long-term brain damage are suspect, at best. For one thing, they derive from studies of *cannabis* users in underdeveloped countries, such as India and Morocco. These studies, furthermore, are skewed by the fact that they used inmates of mental institutions as subjects and assumed a causative relation if they found that the inmates had been users of *cannabis*. Scientific protective devices, such as control groups and blind studies, were lacking. The recent crash program of federal research has not filled this gap, and many experts do not expect that it will do so. In this view, gross organic damage would have been found before now, and long-term subtle damage is difficult to study retrospectively.

The lethal dose of THC for humans has not been determined, but it is known that the cannabinols are not very toxic: There has yet to be a report of a human death due to an overdose of THC. Animal experiments have found that the lethal dose for rats is between 800 and 1,400 milligrams of drug per kilogram of body weight for oral administration. Extrapolating from studies in mice, the ratio of the lethal dose to the effective dose for humans would be about 40,000 to 1. (The effective dose is that amount necessary to produce clinically desired effects. For THC in humans, it is about 50 micrograms per kilogram.) By way of comparison, the ratio for barbiturates is about 10 to 1.[81]

Recent research has found that injected THC has a half-life in the body of fifty-six hours, and that traces can be found in the urine for up to eight days. There is also a possibility that it may accumulate in lung or fat tissue.[82] The clinical implications of these facts, however, are not known.

Psychoactive Effects. The general effect of *cannabis* is "a subtle mood change not easily perceived by the novice."[83] The most common mood encouraged by the drug is a sense of increased well-being, but this is heavily dependent on the setting and expectations of the user. The nervousness that may accompany first use, for example, can negate any reaction to the drug. Set and setting help to produce a wide range of reactions and may be more crucial determinants of the effects of *cannabis* use than those of most other drugs.[84] The effects described below are those observed in clinical trials and obtained from interviews with users.

One important effect is the enhancement of the senses. Sensitivity to colors, sounds, patterns, textures, and taste is greatly increased. Perception of space and time is distorted in ways that can be either pleasing or disconcerting. In particular, time passes very slowly. Inhibitions may be relaxed in a manner reminiscent of the effects of low doses of alcohol. The subject may develop a sense of being in a fantasy or dreamlike state (an effect achieved also by sedatives and anesthetics).

In clinical experiments, large doses of THC have produced LSD-type experiences, but this requires quantities of THC far in excess of the concentrations found in organic *cannabis*. Real hallucinations do not occur.

The dose-response curve of THC has not yet been established; nor have systematic comparisons of THC and LSD been made.

Significant adverse reactions to *cannabis* are rare, but they do occur. They are more common when strong forms, such as hashish, are used. There are four types that may result:

(1) simple depression, (2) a panic state, (3) toxic psychosis, and (4) psychotic break.

Of the four, the simple depression reaction is the mildest and most common. Its genesis is not known. People may be responding idiosyncratically to pharmacological effects of the drug; or the *cannabis* may intensify pre-existing but suppressed psychological states or traits. It is likely, also, that the different explanations might each account for some of the depressions seen. In any event, the reaction ends spontaneously.

The panic reaction occurs when a user interprets the use or effects of *cannabis* as a threat to life or sanity. It is most likely to occur in subjects with no prior drug experience who are ambivalent toward drug use and possibly fearful of police arrest. Verbal and personal support by peers is the most effective therapy; hospitalization and the use of tranquilizers are usually contraindicated unless the person is highly agitated.[85]

Many panic reactions have been misdiagnosed as examples of toxic psychosis—a condition in which the presence of toxins in the body causes organic malfunction in the cerebral cortex and a resultant psychotic state. This reaction is even rarer than the panic reaction and ends when the toxins are flushed from the system. A user is vulnerable to such a reaction when consuming *cannabis* in concentrated forms, especially if the drug is mixed with food and drink. The effects are delayed while the drug is being absorbed, and the user cannot use the effects of the drug as a measure of when he has had enough. In the view of some experts, smoking *cannabis* allows the user to regulate consumption in reaction to the immediate effects of the drug's passing into the blood stream via the lungs.

The view that differences in reaction to the two methods of administration are due to control of dosage can be questioned, however. Dr. Andrew Weil states:

This theory of autotitration sounds nice, but I do not see it happen much. Most marijuana smokers I know smoke as much as they are handed. What is interesting is that one reaches some sort of ceiling in smoking: beyond a certain point, one does not get any higher, only more sedated. With oral ingestion, on the other hand, one can easily get into the toxic range. These observations suggest pharmacological differences between the two routes of administration.[86]

The use of *cannabis* may also trigger a psychotic break in individuals who have normal psychological histories. Although evidence is scarce, the degree of risk is probably very small. A recent study reviewed twelve cases of *cannabis*-related psychotic breaks arising over a ten-month period among soldiers stationed in Vietnam. Only two of the twelve had "significant psychiatric histories and diagnosis of personality disorder." In all cases, the reaction occurred after the first use of *cannabis* and was self-limiting, in that the condition cleared spontaneously.[87] Since about 30 per cent of the 500,000 American soldiers in Vietnam at the time had probably consumed *cannabis* at least once, often in potent form, the incidence seems low.

Other data support this conclusion. During a fifteen-month period, approximately 30,000 persons were treated at the Haight-Ashbury Clinic for a variety of medical and psychiatric problems. An estimated 95 per cent had used *cannabis*. No case of a psychotic break was recorded.[88]

The risk of a psychotic break may be higher for users who have a history of mental disorder. There is some evidence to support this, but there are no statistical data on the degree to which such population is at greater risk than "normals."

Tolerance. Cannabis appears to have the unusual property of "reverse tolerance," in that regular users are more sensitive to the drug than novices. This characteristic has been conventional wisdom within the drug culture for some time; it is supported by a recent scientific study that used radioactive isotope tagging to detect THC in body tissues several days after the drug had been injected. The conclusion was that THC may accumulate in the body, so that a regular user may already have a "basic dose" and require only a small, additional amount to obtain a psychoactive effect.[89]

It is not known whether pharmacological tolerance to *cannabis* develops. Because of the "reverse tolerance" effect, experts have assumed that there was no such tolerance; but, if the effects are cumulative, then "reverse tolerance" in users could be accompanied by pharmacological tolerance. For example, when syn-hexyl, a potent synthetic *cannabis* derivative, is administered, tolerance develops in four to six days.[90]

Physical Dependence. There is little evidence that physical dependence develops with the consumption of *cannabis*, and no significant withdrawal symptoms accompany cessation of use. If dependence of any kind develops, it is probably psychological, but even this appears to be minimal.[91]

Mechanisms of Action. The way in which *cannabis* causes CNS effects is not known.

Additional Sources. A number of comprehensive reviews of marijuana have recently been published, taking up many of the above issues in greater depth. Some of these are

- U.S. Government, Secretary of Department of Health, Education and Welfare, *Marihuana and Health: A Report to Congress,* January 31, 1971 (GPO, 1971)
- Federation of American Societies for Experimental Biology, *A Review of the Biomedical Effects of Marijuana on Men in the Military Environment* (Bethesda, Maryland, December, 1970)
- Lester Grinspoon, *Marihuana Reconsidered* (Harvard University Press, 1971)
- Leo E. Hollister, "Marihuana in Man: Three Years Later," *Science,* CLXXII, No. 21 (April, 1971)

THE MAJOR STIMULANTS

The Drugs.[92] This category of drugs includes those that have the effect of stimulating physical and mental activity and of providing a feeling of such stimulation to the user:

- *Amphetamines* are synthetic drugs that are part of the general category of sympathomimetic agents—a group of drugs whose effects resemble the response to stimulation of certain nerves of the sympathetic nerve system (hence "sympathomimetic"). They are CNS stimulants.
- *Methamphetamine* is a close relative of the amphetamines. The major distinction is that it has a different ratio between

central effects and peripheral actions than do the basic amphetamines. Small doses of methamphetamine produce prominent central stimulant reactions without significant peripheral effects.

- *Cocaine* is an alkaloid of the coca plant. In general effects, it is quite similar to the amphetamines.
- *Methylphenidate* (*Ritalin*) is a mild CNS stimulant, between caffeine and the amphetamines in its effects.
- *Phenmetrazine* (*Preludin*) is also a sympathomimetic agent. Its effects are almost indistinguishable from those of amphetamines.

This section discusses amphetamines primarily, as the prototype. Significant differences are noted as relevant.

Medical Uses.[93]   The amphetamines are used to treat a rare condition called narcolepsy—the inability to stay awake. They are also used in the treatment of obesity because of their characteristic of depressing the appetite centers, but the results in this area are unimpressive. Amphetamines are useful in the treatment of children with hyperkinesis. This condition, which is also called minimal brain dysfunction, is one in which a child shows an inability to concentrate, a deficiency in motor skills, a low frustration level, and often an abnormal EEG pattern.

Quasimedical uses are very common. Amphetamines increase short-term physical and mental performance and are widely used by people who desire this effect, such as students and athletes. They are also used by people who have become dependent on or habituated to them to maintain their normal level of functioning.

Cocaine is not used medically for any of the above purposes, but it is used as a local anesthetic.

Ritalin is effective in treating hyperkinesis and, because it is milder than the amphetamines, may be the drug of choice.[94]

Physical Effects and Toxicity.   In different relative degrees, sympathomimetic agents have the following major actions:[95]

- A peripheral excitatory action on such smooth muscles as those in blood vessels supplying the skin and on salivary and some sweat glands;

- A peripheral inhibitory effect on other types of smooth muscles, such as those in the wall of the gut, on the bronchial tree, and on the blood vessels supplying the skeletal muscle;
- A cardiac excitatory action that increases heart rate and force of contraction;
- Certain metabolic actions;
- CNS excitatory actions, such as respiratory stimulation and others.

Amphetamines follow this scheme. Blood pressure is increased, and the smooth muscle responses, while somewhat unpredictable, are as indicated. The amphetamines are more potent in their CNS effects than other drugs in the group, and it is through the effects on the CNS that they stimulate respiration, depress the appetite, and reverse fatigue. The results of an oral dose of 10 to 30 mg. of amphetamine (the standard therapeutic dose is 10 mg.) are wakefulness, alertness, decreased sense of fatigue, elevation of mood with increased initiative, confidence, and ability to concentrate, elation and euphoria, and an increase in motor and speech activity. Prolonged use or heavy dosage is followed by mental depression and fatigue.

Cocaine has the same effects as the amphetamines. The major difference is that the effects of the amphetamines last several hours, while those of cocaine seem to last only minutes.[96] Ritalin has less motor effect on motor and mental activities than do the amphetamines. Some CNS effect is produced by doses that have little effect on respiration and blood pressure.[97]

The amphetamines can be quite toxic. Severe reactions have occurred with only 30 mg., and death has resulted from 120 mg. of injected amphetamine. The range is wide, however, and doses of 400 to 500 mg. have been survived by nontolerant individuals. Death from overdose is quite rare, possibly because the ratio of lethal to effective psychoactive dose is high for a tolerant user.[98]

Cocaine is toxic because the central stimulation that is the immediate effect of the drug is followed by depression of the higher nervous centers. Death from respiratory depression occurs when the vital medullary centers are sufficiently depressed. The fatal dose of cocaine has been estimated to be about 1.2 grams taken at one time, but severe toxic effects have been reported on doses as low as 20 mg.[99]

The basic symptoms of amphetamine poisoning are extensions of its normal therapeutic effects on the CNS, the cardiovascular system, and the gastrointestinal system. A fatal dose ends in convulsions and coma. Cerebral hemorrhage is a common autopsy finding, but it is rarely massive. "Pathological findings in both man and animals are generally nonspecific and show pulmonary congestion and often congestion of other organs including the brain."[100]

Amphetamines are usually taken orally, but they can be injected. Cocaine is not effective when taken orally, but it can be snorted and absorbed through the mucous membrane or taken intravenously. Medically, cocaine is only applied to body surfaces as a local anesthetic; it is not injected or used internally.

The major, long-term toxic effect of amphetamine use is a paranoid psychosis that is often indistinguishable from a schizophrenic reaction. This can occur after continued use or even after an extremely heavy single dose. It usually disappears within a week if the individual stops using the drug. Cocaine can cause the same condition even more rapidly.

Whether these drugs cause long-term organic damage to the body is at present unknown. Some experts who have worked with amphetamine users believe that there is a long-term deterioration that is explicable only in terms of organic damage. At present, however, this has not been definitely established. In animal experiments, death often results from continued administration of methamphetamine, but the reason appears to be that the animal's disinterest in food, combined with its hyperactivity, results in a malnourished condition that leaves it vulnerable to infection. There have been some preliminary reports attributing arterial disease to methamphetamine use, but these have not yet been substantiated and should not be accepted until further evidence develops.

Hepatitis is very common among amphetamine users. This is to be expected when hypodermic needles are used without proper sterilization, but its incidence goes even beyond the level logically attributable to this cause alone. Some consideration is now being given to the possibility that amphetamine is itself directly toxic to the liver. No clinical evidence on this possibility has been developed, however, and it remains only a possibility.[101]

Psychoactive Effects. When taken orally, amphetamines produce an elevation of mood and feeling of power and intensity that many persons find quite pleasurable. The drugs increase concentration and physical and mental performance and reduce fatigue. Some users claim that orgasms are delayed and made more intense when they occur, but no objective experiments have been done.

The drugs produce the same effect even when taken intravenously. In addition, the user obtains a "rush" that is reputed to be different from, although related to, the effect obtained from opiate injection. Again, sexual analogies are often made by users. It is difficult to know whether the rush is a product of the drug itself or of the process of intravenous injection. Some users actually prefer impure methamphetamine because of the belief that the impurities cause a faster, more intense rush.[102]

As the dosage increases, the experience seems to become more fragmented. Increased ability to concentrate turns either into a compulsion to do repetitive tasks over and over or into a total focusing of attention on some object or toy. Heavy users have a compulsion to take mechanical objects apart and a similar compulsion to try (unsuccessfully) to put them together again. Such repetitive behavior occurs in animals as well as in humans.[103]

Eventually—and fairly predictably—heavy amphetamine use during a limited period of time will result in paranoid ideation and the toxic psychosis discussed above. To some extent, users are aware of this aspect of amphetamine use and can make allowances for it during the experience. They will not act on moderate ideas of persecution or visual illusions. If the run continues long enough, this control will be lost.

Some heavy users may become chronically psychotic, in that they exhibit psychotic symptoms even when not taking the drug. The California experience is that normal functioning returns over a period of six to twelve months, although the user himself may feel some residual disablement.[104]

Cocaine has roughly the same effects as amphetamines in terms of creating feelings of well-being, euphoria, and power. According to the accounts of users, these feelings are even stronger with cocaine than with the amphetamines, but reliable evidence is unobtainable.

Tolerance.[105]   Tolerance to most effects of the amphetamines develops rapidly, and very high dosage levels can be reached. A speed user on a run may inject as much as a gram of the drug every two or three hours around the clock for several days. Whether this is drug disposition or cellular tolerance is not known. The development of tolerance is not uniform, however, and the ability to withstand what would otherwise be a fatal dose does not confer tolerance to the toxic psychosis.

It is not certain that tolerance to cocaine develops. There are reports of very large doses—such as 10 grams per day—but individuals seem able to tolerate the same doses after a period of abstinence as before. It is known that the liver is extremely effective at detoxifying cocaine and can process a lethal dose every hour.

There are no reports of cross-tolerance between cocaine and the amphetamines, but cross-tolerance between amphetamine and the other stimulants has been reported clinically.

Physical Dependence.   For a long time, it was believed that there were no withdrawal symptoms from amphetamines and therefore no physical dependence. At present, it is thought that the prolonged sleep, lassitude, and depression that follow discontinuation of the drug are greater than would be attributable to the preceding loss of sleep and weight. These may be withdrawal symptoms. In addition, the percentage of REM sleep increases after discontinuance of amphetamine, returns to normal when amphetamine is given, and rises again when amphetamine is withheld. This meets the criteria for a withdrawal symptom.[106] The sources are silent, however, on the extent to which these symptoms are dose-related.

Some experts in the field believe that amphetamines are far more dangerous than the opiates. This is related not only to the typicality of the euphoric effect but also to the problems of tolerance and stabilization. Dr. Weil elaborates:

In fact, amphetamine dependence is more serious than narcotic dependence because it is inherently less stable. When a person begins using a tolerance-producing drug, he must soon face the problem of trying to stabilize his use in order to keep his life from being disrupted. More than any other class of drugs, the amphetamines foil the user's attempt to reach equilibrium with his habit because they produce such powerful and unrelenting tolerance. Consequently, users develop erratic patterns of use such as "spree shooting," alternation with barbiturates and, eventually, with heroin. The high correlation of amphetamine use with impulsive and violent behavior is consistent with this pharmacological instability.[107]

Because intensive use of amphetamines is a relatively recent phenomenon, there is little information on such problems as readdiction vulnerability, physiological bases of abuse, or comparative success of different methods of treatment. There is no treatment comparable to methadone, but neither is there any particular evidence that such treatment is needed. The pattern of heavy amphetamine use is probably too hard to sustain for an extended period of time anyway, and there is increasing indication that heavy amphetamine users eventually turn to "down" drugs, such as heroin or barbiturates.[108]

Mechanisms of Action. There are several theories about the mechanisms of the CNS effects of the amphetamines, most based on analogies to their peripheral effects, but none is definitive.[109] While the effects of all the drugs are similar, the mechanisms may be different; for example, there are probably significant differences between the amphetamines and cocaine.[110]

BARBITURATES AND TRANQUILIZERS

The Drugs.[111] Barbiturates and tranquilizers are sedatives (calming agents), hypnotics (sleep-inducing agents), and depressants. The category encompasses a wide range of drugs of different families. For example, over 2,500 barbiturates have been synthesized, and at least twelve are in common clinical use. In the area of nonbarbiturate hypnotics, Sharpless lists twenty-three commonly used drugs belonging to ten different families. In addition to these two groups, there are a number of major tranquilizers that are used in the treatment of psychiatric disorders. More is known about these drugs than about those discussed in previous sections. This is in part because they have been in wide use for a long time, and in part because most of them have more general effects than do other drugs of abuse. Drugs of this category act on a number of bodily systems besides the CNS, and these other systems are more easily studied. This section discusses the effects of the drugs only insofar as these are relevant to their abuse potential.

The major drugs involved are as follows:

- *Barbiturates* are derivatives of barbituric acid; they were first used medically in 1903. The major abused drugs in the series are secobarbital and pentobarbital.
- *Meprobamate* (*Equinil, Miltown*), *glutethimide* (*Doriden*), *chlordiazepoxide* (*Librium*), and *diazepam* (*Valium*) are CNS depressants belonging to several different families. Medically, they are regarded as anti-anxiety agents—not hypnotics—and they and similar drugs are called the minor tranquilizers.

One group of powerful tranquilizers, the *phenothiazines* (*Chlorpromazine*), are not covered. While they are in common use, especially for the treatment of serious mental illness, this class of drugs does not appear to be abused.[112] There is no satisfactory explanation of why they are not attractive to drug abusers. Obviously, their psychoactive effects must differ significantly from those of barbiturates or the minor tranquilizers, but the nature of these differences is unexplored.

The discussion here centers on barbiturates—the most powerful and often abused drugs—and brings in others as relevant.

Medical Uses.[113]   The barbiturates are used as calming agents and as sleeping pills. Some of them are also used as anticonvulsants in the treatment of certain types of poisoning or epilepsy. The tranquilizers are used in any situation where the patient will benefit from an anti-anxiety drug. They are not sleep-inducing, except insofar as insomnia may be caused by anxiety. Both are widely used in the practice of medicine.

Physical Effects and Toxicity.[114]   The barbiturates are general depressants of a wide range of cellular functions in many organ systems. They are not general anesthetics or analgesics, however, and will not prevent or relieve pain. (Some of the ultra-short-acting barbiturates are anesthetics when injected, but this is a minor exception.) They are respiratory depressants, and in high concentrations they have direct effects on the cardiovascular system. Most of the peripheral effects—the effects directly on the organs themselves—occur only at concentrations of the drug that exceed those necessary to affect the CNS and are thus relatively rare. "The CNS is exquisitely sensitive to the barbiturates, so that, when the drugs are given in sedative or hypnotic doses, direct actions on peripheral structures are absent or negligible."[115]

The effect on the CNS can range from coma to mild sedation, depending on the particular drug, the method of administration, and the dose. In some individuals, and in some circumstances, low doses will act as a stimulant rather than a sedative. It is not clear whether this depends on the mental set of the user or on the pharmacological phenomenon that the first effect of a drug is sometimes on brain centers that regulate and inhibit excitatory bodily functions.

For short- and intermediate-acting barbiturates, the hypnotic dose is 100–200 mg., which will give six or seven hours of sleep in the proper environment. The sleep is like physiological sleep, except that the proportion of REM phase is reduced. (The amphetamines also reduce REM.) The usual sedative dose is 30–50 mg., given two or three times daily.

The duration of action varies with the particular barbiturate. Some will last only ten or fifteen minutes, some for more than a day. Performance degradation, however, may last longer than overt effects. A 200-mg. dose of secobarbital (which is known as intermediate in its duration) may cause decreased performance ten to twenty-two hours later. The aftereffect of the drug may be hyperexcitability, even though functioning is, in fact, still impaired.

Taken in large quantities, barbiturates can cause death. The lethal dose varies, but it can generally be assumed that anything over ten times the normal hypnotic dose administered at one time will cause severe poisoning. Moderate poisoning is strikingly similar to alcoholic intoxication, with slurred speech, poor reflexes, and the rest of the well-known syndrome. Severe poisoning is characterized by a deep coma, with respiratory depression, falling blood pressure, shock syndrome, kidney failure, and other complications.

The long-term effects of barbiturate use seem to be in some doubt. The pharmacology books mention only the results of severe intoxication, not the effects of chronic use. At the same time, it is known that alcohol and the barbiturates have many characteristics in common and are to some extent substitutes for each other. Barbiturates will suppress the withdrawal symptoms of alcohol and vice versa; the intoxications are similar, and so are the withdrawal symptoms. In the formal literature, abuse of the two kinds of drugs is linked as "drug dependence of the barbiturate-alcohol type."[116] The destructive effects of long-term heavy alcohol use are familiar, and some authorities believe that barbiturates may have very similar effects on the cells of the liver and brain. Presumably, our knowledge of the toxicity resulting from long-term but moderate use of barbiturates is in the same limbo as our knowledge of comparable use of alcohol.

Psychoactive Effects. The literature contains numerous descriptions of the effects of barbiturates on outward behavior. Intoxication may cause sluggishness, slowness of speech and comprehension, bad judgment, exaggeration of basic personality traits, moroseness, or irritability.[117]

The sources do not contain a description of the subjective effects, however, and the nature of the "high" involved in heavy use is less discussed than is the case for any of the other drugs of abuse. The general effect seems to be one of tranquility and peace. How this compares with an opiate high is not clear.

At doses only slightly in excess of the therapeutic dose, the effect may be one of excitation and mood elevation rather than of tranquilization.

A combination of barbiturates and amphetamines produces more elevation of mood than either taken separately. The reason for this is not known. Nor is it known whether this is the reason for the common drug abusers' practice of taking the two in combination.

The other depressants in this category are abusable and have much the same effects and symptoms as abused barbiturates. Abuse in the sense of self-administration does not seem to be terribly common, however; some of them, such as Librium, have rather minimal euphoriant effects. In general, from the standpoint of the abuser, barbiturates—particularly short-acting ones—are a superior good, with others acceptable as substitutes only if barbiturates are unavailable.

Tolerance.   Both drug disposition and pharmacodynamic tolerance to the barbiturates develop with repeated administration. The first is caused by the activation of drug-metabolizing enzymes in the liver and consequent increase in the speed of detoxation of the drug. A higher dose is then required to maintain a given tissue concentration. The second involves the adaptation of nervous tissue to the presence of the drug. Tolerance develops quickly, and the CNS probably becomes resistant to the effects of the drug during the action of a single administration.[118]

The tolerance, however, is largely limited to the sedative and intoxicating effects of the drug. The lethal dose is not much greater for addicts than for nonaddicts. In addition, the range of tolerance is narrow. An individual tolerant to 1.2 grams of a particular drug may show acute intoxication if the dose is raised as little as 0.1 gram per day.

The other drugs of this class develop tolerance in the same way and with the same limitations as do the barbiturates.

Physical Dependence and Withdrawal.   Severe physical dependence on the barbiturates develops, but, unlike the situation for the opiates, the dosages required for this effect are higher than the therapeutic dose. With pentobarbital, for example, 200 mg. per day can be taken for months without producing withdrawal, and 400 mg. per day for three months will produce EEG changes in only 30 per cent of the cases. The other 70 per cent apparently show no effects. After 600 mg. per day for one to two months, half the subjects will have minor withdrawal symptoms, and 10 per cent may have a seizure. After continuous intoxication with doses of 900 mg. to 2.2 grams, 75 per cent of the subjects may have seizures, and 60 per cent delirium; all experience lesser symptoms.[120]

Defining "major" withdrawal symptoms as seizures or psychoses, the time and dosage necessary to produce severe physical dependence for different sedative hypnotics have been calculated as follows: [121]

TABLE 1–1
ADDICTING DOSES OF COMMON SEDATIVE-HYPNOTICS*

	Dependence-producing dosage (mg. daily)	Time necessary to produce dependence (days)	Drug dosage equivalent to 30 mg. of phenobarbital (mg.)
Drug			
Secobarbital			
Pentobarbital	800–2,200	35–37	100
Diazepam (Valium)	80–120	42	10
Chlordiazepoxide			
hydrochloride (Librium)	300–600	60–180	25
Meprobamate (Equanil)	2,400	270	400

* Dosages sufficient to produce "major" withdrawal signs in humans.

As Table 1–1 indicates, the other sedative hypnotics are thought to produce dependence similar to that caused by barbiturates. They have not been as carefully studied.

We have found no study that divides opiate withdrawal into "major" and "minor" symptoms. Thus, it is not possible to compare the development of barbiturate dependence with that of opiate dependence.

Once physical dependence develops, withdrawal from barbiturates is severe, and—unlike opiate withdrawal—may be life-threatening. For one of the short-acting drugs, for the first twelve hours or so the patient seems to improve as the intoxication clears. He then becomes restless, anxious, tremulous, and weak, and sometimes has nausea or cramps. Within twenty-four hours, he may be too weak to get out of bed, experience severe tremors in the hands, and have hyperactive deep reflexes. The peak is reached on the second or third day, and convulsions may occur. Half the patients who have convulsive seizures go on to delirium, which occurs between the fourth and seventh days. This consists of high anxiety, hallucinations, and disorientation. Once delirium occurs, it may not be suppressed even by large doses of barbiturates. This is contrary to the normal course of withdrawal symptoms, which are quickly suppressed by the drug of addiction. The reason for this anomaly is not known. During the delirium, exhaustion and cardiovascular collapse may occur. The withdrawal syndrome usually clears by about the eighth day, if untreated. For longer-acting drugs, seizures may not occur until the seventh or eighth day, and the general course is slowed down accordingly.[122]

Hallucinations sometimes persist for months, but "this is felt by most investigators to be a manifestation of an underlying psychosis."[123] The sources do not discuss whether barbiturates, like the opiates, have early and protracted abstinence syndromes.

Meprobomate (Equanil, Miltown) follows the short-acting course. Librium follows that of the long-acting barbiturates.

Mechanisms of Action.   More is known about the fate of barbiturates in the body than is known about the other drugs of abuse. It is known, for example, that they are transformed by the liver into a number of inactive metabolites that are in turn excreted. This lessens the concentration of the drug and causes the withdrawal from its site of action in the CNS. The general state of knowledge concerning metabolism, physical redistribution, and excretion is discussed in the sources, as are the general theories of sites of action in the CNS. These are too technical to discuss here. The mechanisms by which barbiturates operate to cause CNS effects are not well understood.[124]

A WORD ON ALCOHOL

Problems of alcohol and alcoholism were not within the mandate of the Drug Abuse Survey Project, and they have not been included in the report or in any of the supporting papers. In the context of this chapter, however, one comment should be made: Alcohol is a drug and could easily be analyzed in the same terms as the drugs that are covered. It has a potent psychoactive effect and is, like most of the drugs with which we are concerned, highly specific to the CNS. Both tolerance and physical dependence develop, and withdrawal can be a very serious clinical condition. The drug causes organic damage. The interplay of physiological factors and psychological factors involves as many uncertainties for alcohol as for the opiates.

In short, the common distinction between alcohol and "drugs of abuse" is based on the fact that alcohol is known and accepted in the culture, not on any pharmacological considerations. It is entirely possible that alcohol is inherently more dangerous than most of the other drugs discussed.

In his listing of the hazards of different drugs, Dr. Samuel Irwin makes the following rankings, starting with the most dangerous: [125]

1. Glue sniffing
2. Methamphetamine
3. Alcohol
4. Cigarettes
5. Barbiturates and hypnotics
6. Heroin and related narcotics
7. LSD and other hallucinogens
8. Marijuana

NOTES

Because the same authors are cited continually in this staff paper, footnotes give only the author, date of publication when necessary, and page number. The complete references are as follows:

Baden, M. Interview by Project Staff.
Ball, J., and J. Urbaitis. "Absence of Major Medical Complications Among Chronic Opiate Addicts," in J. Ball and C. Chambers (eds.), *The Epidemiology of Opiate Addiction in the United States* (Springfield, Ill.: Charles C. Thomas, 1970), p. 301.
Blacker, K. "Aggression and the Chronic Use of LSD," *Journal of Psychedelic Drugs,* III, No. 1 (September, 1970), 32.
Brazeau, P. "Oxytocics," in L. Goodman and A. Gilman, *The Pharmacological Basis of Therapeutics* (4th ed.; New York: Macmillan, 1970), p. 893. (This book is hereafter referred to as Goodman and Gilman.)
Brotman, R., and A. Friedman. "Perspectives on Marijuana Research" (Center for Studies in Substance Use; mimeograph, undated).
Chopra, C. "Man and Marijuana," *The International Journal of the Addictions,* IV, No. 2 (June, 1969), 219–33.

Cohen, S. "Lysergic Acid Diethylamide: Side Effects and Complications," *Journal of Nervous and Mental Disease* CXXX (1969), 30.

Cooper, J., F. Bloom, and R. Roth. *The Biochemical Basis of Neuropharmacology* (Oxford: Oxford University Press, 1970).

Dishotsky, N., W. Loughman, R. Mogar, and W. Lipscomb. "LSD and Genetic Damage," *Science,* CLXXII (April 30, 1971), 431.

Dole, V. "Narcotic Blockade," *Archives of Internal Medicine,* CXVIII (October, 1966), 304, 305.

————. "Research on Methadone Maintenance Treatment," *The International Journal of the Addictions,* V, No. 3 (September, 1970), 359.

Dole, V., and M. Nyswander. "Methadone Maintenance and Its Implications for Theories of Narcotic Addiction," in A. Wikler (ed.), *The Addictive States* (Baltimore, Md.: Williams and Wilkins, Inc., 1968), p. 359.

Douglas, W. "Histamine and Antihistamines: 5-Hydroxytryptamine and Antagonists," in Goodman and Gilman, p. 620.

Eddy, N. Interview by Project Staff.

Eddy, N., *et al.* "Drug Dependence: Its Significance and Characteristics," *Bulletin of the World Health Organization,* XXXII (1965), 721.

Egozcue, J., and S. Irwin. "LSD–25 Effects on Chromosomes: A Review," *Journal of Psychedelic Drugs,* III, No. 1 (September, 1970), 10.

Esplin, D., and B. Zablocka-Esplin. "Central Nervous System Stimulants," in Goodman and Gilman, p. 348.

Fingl, E., and D. Woodbury. "General Principles," in Goodman and Gilman, p. 1.

Goldstein, A. Interview by Project Staff.

Goldstein, A., L. Aronow, and S. Kalman. *Principles of Drug Action* (New York: Harper & Row, 1968).

Grinspoon, L. *Marihuana Reconsidered* (Cambridge, Mass.: Harvard University Press, 1971).

Health, Education and Welfare, Secretary of, *Marihuana and Health: A Report to Congress,* January 31, 1971 (GPO, March, 1971).

Innes, I. R., and M. Nickerson. "Drugs Acting on Postganglionic Adrenic Nerve Endings and Structures Innervated by Them (Sympathomimetic Drugs)," in Goodman and Gilman, p. 478.

Irwin, S. *Drugs of Abuse: An Introduction to Their Actions and Potential Hazards* (Student Association for the Study of the Hallucinogens, 1970).

Jaffe, J. "Narcotic Analgesics" and "Drug Addiction and Drug Abuse," in Goodman and Gilman, pp. 237 and 276.

Jarvik, M. "Drugs Used in the Treatment of Psychiatric Disorders," in Goodman and Gilman, p. 151.

Koelle, G. "Neurohumoral Transmission and the Autonomic Nervous System," in Goodman and Gilman, p. 402.

Kramer, J. "An Introduction to Amphetamine Abuse," *Journal of Psychedelic Drugs,* II, No. 2 (1969), 1.

Lemberger, L., *et al.* "Marijuana: Studies on the Disposition and Metabolism of Delta-9-Tetrahydrocannabinol in Man," *Science,* CLXX (December 18, 1970), 1322.

Mandell, A., and C. Spooner. "Psychochemical Studies in Man," *Science* (December, 1968), p. 1442.

Martin, W. "Pathophysiology of Narcotic Addiction: Possible Roles of Protracted Abstinence in Relapse" (unpublished, 1970).

————, and H. Fraser. "A Comparative Study of Physiological and Subjective Effects of Heroin and Morphine Administered Intravenously in Postaddicts," *Journal of Pharmacology and Experimental Therapeutics,* CXXXIII, No. 3 (September, 1961), 388.

McGlothlin, W., S. Cohen, and M. McGlothlin. "Long Lasting Effects of LSD on Normals," *Journal of Psychedelic Drugs,* III, No. 1 (September, 1970), 20.

Mechoulam, R. "Marijuana Chemistry," *Science,* CLXVIII (June 5, 1970), 1159, 1165.

Meyers, F. "The Pharmacological Effects of Marijuana," *Journal of Psychedelic Drugs,* II, No. 1 (Fall, 1969), 31.

Moore, K. "Biochemical Correlates of the Behavioral Effects of Drugs," in R. Rech and K. Moore, *An Introduction to Psychopharmacology* (New York: Raven Press, 1970).

Morgan, C. *Physiological Psychology* (New York: McGraw-Hill, Inc., 1965).

Pahnke, W., *et al.* "Psychedelic Therapy (Utilizing LSD) With Cancer Patients," *Journal of Psychedelic Drugs,* III, No. 1 (September, 1970), 63.

Phillipson, R. "Methadone Maintenance: Why Continue Controls?" in National Institute of Mental Health, *Proceedings Third National Methadone Conference* (GPO, 1971), p. 1.

Ritchie, J. M., P. Cohen, and R. Dripps. "Cocaine, Procaine and Other Local Anesthetics," in Goodman and Gilman, p. 371.

Sharpless, S. "Hypnotics and Sedatives," in Goodman and Gilman, pp. 98 and 121.

Shick, J., and D. Smith. "Analysis of the LSD Flashback," *Journal of Psychedelic Drugs,* III, No. 1 (September, 1970), 13.

Smith, D. "Acute and Chronic Toxicity of Marijuana," *Journal of Psychedelic Drugs* (Fall, 1968), p. 41.

————. "The Psychotomimetic Amphetamines with Special Reference to DOM (STP) Toxicity," *Journal of Psychedelic Drugs,* II, No. 2 (1969), 73.

————, and D. Wesson. "A New Method for Treatment of Barbiturate Dependence," *Journal of the American Medical Association,* CCXIII, No. 2 (July 13, 1970), 294.

Smith, R. "The World of the Haight Ashbury Speed Freak," *Journal of Psychedelic Drugs,* II, No. 2 (1969), 172.

————. "Traffic in Amphetamines: Patterns of Illegal Manufacture and Distribution," *Journal of Psychedelic Drugs,* II, No. 2 (1969), 30.

Snyder, S. "What We Have Forgotten About Pot–A Pharmacologist's History," *New York Times Sunday Magazine,* December 13, 1970, pp. 26–27, 121–34.

Student Association for the Study of the Hallucinogens (STASH), *Capsules,* II, No. 2 (April, 1970), 1.

_____. "Speed Kills: A Review of Amphetamine Abuse," an issue of the *Journal of Psychedelic Drugs,* Vol. II, Issue II (Fall, 1969).

Talbott, J., and J. Teague. "Marijuana Psychosis," *Journal of the American Medical Association,* CCX, No. 2 (October 13, 1969), p. 299.

Tart, C. "Marijuana Intoxication: Common Experiences," *Nature,* CCXXVI (May 23, 1970), 701–4.

Way, E. L. "Distribution and Metabolism of Morphine and Its Surrogates," in A. Wikler (ed.), *The Addictive States* (Baltimore, Md.: Williams and Wilkins, 1968), p. 3.

Weil, A. "Adverse Reaction to Marijuana," *New England Journal of Medicine,* CCXXVIII (April 30, 1970), 997.

_____. "Altered States of Consciousness," Staff Paper 6.

_____. Interview by Project Staff.

_____., N. Zinberg, and J. Nelson. "Clinical and Psychological Effects of Marijuana in Man," *Science,* CLXII (December 13, 1968), 1242.

_____. Letter to J. V. DeLong, January 14, 1971.

1. This section is based on Morgan, pp. 15–35.
2. Moore, p. 81.
3. *Ibid.,* pp. 82–84. See also Cooper *et al.,* pp. 15–16.
4. Mandell and Spooner, pp. 1443–44.
5. Moore, pp. 95, 102.
6. *Ibid.,* pp. 107–8.
7. Fingl and Woodbury, pp. 16–17.
8. Goldstein *et al.,* p. 52.
9. *Ibid.,* pp. 70–98; Fingl and Woodbury, pp. 17–18.
10. Goldstein *et al.,* pp. 30, 33–34.
11. *Ibid.,* p. 52.
12. *Ibid.,* p. 599.
13. Jaffe, p. 239.
14. This section is based on Jaffe, pp. 237–75.
15. Weil, interview.
16. Jaffe, p. 238.
17. Phillipson, p. 2.
18. Jaffe, pp. 240–41; Goldstein *et al.,* p. 591.
19. Jaffe, p. 243; Goldstein *et al.,* pp. 592–93.
20. Goldstein *et al.,* p. 593.
21. Baden, interview.
22. Ball and Urbaitis, p. 306; see also Jaffe, p. 286.

23. This estimate is based on interviews with several experts.
24. We found no studies on deaths by overdose.
25. Martin, 1970, p. 4.
26. Goldstein *et al.,* p. 592.
27. Based primarily on Jaffe, pp. 239–60.
28. Martin, 1970, p. 4.
29. Jaffe, p. 240; Irwin, p. 5.
30. Goldstein *et al.,* p. 474.
31. Jaffe, p. 279.
32. *Ibid.,* pp. 279–80.
33. *Ibid.,* p. 279; Goldstein *et al.,* pp. 593–94.
34. Goldstein *et al.,* pp. 597–99.
35. Eddy, 1965, p. 721.
36. Goldstein *et al.,* pp. 600, 603.
37. Jaffe, p. 280.
38. *Ibid.,* p. 288; Goldstein *et al.,* pp. 602–3.
39. Martin, 1970, pp. 2–3.
40. Goldstein *et al.,* p. 603; Jaffe, p. 281.
41. Goldstein *et al.,* p. 605.
42. Jaffe, p. 283.
43. Goldstein, p. 605.
44. Jaffe, pp. 281–82.
45. *Ibid.,* p. 282.
46. Dole, 1966, p. 305.
47. Goldstein, interview.
48. Goldstein *et al.,* pp. 474–75.
49. Dole, 1968, p. 364.
50. Dole, 1970, p. 373.
51. Dole, interview.
52. Martin, 1970, pp. 8–9.
53. See Jaffe, pp. 296–97, and Brazeau, pp. 899–900.
54. This section is summarized from the *Journal of Psychedelic Drugs,* September, 1970.
55. Jarvik, p. 196.
56. *Ibid.,* p. 197.
57. *Ibid.;* Jaffe, p. 296; Shick and Smith, p. 16.
58. Egozcue and Irwin, pp. 10–11.
59. Dishotsky *et al.,* p. 439.
60. See Irwin, p. 8; Jaffe, p. 296.
61. McGlothlin *et al.,* pp. 20–31.
62. *Ibid.,* pp. 30–31.
63. Blacker, pp. 32–37.
64. Cohen, p.30.
65. Irwin, p. 9.
66. Shick and Smith, pp. 13–19.
67. *Ibid.*

68. D. Smith, 1969, p. 75.
69. Jaffe, p. 297.
70. D. Smith, 1969, p. 82; STASH, 1970.
71. Irwin, p. 8; Jaffe, pp. 297–98.
72. Jarvik, p. 197.
73. Irwin, p. 9; Jaffe, p. 298.
74. Jarvik, p. 196; Cooper *et al.,* pp. 157–59; Douglas, p. 656.
75. This section was written with the assistance of Peter Wilson.
76. Jaffe, p. 300; Meyers, p. 32.
77. Snyder, pp. 121–25.
78. *Ibid.*
79. Irwin, p. 7; Weil *et al.,* p. 1242.
80. Jaffe, p. 300.
81. HEW, p. 68; Grinspoon, pp. 227–28.
82. Lemberger *et al.,* p. 1322.
83. Jaffe, p. 299.
84. Tart, pp. 701–4.
85. Weil, p. 999.
86. Weil, letter.
87. Talbot and Teague.
88. D. Smith, 1968, p. 41.
89. Lemberger *et al.,* p. 1322.
90. Jaffe, p. 300.
91. Brotman and Friedman, p. 20; Jaffe, p. 300; Irwin, p. 7.
92. See Innes and Nickerson, Jaffe, and Ritchie *et al.*
93. Innes and Nickerson, except as otherwise noted.
94. Esplin and Zablocka-Esplin, pp. 354–55.
95. Innes and Nickerson, p. 478.
96. Ritchie *et al.,* pp. 379–82; Jaffe, p. 293.
97. Esplin anl Zablocka-Esplin, p. 354.
98. Kramer, p. 10; Jaffe, p. 295.
99. Ritchie *et al.,* p. 381.
100. Kramer, p. 11.
101. *Ibid.,* p. 12.
102. Jaffe, pp. 293–94; R. Smith, p. 35.
103. Jaffe, p. 294; Kramer, p. 9.
104. Kramer, p. 7.
105. Jaffe, pp. 294–95; Ritchie *et al.,* p. 381.
106. Jaffe, p. 295.
107. Weil, Staff Paper 6.
108. R. Smith, p. 184.
109. Innes and Nickerson, pp. 503–4.
110. Jaffe, p. 293.
111. Sharpless, pp. 98–134.
112. Irwin, p. 9; Weil, interview.
113. Sharpless, pp. 98–120.

114. *Ibid.*
115. *Ibid.*, p. 100.
116. Eddy, p. 725.
117. Jaffe, pp. 289–90.
118. Sharpless, pp. 107–8.
119. Jaffe, p. 290.
120. *Ibid.*
121. D. Smith and Wesson, pp. 294–95.
122. Jaffe, p. 290.
123. *Ibid.*
124. Sharpless, pp. 101–2, 110–11.
125. Irwin, pp. 3–4.

Drug Education

by Patricia M. Wald and Annette Abrams

Goals of Drug Education • Techniques of Drug Education for Students • Total School Involvement • Out-of-School Drug-Education Programs • The National Media • Films and Audio Visuals • School Curricula • Education for Nonstudents • Sponsors of Current Efforts

GOALS OF DRUG EDUCATION

"Prevention through education" has become the newest panacea of the drug-abuse field. Law enforcement has failed to stem the supply of illegal drugs, and rehabilitation efforts have thus far failed to reclaim many abusers. Everyone now talks of pouring money into education to stop the problem before it begins.

As of any educational undertaking, the first task of a drug-abuse-prevention program is to define the goals sought. If objectives are not understood, developing the educational effort and the techniques to be used is difficult. At present, this is a major problem of drug education. No one is sure what goals are realistic or desirable, and proponents of massive efforts cannot agree on what they hope to accomplish. The most that can be said is that there are a number of possible objectives for youth-oriented, drug-education programs:

- Stopping all experimentation with foreign substances
- Keeping experimentation at the minimum and limiting it to relatively safe substances
- Preventing casual experimenters from becoming habitual users
- Preventing addiction or severe dependence
- Reinforcing the anti-experimentation tendencies of those who have not yet tried drugs
- Presenting information for students to use in making drug decisions for themselves
- Increasing student understanding of the complex factors related to drug use, social attitudes, and policies

For adult audiences, the goals may be somewhat different—for parents, to give them the best information available, to heighten their concern about the effects of drugs, to make them less likely to panic if they find one of their children using drugs, to encourage them to lobby for more education, treatment, or law reform, or to teach them to communicate more openly with their children on the subject. For teachers, counselors, and other "gate-keepers" the object might be to train them to create an atmosphere of communication in their classrooms or to recognize student drug experimenters and abusers, deal with them sympathetically, and channel them into treatment if necessary. Teachers might also be equipped with the tools to stimulate objective discussion of the subject with their students.

The traditional goal of most parents, educators, community leaders, congressmen, and government officials has been to discourage young people from experimenting with illegal drugs at all. In the past, government and privately sponsored education efforts have tried to do this by emphasizing the horrors of addiction and lumping all drugs together as leading to the same ultimate doom. Virtually all experts now agree that such tactics have not proved effective. Indeed, in many cases, they have been counterproductive, causing disrespect, skepticism, and resistance to all advice on drugs. Despite the widespread implementation of this technique, youthful addiction and experimentation with illegal drugs have increased. Consequently, within the past few years there has been a change in emphasis, with more and more programs concentrating on an honest presentation of accurate, factual knowledge about the effects of drugs (insofar as such knowledge is available). The assumption is that drugs are obviously bad, and that telling the facts will be enough to convince young people not to experiment.

Although the approach may have changed, the aim of most public and private antidrug literature remains the same—to discourage young people from trying marijuana, psychedelics, amphetamines, barbiturates, and, above all, heroin. The theme of a nationwide government advertising campaign reflects the traditional broadside approach: "Why Do You Think They Call It Dope?" Many of the recent NIMH posters and television spots are along the same lines: "Will It Turn You On, or Will It Turn on You?" Most "model" curricula for elementary, junior, and senior high schools, even when they present the known facts about drugs fairly, push a strongly negative attitude toward all commonly abused drugs. The measure of success of such programs—although few try to measure success by any formula—is almost always assumed to be total cessation of drug experimentation and use.

In the late 1960's, however, this viewpoint ran into an embarrassing problem: no one was able to develop a factual scientific argument proving that marijuana was harmful. This development had its greatest impact on programs using the scare technique, but it also undermined programs based on the premise that telling the truth was an effective way of discouraging experimentation. This has put education in a difficult position. Most drug-education programs are ambivalent. They profess an honest desire to tell the truth—but only up to a point. When known facts run out or become controversial, as they almost certainly do when the subject comes up, the approach reverts to imposed value judgments, half-truths, or presumptions that the law is right—devices easily seen through by the skeptical young.

Increasingly, drug experts are coming to the conclusion that it is the goal that needs to be changed more than the technique, and that total cessation of all drug experimentation, however desirable in the abstract, is not a realistic goal for an education program. Some experts feel strongly that an education program aimed at stopping drug experimentation of every kind is bound to fail and so alienate students in the process that they will not listen to any of it. Drs. Thomas Ungerleider, Norman Zinberg, and Helen Nowlis, as well as Professor Kenneth Keniston—to name a few experts—appear to define a different goal for drug education: to teach youths to make informed decisions about drugs and indeed about every other kind of chemical subtance they might ingest. This must include a concentration on teaching elementary students a fundamental respect for the human body and the effects of chemical substances.

Teaching young people to make informed decisions on their own about illegal drugs is admittedly a more controversial goal than mechanically urging them to avoid all such drugs. A wholly honest "tell it like it is" approach may cause a decline in the use of heroin, amphetamines, and barbiturates, but it will almost certainly increase the likelihood that youthful listeners will feel more comfortable about trying marijuana and possibly some of the milder hallucinogens. Professor Zinberg reports on a candid talk about drugs to a Massachusetts high school. Before the lecture, 60 per cent of the students said they would not try marijuana; after the lecture, the figure dropped to 35 per cent.[1] This is not a universal occurrence, of course. For example, a before-and-after evaluation at a Temple University educational conference, presenting all points of view, found that attitudes toward marijuana shifted from favoring legalization to a neutral position, especially among undergraduates.[2]

A truly factual drug-education program might also influence attitudes toward commercially advertised and even medically prescribed drugs. When, for example, people discover that some legitimate drugs directly cause more deaths annually than do most abused drugs, they may lose faith in the argument that they should avoid illegal drugs because there is no official quality control or pretesting for safety. Another problem with the factual method involves the source material to be used. Contradictory statements of "facts" could catalyze a "your guess is as good as mine" attitude, and this is an area in which contradictions are common.[3] Nor are the opinions of either laymen or experts always based on scientific fact. Often the opinion comes first and the facts are chosen to fit it.[4]

An impartial factual approach assumes that an individual choice will be made on the basis of medical or scientific evidence regardless of what is forbidden by law. This is a difficult concept for many to accept, even though some young people from time immemorial have refused to obey a given law partly because it *is* the law or have engaged in risk-taking behavior that appalls adults. Today's climate of individuality intensifies the likelihood that they will make their own choices about drugs as well. In some cases, it is precisely the fact that drugs are illegal and risky that constitutes part of their attraction. It may be, therefore, that the most useful educational approach is to give young people the facts upon which to make that choice, so that they will at least keep their risk-taking behavior within bounds. Regardless of the educator's views of what their attitudes should be, effective communication requires that they be dealt with as they are. One survey of elementary, junior, and senior high school students in California concluded that "students feel quite strongly about an individual's right to make decisions concerning his own use of drugs." In the senior high school sampling, 84 per cent of the users and 76 per cent of the nonusers surveyed responded positively to the statement "Decision to Use Drugs Is a Personal Decision."[5]

Even if one is willing to accept increased experimentation with some drugs as the price of decreased damage from other drugs, there are more serious problems. How, for example, can a young child be expected to assimilate all the facts about individual drugs and their effects upon the body and make a reasonable choice about using them? Experimentation with ingestion or inhalation of foreign substances is occurring from age seven on with increasing frequency. How can so young a child make an informed decision? Might he not lean too heavily on his emotions, impulses, and peer-group pressure? Clearly, the "responsible decision" model has its limitations, too.

Other goals for an education program may be identified when those who are to be educated are involved in the selection process. It is highly recommended by the U.S. Office of Education's Drug Education Branch, for example, that young people share more of the responsibility for specifying objectives. Such a partnership arrangement tends to enhance the credibility of a program by "plugging it into" the representative needs of its target audience.

The unfortunate fact is that we do not know whether an exclusively factual approach works with the very young, even to the extent of mitigating the most dangerous kinds of experimentations. Conversely, we do not know whether a concerted attempt by schools and media to control the behavior of the children by propagandizing against drugs and punishing their use works, either, even if it is justified on the basis that the child is not old enough to make a rational choice of his own in so potentially harmful an area. Because of all the problems and unknowns of the "rational choice" approach, relatively few programs have adopted it explicitly, even when they concede the problems of other methods. In general, drug-education programs at the national, college, high school, and elementary levels have not faced the difficult issues involved in deciding among these goals. They have been neither realistic nor frank with the students or themthemselves. In most situations, settling on the goals that are most realistic under the circumstances and acknowledging those goals to the target group would enhance the credibility of the drug-education program. But even more importantly, it is necessary to articulate the precise objectives of any education campaign before it is implemented because they affect the way in which drug education is taught as well as the criteria by which its success or failure is evaluated. Until the precise aims of a program are clear to the sponsor and to the target population, the methodology cannot be sensitively selected and the program's effects cannot be accurately assessed. Such a practice would also allow us to begin to determine which techniques help to accomplish the objectives and which do not.

TECHNIQUES OF DRUG EDUCATION FOR STUDENTS

At present, we know almost nothing about how best to reach students on the drug issue; nor, until recently, have we tried very hard to find out. Only within the last few years have there been even rudimentary attempts to evaluate some of the school programs. Most of the pioneer efforts are very rough, and the outcomes rarely determine, or even significantly influence, the planning and allocation of resources.

Although there is now consensus that evaluation is needed, our lack of knowledge about the effects of existing education programs is not easily remediable. It is difficult to develop reliable evaluation techniques for the programs, although many methods are being tried. In some cases, students are tested before and after a drug course to see how much of the new information has been retained. Other surveys use attitudinal questions about whether participants are more or less willing to experiment with particular drugs after the program; in still other cases, selected students are interviewed intensively in an effort to probe deeply into their attitudes and reactions. Recent evaluative studies test the effectiveness of several factors simultaneously by administering varied instruments. Unfortunately, as Dr. Marvin J. Rosen suggests, existing "methodologies [are] inadequate for the questions being asked, and the designs of evaluation studies are inappropriate for the answers being sought."[6] Evaluations are often *post hoc*, rather desperate attempts to get information out of a program that was set up without regard to the need for it. Even when evaluation is designed into a program, it rarely includes long-range follow-up to determine the program's effects a year or more after its termination.

There are other problems. Little of the scant material that exists on evaluation has been pulled together and published, or even collected in one place. Valid and interesting work may exist unknown to almost everyone. In addition, only infrequent use has been made of the findings of educational-psychology research in designing learning programs on drug abuse for children of varying ages, although other areas have attempted to do so. For example, it is reported that $8 million was spent doing preliminary research on the psychology of learning before airing the *Sesame Street* program, which teaches reading concepts to preschool children.

Finally, there are institutional obstacles, and dedication to evaluation is often more froth than reality. The primary concern of many evaluators is that something be done, and they take a subjective view of the quality of the effort. Program staffs fear that objective study of their efforts will place future activities in jeopardy or believe that they are performing a service that cannot be measured. Some educators feel that evaluation produces only statistical data, which they equate with antihumanism. Program personnel often fail to specify their goals and the means utilized to attain them.

Dr. Helen Nowlis pointed out in 1967 that "at the present time there is no standard or widely accepted model for planning an effective drug-education program. This is an area that urgently needs research, development and demonstration."[7] This statement is still appropriate several years later. The underpinnings for a rational drug-education approach do not exist at the present time. Pronouncements abound on the kinds of programs that should be undertaken, and model curricula are easy to find, but hard data on the effect such programs have on students are virtually nonexistent. Given this situation, the two major priorities in this field are: (1) Well-designed and tested evaluation techniques to measure the attainment of specific goals (once they have been defined) in any school drug-education program. Different evaluative models would measure different goals—e.g., decreasing drug use, more information dissemination among the student body, substitution of less harmful drugs, rational drug use, less use in school, fewer acute health crises, more referrals of students to treatment, more use made of school personnel by students for advice. (2) A formal compilation of what evaluation data exist, which programs have been evaluated, what criteria have been used, and what results have been obtained. This information should be widely disseminated to members of the educational community as well as to those involved in drug programming (treatment, rehabilitation, intervention).

In the absence of this kind of information, we can only turn to the opinions of recognized "experts" in the field, without any real assurance, however, that they are right. Yet, there appears to be consensus (at least for the present) on the following points:

- The common pattern of having physical education or health teachers set aside one unit in the curriculum to lecture on the dangers of drugs is virtually useless. See, e.g., the Report of the Mayor's Task Force on Drug Abuse Education in Washington, D.C.: "To this date, most current crisis-oriented programs cater to the biases of adults, and depend on the faulty theory of emphasizing information or lecture techniques."
- A program must be ongoing, with the opportunity for recurrent discussions throughout the year. Even some of the new, well-motivated programs suffer from a "crisis" approach. An evaluation of programs conducted in four high school classes showed that "short-term programs, even though very sophisticated and intensive, may have little impact on the attitudes of students regarding the abuse of drugs." The study concludes that "the primary value of [the] project is that it adds a note of caution to those who would set aside a single day for drug education and be satisfied with the results."[8] Although countless "one-shot" programs are sponsored nationally, there is little evidence that such programs have any lasting effect.
- Different approaches have to be taken for students of different ages, cultural backgrounds, and levels of drug sophistication. The subtle variations among particular subcultures must be recognized. Drug education of some general kind needs to begin in kindergarten, or even earlier, and should focus on the specific drugs of abuse by fourth or fifth grade. The program for teenage suburban experimenters with marijuana must be different from the program for ghetto heroin users. Each target group must be studied to determine what kind of message will reach it. The information must then be structured so that it relates closely to the students' sophistication and willingness to identify with the subject matter.
- There must be open and free dialogue between students and the teacher or discussion leader in an atmosphere of tolerance for all points of view, free of moralizing and shock reactions.

Use should be made of the comments and experiences of youngsters who have actually used drugs, with confidentiality assured.

- From junior high school on, students should be involved in planning and implementing the drug-education program to assure its relevance to the specific situation in that school. Again, the students' level of sophistication must be accurately assessed. Predetermined curricula are to be avoided unless they are clearly relevant.

- Factual material must be absolutely accurate and honest. Where research does not yet provide clear answers, this must be admitted. Tobacco and alcohol abuse should be treated along with illicit drugs as part of the same over-all problem. The dangers as well as the benefits of legitimate drug use must be frankly acknowledged where they exist.

- The curriculum should not be a passive one, relying solely on pamphlets, lectures, or films. There should be an emphasis on actual experimental data that let the students see the underlying methodology of drug research and the way conclusions are reached. Where possible, students should view actual experimentation with the effects of drugs on animals and, at higher grade levels, conduct these experiments themselves. In Dr. Louise Richards' view: "The expectation is that deeper understanding of the CNS [central nervous system] and effects of psychoactive drugs will result in more profound respect for the hazards of unsupervised use."[9]

- Emphasis should be placed on the motivational aspects of drug use—why people use drugs, what they hope to accomplish and what they hope to escape, and how they can fulfill these needs in other ways. Interviews with high school students in California reveal a strong dislike for repetitive programs focusing on information alone. The students greatly preferred continuing discussions on the reasons for drug use.[10] Again, this is a way of actively involving the student in the learning process and making it a two-way engagement. Equal emphasis should be given to the reasons people do not want to take drugs. Dr. Helen Nowlis points out that college students often seem less interested in the legal and medical facts about drugs than in a personal, philosophical discussion about the limits on an individual's right to self-discovery and expression.[11]

- Education of any kind will have little or no impact on a youngster who is already deeply involved with drugs. A survey of students in nine high schools concluded that "students who have used drugs are not likely to be favorably impressed or to be changed by viewing . . . drug abuse films. In all nine schools the pattern was the same: the students, after viewing the films, said they were likely to continue their behavior as users or nonusers of drugs."[12]

- Alternative behavior patterns should be provided, for many users frequently give up drugs for something else. The "something else" varies but frequently takes the form of intense personal experiences, often of a religious nature, deep interpersonal experiences through the use of transcendental meditation or yoga, participation in sensitivity groups, or free-school activities. (See Staff Paper 6, below.) Such alternative programs, in order to be effective, should be attractive, easily available on a continuing basis, and organized with advice from the student body.

Given this consensus, however, a fundamental dispute still exists over whether the purely factual approach to drugs is more harmful than helpful to young "risk takers." Some experts believe that giving specific factual knowledge reinforces the antidrug propensities of persons not likely to abuse drugs anyway but actually contributes to the "seduction" of vulnerable high-risk groups by romanticizing the negativism that motivates their conduct.[13] Movies, media advertising, rock music, underground newspapers, and commercial films that excite interest in specific drug use transmit the nonverbal message that users get attention and sympathy. Dr. Paul Blachley espouses a different kind of education, focusing on underlying behavioral responses and on why people consciously hurt themselves and those around them. He would convey the over-all image of the drug-abuser as a boring, weak-minded, easily "conned" individual, not as a daring and reckless adventurer. But the student survey quoted above concluded that none of the six drug films examined lured anyone into trying drugs who had not already done so.

Other studies highlight the need for additional investigation into the effects of drug education.[14] Studies by Gilbert Geis (1969) and the California Department of Education (1970) determined that short-term programs (four weeks or less) significantly increased student knowledge about drugs and caused more cautious attitudes toward drug use. However, several studies conducted at the Pennsylvania State University in 1970–71 "showed consistent relationships between better knowledge about drugs and pro-drug attitudes; better knowledge and the use of marijuana; and pro-drug attitudes and the use of marijuana."[15]

A still unsettled question is whether drug education should be integrated into a "life-problem" course that includes such other subjects as sex and relations with parents and peers. Dr. Norman Zinberg, for one, espouses the integrated model. There also appears to be pressure toward this broader model from many students. Even courses labeled "drug education" very often take a motivational approach that examines underlying values and behavioral problems. A comparison of eighth- and eleventh-graders in California revealed that users know less about drugs and drug-related information than nonusers at the same grade level. The study concluded: "While the continued teaching of factual drug information might somewhat lessen student drug use, it could not do the job by itself, but when combined with an affective or attitudinal approach could be of real effect."[16] The Coronado Unified School District consequently led other schools in stressing the need for a comprehensive program covering values, valuing processes (decision-making), value orientations, and their possible effects on human behavior. Advocates of this approach recommend its use with parents, teachers, and students to increase mutual understanding and the ability to cope with the problems of everyday life.

Another fundamental question, especially for schools, is who should do the drug educating. Are regular teachers or knowledgeable outsiders more effective? All experts stress that it must be someone the students like and trust, someone who knows and will present the facts accurately and who feels comfortable and free in open discussion. Few teachers in any school fit that description. It has been observed by some outside speakers that students' questions dramatically increased in sophistication when the teacher left the room. In Washington, D.C., the mayor's task force suggested selecting teachers for drug education on the basis of a "sociogram" asking students to state anonymously to whom they would go for consultation or advice on personal problems. On the other side, several reports and interviews have warned about the possibly insidious effect of teachers who themselves actually promote drug use, wittingly or unwittingly.

Perhaps because of the more personal level of communication encouraged in primary grades, elementary students stand alone in preferring the teacher as a source of information. When surveyed, high school students usually prefer ex-addicts and medical doctors as resource people. Ex-users were considered qualified because of their firsthand experience with drugs. Conversely, doctors were seen as authorities on drug effects but lost credibility when discussing the "feelings" drugs produce. Dr. Thomas Ungerleider, of UCLA, reports that, in his experience, the most successful approach for a medical lecturer begins with an assurance to the students that he is not there for the purpose of persuading them to stay off drugs and does not represent law enforcement, parents, or school authorities, but is there only to tell them the known facts about drugs and the human body and to answer their questions.

Any discussion leader must be able to validate his credentials by showing the students that he knows the facts he states are true. Many schools have drug-education and rehabilitation centers run by, or with the help of, former drug users who present programs consisting of small student group discussions. These are often supplemented by discussions with faculty and parent groups as well. PLACE, in Boston, is an example of a drug-information and service center for hippies, runaways, and drug users, staffed by graduate students and run by the youthful clients with professional supervision. They conduct programs for local schools.

The role of the ex-addict in school programs deserves special consideration. He is the current fad of drug education, on the theory that only one who has been there can tell about it convincingly. There is some truth to this, but apparently different children receive different messages. The ex-addict is perceived by some as a self-promoter capitalizing on his drug experience for admiration or profit. Others get the idea that it is as easy to get off drugs as it is to get addicted, so that there is little risk in trying them. A ghetto youth might well surmise that, if the ex-addict had never become addicted to heroin in the first place, he would be worse off, probably jobless, and without the attention and respect he is now receiving. To some, the ex-addict is a glamorous "anti-hero" somewhat like a rock singer. In one California high school, ex-addict visitors were the recipients of phone calls from girl students seeking afterschool dates. Several schools have had unfortunate experiences with ex-addicts who are not really "ex" and are either pushing or using drugs. Others are akin to religious converts, uttering rigid opinions about all drugs, including marijuana, and denigrating all treatment modalities other than their own. Still others turn out never to have been serious users at all but are merely well-versed in the jargon of the users. Reportedly, some out-of-work rock musicians earn extra money making the school circuit. And, disturbingly, large numbers of ex-addicts reminisce about the actual "high" with an exquisite affection not lost on their young audiences. Some ex-addicts, although off drugs, are currently abusing alcohol. Others are prey to the same myths about drugs as nonusers and pass misinformation on to students.

All this gives the negative side of using ex-addicts, a practice that is sometimes accepted too uncritically. But this is not the only side. Ex-addicts can be excellent teachers, able to speak with credibility and to relate to youngsters, although the mere fact that they are ex-addicts does not ensure rapport. One of the very few carefully evaluated school programs showed, for example, that, while students liked to hear ex-addicts tell of their experiences, they did not give them so much credence when they lectured about drugs generally.[17] Ex-addicts with natural talent in relating to the young and with some training in sensitivity and substance may make very good drug-education teachers, indeed, and their experience may give them extra effectiveness. A good educator who happens to be an ex-addict may have a special and valuable feeling for the factors that lead youths to try drugs.

In ghetto schools, antidrug black-militant organizations often have a special appeal. The ghetto youngster's need for a role model may focus on such a symbol of racial pride. Organizations such as Blackman's Development Center and PRIDE, Inc., in Washington, D.C., have recently entered the drug education field and vigorously propagandize against drugs in schools, sometimes with homemade slides of addiction horrors and appeals to racial unity against a "white man's" scourge. How successful they will be remains to be seen.

The difficulty with most school education programs run by "outsiders" is that they lack continuity in the school itself. The ex-addicts, the graduate students, and visiting doctors come and go, while the students' need for information or help may continue for months. One of the more promising approaches is that used by a San Jose high school, which released a popular young teacher for several months to learn the drug scene intimately by going on "buys" with local police, attending court trials, working with doctors in drug clinics, interviewing patients at treatment centers, and spending time on the streets and in criminology labs. On his return, he took on (apparently successfully) the combined duties of teacher and counselor to students with drug problems.[18]

Dissatisfied with past results, many school systems this year are trying a variety of new preventive-education methods to discourage drug abuse, involving more direction by the students themselves. The New York City Board of Education has announced a trial program in sixteen high schools in which pupils will design and run their own antidrug programs. In Philadelphia last year, selected students from seven high schools (accompanied by a teacher) learned basic drug facts from doctors, treatment experts, and law-enforcement officials and went on field trips. They then went back to their own schools to initiate and run programs of their own choice. Most of them opened counseling services. With regard to peer involvement, there are indications that students should be given a voice in basic approach, curriculum content, and choice of teachers but should not be saddled with administrative chores, which they abhor and often perform poorly. Nevertheless, tapping the enthusiasm of well-selected students can be beneficial in motivating the student body to seek creative antidrug activities.

The notion that young people relate to their peers better than to adults has validity but also limits. They relate only to some of their peers. Rigid social groups exist in many schools, and students chosen by teachers and school officials may not be the ones to lead the group that the antidrug program hopes most to reach. Whenever possible, some student participation in planning and operating programs should come from the group the program is trying to reach, whether nonusers, experimenters, or borderline cases. The student council in an Oregon high school sought the cooperation of ex-users and faculty in creating a youthful "Mod Squad." Teams of experienced students provided successful peer counseling, assistance in crisis situations, and referrals to local treatment facilities and otherwise contributed positively to the school's educational programming.

There is also the "role model" theory that younger children, between the ages of seven and twelve, will learn from and relate better to older youth than to children their own age or adults. "Dope Stop" in Arizona uses high school students, trained by physicians, psychiatrists, or ex-addicts, to counsel grades five to eight. One proposal suggests subsidizing teenaged youth with a reputation for being "in" and "cool" to work with younger boys against drug involvement. NIMH drug-information officials say they are also considering having students of different age groups prepare education programs for the next-youngest age level.

A study of a junior high school drug-education program that featured teachers and ex-addicts produced some illuminating results. The program lasted an entire semester in two junior high schools in the high narcotics area of the inner city, and questionnaires were administered before and after the program as well as in a control school using the traditional lecture method. The results showed that teachers and ex-addicts were hostile toward one another, resenting each other's prerogatives and roles. Teachers resented the time spent on testing for evaluation, and ex-addicts needed feedback on how the students reacted toward them. The students in the experimental schools did better on factual knowledge than those in the control schools. Parent education efforts failed. The students thought the films were "no good" and exaggerated the behavior of drug users, and that the reading material was "cut and dried." They wanted more talking and less reading; also, to hear the ex-addicts relate personal experiences but not to lecture. The students did not like the personal questions on the tests and were suspicious that their answers would not be kept confidential. They wanted more concentration on the drugs used in their own schools; they wanted to see samples of the drugs in order to recognize them.

Discouragingly, however, there is no evidence that most of the new programs being undertaken will be evaluated any more systematically than the older ones have been. Until that happens, therefore, we will not know the best way to educate about drug abuse.

TOTAL SCHOOL INVOLVEMENT

Once again, as has happened so often with complex social dilemmas, the schools have inherited America's number-one "problem child"—the drug-abuse crisis. At present, educators are joining with related disciplines in defining approaches to the problem for use in classrooms, libraries, and counseling offices. Educational institutions have become the testing ground for diverse preventive alternatives. It has become clear that the fundamental areas of school involvement must be to provide relevant educational programs from kindergarten through college and to serve as an avenue for community action involving students, parents, faculty, and other local elements.

According to the Bureau of Narcotics and Dangerous Drugs:

The schools cannot by themselves be expected to rehabilitate youth and their neighborhood environments. Sociologists and others who have worked in the drug abuse prevention field have pointed out that drug education is not a problem for the schools alone. It is a community problem and requires total community effort for its solution. The schools cannot assume the roles of parents, clergymen, enforcement officers, physicians or psychiatrists. But they *can* exercise leadership in facing a problem that the total community, working together, can try to remedy. This is education in its broadest and most important sense. It is making schools relevant to their communities.[19]

An initial effort must be made to formulate school policies that are sensitive to the needs of all elements of the school community. There is no point, for example, in expecting "free" class discussions or adult cooperation when student informers are widely used throughout the school and teachers are required to report all suspected users to the police. If the school intends to act as an extension of civil authority—to investigate and turn users over to the police—it must come to terms with the fact that its effectiveness as an educational force will be substantially reduced. On the other hand, no school administrator can be expected to sit idly by while drug traffic flourishes within the school. Therefore, a major responsibility of school authorities is to give careful consideration to alternative choices in defining the school's action policy toward drug use. Once established, the policy should be clearly explained to students and their parents, as well as to the school staff. The failure of school administrators to communicate with students about policies that they will be expected to obey inevitably creates mistrust of all official advice and information. By seeking and accepting inputs from young people and their parents in the formulation of school policies, school officials not only open up valuable channels of communication but make it possible to develop policies that are relevant to the needs, interests, and aspirations of each member of the school community.

Until recently, schools could do little to deter student use of drugs, because most of them had no announced policy. More and more, administrators are moving to establish such guidelines, for a very good reason: Lacking established policy guidelines, a school has no standard procedure for providing help or discipline when a student is found with drugs. A variety of policies is possible, and it is difficult to say in advance how much effectiveness in one area should be traded for gains in another. Some colleges say that what the student does with his own body is his own business, unless it results in active disruption of classes, threatens the safety of others, or prevents satisfactory academic functioning. This laissez-faire policy, however, is less likely to be acceptable at the high school level. Some schools have opted for the policy that selling or distributing drugs is forbidden, and that distributors will be punished while users will be treated more leniently or ignored. Other schools refuse to initiate disciplinary action for anything that happens off school grounds. More cautious institutions have adopted the theory that drug use spreads in epidemic fashion, and that it is necessary to quarantine and isolate the carrier. They aggressively seek out drug users through urinalysis or locker searches and either expel the users or report them to law-enforcement officials. Some recent court decisions have made it difficult for school personnel to conduct searches of a student's personal belongings, thus imposing limitations on what a school can do to investigate possible drug dealing.

The optimal relationship between school policy and the law-enforcement system is difficult to determine. Some schools have worked out cooperative agreements with law-enforcement agencies in seeking feasible alternatives to arrest (which is viewed as a last resort). Unfortunately, however, most school officials have given little thought to methods of diverting student drug possessors who need help out of the criminal process and into treatment, as witness a booklet published by the National Association of Secondary School Principals in 1969:

> There is a distorted notion gaining widespread acceptance that a school or college is a sanctuary. These institutions are a part of society and are subject to the same laws as the rest of society. Accordingly, the school authorities have the same responsibility as every other citizen to report violations of law. Students possessing or using on school premises drugs prohibited by law should be reported to the appropriate law enforcement officials.[20]

John Langer, of the Bureau of Narcotics and Dangerous Drugs, advises principals to use discretion and judgment in situations that may involve the violation of federal, state, or local laws. He emphasizes that teachers and administrators are not law-enforcement officers but school officials with a responsibility to carry out school board policy.[21]

Continuing lines of communication between law-enforcement agencies and schools (such as the involvement of policemen in teacher-training and community educational efforts, speakers' bureaus, and community-relations programs) are often mutually beneficial in dealing with drug issues. In several metropolitan areas, these efforts have led to the establishment of counseling sessions that must be attended by first offenders and their parents in lieu of a jail sentence. A Hudson Institute study has suggested specially supervised "drug-free" schools for all students found to be using drugs. Opponents of this approach, however, argue that isolation and expulsion will only confirm the occasional user's alienation and result in his further identification with deviant behavior.

Students frequently cited the need for a designated person in the schools to whom they can go for information or help, assured that their confidence will be kept. Helen Nowlis states, "Within any institution it should be made clear who will and can guarantee confidentiality and such guarantees should be respected."[22] Such a person would be an ombudsman-counselor, able to work with parents as well as students to solve drug problems. He must be the kind of person students normally seek out for sympathetic but sound advice. In addition, he should have thorough familiarity with the drug-abuse field as well as access to treatment and intervention programs, so that he can provide referrals in acute situations. (There is reason to believe that this type of counseling resource can be more important for schools than traditional educational programs.) Such a person could also advise the school on general policies and provide drug-usage information. His expertise would be invaluable in conducting drug-abuse education classes.

The ombudsman concept must be carefully considered by the schools. Their wholehearted commitment must be assured, for nothing could be so damaging as to invite confidences and then not to be able to honor them. The legal problems raised when a school official acts in the counselor's role must also be resolved and cooperation obtained from the authorities to prevent pressure on individuals who may not enjoy a technical legal privilege. Because school policies frequently forbid teachers to honor student confidences, many are hesitant to encourage personal involvement, which may place the student in jeopardy.

Many believe that the ombudsman-counselor should provide his services for other kinds of adolescent problems in addition to those related to drugs—family, sex, alcohol, and so on.[23] Classroom teachers often have tremendous influence on students, especially on those who lack parental understanding. They occupy a more neutral position than parents and sometimes are better able to identify behavior requiring special counseling or referral.

Until now, schools have relied almost entirely on classroom teachers to assist student drug abusers in finding help. Public funds earmarked for "teacher training courses" have rarely included guidance-counseling personnel. It is unfortunate that schools have failed to take advantage of the position of those guidance counselors who enjoy the trust and respect of young people. Recently, the American Personnel and Guidance Association began developing a national effort to train guidance workers to deal with the complexities of drug abuse. The program is being held in abeyance until adequate seed money can be procured.

Information alone cannot always help a youthful user. The head of a Mexican-American outreach program in Los Angeles testified before Congress that a large proportion of youth in his area were heavily addicted to barbiturates, but that education could not help when there was no place in the area they could go for medical aid in withdrawal. Teacher and guidance counselors should provide the link between the school and treatment resources that is now lacking in many places. If it is to reach users or experimenters, a school education program not only must supply information on where to go for help but also must have an effective system for getting them there. Teachers or counselors must know, for example, whether the student-user can receive treatment on his own (as in California and Connecticut) or must have parental permission before anyone can treat him (as in most other states). School counselors should be willing to take the initiative in getting the student to the treatment service and in running bureaucratic interference for him. They may even have to help make parents more sensitive to their children's drug problem in an effort to prevent them from acting destructively.

On the other hand, treatment facilities in many areas far outnumber institutions that focus on prevention. Young people who do not use drugs have legitimate questions but find few places to which they can turn for answers. The school counselor can act as an effective source of information.

Any well-balanced school program should harness the support and cooperation of outside community elements in providing help to young abusers. The Office of Education's national teacher-training program challenged schools to consider community motivation as their ultimate long-range goal. OE staff members report that teachers were often unsuccessful in gaining the necessary support of politicians, school board members, principals, and parents in accomplishing this final phase of their program. As a rule, the attitudes of the communities precluded the exploration of innovative ways to prevent drug abuse. What is needed, therefore, is widespread local awareness of the need for unity in making progress—a recognition that educational institutions are merely conduits through which communal efforts must pass.

OUT-OF-SCHOOL DRUG-EDUCATION PROGRAMS

Education does not take place only in school. As Helen Nowlis stated before Congress:

It is learning about drugs that should concern us today, rather than the formal mechanisms for presenting drug information. Information by itself is not education, education by itself is not learning.

How do people, particularly young people, learn about drugs and form their drug-related attitudes? We believe that a series of influences help shape these attitudes: the atmosphere of the school, as well as the factual information presented there; the life-style at home, and the attitude of parents; peer-group pressures; popular culture, including music, films, magazines and nationally publicized events; personal experiences with drugs or drug-related substances;

the availability of alternative mechanisms for carrying out certain kinds of behavior—risk taking, wish fulfillment, etc.[24]

Most of a youth's initial information about a subject comes from his peers. A survey of Maryland high school students showed that they got most of their drug information and attitudes from peers and underground newspapers.[25] In addition, the students most prone to serious drug abuse are often those who are most antagonistic to the school climate. There is general agreement that more out-of-school programs are needed to reach those whom the schools cannot reach. Unfortunately, antidrug programs run by private and public organizations outside the school are of varying quality and totally lacking in evaluation. Nevertheless, the New York Addiction Control Commission alone spent $1 million in 1970 on such "preventive education."

Most prevention programs, besides lacking evaluation, are not grounded on any hypotheses based on field observations. Dr. Irving Lukoff, of the Columbia University School of Social Work, believes that effective prevention programs await basic research to discover what influences young people in heavily addicted areas not to take drugs, why some do use drugs, and how drug use spreads.

The most that can be done at this point is to categorize five basic kinds of nonschool prevention programs:

PEER-GROUP PROGRAMS

Many types of teenage peer-group, antidrug programs have emerged. The following are illustrative:

The members of one national group—the Smarteens—pledge not to use drugs, wear buttons deriding drug use, and distribute posters scorning the drug culture. The psychology is to provide support and reinforcement for youngsters who choose not to use drugs. Such a technique, however, merely widens the gap between the "squares" and the drug users and alienates the latter still further. Those familiar with the group admit it has its greatest impact in middle-class suburban areas.

Members of Project DARE (Drug Abuse Research and Evaluation), in the Los Angeles area, do not use drugs, but participate in the rest of the psychedelic scene—rock music, flashy dress, crafts—so as to show that one can be "cool" without being drugged. Other activities include evaluating drug education films, lecturing to encourage an understanding of today's drug culture, and stimulating the involvement of youth in the solution of community problems.

Two New York City ghetto high schools have experimented with a program in which members of a black youth organization visit the schools, assess the drug situation, and then "penetrate" by mixing at the ball courts and other student gathering places, seeking to identify student pushers and deal with them, either through persuasion or by reporting them to the authorities. Identified users are urged to seek treatment. The organization itself reports a reduction in selling and usage of drugs, but no official evaluation is obtainable.

Teen Challenge is a private, religion-oriented agency with centers across the country that offer treatment to anyone over eighteen. Its premise is that a drug user should be given an opportunity to undergo a religious experience that can give him the strength to overcome his destructive desires and habits.

Private businesses often fund programs offering alternatives to youth. One recently financed a project involving youth groups from Harlem and Nassau County, utilizing peer-group dynamics as an alternative to drug abuse. Films, magazines, and educational materials created by the students are disseminated to schools and community organizations.

Several treatment and rehabilitation facilities have opened their doors to youngsters for whom they organize extracurricular activities. Patients in a Detroit methadone facility have "hit the streets" to provide speakers, peer and family counseling, and neighborhood projects to stimulate political awareness and consumer education. RAP, Inc., a Washington, D.C., therapeutic community, encourages neighborhood children to join a "block club" designed to channel energies constructively. Tutoring services, speakers, and library privileges are extended to members of the group.

Some of the more creative programs involve both drug experimenters and nonusers in activities that seek to explore ways youth can pursue inward and outward experiences that will make drug use less desirable. Dr. William Soskin's Project Community in Berkeley has such a program for 140 youths between the ages of fourteen and eighteen. Acting on the hypothesis that home and school have not provided sufficiently satisfying influences in their lives, the Center seeks to create a "third force" consisting of a group of peers, under supervision, who engage in mutual activities a few hours a day. These activities include inward meditation, body language, poetry, and even active practical jokes for the more aggressive members. Rap sessions and encounter groups as well as active community projects and recreation outings complete the program. Sympathetic counselors are always available to talk to an individual about his problems.

FREE CLINICS AND CRISIS CENTERS

There are a number of free medical clinics for "street people" providing a range of services on a twenty-four-hour basis—not only emergency medical or psychological help for drug crises (bad trips and severe reactions), but also up-to-date information on the quality and effects of drugs currently being sold in the immediate area, long-term treatment, and referral. Their basic purpose is not to proselytize against drugs but to provide help when people need it most and to disseminate accurate analyses of the risks of street drugs. In some cases, for example, there followed a dramatic decrease in the use of particular drugs or batches of drugs after the clinic staff spread the word that a particular product was having bad effects.[26] Free medical clinics reach those in or on the edge of the drug culture, and they enjoy a high degree of credibility. Most crisis centers cater to a variety of needs, including draft, abortion, and family counseling. These facilities sometimes offer temporary residence for runaways and intervention with parents. Usually, they give medical help to those with drug problems and provide speakers and materials as well as information to other community organizations, including schools. Some even provide employment in crafts and work with delinquent youngsters in the community.

Most clinics and crisis centers are run by the youths themselves with professional and medical guidance. Young people are attracted by their neutral attitude toward drug use. What preventive effects, if any, the centers have on continued drug use is extremely speculative, but they fill acute needs for help in immediate health crises and for accurate information.

"Hot-Line" Telephone Services

Anyone can call such a telephone service anonymously with questions about drug reactions as well as a score of other problems. Not infrequently, hot-line staffers are asked to locate lost pets, give advice on domestic squabbles, and make referrals. It is inherent in the nature of such a service that there is no way of telling what happens to callers, or whether they make use of the advice and information given about drugs and treatment services, or whether, indeed, calls are legitimate. Anonymity constitutes the service's main attraction. Ex-users often find positive reinforcement and satisfaction in serving as hot-line operators. Yet, there are cases where constantly talking about drug effects has led these people back to drug use. As a rule, however, their past drug experiences enhance their ability to deal effectively with crisis situations. In cases of extreme emergency, trained professionals are consulted.

Afterschool and Instead-of-School Prevention Programs

As of 1970, New York City's Addiction Services Agency ran sixteen youth centers in poverty areas to discourage drug use by nonusers or early experimenters aged nine to nineteen and referred by parents, schools, police, or courts. Ten centers were funded by OEO, four by NIMH, but all were to be shifted to local and state funding. ASA was asking for money to open four more centers in middle-class neighborhoods.

ASA has estimated that 80 per cent of New York City youths over twelve have experimented with at least one drug. The majority, however, reportedly have no deep-seated mental problems requiring a residential therapeutic community setting. During 1970, about 500 youths were in such afterschool centers at any one time and some 5,440 in all were served.

The focus is on group therapy and counseling to help the youth make basic decisions about his values and life goals. "Disrupters," seriously disturbed youth, and heavy opiate users are not eligible. Parent groups also operate out of the centers, which try to work with the schools, so that teachers too can play a supportive role.

Centers are open five days a week, each handling 50 youths at a time. Youths, if attending school, come to the center in the afternoons, generally for a period of three to six months. If they are not in school, center activities are scheduled during the day. Peer-group sessions, role-playing and psychodrama, individual counseling, recreation, workshops, and seminars are all used. An attempt is made to establish role-model identification with staff members.

These centers have not, to our knowledge, been evaluated systematically. Their aim is to create pressure against the use of drugs. The agency's own assessment is that the centers have had difficulty because the youths referred to them need more supportive services than can be offered.

There have been recurrent proposals for outdoor work or summer camps for drug-using youngsters. ASA would like to create one for 150–180 youths aged twelve to nineteen, modeled on Outward Bound. (This is a program that gets youth into the country, where they increase their wilderness skills in challenging situations, thus increasing their sense of confidence and self-worth.) Group-encounter sessions would be combined with regular camp life. Dr. Gordon Heistad, of the University of Minnesota, has experimented (successfully, he believes) with a camp model combining drug education and regular camp life for high school leaders.

DRUGMOBILES

These vehicles, which follow street youth into their natural haunts, to ball games and rock concerts, have been tried in several cities. Generally, they feature informational exhibits and ex-addict staffers. Counselors answer inquiries on an individual basis and ensure anonymity.

Credible staff is quite difficult to retain, since trained counselors prefer working with more stable programs. In most cases, these mobile units end up having middle-aged discussion leaders with good intentions but little facility in communicating. Many young people suggest that more emphasis should be put on honest discussions and less on "clever" exhibits.

THE NATIONAL MEDIA

A perpetual dispute in the drug-education field involves the influence of the national media on drug-abuse-prevention efforts. What effect do they have? What effect *should* they have? Some who work with young drug users believe that television is more likely to influence them than school programs, because they relate more sympathetically to the medium; others fear that a high-powered television campaign stressing "risks, thrills, scares, fantasies, high tragedy and antiheroism" will increase drug experimentation.[27] Dr. Norman Zinberg points out that television may bend growing children in the direction of seeking experiences that transcend tangible boundaries, such as mind-altering drugs.[28]

The role played by the mass media in any comprehensive drug-education effort depends on the specific objectives of that effort and the methods used to attain them. The current lack of agreement on these matters, however, makes it difficult to conceive of the ideal media program and virtually impossible to predict the benefits to be derived from it. Nevertheless, as the following review of present efforts will show, everybody is doing something.

Between 1968 and 1970, the National Institute of Mental Health conducted a national television campaign against drugs, featuring spots created by the Grey Advertising Company with famous "name personalities," such as Rod Serling and the Everly Brothers. Air time was donated on a public-service basis, and eighteen different films were supplied to every major network station and most independents. Radio stations also aired anti-drug messages, twelve in all. Some fourteen posters and pamphlets were mailed out to supplement the campaign. No one knows what the total effect was, aside from generating 22 million requests for information. Gerald Kurtz, Director of the Office of Communication at NIMH, has been quoted as saying that the effort, which was specifically youth-oriented, was not expected to turn young people away from drugs. Its real purpose, rather, was to heighten the concern of laymen and private organizations and create national awareness of the problem of drug abuse.

In 1970, a new national media campaign was begun under White House sponsorship, based on the same untested assumption that television can "unsell" drug usage. According to the prevailing theory, peer pressure against drugs can be created to reinforce those who have not yet tried drugs or are only very occasional users. The approach still lumps all drugs together under the slogan "Why Do You Think They Call It Dope?" Some black reporters have criticized it as obviously a product of the white advertising world, both in its content and in its style of presentation. It was put together by the Compton Agency, which worked through the Advertising Council. The new campaign started by directing its programs to the preteen group, then moved to high school and college audiences, then to blacks, parents, and the military. While medical hazards are mentioned, the emphasis is on inculcating the attitude that taking drugs is "stupid" rather than on presenting factual information.

Other groups have entered the media fight against drug abuse. In February, 1971, the Corporation for Public Broadcasting began airing eight one-hour programs entitled "The Turned-On Crisis." The series, intended for general audiences, includes programs on several facets of the drug problem. For those more involved in the drug problem, CPB can also provide an in-service training program of six thirty-minute segments for teachers and school administrators and an in-class series of eight twenty-minute programs for junior high school youth.

There are many efforts to develop effective television and radio antidrug spot ads, but whether any such device can counterbalance everyday pressures supporting drug use is doubtful. It has been pointed out that most teenagers listen incessantly to the radio, while their television viewing is sporadic, and that radio spots repeated between rock songs are more likely to reach them than spots on television. But merely reaching the audience is not enough; the ads must be effective. Some stations that carry antidrug spots have complained of a lack of good material but an abundance of poor, ineffective material. The National Institute of Mental Health has provided funds to the

National Coordinating Council on Drug Education to evaluate radio and television material; the results are included in a monthly newsletter, *Tune In,* distributed to approximately 5,600 radio and television stations. Included are reviews of spot announcements, factual programs, interviews, and public-service announcements available to the media for broadcasting.

A black-audience station in Woodside, New York—WWRL— has adopted a more direct approach: It asks listeners to call in the names of pushers, which it then submits to the police; the caller's anonymity is kept, and all tips are investigated. The station contends that thirty-two arrests have been made in six months as a result of this campaign. It also broadcasts a referral telephone number for those who want help with their own drug problems.

Other radio stations are beginning to use the rock sound in communicating antidrug messages. Disk jockeys, for example, play authentic-sounding rock tunes with lyrics describing youthful deaths caused by overdoses or by the ingestion of poor-quality street drugs, in the hope that the young will pay serious heed. But some teenagers resent this attempt to make the scare approach pleasing to the ear.

The subject of rock music raises another question about the relation between national media and the drug problem. Some observers believe that the media are better at aggravating the problem than at solving it. Songs with so-called drug-related lyrics were banned from the airwaves by the Federal Communications Commission because of their alleged potential to glamorize drug abuse. This action was vigorously opposed by underground radio stations, record companies, and private organizations, which castigated the FCC for exercising censorship and imposing an "establishment" interpretation of music on the general public. A booklet put out by the Justice Department's Bureau of Narcotics, entitled *Drug Taking in Youth,* declares that, "Numerous entertainers whose records are played frequently are drug advocates. Many popular songs have hidden or expressed drug allusions. Underground FM radio stations late at night reach many young people with 'acid' rock and their overt or disguised messages about drug use, sources, and availability. Rock festivals are frequently advertised through this medium."[29] The effects of rock lyrics on an individual's decision to use drugs still remain a mystery, however, clouded by the contradictory pronouncements of government spokesmen and rock-music enthusiasts.

Television has also been charged with contributing negatively to the drug problem because of its steady advertising of over-the-counter drugs. In 1969, drug manufacturers reportedly spent $13.7 million for television promotion of seventeen brands of sedatives and stimulants alone. All types of advertising for all proprietary drugs involved expenditures of $282 million. Messages that are criticized for "pushing" over-the-counter medication promise to solve problems and alleviate everyday stresses. The manufacturer of a popular pain reliever supports a successful advertising package attributing love, success, tranquillity, self-confidence, health, and so on, *ad infinitum*, to its product. Another commercial selling children's vitamins shows two youngsters floating through the sky on a magic carpet after chewing the tablets.

Although manufacturers of proprietary (over-the-counter) drugs deny the cause-and-effect relationship between advertising and abuse, many public groups are adamant about eliminating mood drug advertisements. The National Association of Broadcasters, for example, has proposed content restraints and criteria for the broadcasting of such messages. Both the FTC and HEW have been studying the relationship between over-the-counter drug ads on television and drug abuse. Members of Congress are also holding hearings on advertising that urges mood alteration through nonprescription drugs. An HEW-sponsored study concludes:

> By and large, advertising, *per se,* seems to have a relatively low level of general influence upon students, when compared to other environmental factors such as home (parents) and school (peer groups). This suggests that advertising is not, *by itself,* responsible for student behavior toward drugs and/or other products, substances or activities.
>
> At most, advertising operates within the context of the student's

total environment and cannot be uniquely responsible for student values, attitudes and beliefs.

Even though advertising, *per se,* may not be considered uniquely responsible for attitudes towards legal and illegal drugs, the students, nevertheless, feel that it is potentially an influencing agent, particularly on the youngest students.[30]

The study, based on interviews with 560 fifth-, seventh-, and eleventh-grade California students, covered drugs of all kinds, including Compoz, Contac, Alka-Seltzer, Bayer Aspirin, as well as Salem and Marlboro cigarettes. Students questioned after viewing the ads expressed disbelief of the advertiser's claims, as follows: Compoz—46 per cent; Salem—31 per cent; Contac—40 per cent; Bayer Aspirin—19 per cent; Alka-Seltzer—12 per cent; Marlboro —11 per cent. The study also found that "users of illegal drugs tend to be more receptive to proprietary drug ads than non-users." Concluding that such ads may be a "cultural prop in the mainte- the study suggested that the industry initiate an examination of nance of favorable attitudes toward drug usage among the young," promotional programs and more government studies of children's receptivity.

No formal report has been released on the FTC study. Nevertheless, it is the view of a number of FTC staff members, as well as some scientists and some officials of BNDD, that such a relationship does exist in certain cases.[31] In any event, many lawyers are convinced that the FTC has the power to attack many of the suspicious ads without necessarily proving the existence of such a relationship.

A study by four physicians at the University of Southern California pointed out that high-pressure advertising of prescription drugs to physicians depends on a technique of "mystification."[32] The ads identify ordinary human reactions and emotions as symptoms of physical illness and then prescribe a drug as remedy. Tofranil, an antidepressant drug, is cited as one example. The ad suggests that parents agonizing over a runaway daughter might be treated with the drug. The same technique may be applied to television ads for proprietary drugs that impel the listener to seek a drug remedy for the relief of normal tensions arising from interpersonal relations.

Another example is the excessive use of over-the-counter drugs. Richard Blum reports that those who use such drugs heavily assert more frequently than others that medicines make a difference in the way one feels; also, they recall having more medicines in their childhood homes than do light users. Not surprisingly, therefore, they are more likely to use drugs to reduce fear, induce courage, or change mood in social situations.[33] Similarly, many youths learn favorable attitudes about drugs through underground newspapers; yet, these papers often present accurate reports about specific drug dangers and effects. This source of information should not be ignored, even though its ideological slant may be quite different from that of official sources of drug education. If solid research shows that a drug has severe toxic effects, an underground paper may be the quickest and surest way to communicate with those most likely to be damaged by it. For example, Washington, D.C.'s *Quicksilver Times* has printed the pharmacological analyses of street samples provided by the Washington Free Clinic as a warning of the unreliability of certain varieties of drugs then available.

FILMS AND AUDIO VISUALS

The recent emphasis on school drug-education programs has produced a receptive market for drug films and audiovisual materials; in the past few years, the number of these teaching devices has reached approximately two hundred. The potential value of visual teaching cannot be disputed—it makes learning situations more realistic and more acceptable, especially to television-oriented youth. The problem, however, for any school or civic group is how to distinguish between effective material and that which is inaccurate or counterproductive. Certainly, there ought to be readily accessible, up-to-date evaluations of drug films by both experienced adult and student viewers, indicating the content, level of sophistication, target audience, and goal orientation of the films. Different reviewers may well come to different conclusions, but the plethora of drug films now being sold or given away makes a meaningful choice impossible in the absence of some reasonably reliable guide.

The Educational Products Information Exchange, which describes itself as a "nonprofit cooperative conducting impartial studies of learning materials and systems," has published a student rating of several films on drug abuse. It cautioned that, "Educators who run a film in the auditorium as their sole gesture toward curing their school's drug problem are accomplishing nothing and may even be making the situation worse."[34] Several other organizations have begun to circulate listings and ratings of available audiovisuals. The National Clearinghouse for Drug Abuse Information publishes a list of seventeen drug-abuse education films, carefully disavowing endorsement of any one. Significantly, however, the last page of the brochure lists only five that can be borrowed free from regional offices of the BNDD. The titles, such as *Hooked* and *Beyond LSD,* seem to indicate that these are hard-line antidrug films rather than more balanced, impartial reports, such as the *CBS Report on Marijuana.* The University of California's Extension Media Center at Berkeley used large interdisciplinary panels of young people and adults to evaluate ninety-nine drug films. Of the films reviewed, fourteen were rated "excellent" and thirty-two "poor."[35] The National Coordinating Council on Drug Education, financed by contract from NIMH, has rated currently available drug films and audiovisual materials, distinguishing between those that are "unusually noteworthy" and those "using questionable approaches or containing many inaccuracies."[36] The results are available in reports updated quarterly, intended to be used as guidelines in selecting films for various purposes. NCC's latest evaluation mentions a trend toward better films as producers respond to demands for honesty and a more rational approach. One New York congressman has written to schools and libraries in his district, asking them to use the report in removing objectionable films.

Little by little, youth are being given a major role in the development and evaluation of drug-education films and visual materials. Young members of DARE conduct evaluations without adult supervision, and adults find their appraisals credible and responsible. A few schools and private groups encourage student production of visual materials. Sponsors report a double benefit: The students' interest in drug education is enhanced, and so is their mastery of the communication skills involved. Television spots and films created by young people tend to present information that is honest and sensitive to the needs of their peers.

Many evaluators criticize existing films for not conforming to the life-styles of the viewer, for containing technical inaccuracies, and for failing to use either black or Puerto Rican actors or, at least, a Spanish soundtrack. It has been suggested that students do not identify with actors or even with real people in a strange setting, and that movies made in the students' own locale may have more effect. Several drug-treatment programs are planning homemade movies set against familiar backgrounds. Such a series was made in Bedford-Stuyvesant by local talent, under the sponsorship of the Bedford-Stuyvesant Restoration Corporation, and was shown on New York's Channel 13.

Most problems, however, seem to occur once the film is in the teacher's hands, ready for use. Fortunately, most film reports are accompanied by remarks on how to use the materials effectively. Previewing is the essential first step, preferably with students as well as with adult screeners. Films should not be shown if they fail to meet the audience's level of knowledge and sophistication. Next, creative interaction should take place between the audience, the educator, and the film. Students should be allowed to give their own evaluation or to discuss their feelings about the film's message.

A plethora of commercial films focusing on the youthful drug culture has flooded the market. As is to be expected, many such movies sensationalize and exploit the drug-abuse problem. A few, however, present the cruel realities of drug addiction in a sensitive manner, thus meriting their use in student and adult educational programs. The Bureau of Narcotics and Dangerous Drugs feels that "recent films directed to youth . . . initiate them into the drug scene."[37]

The emphasis on student participation has prompted a new method—videotaping the students' own discussions on drugs—that is being tried in many classrooms. Educators are able to gain insights from studying the dynamics of the situation, and students profit from observing themselves in peer-group settings attempting to solve problems and make decisions collectively. Outside the schools, videotapes have been used successfully in adult training courses, especially those focusing on increasing the participants' level of communication. For most, the experience becomes a mirror reflecting strengths, weaknesses, and limitations in dealing with others. Unlike the passive screening of drug-education films, live videotape replays often enhance the ability of teachers and parents to relate to young people. Unfortunately, however, videotape apparatus is too costly for most schools and civic groups.

SCHOOL CURRICULA

Paralleling the proliferation of antidrug films has been the emergence of packaged curricula. Private businesses, state departments of education, local school systems, publishers, pharmaceutical manufacturers, professional associations, consulting firms, and universities have all jumped on the bandwagon in response to the growing demand for ready-made drug courses. These vary tremendously in quality, content, and approach. Some are very useful, while others are aimed merely at exploiting the commercial market, offering little more than the basic facts about drugs with a few suggestions about research projects for students. The better material offers teachers thoughtful background information on specific drugs, suggestions for effective course presentation and teaching aids and flexible lesson plans.

Such publications as the NIMH *Resource Book for Drug Abuse Education* and *Teaching About Drugs: A Curriculum Guide, K–12,* issued by the American School Health–Pharmaceutical Manufacturers Association, contain excellent background material on particular drugs. The National Clearinghouse for Drug Abuse Information will send, on request, eight model curricula from various school systems, again without endorsement or evaluation of their appropriateness for different target groups. As a total package, the booklets provide a valuable diversity of approaches as well as supplemental resources. A few of the education packages encourage self-examination by both teachers and students.

The current emphasis on youthful self-evaluation has given rise to techniques stressing the importance of student values in making decisions about drugs. Those who promulgate the value approach contend that behavior and personal values are inseparable. Richard E. Carney believes that drug abuse can be prevented, or at least explained, if it is viewed as an individual's attempt to actualize his values. In one of his studies, drug users placed significantly less value on such categories as "power" as it related to participation in student organizations, clubs, and "politics"; "affection" and "respect" as they related to their willingness to become involved in parental conferences on important personal subjects; and "skill" as it related to participation in sports and organized activities.[38] But no one knows how students come to hold certain values, or why some values are more prevalent than others. This may explain the adamant refusal of many schools to consider adoption of the value-clarifying curriculum until more concrete data are made available. Channels are opening up, however, and skeptical educators are becoming more tolerant of "radical" approaches to education. Several counties in Maryland, for example, recently adopted a value-oriented curriculum package developed by Drug Central, a division of Washington, D.C.'s Council of Governments. As is often the case with new methods, the Maryland teachers are in need of special training programs to assure positive results in the classroom. At present, increasing numbers of schools are adopting this approach and report favorable responses from students and teachers alike.

Other imaginative innovations in the field are receiving favorable support from the educational community. The Creative Learning Group in Cambridge, Massachusetts, has integrated materials available for elementary and junior high schools focusing on problem solving and teaching younger children how to make decisions about life and drugs. A vast array of unique teaching aids is offered for classes, and teachers are equipped with a comprehensive manual containing drug-abuse information, sound medical information for use in emergencies, and suggestions for generating group discussions. The group's services will be broadened to include short-term programs, guides for student counselors, preschool film strips, and materials for inner-city, Spanish-speaking youngsters.

Macro Systems, Inc., has a complex package consisting of a

self-discovery kit for use by the teacher in finding out his own position on drugs and exploring his own biases, before proceeding to lead an objective and probing discussion among his students. It also contains a consensus map for the classroom that enables students to plot their own attitudes compared with those of their peers.

It is encouraging to note that at least one group, New Dimensions Publishing Company, has responded to the scarcity of materials for minorities. This New York City firm produces books in Spanish and English for blacks, Puerto Ricans, and Mexican Americans at the elementary level.

There are undoubtedly other good materials that we did not happen to find. As yet, no one can prove that any particular package or curriculum has an edge over others. There is no present basis of comparison, since distributors rarely make provisions for evaluation, student testing, periodical re-evaluation, or updating of their materials, although the Office of Education is funding efforts in the area.

For any curriculum, it is essential that teachers be sensitized to the philosophy, techniques, and goals of the materials. If the instructors fear the subject and doubt their ability to teach it, the odds are that they will not succeed with young people, regardless of the caliber of the materials.

EDUCATION FOR NONSTUDENTS

Despite massive expenditures on public drug-abuse-education programs, there is still widespread ignorance of basic drug facts among the population at large. For instance, a New York Addiction Control Commission survey of 6,000 persons aged thirteen and up found that one out of every four regarded drug abuse as among the top four problems facing the nation. Yet, 67 per cent had no idea what should be done about it; 60 per cent did not know what state agencies were at work on the problem; and 50 per cent did not know what effects heroin or amphetamines had on users.[39] A Gallup poll in December, 1970, showed that 64 per cent of the adults and 39 per cent of the students interviewed thought drugs were a serious problem in the public schools.[40]

In most cases, parents, teachers, and community leaders are more in need of accurate information about drugs than students are. Parental responses to a student's involvement in drugs can curb or accelerate further experimentation. It is therefore unfortunate that most school drug-education programs have not prepared parents to deal with the complex drug issue. For parents need not only accurate information but also the ability to discriminate between the effects of experimenting once with marijuana and those of heavy involvement with drugs as well as the ability to establish and maintain lines of honest communication with their children. Thus, to begin with, school-education programs should include a parent component. Several sessions could be designed to encourage adult participation and interaction with groups of young people. Community information and education programs sponsored by private and public organizations could also serve to reach and inform parents. Even more importantly parents need a place to go for specific help when they find drug abuse in their own family. As noted in a newspaper article, "This is sheer panic that simply cannot wait. If advice is not quickly available, fear, anxiety, rage or protectivism takes over. If action is taken during the panic and without advice, irrevocable damage may be done to the sick victim as well as to the total family structure and relationships."[41]

As a general rule, parent "help" programs should impart sympathy and counseling together with facts. The guilt, fear, and anger parents are likely to feel when a family drug crisis occurs should be channeled into constructive action through effective self-help programs. Parents of drug-dependent children can also help each other. It is often beneficial to talk to someone else who has been through a family drug crisis in trying to approach the situation calmly and objectively. No one is better prepared to provide this assistance than those parents who have been forced to deal with their own children's abuse of drugs. Opinion varies concerning the value of involving parents in group discussions with their own children. Some planners insist that direct family interaction is always counterproductive, while others advocate the confrontation of familial problems after the initial ice-breaking session.

New York's ASA runs programs for parents and relatives of serious drug-users and for community residents worried about the problem in their neighborhood generally. Several school programs (as in Nassau County, New York, and in Los Angeles) also run special sessions for the parents of children enrolled in the schools. In some, parents participate with youngsters (not their own) in group discussions on why young people use drugs. There are, of course, a multitude of drug-information programs run by civic groups, eager to involve parents. (In Miami, for instance, about two dozen organizations have drug-abuse education programs.) Many parent-oriented programs focus too heavily on how to recognize the symptoms of drug usage and may provoke needless confrontation between parent and child. Many are not prepared to help in actual cases. Until very recently, most urban centers had no place where parents could go for balanced personal advice about what to do when they suspected, or discovered, their child was using drugs.

Experts do not agree on how a parent should react when confronted with a drug-abuse crisis. They all begin by urging the parent not to panic but differ markedly on what should be done in coping with the crisis. Some suggest that the parent compel the child to seek treatment, even by threatening to throw him out of the house. Others counsel the parent to be patient and understanding in an effort to get at the underlying problems. Dr. Paul Blachley suggests that relatives of a drug user be told that "bailing him out" encourages continuation of dependence and drug use and advises that they not be accessory to the problem.[42] Sidney Cohen, former director of NIMH's drug program, advocates a middle course, urging parents to demonstrate an attitude of "I love you and I will help you, but I won't support you if you persist in behavior that I believe to be detrimental to you."[43] He further advises that these decisions must be made on an individual basis, depending on the drugs involved, the child's age, and his willingness to seek help voluntarily.

Of course, other adults who come into contact with youth need accurate information on drugs—especially teachers, counselors, policemen, and doctors. How much information is needed has yet to be assessed. Nevertheless, NIMH recently funded the Bureau of Social Science Research to study the knowledge levels of professionals who have contact with the drug scene in Baltimore and San Francisco. The study will focus on eleven occupational groups, including policemen, probation officers, pediatricians, general practitioners, psychologists, social workers, teachers, school administrators, and counselors. Results should cast some light on the level of knowledge in the various professions, as well as on prevailing attitudes, and should indicate methods of upgrading levels of education.

The current emphasis is primarily on training teachers, especially through the Office of Education. But other youth workers deserve attention as well. The National Coordinating Council on Drug Education points out, with a note of lament, that, in 1971, half of the administration's funds for drug-abuse education were spent on teacher training. In contrast, New York City's ASA would put primary emphasis on a training institute to prepare a "virtual army of skilled addiction specialists" to interact with drug-prone youth within the framework of existing institutions—schools, churches, recreation programs, settlement houses, block associations, and other groups.

To enhance the effectiveness of local efforts, the National Coordinating Council on Drug Education has put out a manual for community action—*Common Sense Lives Here*—that sets out a process whereby interested community people can define their community drug problem and work together to solve it. Not a "how to" manual, the pamphlet, together with an accompanying film, encourage each community to mobilize its own resources and seek the local causes and cures for increasing drug use before attempting to formulate a plan of action. It advocates federal planning grants for communities to finance this preparatory process. (It is possible that such grants could be made under Title I of the 1970 Drug Abuse Prevention and Control Act.) Also, it cautions against rushing into any major educational effort until the nature of the local problem is clearly perceived and adequate support has been gained.

SPONSORS OF CURRENT EFFORTS

THE FEDERAL GOVERMENT

A number of federal agencies participate in drug-abuse-education programming, but only five have a substantial involvement— the National Institute of Mental Health, the Law Enforcement Assistance Administration, the Office of Education, the Department of Housing and Urban Development, and the Bureau of Narcotics and Dangerous Drugs. Their expenditure levels and basic activities are described in Staff Paper 5.

There is general agreement among these primary agencies that their present system of program development and funding is piecemeal, uncoordinated, and inefficient. It involves various agencies independently supporting different drug-abuse programs without regard for the resulting duplication of effort and wasted resources. Ongoing programs, too, are poorly evaluated or not evaluated at all. Consequently, the agencies have reached a dead end. They are finding it virtually impossible to judge the success of programs or even to design cost-benefit analyses without comprehensive assessments. Only one fact is certain: Millions of dollars are being spent. Just how effectively funds are being used is still unknown.

STATE AND LOCAL EFFORTS

Virtually every sizable community in the country now has at least one public or private drug-abuse prevention and education program. The quality of these efforts varies from one area to another, depending, for example, on the flow of funding information from Washington, the attitudes and concerns of local citizens, the fiscal condition of the locality, and the number of agencies active in prevention programming. State education administrators agree that there are too many crash programs concentrating on drug education in isolation; that there is not enough coordination of effort where many agencies are in the same field; that there is too much attention to medical and legal factors and not enough to social and psychological factors; and that, finally, there is too little an attempt to relate specific drug use to the "drug culture," and too much reliance on one-way education (i.e., handouts, lectures, films, and speakers).

States also suffer from a lack of support from school administrators and local political structures. The National League of Cities/U.S. Conference of Mayors and the National Association of Counties are responding by planning educational programs beamed at local office holders.

This chaotic situation is further complicated by the innumerable commercial firms entering the field, putting out an avalanche of gimmicks as well as legitimate drug-education materials, along with model school curricula, films, and cartoon books. State planners have been inundated by the tide of mass-produced course materials and usually have been unsuccessful in sorting the good from the bad.

Different agencies in different states provide drug education funds in response to the variety of laws. A 1970 compilation by HEW of drug-abuse education programs supported by state education agencies shows that twenty-one states have legal requirements for school drug (and alcohol) education and are "complying" with them. Four other states have programs in all educational districts, despite a lack of legal requirements. In eleven states and Puerto Rico, some, but not all, districts have school programs. A parallel survey of drug programs supported by state health authorities, conducted by NIMH in 1970, found that twenty-two states had such health-related programs, and sixteen more had them in the planning stages.

A major problem at the state level is lack of effective coordination. Most states are plagued by a lack of cooperation between existing programs, by unnecessary overlap and duplication of effort, and by an insufficient flow of information from the grassroots level to the legislature to stimulate effective policies and leadership. A few states, such as Arizona, California, and now Florida, have statewide councils to coordinate and give direction to public and private agencies in the field. California alone has 300 community-based drug-abuse programs, all of which have sprung up in the past two years. New York City has 47 identifiable drug-education programs, and New York State has Community Narcotics Education Centers in sixteen localities, manned by professionals, as well as 57 local narcotics-guidance councils to coordinate local programs.

To eliminate the fragmentation that exists among the states, a National Association of State Drug Abuse Coordinators was organized recently. Since it is still in the organizational stages, however, its impact remains uncertain.

PRIVATE ORGANIZATIONS

A plethora of professional organizations, social-welfare associations, charitable volunteer organizations, and other groups also conduct community education programs. Few, if any, of these programs have been evaluated with regard to their impact on a target population or their record of accomplishing specific goals. They rarely assume an action-oriented role, preferring instead simply to disseminate educational brochures and audiovisuals. Their programs all look rational and successful on paper, but no one has any real notion of their effectiveness, except, perhaps, for a pervasive feeling that nothing they have done so far has made much difference. In fact, they are often criticized for jumping into the drug field without first asking for experienced advice on what their role ought to be. Also, the huge sums of money they expended on mediocre printed materials would, according to people involved in delivery of service programs, be better spent on the treatment and rehabilitation of addicts.

On the other hand, some private groups do make successful use of low-key approaches in performing unique and valuable services. Several minority professional associations, for example, sponsor clinics that provide dental care for addicts and support halfway houses that offer counseling, job placement, and training to hard-core, youthful drug abusers. Undergraduate chapters of black fraternal organizations educate members of their campus communities, while their graduate counterparts initiate the involvement of local groups in educational programs and "action" workshops. Another case involves student professionals who spend their summer months working in interdisciplinary teams, providing improved health-care delivery (including drug treatment and related legal services) to inner-city residents. Finally, several organizations whose main focus is drug abuse not only encourage research and conduct training sessions for professionals but offer free consultation to people setting up treatment centers.

Inherent in the structure of national groups is a widespread network for the dissemination of materials and information. These expansive communication mechanisms are frequently used to support legislative reform efforts and to provide information to the media and the public on the subject of drugs.

Federal money is not being spent to evaluate ongoing educational programs. As the National Coordinating Council on Drug Education has testified:

> There is a danger from continued massive education programming without first taking the time to evaluate what has been done, what needs to be done, and what can be done. Unexamined and unevaluated information and education programs are certainly no answer; and it is safe to say that in some instances they may be as harmful in the long run as no program at all.[44]

Most private efforts are limited, and many are local in scope. A few, however, are important forces nationally. With public attention being focused on the drug-abuse problem, increasing numbers of national drug organizations have begun to emerge, and many of them project coordination as their main function. The most inclusive of these is the National Coordinating Council on Drug Education, formed in 1968 as a coordinating group for public agencies and private organizations involved in drug-abuse education. The Council's philosophy emphasizes rational approaches to drug-related issues. Any interdisciplinary regional, state, or local organization whose purpose relates to drug education is eligible for membership. National organizations wishing to cooperate with NCCDE in achieving its goals may also join. At present, most members are white, middle-class organizations, although there are a few black groups, again primarily middle-class. Federal agencies are assured of the Council's cooperation. The National Coordinating Council has been financed by government contracts, private foundation funds, contributions from private industry, and donations from its members.

NCCDE has been quite independent despite its government

funding. It refused to join in National Drug Abuse Prevention Week because it felt that such one-shot crash campaigns were useless; it criticized the national advertising campaign; and it filed suit against the Federal Communications Commission, challenging its ban on rock music. Whether it will continue to receive government support is doubtful.

The Student Association for the Study of Hallucinogens (STASH) is an independent, nonprofit group run by the students themselves. It publishes the *Journal of Psychedelic Drugs*, provides reprints, issues a bibliography on hallucinogens and other drugs, and holds regular conferences on drug abuse and related problems; it has a good (and computerized) library containing 90 per cent of all the literature in English on marijuana and hallucinogens and has compiled a directory of drug-information groups. STASH is objective and scientifically oriented and, for the sake of credibility, will not accept any government money. It expects, in time, to support itself totally from membership and publication fees.

BUSINESS AND INDUSTRY

The increasing extent of drug use in industry began to be recognized during the last year by management and personnel officials. Nationwide interviews with 6,000 workers in the automobile industry recently compiled by the Alliance for Labor Action found that about 46 per cent of the workers interviewed who were under thirty years of age had used drugs at least once.[45] Of approximately 222 major businesses surveyed about drug abuse among blue-collar workers and alcoholism among executives, nearly two-thirds saw drug abuse as a major industrial problem, either now or in the immediate future, and 53 per cent had already discovered some form of drug abuse in their organization.[46]

The existence of drug abuse in a business creates serious problems for an employer. It is legitimate for him to consider whether the employee's behavior on the job endangers other workers or consumers, or even the image (or profits) of the business. He can also be encouraged to understand the underlying problems that may have led to the drug use, to help the user find treatment, and to allow him to continue to work under supervision. Although most businesses still maintain a "find them and fire them" policy, an increasing number of executives realize that they cannot find and do not wish to fire all employees who use drugs. Such employers are instituting education programs in an effort to wean employees away from drugs and to teach management how to recognize serious drug problems and channel workers to helping agencies when necessary.[47]

Business must also be involved in another urgent problem—providing employment opportunities for ex-addicts who are in or have completed a treatment program. Long-term rehabilitation requires that an ex-addict be able to find a job. Governmental and social-service agencies can contribute greatly to this—the Vera Institute and the City of New York are pioneering the employment of patients who are in treatment in specially supervised work projects—but real progress will depend upon the tolerance and assistance of far-sighted employers. More experimental work is needed, of course, to determine the problems, possibilities, and legitimate expectations of employment programs.

CONCLUSION

This examination of current drug-education efforts indicates that additional money is not the most urgent requirement. Creative individuals are needed to act as catalysts for the growth, testing, and support of creative educational approaches. Evaluation is vital, as is a climate that encourages the translation of research findings into action. Educational programming must respond to differences among addicts in ethnicity, age, and mental set. Finally, concerted efforts to clarify goals, drug knowledge, and institutional responsibilities are essential.

NOTES

1. Norman E. Zinberg. Personal communication.

2. John D. Swisher and Richard E. Horman, "Evaluation of Temple University's Drug Abuse Prevention Program," *Research Report Contract* J-68-50 (U.S. Department of Justice, Washington, D.C., 1968).

3. See Lester Grinspoon, *Marijuana Reconsidered* (Harvard University Press, 1971), for a discussion of different beliefs about one drug.

4. See Norman Zinberg and John Robertson, *Drugs and the Public* (in press).

5. California State Department of Education, "A Study of More Effective Education Relative to Narcotics, Other Harmful Drugs and Hallucinogenic Substances" (a progress report submitted to the California Legislature as required by Chapter 1437, Statutes of 1968), Sacramento, California, 1970, pp. 16–27.

6. Marvin J. Rosen, "An Evaluative Study Comparing the Cognitive and Attitudinal Effects of Two Versions of an Educational Program About Mind-Affecting Drugs," San Francisco, California, Evaluation and Research Associates, July, 1970, p. v.

7. Helen H. Nowlis, *Drugs on the College Campus* (Garden City, New York: Anchor Books, 1969), p. 60.

8. John D. Swisher and James L. Crawford, Jr., "An Evaluation of a Short-Term Drug Education Program," *The School Counselor* (March, 1971), p. 272.

9. Louise G. Richards, "Psychological Sophistication in Current Drug Abuse Education," *Rutgers Symposium on Communication and Drug Abuse* (October 14, 1969), p. 15.

10. California State Department of Education, *op. cit.*, note 5, p. 26.

11. Helen H. Nowlis, *op. cit.*, note 7.

12. "Ten Drug Abuse Films: What Students and Professionals Think of Them," *Educational Product Report*, III, No. 7 (April, 1970), 16.

13. Paul Blachley, *Seduction: A Conceptual Model of Drug Dependencies and Other Contagious Social Evils* (1970).

14. Swisher, Crawford, Goldstein, and Mura (1970); Swisher and Warner (1971); Swisher, Warner, Upcraft, and Spence (1971).

15. Richard W. Warner, "Evaluation of Drug Abuse Programs" (unpublished article), Pennsylvania State University, State College, Pennsylvania, 1971, p. 6.

16. Herbert O. Brayer, "A Comparative Analysis of Drug Use and Its Relationship to Certain Attitudes, Values and Cognitive Knowledge on Drugs Between Eighth and Eleventh Grade Students in the Coronado Unified School Districts," Coronado, Calif., 1970, p. 53.

17. Gilbert Geis, "Impact of an Experimental Narcotics Education Program on Junior High School Pupils" (1967).

18. Thomas Ungerleider, "Drugs and the Educational Process," *The American Journal of Psychiatry*, XXV (June, 1969).

19. Louise G. Richards and John H. Langer, *Drug Taking in Youth* (Bureau of Narcotics and Dangerous Drugs, Washington, D.C., 1971), p. 37.

20. *The Reasonable Exercise of Authority*, National Association of Secondary School Principals, Washington, D.C., 1969.

21. John H. Langer, "School–Law Enforcement Cooperation," *Guide-*

lines for Drug Abuse Prevention Education (Bureau of Narcotics and Dangerous Drugs, Washington, D.C., April, 1970), pp. 13–14.

22. Helen H. Nowlis, *op. cit.,* note 7, p. 66.

23. Thomas Ungerleider and Haskell Bowen, "Drug Abuse and the Schools," *American Journal of Psychiatry,* XXV (June, 1969).

24. U.S. Congress, Senate Committee on Labor and Public Welfare, Special Subcommittee on Alcoholism and Narcotics, *Hearings* on S. 3562, 91st Cong., 2d sess., March, 1970, pp. 176–77.

25. Montgomery County Joint Advisory Committee on Drug Abuse, *Final Report,* March 10, 1970.

26. Frederic Meyers, "Incidents Involving the Haight-Ashbury Population and some Uncommonly Used Drugs," *Journal of Psychedelic Drugs,* I, No. 1 (Fall, 1968).

27. Robin Nelson, "Dragon Slayers on an Ominous Crusade," *Marketing Communications* (September, 1970), p. 20 (quoting Dr. Nes Littner, Director of the Chicago Institute for Psychoanalysis).

28. Norman E. Zinberg, "Why Now?: Drug Use as a Response to Social and Technological Change," lecture, Aspen, Colorado, August 29, 1970.

29. Richards and Langer, *op. cit.,* note 19, p. 29.

30. Donald L. Kanter, "Pharmaceutical Advertising in Youth: A Monograph Reporting upon a Quantitative Pilot Study" (mimeograph), December 30, 1970, p. 15.

31. Henry Lennard *et al.,* "Hazards Implicit in Prescribing Psychoactive Drugs," 169, *Science* 438 (1970). The authors cite examples of such statements as follows:

1. "The epidemic of drug abuse is rapidly becoming a national emergency. Part of the responsibility for this must be borne by the drug industry, radio and television. Just as cigarette commercials made smoking romantic, manly, relaxing, smart, and 'in,' drug advertising has helped 'turn on' our civilization, especially our youth. We are constantly bombarded by people on television with an easy solution to any of our troubles, most of it half truth or lies. The continuous selling of drugs on television and radio must be stopped. All drug advertising should be prohibited from the mass media, a small step toward regaining our children." (Letter from Robert A. Levine, M.D., to the editor, 282 *New England Journal of Medicine,* pp. 1378–79 [1970].)

2. "Our technology provides us with highly potent synthetic materials and through the mass media means to inform any person who can read, listen, or look about these dangerous substances. In this situation it is all too easy for anyone of any age who does not like the way he lives to try a drug 'high' in search of a mystique of esoteric meaning, of euphoria, or of oblivion." (Stanley F. Yolles, M.D., "The Drug Phenomenon," NS10 *Journal of American Pharmaceutical Association,* p. 403 [1970].)

3. "Our culture and communications media teach children that one solves almost all problems by 'turning on'—drugs for headaches, constipation,

172   *Patricia M. Wald and Annette Abrams*

sleeplessness, 'nerves,' and for whatever other maladies beset us." (Allen
Y. Cohen, Ph.D., "Inside What's Happening: Sociological, Psychological,
and Spiritual Perspectives on the Contemporary Drug Scene," 59 *American Journal of Public Health*, pp. 2090, 2093 [1969].)

4. "The impact of mass media advertising . . . tends to create a psychological dependence upon drugs as a palliative for the strains and stresses of contemporary society." (Dr. Donald C. Brodie, *Drug Trade News*, June 15, 1970, p. 8.)

32. *Ibid.*

33. Richard Blum *et al.*, *Society and Drugs*, I (San Francisco, California: Jossey Bass, Inc., 1969), 262.

34. *Educational Product Report, op. cit.*, note 12, p. 16.

35. "99 Films on Drugs +," University of California Extension Media Center, Berkeley, California, 1970.

36. *Drug Abuse Films*, 2d ed., National Coordinating Council on Drug Education, Washington, D.C., 1971, p. vii.

37. Richards and Langer, *op. cit.*

38. Herbert O. Brayer, *op. cit.*, note 16, pp. 54–55.

39. Glaser and Snow, "Public Knowledge and Attitudes on Drug Abuse," *NACC* (1969).

40. *Washington Post*, December 10, 1970.

41. *New York Times*, April 27, 1970.

42. Paul Blachley, *op. cit.*, note 13.

43. Sidney Cohen, "The Drug Dilemma: A Partial Solution," *Resource Book for Drug Abuse Education*, National Institute of Mental Health (October, 1969), p. 15.

44. U.S. Congress, *op. cit.*, note 24, p. 176.

45. Alliance for Labor Action (ALA) is an organization representing the United Auto Workers and the Teamsters Union whose "Drugs in Industry" survey results will be available early in 1972.

46. Harold M. F. Rush and James K. Brown, "The Drug Abuse Problem in Business," *Conference Board Record* (March, 1971).

47. Carol Kurtis, *Drug Abuse as a Business Problem: The Problem Defined with Guidelines for Policy* (New York: New York Chamber of Commerce, January, 1971).

Treatment and Rehabilitation

by James V. DeLong

Introduction • Abstinence Programs • Methadone Main-
tenance • Antagonists • Multimodal Programs • Heroin
Maintenance • Treatment of Users of Nonopiates •
Conclusion

INTRODUCTION

HISTORY OF TREATMENT

The beginnings of our current narcotics problem go back over
a century. As many authors have noted, the United States had a
large number of opiate addicts in the period between the Civil
War and the passage of the Harrison Act, which limited the availability of drugs, in 1914. These addicts were primarily white, female, rural, lower to lower-middle class, and middle-aged.[1] They
regularly injected morphine or took morphine or opiated patent
medicine orally. Opiates were freely available from the local
pharmacy, so they were not criminals.

Some of them did not even know that they were addicted to
narcotics. Patent medicines were not always labeled, and the user
may have known only that he felt sick when he did not take a

particular medicine, not realizing that the problem was withdrawal from the medicine itself. Most were knowingly addicted, of course, and addiction was a matter of great individual concern. Physicians had developed many different "cures" between 1856 and 1914, and the effort continued thereafter. In 1928, Dr. Charles Terry and Mildren Pellens, after reviewing these efforts extensively, stated:

> . . . for the most part, the treatment of this condition has not emerged from the stage of empiricism. The various methods described in general indicate that the basis of the majority of them is merely the separation of the patient from the drug. Very few of those who have described the details of treatment have given a rationale for their procedures but rather have outlined dogmatically the adoption of certain measures whose primary object is the withdrawal of the drug and have stated or left the reader to infer that the completion of the procedure brings about cure.[2]

True to the spirit of the age, there were also numerous patent medicine "cures" available, some of which were themselves laden with opiates.

It is difficult to recapture the dominant attitudes toward addiction during this period. Terry and Pellens cite contemporary sources contending that addiction was a vice, a physical disease, a moral perversion, a product of neurotic inheritance, or a result of morphine poisoning.[3] Much of the debate is cast in terms of virtue and vice, and it is hard to tell what these terms meant to the participants. On the whole, however, the arguments are remarkably similar to those used in current debate about addiction.

While there was no consensus on the nature or causes of addiction, by the early 1900's it was recognized as a significant public-health issue, and pressure for legislative action developed. The passage of the federal Harrison Act in 1914 changed the problem dramatically. For the first time, opiates were to be controlled and prescribed by physicians rather than freely available on the open market.

It is not clear what response the lawmakers expected from the medical establishment. They may have expected doctors to keep on supplying existing addicts while avoiding the creation of new ones; they may have expected doctors to force addicts to give up their habit by refusing to prescribe narcotics; they may not have thought about it at all. In any event, at passage of the Harrison Act, the country had at least 200,000 to 300,000 opiate addicts who were now cut off from their normal sources of supply and unable to receive drugs except through physicians.

One result was predictable, although not necessarily predicted: Physicians were deluged with addicts seeking drugs.[4] A survey conducted by a Treasury Department committee in 1918 that reached 31 per cent of the physicians in the United States found that they had 73,150 addicts under treatment. Treatment, the committee believed, meant supplying drugs.[5] In addition to, and partly in replacement of, private physicians, more than 40 maintenance clinics were opened from about 1918. Most were sponsored by cities.

Whatever the lawmakers may have thought about the nature of addiction, the law enforcers considered maintaining existing addicts on opiates unacceptable. This group believed that, once the drug was removed and the addict had gone through withdrawal, he should have no further problems. Rufus King has given some examples of this view:

. . . the medical conclusion, propounded as not open to question . . . , [was] that drug addiction was a correctible and curable condition, viz. the following preface to the Prohibition Bureau's Regulations: "It is well-established that the ordinary case of addiction will yield to proper treatment, and that addicts will remain permanently cured when drug addiction is stopped and they are otherwise physically restored to health and strengthened in will power."

Moreover, a small but strident segment of the medical community went even further than the authorities . . . In 1921 a member of the American Medical Association's Committee on Narcotic Drugs, purportedly speaking officially for the Association, was quoted [as saying]: "The shallow pretense that drug addiction is a disease which the specialist must be allowed to treat, which pretended treatment consists in supplying its victims with the drug which has caused their physical and moral debauchery . . . , has been asserted and urged in volumes of literature by the self-styled specialists."[6]

To people with this mental set, the maintenance clinics served no useful purpose; they simply prolonged the addictive state instead of curing it. If one assumes that abstinence is relatively easy, then drug maintenance does appear to be the equivalent of drug pushing. The government put severe pressure on the clinics, and the last one was closed in 1923.[7]

At the same time, a very tough policy toward physicians was maintained. The Narcotic Division of the Treasury Department arrested or threatened 14,701 persons registered to dispense drugs under the Harrison Act in 1918, 22,595 in 1919 and 47,835 in 1920.[8] Between 1914 and 1938, 25,000 doctors were arrested for supplying opiates, and 5,000 of them actually went to jail.[9] Those doctors who maintained that addiction was more complicated than what the official view held, and who advocated maintenance, were purged from the field.

It is tempting today to condemn this enforcement policy as both cruel and ineffective. It was certainly cruel, but its real effect will never be known. To begin with the most elementary question, no one knows whether the policy of closing off legitimate sources of supply decreased the total number of addicts. The Federal Bureau of Narcotics has estimated that the number of addicts declined from 200,000 at the time of the Harrison Act in 1914 to 118,000 in 1930, 60,000 in 1936, and 20,000 in 1945. Dr. Alfred Lindesmith has pointed out that these estimates are improbable, since they depend on the proposition that new addicts were not being recruited to replace those who died or quit the habit. If this were true, the average age of addicts would have risen as the population aged. In fact, the average age declined steadily throughout the period, and the other demographic characteristics of the population also changed, so there must have been substantial recruitment. Lindesmith reached no firm conclusion on absolute numbers, but pointed out: "Since the range of estimates of the addicted population at present is at least as great as it was before 1914, one can make out a case for any trend one chooses by judiciously selecting the estimates."[10]

One can argue that the policy worked fairly well for the addicts of the early part of the century, who were 60 per cent female, 90 per cent white, rural rather than urban, and middle or lower-middle class rather than impoverished. By 1945, the addict population was about 85 per cent male and only 75 per cent white, a substantial change in character. Since then, the addict population has remained about 85 per cent male and become steadily younger as well as more minority-group-concentrated. In New York City, for example, the Narcotics Register shows 47 per cent of the addicts to be black, 27 per cent Puerto Rican,[11] and 26 per cent white. During the last two or three years, addiction has been spreading back into the middle class, but this is not a marked trend as yet. Clearly, the population of the 1910's and 1920's did not replace itself, and this could be judged a successful result of sorts.

By any account, a hard core of addicts remained after the closing of the clinics. During the 1920's, they were largely ignored, and treatment for opiate addiction disappeared for a decade. Then, in 1935 and 1938, the Public Health Service clinics in Fort Worth and Lexington were opened, largely because of problems created by addicts in the prisons. The basic theory of treatment remained unchanged since the earlier period—if an addict could be separated from his drug for a time, he could be counted as cured. It was generally believed by this time that the horrors of withdrawal were so great that few real addicts would undertake it on their own, but that a few months at one of the clinics would see them through withdrawal and allow them to recover. Once they went back to the community, it was presumed, they would never want to go near the drug again because of their fear of withdrawal.

Subsequent studies have indicated that the PHS clinics did not work very well.[12] This was not generally recognized at the time, however, and there was another hiatus in the development of new treatment techniques until the explosion of urban addiction in the 1950's and 1960's. During the latter part of this period, several new methods came into being in response to the obvious inadequacies of the old ones.

Synanon, founded in 1959, became the precursor of a line of therapeutic communities that emphasized the psychological component of readdiction and tried to restructure the addict's character. During the next decade, many such communities were founded across the country. The apogee of the movement was probably reached in New York City's Addiction Services Agency between 1965 and 1968. At the same time, civil-commitment programs more or less on the Lexington model were applied on a large scale by California starting in 1961 and by New York State and the federal government starting in 1967.

In 1964, Dr. Vincent Dole pioneered in the use of methadone, a synthetic opiate substitute for heroin. Methadone maintenance has grown rapidly in the last few years, and, as of 1971, it is the technique into which most new money is going.

Contemporaneously with methadone, researchers at Lexington in 1965 began experimenting with the use of antagonists—drugs that block the effects of opiates without themselves being addictive. This method, however is still experimental, has a great many problems, and is not yet an operating modality.

At present, the dominant treatment modalities are therapeutic communities, civil commitment, outpatient abstinence, and methadone maintenance. A large number of hybrid programs, however, have developed in response to the concern over addiction during the late 1960's. Some are explicitly multimodal, utilizing all the major techniques. There are also detoxification programs that simply take an addict through withdrawal, often using methadone but sometimes not; there are also crisis intervention centers, and programs that supply very small doses of methadone on demand. Many community organizations have become active in the field, with operations of all types and combinations.

For purposes of clarity, this paper imposes more order on the field than exists in practice. Methadone receives by far the most detailed analysis. In part, this is because methadone treatment is expanding very rapidly, and thorough analysis is therefore especially important. It is also due to the fact that, since methadone maintenance has been in the hands of physicians and scientists who believe in records, evaluation, and research, information on these programs is more readily available.

GOALS OF TREATMENT

The apparent goals of treatment are obvious. Society wants the addict to stop using heroin and committing crimes and, instead, to find a job, stabilize his personal life, generally improve his character, and become a useful and productive citizen. Analyzing programs in terms of these objectives presents a series of problems, however. The first is mechanical, although important: It is extremely difficult to get good information on the results of programs in terms of these or any other measures of success.

The second is more subtle. Even when information on treatment results can be obtained, it tends to focus on whether the patient has stopped using heroin. This represents in part a moral judgment that this is the most important goal of treatment and in part the belief that abstinence is a valid proxy measure of the achievement of the other objectives. Historically, there has also been a tendency to believe that treatment has failed if an addict subsequently uses narcotics for any length of time whatsoever, on the assumption, perhaps, that *any* relapse automatically means *total* relapse.

Increasingly, experts have become aware that this concentration on abstinence is questionable. While abstinence is to some extent a proxy for the other possible benefits of a treatment program, it is not completely accurate. The many facets of the addicted life-style are not totally inseparable, and, equally important, they need not all be treated at once. After treatment, an addict might hold a job, support a family, refrain from criminal activity —and still go on occasional benders of drug use. Or, he might continue to commit crimes, but fewer than before. His physical health might be improved even if nothing else were changed. It is also possible for a program to have a reverse effect. It might, for example, eliminate opiate addiction at the price of alcoholism, a dubious bargain.

In short, there is a range of possible benefits and adverse effects that can be produced by treatment programs. Different programs attach different importance to each; conflicts of value are inherent in comparisons of effectiveness. Since such questions are not easily resolvable, an objective examination of treatment programs should, ideally, use varying measures rather than only two categories—success (total abstinence) or failure (anything else). Abstinence, stabilization on methadone (or, in fact, stabilization on heroin), employment, decreased criminal conduct or noncriminal conduct, support of a family, improved physical health and psychological functioning—any of these outcomes represents at least partial success for a treatment program and should be so regarded.

Despite the strong reservations about using abstinence as a measure, this paper repeatedly uses freedom from drug use as the major criterion of the success of treatment programs. While evaluation of even this factor is fragmentary, it is far more common than evaluation in terms of other possible measures. Anyone trying to analyze program results has to use it as a proxy or refrain from any judgments at all, and it is sufficiently important to be of use. It should be emphasized, however, that good multifactor evaluation might drastically change many of the conclusions contained here.

The third problem is even more fundamental. No one knows whether the goals of treatment as set forth in the beginning of this section are realistic or even desirable. Since no one knows why people become narcotics addicts, no one knows either how to make them stop or what will happen to them if they do stop. For example, NIMH officials recently stated that about 25 per cent of the addict population are people who suffer from depression and chronic anxiety, another 25 per cent are hedonists who like to get intoxicated, and the rest are psychopaths who need immediate gratification and are not particular about how they obtain it.[13] Other researchers have also concluded that there is no one addict type, and that addiction can serve as a functional and adaptive characteristic for people with different types of psychic problems.

Yet, there are also a number of researchers who, denying this stress on psychopathology, contend that people are inducted into drug use through peer pressure and that large numbers of addicts may not suffer from severe psychopathology. The argument can be made that whatever characteristics addicts appear to have in common are forced upon them by the requirements of sustaining the addiction once it exists. Still another view is that addicts do have psychological problems but that these are in many cases no more severe than those shown by many nonaddicts. If one conducted a mental-health survey of the population from which most addicts are drawn, one might discover as many symptoms of mental disorder among the nonaddicts. Finally, some argue that heroin itself causes a metabolic change in the body that makes it difficult to cease being an addict. Thus, one can become addicted casually and then be unable to rid oneself of the addiction no matter what therapeutic techniques are brought to bear.[14]

Treatment programs have disparate philosophies on these questions. Some, though by no means all, methadone programs assume some physiological basis of addiction. Most therapeutic communities probably assume a character disorder that can be helped by group therapy. Some outpatient abstinence programs assume that addiction may be an almost accidental event for many addicts, and that they can be helped with minimal intervention. But these assumptions are not constant within any modality, and almost all spectrums of opinion exist in each.

In short, there is no uniform theory of addiction and no adequate description of the addict population. Further, addiction has spread rapidly in recent years, and we know less about the new population than we do about the old. And we knew little enough before.

The difficulties these factors create in judging treatment programs are obvious. We do not know what expectations are realistic or desirable. We do not even know for certain that it is good for addicts to stop taking drugs. Some programs may be better for certain types of addicts than others, but we are not sure what types, or whether the programs are attracting the type with which they do best.

All the figures given in this paper are gross figures—the programs are judged by effects on the total number of people who were involved without any breakdown of results for different hypothetical subgroups of the addict population. The conclusions, therefore, are tentative, at best.

ABSTINENCE PROGRAMS

DETOXIFICATION

The most straightforward way to help a heroin addict is to detoxify him—reduce his daily heroin intake to zero and see him through withdrawal. The addict can be maintained on an in-patient basis without any drugs for the five-to-ten-day period nec-essary for primary withdrawal symptoms to disappear; or he can be treated with tranquilizers but not opiates; or methadone can be used to decrease his opiate dosage gradually until he is drug-free.

Detoxification services are offered in many places and modes across the nation—in hospitals, therapeutic communities, free clinics, and government programs. There is no way of learning how many addicts receive them each year.

Detoxification has several clear benefits for both the addict and society. Even if the addict does not intend to stay off drugs, it reduces his habit and decreases its cost. This spares him the hassle and society the crime costs of his addiction for some period, even if only a few days, after the process is complete. For some addicts, it is also a step toward rehabilitation. After repeated failures to remain detoxified, they become ready for other modali-ties.

On the whole, however, it is not clear that detoxification itself contributes greatly to the achievement of long-term abstinence. One program that used methadone in decreasing doses found that 74 per cent of the patients either did not finish the withdrawal program or relapsed to drug use within 48 hours after leaving it. Another, which effects withdrawal without opiates, found that only 10 per cent successfully completed the withdrawal, and almost all of these soon relapsed.[15] The New York Narcotic Ad-diction Control Commission has estimated that only 24 per cent of those who receive detoxification without other services "remain drug-free for any length of time."[16]

The Haight-Ashbury Clinic in San Francisco has been experi-menting with outpatient withdrawal, utilizing analgesics but not opiates. It reports the results with 450 patients:

- 56 per cent dropped out before they were clean and were lost to follow-up for at least two weeks; 5 per cent of these resumed their habit, 22 per cent were in treatment, and the rest were apparently not known.
- 12 per cent had decreased their habit to "chipping" no more than once a week.

- 5.5 per cent had been clean for one month or more.
- 38 per cent were lost track of after only one clinic visit.[17]

This population differs from the standard drug-addict population because it includes individuals who are basically middle class and who began using heroin after being involved in the San Francisco speed scene; many have not been addicted for long. No one knows whether this population is harder, or easier, to work with than the more familiar ghetto populations. Other program examples could be cited—some better and some worse—but the general picture remains: Detoxification does have some benefits, but it is primarily a service for the drug user who needs a respite and a short-term way of protecting society against crime rather than a long-term treatment for addiction. As such, it is valuable, especially for anyone who believes that addicts should be treated more humanely than they are at the present time and that band-aids can be valuable things. But expectations should not be too high.

CIVIL COMMITMENT

In theory, civil commitment is the nonpunitive incarceration of an addict for purposes of rehabilitation. This method of treatment was started in the 1930's at the Lexington and Fort Worth hospitals, where the programs were part voluntary and part coercive. In the 1960's, civil commitment was applied on a wider scale, first in California then in New York. Subsequently, the federal government started using civil commitment as an alternative to imprisonment through the Narcotic Addict Rehabilitation Program. Dr. John Kramer has traced the relationship between the earlier programs and the massive investment of the 1960's:

> The roots of these commitment laws can be traced to the federal narcotics hospital in Lexington. In recounting the initial expectations for that institution Isbell writes . . . "Drug addicts were to be treated within the institution, freed of their physiological dependence on drugs, their basic immaturities and personality problems corrected by vocational and psychiatric therapy, after which they would be returned to their communities to resume their lives. It seems to have been tacitly assumed that this program was the answer and would solve the problem of opiate addiction. Within a

year it was apparent this assumption was wrong . . . a more adequate treatment program [required]: (1) Some means of holding voluntary patients until they had reached maximum benefit from hospital treatment. (2) Greater use of probation and parole. . . . (3) Provision for intensive supervision and aftercare. . . ." Isbell goes on to say that the reasons why these problems were not solved were complex. "In 1961 the California Legislature enacted laws establishing a commitment program for addicts which was designed to accomplish those objectives recommended but never carried out at Lexington."[18]

It is generally thought that the programs started in the 1930's were almost total failures. Between 1935 and 1964, there were 87,000 admissions to the two centers, of which 63,600 were voluntary and 23,400 were federal prisoners. Of the voluntary patients, 70 per cent left against medical advice. A series of studies of addicts released from the abstinence facilities found that up to 90 per cent of those followed up relapsed into drug use within a few years.[19]

As is true of almost every other aspect of the field, this conclusion is debatable. Recent research has suggested that it may exaggerate the failures. Dr. John O'Donnell points out that all the studies had problems with data collection and with categorization of those addicts who could not be found. He also questions the assumption that any relapse—any use of drugs—should be regarded as a failure, an assumption that was made by several of the studies. As has been pointed out, an addict may become basically abstinent, even though he does relapse a few times; and, even if he relapses regularly, he may spend more time off drugs than he would have without the treatment. This is also a net social gain.

O'Donnell uses the following example. If one has 2,000 ex-addicts in a two-year study (a total of 4,000 man-years) and defines relapse as a two-week period of heroin use at any time, then a 90 per cent relapse rate could mean that anywhere between 72 and 3,600 of the 4,000 man-years were spent in a state of addiction. That is, 90 per cent of the addicts could have relapsed for exactly two weeks each, or, at the other extreme, 90 per cent could have relapsed for the entire two years, or anything in between.[20] The social and individual consequences of these polar possibilities are very different.

The revisionist approach to the Lexington experience has caused many observers to soften their adverse judgments somewhat. Most still believe that it was not effective with very many addicts but concede that the question probably cannot be answered definitely. The data that would allow methodologically acceptable studies are lost. This does not seem to bother anyone too much, however, because the Lexington population drew heavily from rural white populations, and the exact results would be of marginal relevance to our present situation.

The three programs that were started in the 1960's built on the Lexington model, although they tried to improve it. They appear to have been started because addiction was either increasing or becoming more visible, and was thus becoming a political problem. In 1961, there was simply no treatment modality available except civil commitment, and even by 1966 it did not appear that there was any clearly better alternative. Under pressure to do something, state and federal authorities picked up the only available model, apparently on the premises that: (1) The failures of the Lexington program were due in part to the fact that the duration of treatment was too short (six months or a year); (2) Improved vocational and counseling services would be helpful; (3) Some careful studies had indicated that better supervision in the community after release would improve the success rate;[21] (4) Civil commitment would at least get addicts off the street.

The California program, instituted in 1961, provides for commitment on court order in lieu of sentence or prosecution. Voluntary commitment and commitment by relatives are also possible, but over 90 per cent of the inmates are there involuntarily, after conviction.[22] In fact, the program is structurally and functionally very similar to imprisonment. The main center, in Corona, California, is a maximum-security facility under the direction of the Department of Corrections. There are armed guards and barbed-wire fences, and most of the personnel are corrections workers. The minimum institutional stay is six months, and the average is about 14 months. After leaving the institution the addict is required to undergo a three-year period of "community aftercare," which is essentially "parole." During this time, he follows the same regimen as ex-felons, with the additional requirement of regular urinalysis testing and group counseling. Violations of "parole" can and, in the case of relapse to drug use, usually do mean return to the institution. Attempted escape from the institution and serious parole violations are felonies in themselves.

The facility does provide inmates with a modified form of encounter-group therapy, based on the hypothesis that drug use is a symptom of aberrant personality patterns which must be changed. However, a study of the program's results concluded that the program was interpreted by addicts and professional visitors as more punitive than therapeutic. Whether one were released depended in large part on how well one played the game at group sessions. This was not conducive to the honesty that real group therapy demands.

Evaluation showed that between 1962 and 1964 there were 1,209 persons on release status at some time. At the end of the year, only 35 per cent were still in good standing and only 16 per cent maintained this status after three years. The majority who fail in aftercare do so for drug use, "poor adjustment," failure to report in, or new arrest. During the first year, 56 per cent were detected using drugs and 20 per cent convicted of new crimes. In the three-year period, 81 per cent had been suspended from release status at least once. The usual pattern for the inmate consisted of periods spent in the facility followed by periods of abstinence in the aftercare phase, and then return to the facility in Corona. As a result of this pattern, inmates who would have been serving a felony sentence (70 per cent) actually spent less time "incarcerated," while those who were guilty of misdemeanors (16 per cent) were "incarcerated" longer than if they had served an ordinary prison sentence. No later results seem to have changed this pattern. Felon addicts who receive no therapy while in prison do as well as or better than California Rehabilitation Center addicts while on parole.[23]

The New York program, adopted several years later, differs somewhat in conception.[24] Like California, New York provides for commitment in lieu of sentence or prosecution, for voluntary commitment, and for commitment by relatives or other persons, such as school officials or prosecuting attorneys. Unlike the California system, New York's system is under the direction of an independent Narcotic Addiction Control Commission (NACC) and has a mental-health orientation involving the use of professional mental-health personnel. NACC is also more committed to research and community aftercare programs.

New York's total program, by far the largest in the United States, has spent $475.3 million in the last four years, including its investment in methadone and therapeutic communities as well as in civil commitment. The direct annual investment in the civil-commitment program appears to be at least $50 million out of a total budget of $88.5 million. As of the end of 1970, NACC had 10,764 addicts in its own facilities, and another 10,419 were in facilities accredited or funded by NACC. These population figures were not broken down by modality.[25]

Despite the dominance of a mental-health approach and professionalized therapy, the emphasis on security and remote institutions has apparently produced a penal atmosphere at many of the NACC facilities. Recreational and entertainment facilities appear to be lacking, and life in a NACC institution has been described as a dreary round of a few hours in a classroom or workshop, some time in group meetings led by civil servants, and the rest of the time watching television or loafing. The peer pressures, ex-addict, encounter-group leadership, and meaningful work assignments needed to create an effective therapeutic environment are absent.[26] The program has been subject to some fierce attacks, as in the 1970 New York gubernatorial campaign, when one candidate claimed that in three years NACC had spent $345 million and cured 120 addicts.[27] It is difficult to know whether all of these accusations are justified. But it is equally difficult to find disinterested observers who contradict them.

NACC officials state their results fairly carefully. In June, 1971, the research director testified that "a relatively small number of people" had been processed through the entire civil-commitment procedure (the three to five years), and that, of those who had gone all the way through, 25 per cent "are currently abstinent, according to a physical follow-up." Another 25 per cent had either recertified themselves to NACC or had entered other treatment programs. The rest (50 per cent) were in jail as a result of new drug-related offenses or had returned to drugs.[28] This statement does not reveal how many addicts had completed the program, how many were able to drop out or escape in some way, or what level of functioning the abstinent addicts were maintaining. The population is referred to as "small."

The federal NARA program of civil commitment for addicts includes three separate programs. Title I provides for addicts charged with violating federal laws (nonviolent crimes only). In lieu of prosecution, the addict can be committed to a three-year treatment period involving both institutional and aftercare treatment facilities. Admissions under this title have been few. Between July, 1967, and June, 1970, only 207 persons were examined and 179 accepted, although a case load of 900 per year had been anticipated. The main reason seems to be a general disinterest by U.S. Attorneys.[29]

Title II offers treatment in lieu of sentencing for addicts convicted of federal crimes. This program is administered by the Bureau of Prisons, which provides facilities for treatment within regular penal institutions. The time of incarceration is not to exceed ten years, and the addict can be released to aftercare services after six months. Only about 375 addicts are currently being serviced under this title.[30]

Title III provides for voluntary commitment by addicts who are not involved in criminal proceedings. The commitment is for a period of three years, most of which is spent in aftercare facilities. The term of the institutionalization itself is to be determined by the patient's progress but is not to exceed six months.

Until recently, Title I and Title III patients were sent to the Lexington or Fort Worth facility, under the Surgeon General. (Fort Worth has now been transferred to the Bureau of Prisons and will no longer be used for addiction treatment.) Title III patients receive their initial evaluation at Lexington, but many are channeled into community or state programs funded by NARA grants and contracts. The Lexington facility is the most open of the institutions and has a more relaxed policy toward escape or attempted escape. The primary treatment methods employed are detoxification, counseling, and some work and recreation therapy. They have begun an experiment with a small therapeutic community (Matrix House) but require a longer time commitment for patients in this program.

The initial evaluation determines whether the addict is suitable for treatment. The rejection rate is about 55-60 per cent. The grounds for rejection are not clear. Some officials claim that suitability is based on an assessment of motivation—whether an addict has sufficient self-control to be able to function in a relaxed and open environment, and, if not, the availability of other types of treatment facilities. Another view is that decisions on suitability are made on the basis of objective criteria, such as current legal status, criminal record, age, employment, history, prior drug experience, and mental state.

In a study of the first 27 months of operation under the new Act (1966–69), about 2,000 addicts were tested at Lexington. As of September 30, 1969, there were 802 Title I and Title III patients on an aftercare status; 26 per cent had been recommitted to the institution for aftercare violations, and 5 per cent had been discharged. As of March, 1971, 2,000 patients were in the civil commitment program, of whom 1,300 were in aftercare. Of the 2,000, 60 per cent were white. Average age was in the late 20's.[31] In June, 1971, the Director of NIMH stated:

> In the civil commitment program, a study of 1,200 patients who were in aftercare in 1970 showed that approximately 85 percent were employed, 70 percent were not arrested and spent no time in jail during that period, 35 percent were in self-help therapy, and 33 percent were pursuing their education. Patients who had been [in] aftercare for 3 months or more were, on the average, drug-free 80 percent of the time. A similar statement can be made regarding the heroin use of patients who were in the community treatment programs. As you know, many patients during the treatment of their addiction may abuse drugs other than heroin occasionally, such as cocaine, marijuana, amphetamines, or barbiturates. Of the patients in the civil commitment program who had been in aftercare for 3 months or more, 60 percent were not abusing any drugs. The same is true of patients who had been in the community treatment program for 3 months or more. Of the patients who are in the civil commitment aftercare phase, we know that 60 percent do not be-

come readdicted during their first year in aftercare. Of the remaining, 25 percent do abuse some drugs or become readdicted and require further hospital treatment. About 15 percent were dropouts.[32]

It is difficult to know what to make of these results. Even allowing for selectivity in acceptance into the program, they are far better than the New York or the California experience would have led one to expect. Since the detailed studies on which this statement is based are not available, one can only reserve judgment.

The Bureau of Prisons has analyzed initial results from its care of inmates committed under Title II of NARA. As of the end of 1971, 896 inmates had been examined for program eligibility, and 70 per cent (630) had been accepted. The program had released 414 inmates to aftercare after an average institutionalization of 15 months, and 297 (72 per cent) of these were still active. The other 28 per cent had "violated or absconded." Over five thousand months of "successful aftercare" had been accumulated, but the meaning of that term as used in the report is unclear.[33]

Many drug experts believe that programs of civil commitment offer little more than custodial care in a predominantly penal setting. Counseling and therapy, when employed, are imposed on the patients by the staff and are of questionable value. Apparently, most addicts are committed as an alternative to criminal prosecution or sentencing, and view commitment as such. Most do not appear to be motivated toward inner change, and those that do succeed might succeed equally as well in a voluntary community program. In addition, civil commitment is expensive. It requires secured facilities, around-the-clock guards, and large staffs. (Cost estimates for all three of the large programs are $10,000 to $12,-000 per year per addict while the addict is in the institution. It is not clear whether this represents full costs, including capital expenditures, or operating costs only.) In spite of these costs, the chief function of civil commitment seems to be nothing more than to keep the addict out of circulation for intermittent short periods.

The NARA information cited above seems to indicate that civil commitment for a limited term followed by aftercare is more promising than this conclusion suggests. The California program was structured in somewhat the same manner—although with a more open law-enforcement orientation—and it may be that it shows worse results than NARA because it was more carefully evaluated and the patients were more carefully controlled. A definite answer to this will have to await more detailed information on NARA.

THE THERAPEUTIC COMMUNITY

"Therapeutic community" (TC) is a generic term used to describe an institution that attempts to treat the addict by dealing with the underlying causes of his addiction. The basic concept of the TC modality, as of the civil-commitment programs, is that addiction is the result of psychological problems, and that intensive therapeutic techniques utilized within the structure of a residential community can restructure the character and personality of the addict to the point where he no longer needs to use drugs. Although heroin addicts constitute the major part of the TC population, most TC's service users of nonopiates as well. As of mid-1970, there were probably 40–50 therapeutic community programs in the country with approximately 4,000–5,000 residents.[34]

The growth of therapeutic communities is in some ways as much a quasi-evangelical movement as a drug-treatment modality, and it is difficult to describe them without distorting the views of at least some of the participants.[35] The flavor of this modality can be partly conveyed by tracing some analogies and intellectual roots. First, there is a parallel between the TC and Alcoholics Anonymous. Synanon, the original addict-oriented TC, was founded in 1959 by an ex-alcoholic as a treatment program for alcoholics modeled after AA. It drifted into treatment of opiate addicts largely by accident. Many of the TC's retain some of the basic AA characteristics—the concept that there is no such thing as an ex-addict, only an addict who is not using at the moment; the emphasis on mutual support and aid; the distrust of mental-health professionals; and the concept of continual confession and catharsis. However, the TC has extended these notions to include the concept of a live-in community with a rigid structure of day-to-day behavior and a complex system of punishment and rewards.

The rise of the TC also parallels the rising popularity of group therapy generally. Encounter groups, support groups, and marathon sessions are as prevalent in the "straight world" as in the TC's, and the many differences in group-therapy methods that exist outside exist in the TC's as well. One reason for the frequent confusion about the different TC's is that they reflect the many variations in approaches to group therapy.

The growth of TC's has occurred at the same time as the growth of interest in communes, and some TC's have an element of the commune in them—the residents are rejecting a dishonest world in favor of a better way of life. Synanon, for example, has residents who have never been addicted to anything but who prefer the Synanon life-style. Dr. John Kramer has referred to Synanon as "the third community," different from the drug-using community and the "square" community. He points out that there is a fundamental difference between Synanon and many of the TC's in that "the Synanon ideal is to retain members in the group indefinitely and to expand steadily, drawing in more and more members, squares as well as addicts. Other TC's differ in that they do expect their members to re-enter the square community."[36]

The past decade has seen a movement toward community action and a rejection of services furnished exogenously. Community control is a familiar slogan, and the beliefs that only the poor know what the poor want and only blacks can help blacks are also common. To some extent, TC's reflect this movement. Many of them have adopted the view that the nonaddict does not really understand the problems and world of an addict and therefore cannot contribute as an ex-addict can. Since addicts are often poor and black as well as addicted, this concept is a powerful force.

Finally, the quasi-evangelical aspect of the TC creates an interesting, although certainly not documented or provable, situation. The addict may be replacing his addiction to heroin with an "addiction" to being an ex-addict and to the encounter therapy. The philosophy of the TC becomes a religion for the addict. It is something to believe in and a message to spread to his fellow addicts in the world. The "religious fervor" involved exists in varying degrees. In Dr. Kramer's words:

> It has been undiplomatically stated that religiomania is a cure for narcomania. This observation is valid, particularly if one defines religiomania broadly as the devout acceptance of clearly defined tenets of a faith and its principles of behavior, and persistent participation in its prescribed rituals. The faith and its practice will usually encompass all the life activities of the communicant and in its practice he will have the opportunity for both penitence and ecstasy. Obedience is part of it as is the sense of being an accepted member of the congregation, however lowly, and thus possessing an attribute not possessed by anyone outside the sect.
>
> The requirements can be fulfilled not only by formal fundamentalist religious groups such as Teen Challenge but by such an organization as Synanon and other programs which have been modeled on it.[37]

In terms of structure and program, some common features of TC's can be identified, despite wide individual variations. Most have three identifiable phases to their program. The first of these is a testing for admission; the addict must show the genuineness of his desire to become drug-free. In some places, the addict must become drug-free on his own and remain so for a given period of time before he is admitted. In some, he must work in a storefront center for a time, showing the proper attitude. Others do not require abstinence in advance and will have a patient detoxified on methadone or go through withdrawal after formal admission. In some TC's, an addict is put through an encounter session with present residents to test his dedication.

The methods vary, but at some point early in the process every TC tests the candidate's motivation. As might be expected, there is a high loss rate at this point, although numbers are difficult to find. The different entrance procedures must be kept in mind in evaluating TC's, because they can obviously make a substantial difference in the statistical records of the program. A community that does not formally admit addicts until they have passed stringent tests is likely to show a higher success rate than a community that does its weeding out after formal admission.

Whatever the form of testing used, relatively few addicts pass it. In most TC's, somewhere between 50 per cent and 90 per cent of the applicants are rejected or quit at this initial stage. Once admitted, the addict enters a treatment ladder. The program of treatment is usually highly structured and extremely rigid, with an enforced system of rewards and punishments. The resident starts at the very bottom of the ladder, with little freedom, no responsibility, and the lowest types of tasks. As he proves himself, he begins to acquire more freedom, better jobs, and increased responsibility. This period of treatment lasts at least a year and is characterized by clearly marked stages in status. The emphasis is usually on confronting the addict with the immaturity of his past behavior and his need to learn responsible patterns of dealing with the world. Group therapy is emphasized, and the encounters can be extremely rough. It is part of the ethos, however, that the motives behind the encounters are concern and love rather than hostility.

Finally, the resident arrives at the re-entry phase. During this period, he begins to have a life outside the community again—he takes educational courses, spends weekends with his family, works, etc. When he has established a stable pattern outside the community and is considered responsible by the professional staff and/or peers, he may be discharged. (At Synanon, there is no re-entry phase. Family life, education, and work are all incorporated into the community. To Synanon community members, the straight world outside the community has not changed, and the pressures and problems that resulted in their addiction in the first place are still there. Return to the outside means return to heroin addiction, alcohol, or whatever drove them in.)

A major problem in evaluating therapeutic communities is the difficulty of ascertaining facts. Even a matter so rudimentary as the costs involved is a matter of dispute because of differences in calculating capital and operating costs, treatment of welfare expenditures that go to support the community, allocation of funds from different government agencies, appraisal of donated goods and services, and simple lack of records. Costs range anywhere from $3,000 to $10,000 per year per resident.

Even more difficult to assess is the result of the effort, since little careful evaluation has been done. One multimodal program analyzed the "split rate" from the TC component of its program. They found that, of 122 entrants, 40 per cent left within three weeks, 50 per cent within seven weeks, and 85 per cent within one year. A TC that appealed mainly to white, middle-class residents found that, during one year, almost 700 persons entered the program, 535 left voluntarily, and 23 were expelled. Of those who left, 175 came back. The program graduated 38 residents during the year. Of 113 graduates of the program over a four-year period, 13 had relapsed to drug abuse. Of the remaining 100 graduates, 25 were employed in the subject TC, 51 in other addiction programs, and 19 in the community at large; five were unknown.[38]

These are only fragments, because there is very little hard information on the results of TC's. In part this is because evaluation is expensive and difficult and many organizations do not have the money to spend on it. Also, some program operators oppose evaluation on philosophical grounds—they believe that what they are doing is humane and valuable and that their work is demeaned by attempts to judge it in quantitative terms. They may also believe that evaluation has negative effects on the program. If it shows many failures the residents will come to believe that they, too, will fail, and the prophecy will be self-fulfilling.

Finally, there are sound bureaucratic reasons for avoiding evaluation as much as possible. All the preliminary and anecdotal indications are that, while a few people are helped greatly by TC's, an overwhelming majority are not. In the hard competition for government drug-treatment money, evaluation might well hurt the TC's more than it would help them. The incentive to permit evaluation, let alone fund it, is minimal.

Looking at all the available evidence and the impressions of experts in the field, it is hard to escape the conclusion that TC's are, at best, good for a very limited number of drug addicts. As a rough guess, considering the initial rejection rates, the split rates, and the relapse rate, it would be surprising if careful evaluation showed that more than 5 per cent of those who come into contact with the program are enabled to lead a reasonably drug-free, socially productive life.

There is also a major question about the type of addict for

whom the TC is the proper solution. Some experts believe that the TC works best for the sociopath who is tough enough to take the encounters but not for those with less serious psychological problems or those who are the least alienated. Other experts have different categorizations.

The TC's may have advantages in dealing with particular subgroups of addicts, however. Although exact population breakdowns are seldom available, it is generally recognized that the mean age of the residents is lower than that of either addicts in the methadone programs or the total addict population. This could mean that the TC is especially attractive to young addicts, but this is not certain; the same result would ensue if it were less attractive to older addicts. It may also be effective with multidrug users or with young experimenters, but this has also been unproved.

In terms of any national program of treatment of heroin addicts, it is difficult to see a major role for the TC, simply because the success rate is too low and the cost too high to make an important impact on the problem. At the same time, most drug experts, when they discuss the necessary elements of a comprehensive drug-treatment program, include a therapeutic community, but whether this is based on a genuine belief in its utility, on the hope that utility might be demonstrated, or on simple politics is unclear. In the long run, it may turn out that the TC is much more interesting outside the drug context than within it. By setting itself the task of rehabilitating drug addicts—a notoriously hard group to rehabilitate—the TC movement may have destined itself to look bad. The real contributions that such methods might make to improvements in the condition and functioning of more tractable populations are easily lost sight of by appraisers who are concerned with the drug problem.

OUTPATIENT ABSTINENCE

Many programs have a component that treats outpatients and attempts to get them to abstain from heroin use. Of 142 programs covered by an NIMH survey, only 23 were for inpatients only, and only 43 of the 142 engaged in methadone maintenance;

therefore, at least 76 were operating some form of outpatient abstinence program.

These programs differ as much as or more than the therapeutic communities. The major components are community outreach to find people who need help; group and individual therapy of various types; vocational and social counseling; intervention with authorities, employers, or schools on behalf of the patient; vocational training and education; and family counseling. The programs emphasize these elements in varying degrees, of course, and most probably do not offer a complete range of services. Another variable is the intensity of the patient's involvement with the treatment center. Some are halfway houses, where the patient spends the whole day and goes home only at night. At the other extreme are agencies that have only one or two sessions with a patient or that are more or less social centers. Most programs are, of course, between these extremes.[39]

This method of treatment is not based on any constant theoretical beliefs. Some people believe that addicts suffer from underlying character disorders and can be changed only through heavy involvement in therapy. Others believe that helping with the immediate problems of the patient will enable him to help himself. Still others are desperately trying to fend off the total catastrophe that may overwhelm the patient if he does not receive aid.

Very little evaluation of these programs has been done, and there are no reliable data on the results. Most observers believe that the attrition rates are very high, the number of patients who remain drug-free is small, and the impact on such areas as employment and criminal activity is minimal. Dr. Robert DuPont, Director of the Washington, D.C., Narcotic Treatment Agency, has found that only 15 per cent of the patients who selected NTA's abstinence program remained in it for six months, although those who did remain did well.[40] A D.C. Department of Corrections study of the performance of abstinence patients in NTA facilities (all of whom had been referred to NTA by the Department of Corrections) came out with somewhat better results: 50 per cent of 165 referees were failures after six months. If "escape" was removed as a category of failure, then the failure rate was only 25 per cent.[41] Programs connected with the criminal-justice system usually have the spur of return to jail if the patient fails, of course.

The Office of Economic Opportunity enlisted a contractor to do a thorough evaluation of eight OEO-funded projects; but the data-collection problems were great, and it was impossible for the evaluators to reach any meaningful judgments.[42] OEO is now trying again, but the results have not yet been published.

In general, the conclusions for these programs are about the same as for the therapeutic communities and the detoxification centers: They help a few people a great deal and more people to some degree, but the failure rates are very high. They have a considerable cost advantage over the therapeutic communities because they do not need extensive and expensive residential facilities. Their over-all, long-term contribution to the drug problem is in some doubt. The major imponderable is the extent to which changes in the addict population may invalidate pessimistic conclusions drawn from past experience. Addiction may have spread to people who are not so intractable as the groups on which these conclusions are based. They might become abstinent with the help that can be given by the outpatient facilities.

Most important is whether these programs have an impact on the juvenile who is dabbling in the drug scene but has not yet become a confirmed addict. This is the target population for many such programs and would seem to be the area in which they have the most to offer. At present, the answer is an enigma. Some of the conclusions reached and questions raised in 1969 by Judith Calof of New York's Community Service Society are still valid:

> Voluntary treatment agencies have always emerged in response to the neglected needs of segments of the community. In the addiction field, there are still grave unmet needs. For one, the number of school-aged addicts has been growing, while voluntary and public agencies continue to concentrate on the older addict. Are special techniques needed for reaching and treating this young age group?. . .
>
> A major unmet need is addiction prevention. Do voluntary treat-

ment agencies have a major contribution to make in prevention? Could their coordinated efforts succeed in identifying and reaching those most vulnerable to this disease?

The limited success of the voluntary treatment agencies should not be interpreted as failure, but should be viewed in long-range terms. Pioneering means trial and error, with inevitable setbacks and frustrations, but it reveals the assessment of a situation. Voluntary treatment agencies have already demonstrated the enormity of the addiction problem and the immense difficulties in rehabilitating heroin addicts. The results of their dedicated efforts should serve as a warning against unrealistic expectations. Their experience can prevent catastrophe in a massive government program, and refusal of the public to allocate further funds for treatment.[43]

METHADONE MAINTENANCE

CHARACTERISTICS OF METHADONE

Methadone is a synthetic opiate. For purposes of understanding its use in the treatment of heroin addiction, its most important characteristics are as follows:

- It is a substitute for heroin, in that it will prevent an addict from having or feeling withdrawal symptoms if he replaces his usual drug with methadone.

- Unlike the heroin available in this country, it is effective when taken orally.

- If the dosage is sufficient (the exact level depending on the addict's level of tolerance to heroin), the methadone will block the action of heroin, so that the addict receives no euphoric effect if he tries heroin. At lower doses, methadone will not block this effect of heroin, but it will suppress the "narcotic hunger"—described by Dr. Jerome Jaffe as a "felt sense of physical abnormality"—that an addict feels without his drug.

- The effective action of methadone is about 24 hours, as opposed to about six hours for heroin. Thus, it needs to be taken only once a day.

- When taken orally in constant doses, methadone does not produce a euphoric effect.

- To date, no significant deleterious side effects have been reported.

THE PROGRAMS

Starting with a 1964 experimental project sponsored by the New York Health Research Council and conducted by Drs. Vincent Dole and Marie Nyswander, programs that maintain addicts on methadone have grown steadily. Despite some differences in theory and practice, in all maintenance programs an addict receives a dose of methadone every day, either at a clinic or, if he has proved himself, at home. He may also receive ancillary services—group or individual therapy, individual or family counseling, vocational rehabilitation, employment services, use of social center facilities, and medical and dental care. The extent and quality of these varies greatly, but almost all programs provide something.

There are wide variations in the modes of operation of methadone programs.[44] For example, a study of 47 methadone programs found that 27 programs used ex-addicts on the staff, while the others did not; 6 had inpatients only, 19 had outpatients only, and the rest had both. Only 8 of the 47 provided chemotherapy without any group work.

Table 3–1 lists the types of service offered by the 47 programs in terms of the numbers of programs and the per cent of the total sample offering the service.

More detailed statements obtained from 25 of the methadone-maintenance programs showed that 14 favored narcotic-free rehabilitation as the ultimate goal, and only 11 favored prolonged maintenance. Also, 18 preferred high-dose administration (50–180 mg.) and 7 preferred low-dose (20–40 mg.). Not surprisingly, there was a correlation between preference for narcotic-free rehabilitation and preference for low doses.

The precise number of persons now in methadone-maintenance programs is not known. At the Third National Methadone Conference in November, 1970, Dr. Vincent Dole estimated that there were then about 9,000 people on methadone maintenance in the United States and Canada.[45] This estimate was based on a

TABLE 3–1

TYPES OF SERVICE OFFERED BY METHADONE-MAINTENANCE PROGRAMS

	Number	Per cent
Detoxification		
Methadone	30	64
Tranquilizers and other drugs	6	13
Drug free[a]	4	8.5
Chemotherapy		
Methadone maintenance	47	100
Cyclazocine maintenance	8	17
Naloxone and other	3	6
Group work		
Therapeutic community	8	17
Group psychotherapy	36	76
Group discussions and programs	9	19
Individual psychotherapy	35	74
Medical-surgical treatment	23	49
Educational classes	8	17
Religious counseling	5	11
Work assignments	3	6
Rehabilitation services		
Vocational rehabilitation	20	42
Employment counseling	24	51
Social and family services	16	34
Occupational therapy	10	21
Recreational programs	8	17
Prevention	6	13
Research	17	36

[a] Drug-free detoxification is not a feature of the methadone program.

variety of inputs, including discussions with the manufacturer of methadone. It was in rough accord with the numbers of patients recorded in publications by the major projects and was probably fairly accurate.

Growth has been quite rapid, however. The NIMH treatment directory listed 44 methadone-maintenance programs as of 1968–69, and many of these had small patient populations. As of April, 1970, 64 programs had acquired or applied for Food and Drug Agency authority to use methadone for maintenance, although not all of them were in operation. At that time, the best estimates were that between 50 and 60 programs were actually operating.[46] By June 1, 1971, the FDA had given permission to 257 sponsors representing 277 methadone-treatment programs, some of which included several clinics. Of these, 185 programs were in institutions and the other 92 were private. The number of programs now in actual operation is not known.[47]

The FDA estimated, in June, 1971, that there were 20,000 to 30,000 people on methadone maintenance at that time. Dr. Bertram Brown, Director of NIMH, testified at the same hearings that 20,000 was probably the best estimate.[48] As of December, 1971, the FDA has doubled its estimate again. It now believes, according to Dr. Elmer Gardner, that there are between 40,000 and 50,000 patients on methadone maintenance.

Costs. Costs of methadone programs are hard to determine. Many figures are given, but it is never clear whether all costs (such as plant and equipment or the value of volunteer help, for example) are included. As a rough estimate, the cost of the programs is between $500 and $2,500 per patient per year, depending on a number of factors.

- Methadone itself is not an important cost, since it can be procured for about $.05 per day per addict.
- Controlling and administering the methadone is a significant cost, since it requires a staff.
- Determination and preparation of individual doses are significant, since determination requires physician time, preparation requires careful work by a pharmacist, and keeping track of individual doses takes staff time. Whether individual doses are more effective therapeutically than standardized ones is an open question.
- All programs use urinalysis to test the patients' use of heroin and other drugs. This costs $1 to $3 per test, depending on the frequency, the laboratory, and the number of samples tested. Obviously, this is a significant cost element: Testing three times a week at $3 per test would cost $468 per addict per year. There are some ways of avoiding these costs through random testing, which is effective for some purposes. There may also be cost-reduction possibilities for the tests themselves.
- The method by which an addict is initially switched from heroin to methadone makes a large cost difference. If the

addict is switched to methadone as an inpatient in a hospital (as was done for most of the patients in the Dole-Nyswander project, for example), each addict admitted may cause $200 to $1,400 for initial hospital expenses.

- Physical plant and facilities obviously make a difference in costs.
- Legal requirements are important. To the extent that jurisdictional law requires that elaborate information be obtained and records kept, the costs are increased.
- Any research component adds expenses.
- The level of ancillary services is important. An effort to supply group therapy, counseling, vocational or educational rehabilitation, and other services—all of which require high staff-to-patient ratios—will increase expenses substantially. Many of the public statements on costs regard this as the major variable involved. While most programs pay lip service to the need for these services, careful evaluation of the extent to which they influence the success or failure of the program is only beginning.
- The rate of expansion of a program makes a significant difference in average cost. An addict will probably require more services and control in his first year than later, when he is stabilized in a new life-style, so that a new or expanding program should show higher average costs than a static one.

These variations account for the wide range of the basic cost estimate. At present, $500 per addict per year seems about the minimum for a program that uses standardized dosages, outpatient induction, fairly cheap urinalysis, and no services except those supplied by the addicts themselves. A reasonable estimate for a program with individual doses, some inpatient induction, frequent and expensive urinalysis, and many ancillary services is $2,000, although, of course, the cost for each patient stabilized in the program would be much lower.[49] This figure could be raised almost without limit by the provision of more extras, of course, a phenomenon sometimes referred to by program operators as the danger of "Taj Mahalism"—providing very elaborate services to a few addicts rather than minimal effective services to many.

Population Characteristics. Because of regional differences, the demographic characteristics of the over-all methadone population are hard to describe. The patient population of the Methadone Maintenance Treatment Program (MMTP) in New York City, for example, is about 40 per cent black, 19 per cent Puerto Rican, 40 per cent white, and 1 per cent Oriental. This breakdown compares with the ethnic breakdown of the New York City Narcotic Registry, which, as of December, 1969, was 47 per cent black, 27 per cent Puerto Rican, and 26 per cent white.[50] The Santa Clara County (California) Methadone Program reports a patient population of 55 per cent Mexican-American, 6 per cent black, and 39 per cent white.[51] Other programs also exhibit ethnic breakdowns, indicating that methadone maintenance appeals to minority-group addicts. The Washington, D.C., program, for example, is 95 per cent black.[52] The ethnic composition of any methadone project is probably not too dissimilar from that of the local addict population of comparable age, although it may be skewed slightly toward overrepresentation of white addicts.

Methadone has not had similar success in attracting younger addicts. Although the minimal age required for admission to most programs is 18, the mean age of the patient population is usually between 30 and 35. In addition, the average length of addiction for the patient population on methadone is 10 to 15 years, although most programs require only two years, and some now require only one. There are reports, however, that the mean and median ages and length of addiction are now falling.[53] Unfortunately, no treatment method has been developed that attracts the majority of young addicts. Most members of this group do not seem to be sufficiently disenchanted with either the life-style or the effect of heroin to seek treatment of any type, or are as yet unconvinced that they are truly hooked.

Results. Most methadone programs have made an effort to evaluate their effect on the patients. The criteria employed usually follow those developed to evaluate the MMTP in New York —remaining in the program, employment, freedom from drug use, decrease in crime, and willingness to accept help for personal problems.

The New York program is not only the largest but also the best-evaluated over time. Consistently, the evaluation committee, headed by Dr. Frances Gearing of Columbia University's School of Public Health and Administrative Medicine, has found the program successful with a large percentage of the addicts. The findings of the evaluation, as of October 31, 1970, are as follows:[46]

Population. Most of the patients had been selected under criteria that required them to be 20 years old, have a five-year history of addiction, display no serious psychiatric problems, and have no addiction to drugs other than heroin. Although in 1969 the requirements were reduced to age 18 and two years of addiction, this had little impact on the age distribution of the treatment population because of the waiting time. The mean age at admission remained about 33—higher than the 27.9 mean age of the addicts on the New York City Register. Whites had a mean age at admission of 31, blacks of 35, and Puerto Ricans of a year in between.

Retention. A total of 4,376 patients had been admitted since the inception of the program in 1964. Of this group, 3,485 (80 per cent) were still in treatment at the time of evaluation. The others had left voluntarily or had been discharged because of excessive use of other drugs or alcohol, death, incarceration, or antisocial or generally uncooperative behavior. Of the 2,424 originally inducted on an inpatient basis, 74 per cent were still enrolled. Of the 1,952 who had been admitted directly as outpatients, 88 per cent were still enrolled. (This group had not been in treatment as long as the others, since outpatient induction was started only in 1968. They were also a selected group.)

Special studies of three 500-patient cohorts have been done. One of those covered the cohort for 21 months, one for 33 months, and one for 48 months. About 23 per cent of each cohort had been discharged by 21 months after admission, 34 per cent of two cohorts by 33 months after admission, and 42 per cent of one cohort by 48 months after admission.

As is shown by the cohort studies, the commonly cited 80-per-cent success rate is misleading. The statistic includes a large number of addicts who have been in the program for a relatively short period and does not fully reflect the attrition over time. For example, the total admissions, as of October 31, 1969, were 2,325. As of October 31, 1970, they were 4,376. Thus, the data for the latter date included 2,051 patients who had been in treatment for less than one year, and half or more of these may have been in for six months or less. (The cohort studies show that the attrition rate during the first six months is about 10 per cent, and over the first year it is about 16 per cent.) Maintenance of the over-all average of 20 per cent attrition is therefore dependent on continuing expansion of the program.

There is another side of this argument, however. MMTP has fairly strict standards for behavior and drops people for violation of those standards; a large proportion of those listed as failures were therefore dropped by the program (they themselves did not want to leave). A study of 138 terminations found the following causes: [55]

Involuntary terminations		81.2%
Uncooperative behavior	17.4%	
Antisocial behavior	7.2	
Unreachable psychopathology	7.2	
Drug abuse	8.7	
Alcohol abuse	10.9	
Arrested	15.2	
Medical disability	2.2	
Death	12.3	
Voluntary terminations		15.9
Voluntary discharge	14.5	
Loss of contact	1.4	
Administrative terminations and unknown		2.9
Administrative	.7	
No information	2.2	

One can question whether a methadone program should terminate patients for all of the causes given. Even if the patient has serious problems remaining, the program may have substantial beneficial effects. One can argue that the only patients who should be counted as failures are those who drop out voluntarily. If this criterion is applied to the 500-patient cohort that had a 42 per cent attrition rate over 48 months, and if we assume that only 15.9 per cent of these dropouts were voluntary, then only 34 of 210 dropouts would be counted as failures. By this standard, the MMTP may claim that it has at least partial success with 93.2 per cent of all addicts who are admitted to the program.

Again, this is not totally satisfactory, for several reasons. For example, it is difficult to know how to categorize those who die or are discharged for medical disability. Some of the voluntary patients moved to programs in other cities. Some patients who were expelled might have dropped out voluntarily at a later time. Thus, 93.2 per cent may be unrealistically high. But it does show that a 42 per cent termination rate over four years probably understates the value of the program somewhat.

To sum up, if one adopts MMTP's own standards on the retaining power of methadone, the common figure of 80 per cent success errs on the high side. If, however, one argues that those standards are too stringent, excluding too many patients who are receiving worthwhile benefits from the program, the 80-percent figure may be too low. (It should be noted that the same problems exist in assessing the effects of nonmethadone programs. They are just more obvious in this context.)

Employment. For the group that stayed in the program, employment rose markedly. About 26 per cent of the men were employed when they entered. This figure rose sharply to about 57 per cent and 66 per cent for those in the program six and twelve months, respectively, and then rose more slowly to about 78 per cent for those in the program for 48 months. Because of attrition, this percentage rise represents a much smaller absolute rise in employment. Out of a cohort of 100 entrants, 26 would be employed. After four years, 58 members of the cohort would still be in the program, of whom 45 (78 per cent of the 58) would be employed. So, out of any group of 100 entrants, only 45 would be employed after four years.

Criminal Activity. For the group that stayed in the program, criminal activity apparently decreased. In the three years before admission to the program, the methadone patients had 120 arrests and 48 incarcerations for every 100 man-years. In the four years after admission, they had 4.5 arrests and 1.0 incarcerations.

A group of detoxification patients studied for purposes of comparison showed 131 arrests and 52 incarcerations per 100 person-years in the three years prior to detoxification and 134 arrests and 63 incarcerations for the four years after detoxification. A separate study of 912 patients admitted over a four-and-a-half-year period showed a 90-per-cent drop in criminal convictions.[56]

Drug Use. While most patients test the methadone blockage a few times while on methadone, none had returned to regular heroin usage while still in the program. About 8 per cent have problems with chronic alcohol use and 10 per cent with continuing use of amphetamines, cocaine, and barbiturates.

Fate of Dischargees. A Gearing Committee study of 281 ex-patients six months after discharge had the following findings:

	Left voluntarily		Discharged for cause		Total discharge	
Arrested or jailed	10%		26%		23%	
Dead	2		2		2	
Detoxification	13		20		19	
Other Rx program	11		4		7	
Medical or psychiatric facility	—		3		2	
Private M.D.	2		2		2	
Moved	7		1		1	
Readmitted	33		6		11	
No reports found	22		36		33	
Total sample	100	(45)	100	(236)	100	(281)
Total N		(90)		(472)		(562)

Two other studies have produced similar results.

Previous evaluations of MMTP have been criticized on the ground that the original selection criteria (since eased, as we have noted) picked only those addicts most amenable to treatment. Another criticism is that the ambulatory induction program has required that the applicant have either a job or a family. This may also select the strongest candidates. Finally, the fact that there is a waiting period may also operate to select patients who are most amenable to treatment. The Gearing evaluations through 1970 do not include any analysis of attrition rates from the waiting list or any comparison of those who enter treatment and those who drop off the list.

These criticisms seem at first glance to have weight. There are several compelling arguments that they do not, however. Dr. Carl Chambers, Research Director of the New York Narcotics Addiction Control Commission, headed a study that utilized single-factor analysis to compare patients who stayed in the program and patients who did not. He found that continuing in the program was not related in any statistically significant way to the patient's sex, marital status, multiple abuse of drugs, abuse of alcohol, ethnicity, education, age at onset of heroin use, or number of prior treatments. Continuing in treatment was marginally related to conviction history, in that there was a significant difference between those with three or more convictions and those with two or fewer. It was related to the length of abuse of narcotics, in that 90 per cent of those who had abused five or fewer years and only 77 per cent of those who had abused more than five years remained in treatment for two years. There was a relationship to the employment status of the patient at time of admission—88 per cent of those who were employed and 77 per cent of those who were not remained in treatment for at least two years. The item with the greatest predictive power was the number of convictions—the fewer the number, the greater the chance of remaining in treatment. Combinations of these characteristics do have some predictive value. For example, the Chambers study concluded that a patient with seven or more convictions who had no marketable employment skills was least likely to remain in treatment two years (55.6 per cent of these did remain), and that a patient with few convictions and no multiple drug or alcohol problems was most likely to remain in treatment (95.8 per cent).[57]

In short, the original admission criteria may exercise some influence on the success rate as measured by retention, but it seems to be minimal. Some admissions criteria, such as the four years of addiction, would operate against success. Others, such as freedom from severe psychiatric problems (which would probably result in a higher percentage of employed addicts than the number in the population at large), would operate in favor of success. But none seems to be very important.

Some special studies indicate that problem groups of patients do respond to methadone, although not quite so well as the normal groups. Of 269 patients on probation or parole—a group that would be especially difficult to work with—72 per cent remained in the program in good standing.[58] Even more convincing is the fact that the Dole-Nyswander results have been replicated by reputable researchers in other places. At the National Methadone Conference, sponsored by NIMH and the National Association to Prevent Addiction to Narcotics, a succession of researchers from different parts of the country recited results comparable to, though usually not quite so good as, those achieved by the Dole-Nyswander program. Results have been generally good no matter how few the restrictions placed on patient characteristics.[59]

Interpreting these reports is complicated by the fact that, while the basic criteria remain fairly constant, there are variations in the exact methodology of evaluation—in the extent to which information from addicts is verified independently, in the frequency of urinalysis, in the relations between the police and the program (in some places, for example, the police may cooperate with methadone treatment by not prosecuting addicts in the program except for very serious crimes), in the sampling techniques used, and in the definition of retention. In addition, some programs use outside evaluation teams, and some rely on internal information systems or on special studies done by their own staff. At present, no two major programs have been thoroughly evaluated by the same team of outside experts, although the Columbia group that evaluated the MMTP will probably also evaluate the Narcotics Treatment Agency in Washington, D.C.

Nevertheless, the basic consistency of results is quite impressive. Although we may not yet know exactly how good methadone maintenance is, its essential efficacy is as well established as anything in this field can be. It is now generally acknowledged that methadone is medically safe, acceptable to many heroin addicts, effective, and administratively feasible for large-scale programs.[60] Clearly, methadone should not be regarded as a miracle cure. The majority of program operators believe that most addicts on methadone try heroin a few times, partly out of curiosity as to whether the block works, partly because of the desire for euphoria. Judging a program in terms of whether an addict ever relapsed might well make it appear to be a failure. Methadone addiction avoids the large swings and demanding schedule of heroin addiction, thus making it easier for an addict to hold a job and support his family, but it is likely to take months for an addict to revamp his life-style into a new pattern. Underlying psychological problems remain, except for those caused by the demands of heroin addiction itself. Addicts tend to abuse some other drugs, such as amphetamines and alcohol, to about the same degree that they abused them while on heroin.[61]

From society's point of view, the most important of all the evaluation criteria is remaining in the program. An addict who is using methadone is not continuing either extensive heroin use or heroin-seeking behavior, and his criminal behavior will probably be reduced because he does not need the money to purchase the drug. He is not spreading hepatitis contracted from infected needles by selling his blood to hospitals.[62] He is not trying to sell heroin because he needs money for a fix. He is not hanging out in a shooting gallery or on the street serving as a role model for the neighborhood adolescents. And he is not helping to provide the mass market for heroin that makes investment in its importation and distribution economically attractive despite the risks. It should be emphasized, however, that the addict will still have the criminal skills he has learned and may choose to use them to support himself. In such case, the decrease in crime would be the difference between the amount needed to support the habit and the addict and that needed to support the addict alone. Some patients may continue to commit crimes at the same level as before, using the extra money to raise their standard of living or to build up a nest egg. Criminal activity, according to several experts, declines slowly, over a period of a year or more.

BASIS FOR THE SUCCESS OF METHADONE

The expansion of methadone maintenance has been based on empirical evidence of its utility, not upon any solid understanding of the pharmacological reasons for its success. While, obviously, this success is due to its nature as an opiate and long-acting substitute for heroin, an understanding of the nature of addiction itself is missing. It is not known whether methadone is more effective than other modalities because addiction has physiological components that only another opiate can offset or because of factors rooted in the psychology of addiction.

The issues concerning possible physiological components of addiction can be stated succinctly:[63]

- Are some persons physiologically vulnerable to heroin, in the sense that it causes physical changes in them that it does not cause in "normal" people?
- Are there inherent physiological factors that make some people seek heroin—is there some pre-existing felt physical need that does not exist in most people?
- Does taking heroin cause a permanent or long-term physiological change in the addict that makes him crave the drug after he becomes abstinent?
- Does heroin addiction create a physiological change that makes an ex-addict particularly vulnerable to stress after he becomes abstinent?

There is no clear answer to any of these questions. Yet, most scientists would be inclined to think that the answers to at least the first two are "No." Dr. Vincent Dole, in the past, has hypothesized that narcotics addicts may have an inherent neurological vulnerability to the drug, but recently he seems to have modified his view.[64] The second two questions are the subject of debate among experts. Dr. Dole does seem to think that opiate addiction causes a metabolic change in the addict that, in turn, causes drug hunger. Whether he thinks this change is permanent or only fairly long lasting (i.e., well beyond the period during which overt withdrawal symptoms are present) is, however, unclear.[65] In either event, giving methadone to an addict, in Dr. Dole's view, simply corrects the metabolic imbalance that has already been caused by his heroin addiction. In this sense, he believes the analogy between methadone for an addict and insulin for a diabetic is valid. Others are skeptical.[66]

Dr. William Martin has hypothesized a more elaborate physiological model. In his view, an opiate such as heroin or methadone causes a metabolic change that makes the user more vulnerable to stress.[67] An addict may become abstinent, but stress will trigger a physiological reaction that makes him crave the drug again. Furthermore, this effect may increase with continued or increased doses of opiates. Thus, when an addict is maintained on a methadone dosage higher than his prior heroin dosage, as is true in many programs, the underlying physical problem is aggravated. This, in turn, makes it even less likely that he will ever be able to become totally abstinent. Dr. Martin is uncertain whether the opiate-induced change is reversible.

Which, if any, of these theories are correct is obviously an important question. A finding that there is an inherent neurological vulnerability or that addiction causes an irreversible or long-term metabolic change that induces drug hunger, either inherently or as a response to stress, would have important consequences for law enforcement, treatment, education, and research.

To reiterate, the metabolic theories are far from proved at present. They may turn out to be wrong, or it may develop that there is a physiological change that is reversible over a period of months or years. Such a finding would pose very difficult public-policy problems, because methadone might be prolonging and aggravating a physical condition that could be reversed if an addict could endure abstinence from opiates for some period that, in practice, most addicts cannot endure.

There are other hypotheses about the reasons for the success of methadone maintenance that are alternatives or supplements to the metabolic theory. Some of these are as follows:

• To some extent, abstinence symptoms may be a conditioned response to environmental factors. In turn, self-administration of heroin is a conditioned response to the existence of these symptoms, in that for the addict it has been a successful way of eliminating them in the past. (There are reports, for example, of men who have been in prison and "clean" for years experiencing withdrawal symptoms upon return home.) By blocking the effect of heroin, methadone extinguishes the reinforcement for its self-administration.[68]

- Heroin has a short duration of action and involves wide emotional swings, from euphoria after administration to the threshold of withdrawal six hours later. The rapidity of this cycle forces a totally drug-oriented existence on the addict. If he does not concentrate on procurement of the drug to the exclusion of virtually everything else, he is not going to have it when he needs it. Methadone, with its twenty-four-hour action and gentler swings, allows the addict the luxury of thinking about something besides drugs.

- Methadone programs, with or without supporting services, gives the addict a good deal of psychological support. The staff is concerned with his well-being and is giving him a medicine in which they have obvious confidence. Medical practice has long known that this placebo effect is important.

- Heroin addiction imposes a structure and purpose on the addict's life—getting the drug. Daily visits to the methadone clinic may provide comparable structure.

- The life-style and personal associations of an addict provide great pressures to relapse after a period of abstinence. An abstinence program located where the addict will not live in the future (e.g., Lexington) does nothing about this problem, because the addict does not build up an alternative life-style and alternative associations and will probably return to the old ones after release. Methadone protects him from heroin while he builds new patterns of behavior and loses touch with the addict culture. In this view, after new patterns have been developed, it might be possible to withdraw the addict from methadone because his altered environment would not put pressure on him to relapse.

- There is some evidence that a substantial number of addicts —perhaps as many as one-third—"mature out" of addiction when they reach their 30's and 40's. Some of the patients who do well on methadone may come from this group.[69]

- Studies have indicated that monitoring an ex-addict is an important factor in keeping him off drugs.[70] The crucial ingredient of methadone treatment may be not the methadone per se but the urinalysis. Addiction to methadone is necessary only to force the patient to come to the program.

• At present, one can do little but note these differences; one cannot know how these vary in validity for different addicts or groups, or, in some cases, even how they could be researched.

ISSUES CONCERNING METHADONE

Dosage Level. The first question about dosage levels is how much methadone should be given to an addict. Most people have a general preference for administering the least amount consistent with success. This is based partly on moral feelings that one should give as little of an opiate as possible and partly on a desire to minimize unknown side effects or metabolic disruption. The problem is to determine this minimum level.

The general rule of thumb is that a daily dose of 100 mg. will block any effect of heroin for almost all addicts. Most programs administer a maximum of 180 mg., although a few may go as high as 300 mg. in selected cases. A program that administers 80 mg. or more is probably aiming at a blockage dose. A lower dose will not block the effect of heroin—an addict can achieve euphoria if he tries. However, the lower dose will block the narcotic hunger and thus remove some of the pressure for heroin use. For most addicts, a dosage of 40 or 50 mg. is enough to eliminate this craving, but an even lower dose may be enough if the addict has a light habit.

In the early methadone programs, it was apparently assumed that any addict who found that he could break the block would do so, and that the higher, blocking doses were necessary. In the last few years, some experiments have been made comparing the efficacy of high and low doses. Dr. Avram Goldstein, at the Santa Clara County Program, maintained three groups of randomly chosen addicts on blind doses of 30, 50, and 100 mg., respectively. (Blind dosage is not discussed with the patient, who is not aware of how much he is receiving.) The addicts receiving the lower doses did tend to use heroin more often during the first month, but by the third month in treatment there was no significant difference among the groups in either heroin use or retention in the program.[71] Dr. Jerome Jaffe, of the Illinois Drug Abuse Program, has done similar research with roughly equivalent results. For the first month or so, the high-dose group has a higher retention rate; thereafter, the two groups do about the same in terms of retention, employment, and arrest rates.[72] Dr. William Weiland came to the same con-clusions after similar experiments in Philadelphia with groups of 52 patients on 50 mg. of methadone and 52 on 100 mg. for a period of 60 days.[73] There are few dose-related side effects.

These results suggest that suppression of the narcotics hunger may be more important than the blockage effect, at least for motivated addicts. The results are only suggestive, however, because the time spans involved in these experiments are limited, and it is not known what the results of a more extended experi-ment might be. The results might also be different if the popula-tions involved were younger or less motivated. Drs. Dole and Goldstein, among others, regard these experiments as very inter-esting. The low dose does mean that some addicts will drop out in the initial stages who might have been retained with a higher dose. In addition, it exposes the patient to the medical risk of relapse. Given these known costs and risks, and given the lack of any solid reason to believe that a 100-mg. dose is in some way more harmful than 50 mg., some doctors are reluctant to use a low dose. The major reason for doing so is that it minimizes leakage into the community from patients who take their metha-done home, minimizes side effects, and safeguards somewhat against unknown side effects or long-term effects.

Some programs use doses even smaller than those described above, but none has been scientifically evaluated. Colonel Hassan Jeru Ahmed, of the Blackman's Development Center in Washing-ton, D.C., claims to give a number of addicts as little as 5 mg. per day with good success. Without controlled experiments, it is hard to know whether his opinion is accurate. Theoretically, such a dose might suppress the hunger in an addict with a very low habit, or there might be some placebo effect involved. Since Colonel Hassan's aim is abstinence rather than maintenance, this might also be a method of slow detoxification.

A second issue about dosage involves expense. Most programs have assumed that the specific dose should be tailored to the individual addict and therefore give doses of anywhere from 25 mg. to 180 mg., depending on the individual. From the stand-point of administrative efficiency, this is costly. To work with a few standardized doses would allow programs to treat more addicts with the same expenditure. Dr. Goldstein has done an experiment to determine whether the individualized dose is really more effective and has concluded that it is not.[74] To test this, he used a blind dosage procedure. (This procedure not only is necessary for research on dosage but also has substantive benefits as well. The most important of these may be that the "dosage game" is part of the addict's life style of "conning," and eliminating it contributes to over-all rehabilitation.) An initial dose of 30 mg., increased by 10 mg. a day until final stabilization at 100 mg., was equally effective for all patients.

Ancillary Services. Most program operators declare that ancillary services are a vital part of methadone treatment. Group and individual therapy, job training, job placement, family counseling, medical and dental care, and education are all regarded as crucial to the process of helping addicts make the adjustment to a new life-style once they have broken the heroin habit. MMTP, for example, provides extensive services, which is one reason the total cost is estimated at about $2,000 per year per patient. (The cost for each patient who has finished the induction stage is about $1,000 per year.) In its evaluation reports on MMTP, the Gearing Committee always emphasizes the importance of services.[75] Dr. Jaffe, whose Illinois Drug Abuse Program also offers services, agrees. In particular, he believes that the techniques and group procedures developed in therapeutic communities are helpful in stabilizing addicts on methadone because they create an environment in which patients not only can be relieved of narcotics hunger but also can begin to develop attitudes that may be useful to them in achieving social rehabilitation.

There are some programs that operate with a minimum of extras, however, and their success rate does not seem markedly lower than the others'. In New Orleans, most addicts are treated in private clinics and pay about $10 per week.[76] The program has limited ability to finance additional facilities. The Santa Clara County Program, which also operates at a cost of about $10 per addict per week, is equally limited in its services.[77] About 10 per cent of the patients receive psychiatric help outside the program, and there is some vocational counseling. There is also some group work by the patients themselves without professional involvement. Since the initial retention rate of the Santa Clara County Program is relatively close to that of the MMTP, additional ancillary services might contribute little as compared with their costs. (An important aim of the program has been to study this question.) The Santa Clara Program did include a vocational counselor, which many observers feel is the most important single service that can be offered. It also emphasizes peer-group therapy as a key to rehabilitation.[78] Drs. Jaffe and Dole have experimented with giving methadone without services to people on waiting lists. Preliminary results from MMTP are good.[79]

Although one could easily find widespread agreement that ancillary services would be clearly desirable if they were free, one seldom finds any explicit analysis of the cost/benefit aspects of the issue. The key fact is that, as long as the supply of addicts holds out, a minimal program can treat many more patients than an elaborate one at any given level of expenditure. A program costing $500 per year per addict, with a retention rate of only 50 per cent, can treat more people than a program costing $2,000, with an 85-per-cent success rate. With $1 million, for example, the cheaper program could treat 2,000 addicts for a year and would retain half of them. The more expensive one could treat only 500 addicts, even though it would retain 425 of them. The economic advantages of the cheaper program are even greater when the comparative outputs are analyzed over time. Still, assuming a limited budget and an unlimited supply of addicts (and, at present, almost all methadone programs have waiting lists), each type of program will be losing its failures and retaining its successes. After some period, each would have a success rate of 100 per cent, because only the successes would remain; but the $500 program would be maintaining four times as many addicts for the same amount of money.

This analysis holds even for gross differences in success rates. Since, as New Orleans and Santa Clara show, the actual differences may be limited, or even nonexistent, the case for the cheaper program is even stronger. Any city with a large addiction problem and limited funds should probably choose a methadone program with minimal services rather than full ones. The principal argument against this conclusion is that services might make a crucial difference for the hard-core addicts, and that this is the population that causes most of the crime. But, while it is true that addicts with long criminal records are less successful on methadone than are others, it has not yet been proved that the services make a crucial difference for this group. In addition, the proposition that society should condemn four treatable people to addiction in order to treat one other addict who is causing more trouble is a hard moral position to defend. It might be better to put the hard-core addict on heroin maintenance and treat the others with methadone.

Another argument sometimes used in support of extensive services is that society should spend the money necessary to give full treatment to all addicts, thus obviating the whole question and avoiding the need for moral choices. In the practical world, however, everyone knows that the cities are in financial trouble and have tremendous demands on their limited resources. It is neither possible nor desirable to give narcotics addicts a prior claim to limited public resources that might otherwise be spent on education, health, welfare, or countless other pressing areas. The best model may be one in which the patients are encouraged to develop their own services, with the expensive ancillary services targeted on the hard-core.

Outpatient Induction. The MMTP originally inducted patients into the methadone program by putting them in the hospital for a week or two during the transition from heroin to methadone. Because this is expensive, and because the limited number of available hospital beds imposes a constraint on the number admitted to the program, there has been much interest in ambulatory induction. Starting in 1968, MMTP has adopted such a program for some of its patients. As of 1971, about 1,952 of its 4,376 patients had been admitted in this fashion. Preliminary data indicate that rates of attrition are almost identical whether patients are inducted as inpatients or outpatients. After 24 months, about 72 per cent of each group remains.[80] This figure is not entirely valid because of the special characteristics of the ambulatory group. Having a job or family was a requirement for admission to the ambulatory component, and 79 per cent of admittees were employed or in school. Whether a patient is employed, as we have seen, is a statistically significant predictor of whether he will remain in treatment.

Other programs have also used ambulatory admission with consistently good results, and the effectiveness of this method is no longer in doubt.[81]

Withdrawal. Eventual withdrawal from methadone rather than perpetual maintenance is regarded as a goal by drug experts —in part because of a moral feeling that people should not and do not need to be drug-dependent; in part because of a desire to free the addict from his ties to the clinic; in part because of the wish to minimize any unknown long-term effects of opiates on the human body.

At present, it is uncertain whether withdrawal is possible. In a study of 350 patients who withdrew from the MMTP, Dr. Dole found that "narcotics hunger" returned in almost all individuals immediately after they ceased taking the methadone, whether their withdrawal was voluntary or involuntary. Since this is a somewhat special population—a high proportion were treatment failures—the results are not conclusive, although they are suggestive that withdrawal may be difficult. Dr. Dole has also found in blind experiments that a patient stabilized on methadone and free from drug hunger may have a return of drug dreams if his medication is withdrawn. He believes that, for most addicts, maintenance has to be a permanent way of life. It is important to note, however, that the return of "narcotics hunger" does not automatically mean a return to heroin use; some individuals are able to live with the hunger without returning to drugs. But hunger does make successful abstinence substantially more difficult.[82]

Dr. Jaffe believes that withdrawal from methadone can be successfully accomplished, although his work in this area has not yet been extensive. In a study of 53 patients in active treatment, he found that 29 per cent had voluntarily withdrawn from methadone but remained affiliated with the methadone units,

either participating in group therapy or transferring to therapeutic communities or aftercare systems. Not all those observed
on withdrawal remained abstinent, although some patients observed after six months had been able to do so. Dr. Jaffe seems
to feel that continued therapy techniques are helpful in maintaining abstinence.[83]

Dr. Avram Goldstein has done experiments showing that the
methadone dosage can be reduced without discomfort to the
patient if it is done slowly at a weekly reduction rate of no more
than 10 per cent. Withdrawal from a moderate methadone
stabilization program would then require about six months.[84] But
follow-up results are not yet in.

Although the results to date are ambiguous, it seems certain
that substantial experimentation with withdrawal from methadone
will be undertaken. Some black activists, in particular, are
strongly opposed to the concept of permanent maintenance and
will accept methadone programs in their communities only if
they are seen as intermediate-term therapies with the ultimate
goal of abstinence. Dr. Beny Primm, of Addiction Research
Treatment Corporation in New York City, for example, told us
that his explicit goal is to get everyone off methadone and into a
drug-free state. Dr. Goldstein has also suggested that methadone treatment should be thought of as "methadone temporary
support rather than methadone maintenance, with its implication
of life-long medication." An addict could join the program, become stabilized on methadone, eventually taper off slowly and
become drug-free, but be able to return to methadone if the
urge to take heroin became overwhelming.[85] Ultimate determination of the possibilities of withdrawal must await determination of
the metabolic-change issue. Meanwhile, the only way to find out
if withdrawal is possible is to try it. Since we do not know
why methadone works, there is no way of telling *a priori*.
Some programs have reported an unexpected phenomenon that
might be called "the 20-mg. barrier." The patient undergoing
withdrawal does well until the dose is reduced to about 20 mg.
At this level, there is a sudden increase in physical complaints
and heroin usage.[86] What this means for permanent withdrawal
is a question that needs study.

Benefits to the Addict. Methadone maintenance is sometimes criticized on the ground that it is society's way of dealing with the addict crime problem without regard to the addict himself. This view is especially strong among so-called militant black groups. On the whole, however, the idea that methadone sacrifices the addict for the sake of society does not seem valid. Although many communities adopt methadone programs in an attempt to solve their crime problem, the program results showing increased productivity and family stability of the patients suggest that they themselves benefit from the changed life-style and reduced crime as much as or more than the community at large. Since most programs operate primarily on a voluntary basis, the patients themselves must prefer methadone to the addicted life. Even when an addict is coerced into treatment by law enforcement, simply staying in treatment is a vote against the former life-style.

Finally, even if one were to concede the truth of the criticism, the logical rejoinder would be "So what?" There is no good reason for society to tolerate crime simply because the criminal is a heroin addict when it can eliminate the crime by forcing him to switch to being a methadone addict. It is not as if one could choose between methadone and an equally effective but more expensive alternative: The other alternatives do not appear to work so well. Even if they did, it would be difficult to argue that addicts deserve priority in allocating scarce public resources that could be devoted to the general welfare of the groups in society that furnish most of the addicts. In general, to the extent that the criticism represents the truth of the situation, its use as a criticism seems based on wishful thinking rather than sound analysis. Its proponents wish there were another, equally effective treatment method or wish that public resources were unlimited.

If the metabolic theories of addiction should prove accurate, the issue will become more acute. Dr. William Martin, for example, poses the issue as the "medical dilemma of methadone maintenance, namely, the creation or continuance of a serious medical disorder, physical dependence, in order to decrease antisocial behavior."[87] If this dilemma is a real one, all the choices would be unpleasant. The nation could legalize heroin or move to a massive system of heroin maintenance, but this would pose exactly the same moral problems as administering methadone. It could continue to keep heroin illegal and prosecute addicts for crimes committed to obtain it while refusing them methadone, but this seems both morally wrong and politically impossible. It could declare that addicts are not responsible for crimes committed to obtain heroin because of the physical duress involved. This would necessitate either heroin or methadone maintenance, however, since no one can be given such a license to steal without some counteraction by society. Despite the problems stated by Dr. Martin, methadone seems the best choice.

Methadone and the Law-Enforcement System. Some program operators are strongly opposed to the development of close relations between methadone maintenance and the law-enforcement system. In their view, a coercive system that forces an addict to accept methadone as a condition for probation or parole is an intolerable violation of civil liberties. Others, with equally strong opinions, disagree. They believe that the realistic choice lies between having the addict on methadone and having him in jail, and that the authorities will not often impose a methadone requirement on a man who would otherwise have been released. In this view, accepting treatment set by courts or parole boards gives addicts an option that would not have been available otherwise. All agree that participants in the methadone program should avoid becoming informers for the law-enforcement system. Because of the need to maintain the confidential doctor-patient relationship, patients should not be reported by the treatment agency for violations of probation or parole.

Methadone and Causes of Addiction. Addiction is often seen as a sociopsychological disorder, stemming from basic personality defects. In this view, it is useless and wrong to treat addiction by administering methadone without, at the same time, treating the underlying disorder. A better way to approach the problem is to deal with the basic pathology; when this is done, freedom from drug use will follow naturally. As stated by a Manhattan probation officer:

My objection to the methadone program . . . is predicated on the observation that while the drug methadone removes the physical craving for the other opiates it nevertheless fails to combat in any way or deal with the various emotional or other difficulties that permitted the individual to initially become and remain involved with drugs. Since the drug problem has, so to speak, been eliminated, that basic problem has not been dealt with; that of the inadequate, ineffective person unable to cope with the reality of his situation. In essence, an aspect, the symptom, has been treated not the entire individual, with the result that they then frequently resort to other avenues of escape including amphetamines, barbiturates, wines, and liquor, or they begin to manifest serious forms of instability.[88]

Most proponents of methadone would readily agree that methadone *per se* does not cure any personality disorders that might cause addiction. (Not all would; it is entirely possible that the opiates constitute an effective treatment for certain as yet undefined psychic states.[89]) Those who do agree would respond to the basic criticism as follows:

- No consistent pathology has been found. No psychiatric diagnosis can be shown to apply to all heroin addicts or even to a majority of them. Thus, while addicts tend to be depressive, they are not so depressive as neurotic nonaddicts. While some addicts are schizophrenic, 80 per cent to 90 per cent are not. Some are psychopathic, but the great majority are not. In short, no satisfactory explanation of the psychological roots of addiction has been found, much less developed to the point where it is operationally useful for treatment purposes.[90]
- The view that an underlying pathology is responsible is an assumption rather than a proved fact. One can construct equally plausible theories that experimentation is caused by exposure and normal psychological processes, and addiction is caused by physiological factors. Dr. Dole, for example, believes that the observed common characteristics of addicts are simply those forced on them by the nature of the life-style required to maintain a heroin habit. Other experts also believe that, even for addicts with marked problems, it is the addiction that causes the problems rather than vice versa.

- Even granting the argument that pathology is at the root of addiction, it is easier to work on underlying causes with an addict who is on methadone and free of drug hunger and the heroin life-style.
- Again granting the argument that pathology is at the root of addiction, the success rates in attempting to cure such pathologies—especially among the socioeconomic groups that furnish most of the addicts—are not very high. Thus, one has no realistic choice except to accept the second best solution of methadone maintenance, which has very great benefits for society and for the addict, even though it is not a complete cure.

Perhaps the best summary has been given by Dr. John Kramer, discussing the psychopathology of addiction generally, not just methadone:

It is generally conceded that traditional psychiatric techniques have not been useful in the management of opiate dependence. In a psychoanalytic frame of reference symptoms are considered to be the behavioral or somatic representations of an underlying intrapsychic conflict. Once the conflict is resolved or reduced to manageable proportions, the symptoms will diminish or disappear.

This conceptual model fails to account for two different issues, either or both of which may play a role in people who abuse drugs. First, though intrapsychic determinants may play a part in whether a person uses drugs, other circumstances such as drug availability, subgroup attitudes, peer pressures, and plain chance are very often more important. In other words, in some individuals, there may be no serious underlying conflicts, though there may be considerable conflict with the community. Second, whatever the original determinants of drug use may be, the symptom, dependency on drugs, can become so central an issue that it, so to speak, assumes a life of its own, and even solving the underlying conflicts may have no influence on the drug dependence itself. An analogy may be drawn with a depressed person who in an attempt at suicide breaks his neck and becomes paraplegic. Psychotherapy may relieve his depression but will not restore function to his legs.

Because drug use has been invested with such great importance in our society (an importance it did not always have) it is assumed that the intrapsychic events which cause, or contribute to it, are of equal magnitude. Hence the view, that since drug use potentially subjects the person to such serious consequences, the psychological problem he has must be equally big. Experience with drug users does not validate this view. Some do indeed have clearly definable psychiatric problems, but many do not. Where it is sought, some subtle psychiatric defect can always be found, as has been the case with addicts. Further investigation may clarify this question. In the meantime a functional approach, handling the symptoms, educating and giving practical assistance as well as offering psychotherapy in selected instances seem desirable.[91]

Multiple Drug Use. If a heroin addict is involved in the use of other drugs, methadone will do nothing about that use. There is evidence, however, that methadone patients do not increase their use of other drugs—a charge that has been made—although they do tend to maintain it at about the same level. The Santa Clara County Program found that, both before and after going on methadone, about 20 per cent of the patients overused alcohol, 5 to 10 per cent used amphetamines, 45 per cent used marijuana, and 30 per cent used nothing. The only significant difference was that 20 per cent abused barbiturates before going on methadone, and only 6 per cent did so afterwards.[92] Since barbiturates create a dangerous addiction if used too much, this is an important shift.

We know of no other before-and-after study of drug use by patients on methadone. A recent study of multiple drug use by heroin users, however,[93] supports Dr. Goldstein's conclusion that the use of other drugs does not increase. A sample of 422 heroin users were asked whether they had used certain drugs more than six times. The per cent who had done so were: marijuana—86 per cent; cocaine—47 per cent; barbiturates—34 per cent; and amphetamines—33 per cent. (They were also questioned about other drugs, not recounted here.) In general, it had not been thought that multiple use among heroin addicts was as high as this, and there may have been some tendency to assume that multiple use among methadone patients was a new pattern for them rather than the continuation of an old one.

Leakage of Methadone. As more large methadone projects come into existence, it is reasonable to anticipate that some of them will be lax in their control of methadone, permitting leakage into the community at large. Several possible consequences of such a development cause concern. First, there is a fear that the drug will become available in an injectible form that is an acceptable, if not a totally satisfactory, euphoric substitute for heroin. Secondly, the availability of even oral methadone will create a new group of addicts. Thirdly, nonaddicts, particularly children, may take methadone and die.

These fears have a sound factual basis. Indeed, methadone can already be bought on the street in any major city, although it is unclear whether the source is diversion from the programs or independent manufacture. The major concern is injectible methadone. Many addicts regard it as a very good drug, and it could result in a substantial addition to the present addiction problem. This is probably a controllable problem, however. Methadone can be mixed with Tang or some other substance before dispensation (as is true in almost all programs at present), so that it is suitable for oral administration only. More important, the drug companies have developed a methadone disk that requires a large volume of water for it to dissolve. This makes it difficult, although not impossible, to inject.[94]

The second concern, the leakage of oral methadone, is more crucial. The rapid expansion of methadone programs is highly probable. With this will inevitably come carelessness about staff and about control of methadone. If there is a market for the drug, there will also be some corruption. It will be surprising if there are not some major scandals involving the diversion of methadone from treatment programs.

In some ways, leakage may not be very important. While there are some methadone addicts who are not involved in treatment programs, oral methadone is not so euphoric as heroin, and few current heroin addicts would prefer it to heroin as a euphorogenic.

There is no reason to believe that methadone addiction is physically more harmful than heroin addiction, and, if the methadone is pure, there is good reason to think it less harmful. There is substantial evidence to the effect that methadone addiction is psychologically less harmful than heroin addiction. In general, while a few addicts might make oral methadone their drug of choice, it is probable that the major market for illegal methadone will consist of addicts who are on do-it-yourself methadone maintenance, who tide themselves over with methadone when they cannot get heroin, or who want the euphoric effects of heroin only occasionally. In these cases, both society and the addict are better off if they can get methadone to substitute for heroin.

There is some possibility that methadone will make addicts of persons who would not otherwise have become addicted. Heroin has two major defects that may exert some deterrent effect on potential experimenters: It often contains dangerous impurities; and it is not effective when taken orally. On the whole, however, it seems unlikely that these factors are very influential. For those who might not like to inject a drug, heroin can also be snorted. (This is, in fact, the usual method by which neophytes take the drug.) The impurities point might be valid, but it is difficult to believe that anyone willing to get into the general life-style of addiction is going to be deterred by the marginal additional disadvantage of impure drugs. It does seem likely, however, that, as methadone becomes increasingly available, it will be used as the drug of initiation by persons who would otherwise have tried heroin.

More difficult to accept are the overdose deaths that are already starting to occur—most poignantly, among children who find and drink methadone-laden Tang. Recurrences could be prevented by insisting that methadone patients keep methadone in a locked box outside the refrigerator. The drug will keep a week without refrigeration, so that this is perfectly feasible.[95] Noninjectible methadone could also be given in a tablet form that is too large and bitter for children.

Other deaths occur among people who use methadone to achieve euphoria. Because methadone is slower-acting and longer-lasting than intravenous heroin, even a veteran heroin addict may take methadone, decide that the drug is not having an adequate effect, take more, and overdose when the peak comes two or three hours later. Self-education within the drug subculture might keep such incidents to a minimum. But some deaths will occur, and it is reasonable to expect that the more methadone available, the more deaths it will cause.

The only effective answer to this argument is to point to the large number of heroin deaths caused by overdose, disease, and infection and to the other deaths caused by addict-committed crime and by such practices as the sale of infected blood by addicts. Almost certainly there will be an over-all decrease in opiate-related deaths as methadone replaces heroin in the community.

Side Effects.[96] A number of possibly undesirable side effects of methadone have been hypothesized, ranging from impotence to damage to the bones and teeth. So far, clinical studies have found no evidence of birth defects and no indication of physical damage. Drowsiness is a frequent complaint of program initiates, but this is a natural consequence of an increase in the opiate dose and disappears as the addict develops tolerance for the new level. Some addicts continue to complain of the loss of libido, but the best evidence is that, for most, sexual performance is better when they are on methadone than when they are on heroin. In short, although it cannot be stated categorically that there are no serious side effects, clinical investigation so far has failed to find any. To date, however, research has concentrated on possible physical effects; there do not seem to be detailed studies of the effects of methadone on intellectual or motor functioning, and we do not know how methadone affects a wide range of important functions, from problem-solving ability to the ability to operate a car or often complex machinery. Since methadone is a powerful tranquilizer, it may well have effects in these areas. It is also possible that tolerance to tranquilization develops, as may be indicated by the disappearance of excessive drowsiness.

THE FUTURE OF METHADONE

It is virtually certain that methadone maintenance will increase rapidly in the next few years. While many observers have reservations, the cost/benefit and cost/effectiveness advantages of methadone have become obvious. Since the relationship between addiction and crime has been widely publicized, political pressures to do something about crime are great enough so that the government will probably support methadone, and vigorously.

While the federal subbureaucracies involved—the National Institute of Mental Health, the Bureau of Narcotics and Dangerous Drugs, and the Food and Drug Administration—have never been fond of methadone maintenance, its social and political advantages should now be obvious enough to induce large-scale federal funding in the near future. Most informed observers regard the Administration's proposal to create a Special Action Office on Drug Abuse Prevention and to increase funding dramatically as confirmation of this. At this writing, the Food and Drug Administration is on the verge of liberalizing the rules under which methadone is approved for use.

As the programs expand, several issues in addition to those already discussed will become important:

Administrative Problems. There are clear differences between operating small, experimental programs and operating mass programs. Such issues as the extent to which ancillary services should be supplied, the extent of monitoring through urinalysis, high doses versus low doses, standardized doses versus individual ones, and control of leakage will arise over and over. In addition, there will be the problems of recruiting and training staff common to any expanding area. At present, there are not enough people experienced in methadone programs to double or triple current programs. One can expect a period of raiding of existing programs (with a consequent decline in their effectiveness) and increasing use of less qualified and less dedicated people. The difficulties of hiring good staff will compound the leakage problem. It will also create pressures to use the cheapest methods available. Most of the higher costs of the more expensive programs are caused by the increased staff required for added services; if the trained staff to provide these services is simply not available, they either will not be provided or will be done poorly. Analysis of the impact of these services is therefore urgent.

Community Problems. As noted, some black militants are opposed to methadone maintenance because they regard it as a device to keep the black community "drugged and enslaved." Many of the rumors of side effects are also believed. These fears can be countered as long as there appears to be a possibility that methadone maintenance leads to abstinence; but, if experiments indicate that this is not a reasonable hope, the situation may become more difficult. This is not the type of problem that is amenable to rational solution, or even advice. Methadone-program operators, however, can do at least three things to meet the challenge:

1. Maintain close contact with various elements of the community, to explain what they are doing and why it is good for the addict and the community.

2. Provide facilities to ensure that any methadone patient who wants to try to become totally drug-free will receive the best possible support for his effort.

3. Involve the community in the staffing and administration of the project.

Since these are all good policies irrespective of any militant reaction against methadone, programs should follow them whether or not they foresee any problem. Some program operators believe that the fear of adverse community reaction is exaggerated and is likely to decrease over time. The area in which the addict lives, after all, bears the crime costs and the risk of a spread in addiction. As a methadone program becomes operational, the surrounding community comes to appreciate it, and strong opposition dissolves. Dr. Robert DuPont, of Washington's Narcotic Treatment Agency, has told us that methadone patients become the best missionaries in the community.

Long-acting Methadone. The effect of the methadone used at present lasts only about 24 hours. Drug companies have been experimenting with a drug (acetylmethadol) that will last up to three days, and it is expected that this will become generally available soon.[98] This will have several significant effects on methadone maintenance. It will cut costs by reducing the expense of preparing and administering the drug. It will also make it more difficult for the patient to skip his dose and try heroin. Another effect may be to allow the patient greater mobility and weaken the ties between the patient and the program. In the view of some, this will be a good thing because it will enable the patients to lead a more nearly normal life. Others speculate that it will be counterproductive, in that the routine daily visit provides an important element of structure in the patient's life and has positive therapeutic benefits. There is no way of resolving this dispute *a priori.*

Changing Patterns of Addiction. There is consensus that the primary reason addicts volunteer for methadone programs, or stay in them once assigned by the law-enforcement system, is that they are tired of the life-style of an addict, with the constant need to make a connection, the strains of criminality, the jail time, and the risk of infection and death. Participation in a methadone program and abstinence from heroin become a more attractive choice. Whether he procures methadone on the street or through a clinic, as long as it is cheap he can maintain his opiate habit at low cost and then occasionally obtain the desired euphoria by skipping the methadone and using large amounts of heroin. Since the data from existing programs indicate that many addicts do use heroin occasionally—anywhere from 10 to 50 per cent, depending on the program and length of time in treatment—this may already be a common pattern.

This problem presents a difficult choice to program operators. To eliminate this last increment of drug use might require expulsion of addicts for occasional heroin use. This would certainly return some patients to the addicted life, with all the social and personal costs involved. If an addict is adjusting well in other ways, this cost is not justifiable. Eliminating the last vestige of heroin use in such a case is essentially a meaningless concession to moralism.

There is a more serious question involved, however. There is no way of knowing the extent to which the negative aspects of the addicted life have a general deterrent effect that keeps people from experimenting with heroin. Clearly, almost anyone exposed to heroin is also exposed to the addict community generally and knows the risks involved in becoming addicted. It is possible that the existence of large methadone programs would indicate to some portion of the nonaddict population that they could attain the euphoria of heroin without having to adopt the life-style as a whole, and they might find this option more attractive than either abstinence or full-scale heroin addiction. Present evidence indicates that there may be a curious gap of belief in people who become addicted to heroin. They know full well that the drug is addicting and that the life-style is terrible, but they do not doubt their own ability to handle the drug without becoming addicted. For all we know, the unattractiveness of the life-style may be exercising a potent deterrent effect on others who are curious but more realistic about the danger of becoming addicted. Opening up the methadone choice might make these people more willing to run the risk. Since we know little about the causes of addiction and even less about deterrent effects, we do not know whether this is a matter for real concern. If it turns out to be an important phenomenon, it will create some painful public-policy choices.

Total Size of Methadone Programs. A final question concerns the portion of the addict population that is amenable to successful methadone treatment. Any figure is only an educated guess based upon the observer's estimate of the total number of addicts, observations about the results of existing methadone programs, and judgments about the criteria of success.

Official U.S. Government calculations seem to agree that 25 to 33 per cent of the addicted population will be helped by methadone.[99] This estimate may well be too low; some program operators have estimated that their methadone programs drew almost 50 per cent of the addicts in an area within a year or so after beginning operations.[100] Considering that many addicts believe street rumors adverse to methadone, and that one would not expect any program to reach its full potential right away, an estimate of 50 per cent probably represents a more realistic, but still conservative, figure, if one assumes that "success" means "derives substantial benefit from methadone maintenance."

ANTAGONISTS

Antagonists are drugs that prevent opiates from having any effect if the antagonists are administered before opiate injection and that precipitate withdrawal if administered after injection. The possibility of using these drugs as a major treatment modality has intrigued researchers for the last six years, but at present the antagonists remain experimental.[101]

There are two basic antagonists currently in use for the treatment of heroin addicts, cyclazocine and naloxone, but an excellent survey by New York's Health Services Administration noted that there might be several hundred others already in existence, as yet untested.[102] The most important characteristics of these drugs are as follows:

- Cyclazocine produces unpleasant side effects, such as nausea, sweating, a drunken feeling, anxiety, and hallucinations, but tolerance to these effects does develop. Naloxone does not appear to have significant side effects.
- Cyclazocine is effective when taken orally and has a duration of action of 12 to 24 hours. Naloxone is effective when taken intravenously but is relatively ineffective when taken orally. There does not appear to be any information on subcutaneous administration, though presumably it would be less effective than intravenous but more effective than oral administration.
- Small doses of an antagonist are effective. Thus, 4 mg. of cyclazocine will block the effects of 15 to 25 mg. of heroin for one day. Naloxone is even more powerful if used intravenously: 1 mg. will block the effects of 25 mg. of heroin for ten hours. (Taken orally, it requires 200 mg. to block the effects of 25 mg. of heroin for six hours.)
- Cyclazocine has addictive qualities, in that an abstinent user will show some withdrawal symptoms. Users do not crave the drug even when they are in withdrawal, however. Naloxone does not have addictive properties.
- The antagonists do not reduce the "drug hunger" felt by the opiate addict.
- Most experimentation to date has been done with cyclazocine, largely because the short duration and ineffectiveness of oral naloxone makes it an unsuitable candidate for mass treatment.

The NIMH Addiction Research Center is now experimenting with a new antagonist, EN-1639A. It is two to three times more potent than the other two, is effective orally, and has a longer duration of action than naloxone.[103]

Besides the mechanical problems of dosage and delivery, there are several major problems in using the antagonists as a treatment modality. Because they do not eliminate the "drug hunger," the patient is constantly tempted to miss his dose and take heroin. As the HSA paper points out, the fact that addiction to the antagonist itself is minimal means that it is possible for him to do this. A methadone patient is tied to the program by his addiction; an antagonist patient is not. Because of this problem, and also because of the short duration of action of many possible antagonists, a major search is under way for a capsule that could be implanted in the patient to release the drug slowly over an extended period. It is likely to be some time before success is achieved, however.[104] The civil-liberties questions involved are also substantial.

Two apparent disadvantages may be due to the experimental nature of the programs. So far, the costs have been high ($3,000 to $5,000 per addict per year), partly because of the need for inpatient care common to all experimental programs and partly because of the scarcity and high price of some of the drugs. The success rate so far is hard to calculate, but, at best, it has been about 40 per cent over all, judged by the criterion of remaining in the program.[105] However, some of the failures may reflect the fact that dosages had to be worked out and supportive services developed. Future experiments may do better. One can, of course, argue the opposite—that future, larger projects will be less successful because the Hawthorne effect of participating in a new experimental program will be gone. In addition, there is some evidence that the success rate for outpatients may be considerably lower than for inpatients.

It is as yet unproved that the antagonists will ever be a useful treatment modality. Nor is there any reason at present to believe that the side effects of any antagonists would be less adverse than those of methadone. It could easily turn out to be the reverse, with the antagonists having more serious adverse effects. If an addict is going to be dependent upon long-term chemotherapy, there appears to be no reason at present for preferring that he be dependent on an antagonist rather than on methadone.

Under some theories of addiction, the antagonists could be useful adjuncts to treatment. If one takes the view that it is important to extinguish reinforcement of the desire to use opiates, the antagonists may turn out to be successful. One can also argue that the use of an antagonist, combined with supportive services, would force the addict from the addicted life-style and give him an opportunity to forge a new one. Finally, and probably most important, is the possibility that use of an antagonist might turn out to be the only practical way an addict on methadone can become abstinent. If research should ultimately show that opiate use does create a drug hunger that persists for a long period after obvious withdrawal is complete, then antagonists might be developed that would help the addict survive this period without readdiction. Dr. William Martin has found that secondary withdrawal symptoms persist in animals for at least six months after withdrawal from opiates. If the drug hunger is such a symptom, and if it persists in humans in similar fashion, there is at present no way for an addict to leave a methadone program without enduring six months of craving opiates. As is obvious from the failure rates for abstinence programs, few manage to do this. If an antagonist could prevent relapses from leading to readdiction during this period, it would be valuable.[106]

Dr. Martin is cautious about the antagonists. He states only that, if the research goals are achieved, "I believe that certain motivated addicts can be benefitted by this approach. . . . [They] may find a role in the treatment of the juvenile experiment."[107] Others are more enthusiastic, and suggestions of mass inoculations are occasionally heard. The wisdom of such ideas is questionable.

MULTIMODAL PROGRAMS

Several programs now contain components of all the different modalities. The Illinois Drug Abuse Project (IDAP), in Chicago, the Narcotics Treatment Administration, in Washington, D.C., and the New Haven Mental Health Center, for example, include methadone, therapeutic communities, detoxification, abstinence, and supportive services for all types of patients. The Community Mental Health Center in New Haven has an experimental naloxone group as well, and IDAP at one time tried cyclazocine on some patients. While the approach is promising, rigorous comparison of multimodal and unimodal programs has not yet been done, and one can only set forth the present arguments for and against the multimodal approach.

The arguments in favor run along the following lines:

- Most observers believe that different programs work best for different addicts, although the typologies are not worked out and no tool has predictive value at present. If a program has several modalities, an addict can readily transfer from one to another if he or the staff feels that his performance could be improved by the change. In addition, failure in one modality does not mean total failure, because the addict can try another with minimal delay.

- Different modalities attract different types of addicts. Therapeutic communities, for example, may have more appeal to younger addicts; methadone, to older. Differences in age, education, employment, or criminality may also be significant. But the modality that attracts an addict may not be the one in which he will ultimately do best. Combining the modalities makes one an intake center for each of the others, to the benefit of all.

- In some cases, the modality to which an addict applies is an accident of geography and personal contacts. Centralized administration can make this choice more rational and productive.

- Each modality has something to contribute to the others. The group-therapy techniques and intense environment of the therapeutic community may help methadone patients by encouraging them to become abstinent or by improving their understanding of the factors that led them to addiction. They may also have an impact on abuse of other drugs by methadone patients. Conversely, TC residents and other abstinent patients may benefit from knowing that there is a back-up program if they do not succeed in remaining abstinent.

- A multimodal program will find it easier to develop new strategies for the treatment of addiction. For example, it may be possible to have patients who are basically abstinent but receive low doses of methadone if they feel the craving for drugs is about to overwhelm them. This could be a particularly important technique for teenagers. It would be difficult to operate such a program in connection with any single modality, because both the administrative structure and the ambience would be against the experiment.

- Politically, it is advantageous to combine the modalities, so that they will stop fighting each other and unite to get more support from the government.

The primary arguments against multimodal programs are as follows:

- Most of the benefits to be gained from eliminating accidental assignment, allowing rapid reassignment, and experimenting with new programs may be achieved just as well by better administration and coordination of separate modalities.
- Multimodal programs have the basic problem that they transmit contradictory messages to the patients. The ethos of most such programs is that abstinence is superior and that methadone patients, while not so bad as heroin addicts, are definitely second-class. This lack of psychological support makes it more likely that the methadone patient will fail. It may also make it difficult for a patient who is not doing well on an abstinence program to change to methadone—he may leave treatment entirely rather than accept what he and his peers view as a demotion. If such an attitude does not pervade the project, the reverse problem may occur: The abstinent patient may not see why he should endure drug hunger while others are receiving methadone.

   In this view, faith is a very important part of every modality. The evangelical nature of the TC has been discussed, for example, and it may be a necessary part of the therapy. Part of the success with methadone may be due to the fact that patients come to believe that they have a metabolic disease and are going to receive a medicine that will help them. In short, mixing different modalities may undermine all of them by confusing the patient about the expectations and possibilities of the program.

Resolution of this issue must await further research that explicitly compares the success of the different components of multimodal programs with that of comparable techniques used alone. Since multimodality is a growing trend, such evaluations should be performed soon.

HEROIN MAINTENANCE

One treatment modality that is not used in the United States at present is maintenance of addicts on heroin or morphine. While many, perhaps most, observers react negatively to the idea, there are good reasons for trying it on an experimental basis. The major argument in favor is that heroin maintenance might attract two important groups of addicts: those who do not succeed on methadone maintenance and those who do not volunteer for it in the first place. If this were the result, addiction-related crime would be decreased, because the costs of the heroin habit would be eliminated and, as a benefit to the addict, the chances of infection, overdose, and imprisonment would be lessened. In addition, since remarkably little is known about the etiology of addiction or the effects of heroin, controlled clinical experimentation with heroin maintenance would allow some important questions to be studied. It is also possible that heroin maintenance would break the market for heroin and remove the impetus for expansion caused by the high profits of illegal distribution. (The English experience, described by Edgar May in Staff Paper 7, is, of course, instructive.)

The most important objections to heroin maintenance are as follows:

- The administrative expenses would be high. If the drug were administered in clinics, it would have to be made available about four times a day. Also, because heroin is relatively ineffective orally, medical personnel might be required to give injections to ensure a sterilized procedure. Both factors would increase expenses. If the English system were adopted and the heroin were dispensed from pharmacies on prescription, it would be difficult to control the dosages, track the patients, secure the heroin, and avoid infection and disease.

- Because of heroin's sharp peaks and short duration of action, it may be a difficult drug on which to find and maintain a constant dosage even if the patient desires stabilization. There is always physical pressure on the patient to increase his dosage. To make this problem worse, a maintenance program would draw addicts who were not willing to give up the effort to attain the euphoria of heroin. Thus, they might take their maintenance dose, buy more on the street, and then demand that the clinics maintain the new, higher dosage. While there may be a pharmacological ceiling beyond which the drug has no additional euphoric effects, this is not definitely known. Addicts on heroin maintenance might quickly reach levels of 100 to 200 mg. of heroin per day, a dose higher than that of almost all present addicts. The physical effects of this dosage are not known.
- Many members of the black community would oppose heroin maintenance, interpreting it as a scheme to keep the black community tranquilized and quiet or as an indication that society is concerned only with the crime caused by addiction, not with the addicts themselves. Still others, who believe that continuing use of heroin causes long-term organic damage, might regard heroin maintenance as a form of mass murder.
- The high doses that would tend to prevail in such a program would tranquilize addicts and make them function ineffectively. This would make rehabilitation efforts impossible.
- Heroin maintenance might draw patients away from methadone, thus transferring them from a program with proved effectiveness for rehabilitation to one that is probably counterproductive in terms of reformation of the addict's life-style.
- The existence of heroin maintenance would remove an important deterrent to experimentation with heroin—the obvious degradation of the addicted life.

These objections have force. It seems doubtful that society would wish to move to a large-scale heroin-maintenance program at the present time, especially if doing so would undercut methadone. However, there are limitations on the effectiveness of methadone and on the extent to which it can eliminate the addiction problem. If, for example, only 50 per cent of the addicts are helped by methadone, the country may be left with a sizable addiction problem even after methadone has reached its full potential. Despite the problems, it is likely that heroin maintenance will begin to receive serious consideration. It would be wise to start accumulating solid knowledge on its workings and effects, and on the validity of the objections to it, before proposals for large-scale programs make the matter urgent. There will not be time to do so afterwards. Careful experimentation is desirable.

TREATMENT OF USERS OF NONOPIATES

Treatment of users of the amphetamines, barbiturates, hallucinogens, and cannabinols has two distinct aspects. The first is "crisis intervention"—emergency assistance to those who are suffering from adverse effects of drugs. The second consists of long-term programs designed to prevent future drug use.

CRISIS INTERVENTION

Overdoses of opiates and barbiturates constitute a medical emergency, and death results unless steps are taken quickly.[108] For other drugs, the adverse effects are more psychological than physical—usually the user is having a severe mental disturbance as a result of the drug and needs psychological support until the body clears the drug from the system.[109]

Until recently, users of nonopiates suffering from adverse effects of drug taking had nowhere to go except hospital emergency rooms. Most users were reluctant to do this, both because hospitals often felt compelled to report the illegal drug user to the authorities, and because emergency-room personnel treated them demeaningly. In addition, drug users came to believe that the treatment received in hospitals was not very helpful. In fact, the reaction of the medical personnel tended to intensify and prolong the user's own panic. In the words of one observer, "Modern medical science can keep a panic reaction going for about five days." The hospital use of strong tranquilizers is regarded by experienced drug users and drug-treatment doctors as unnecessary and possibly damaging. Chlorpromazine, the usual drug given, has strong side effects[110] and is unpleasant in its psychoactive characteristics.[111]

Free clinics, manned by interested professionals, experienced youths, and volunteer doctors, have sprung up in many cities. The Haight-Ashbury Clinic in San Francisco seems to have been the prototype. The Langly Porter Youth Drug Unit at the University of California is another. It is not known how many there now are, but it is probable that every large city has at least one, some have several, and the movement is spreading rapidly to suburban communities.

The treatment provided to drug users on a "bad trip" consists primarily of "talking down" the patient, which can be done by peers who have had similar experiences. "Quiet rooms" for such "talk downs" have been recommended as a component for all emergency medical centers that treat youthful drug users. The patient is not left alone and is constantly reassured about who he is and where he is. Establishment of verbal contact with the patient is recommended, and there is little or no use of tranquilizers. When tranquilizers are used, chlorpromazine is the most common, given either orally or, preferably, intramuscularly, which avoids adverse gastrointestinal symptoms. Experimentation is going on using short-term barbiturates instead. As of 1970, the Berkeley Free Clinic claimed to have given only three tranquilizing injections to "freakouts" since the clinic began; the rest were talked down.

Heavy amphetamine users and barbiturate addicts present different detoxification problems. The barbiturate addict needs to be withdrawn from his addiction under a carefully supervised medical regimen in an inpatient hospital setting, for the withdrawal process itself is life-threatening.[112] Heavy amphetamine users are apt to suffer from paranoia, sometimes leading to violence; they need a quiet recovery room away from strangers whom they may consider enemies. They often shy away from hospitalization for fear of arrest.

Treating soft-drug users for adverse reactions is an important health measure to prevent possible deaths, suicides, or bizarre and self-destructive behavior. Since most facilities that perform this service do not have a follow-up capacity, there is no way of telling how many patients return to drug use and how many abandon it after experiencing adverse reactions. The treatment process itself is not concerned with abstinence but with the immediate problem. Many of the patients seen in these clinics are only occasional experimenters or sporadic users.

Before the drug legislation of 1970, there was no basis for federal funding of these crisis clinics. The law now provides that HEW can make grants for such partial services to drug users. Some of the clinics are not enthusiastic about federal backing, fearing that it will lead to greater conformity in approach and a decreased ability to utilize ex-drug users in new roles. Federal or state governments might also impose bureaucratic standards on staff training and facilities without contributing enough money to meet the costs of these requirements. There is also a fear that government backing will turn away some clients.

LONG-TERM THERAPY

While the crisis centers provide necessary emergency services, it is unlikely that they have much permanent impact on drug users. There is therefore a movement to expand the centers to include programs that will have some effect on the drug-using behavior of patients. As a result, the crisis centers are beginning to offer long-term therapeutic help as well as emergency services.

This expansion is not limited to the treatment of drug users. Most clinic staff members view drug problems as only one aspect —and not always the most serious—of human malfunctioning for which help should be provided. For example, the Center for Special Social and Health Problems in San Francisco, according to its descriptive materials, is concerned with drug abuse, sexual problems, violence and hatred, compulsive gambling, suicide, management of death and dying, crime and delinquency, inability to manage finances, obesity, and insomnia. While this list is more ambitious than most, it illustrates the general trend toward broadening the scope of the crisis clinic. In a way, these organizations are becoming privately run community mental-health centers.

The techniques and operations of these programs are about the same as those of the therapeutic communities and outpatient abstinence programs. Since, at present, there is no chemotherapy for soft-drug use, no treatment comparable to the methadone movement is possible. The basic problem with nonaddictive soft drugs is that continued use reflects the user's desire to keep taking them or a psychological dependence on them, which can be even more difficult to deal with than a physical craving. As one study points out, "Student drug users are, as a group, knowledgeable about the undesirable effects of drug abuse. In general, it is not difficult for most student drug abusers to stop. The issue is to get them to want to stop."[113]

While some soft-drug users are in TC's, the majority of those receiving help are in some form of outpatient program, usually the same programs described in the section on outpatient abstinence for opiate users. Often, the patients themselves are the same. A number of heroin addicts use other drugs as well, and youthful drug users are increasingly experimenting with heroin as one of several drugs they try. Whether it is possible to sustain a pattern of sporadic heroin use without becoming addicted is as yet uncertain. The "speed culture" in the Haight-Ashbury section of San Francisco has produced some evidence that speed users, who first use barbiturates to ease the "crash," soon learn that heroin is an even smoother way to achieve this purpose. Eventually they may abandon speed entirely and become heroin addicts. It is possible that a pattern of multiple drug use that includes heroin is an intermediate step toward full addiction.[114]

It is even more difficult to determine the success of these programs with soft-drug users than with narcotics addicts, in part because most experts believe that youths who become heavily involved with cannabis and hallucinogens do not usually stay involved for a long period of time.[115] This fact, of course, increases the difficulty of evaluating the impact of any drug program, because abstinence is a poor indication of the program's effect.

Some work is going on in the area of chemotherapy. An effort is now being made to find antagonists to some of the more common drugs. Researchers tentatively claim to have found a drug that is an antagonist to amphetamines, although it has not yet been fully tested, and some work is being done on antagonists to LSD. However, it is not clear whether these drugs, when and if they are perfected, will have a significant impact on drug use, since soft drugs are taken without the spur of physical necessity. Unless a policy of forced implantation is followed, the drug user will always have a choice about taking the antagonist, and in most cases the choice would probably be to continue drug use.

There are, however, two hypotheses under which the antagonists might be useful. The amphetamines appear to be physically addictive to a limited extent, and this could exert some pressure on the amphetamine user to continue his use.[116] An antagonist might prevent the constant renewal of this physical dependence and give the user's body a chance to become free of it. Secondly, if one adopts a conditioning theory of drug use, an antagonist would eliminate the reinforcing effect of gratification from drug use and might in time extinguish the conditioned response of taking drugs.

One of the most carefully evaluated methods of decreasing soft-drug use is transcendental meditation. A Harvard Medical School Study gave questionnaires to 1,950 subjects who had been practicing transcendental meditation for three months or more. Of these, 1,862 completed the questionnaire. The decrease in drug use was quite striking. The study says:

Following the start of the practice of transcendental meditation, there was a marked decrease in the number of drug abusers for all drug categories. . . . As the practice of meditation continued, the subjects progressively decreased their drug abuse until after practicing 21 months of meditation most subjects had completely stopped abusing drugs. For example, in the 6-month period before starting the practice of meditation, about 80 percent of the subjects used marijuana and of those about 28 percent were heavy users. After practicing transcendental meditation 6 months, 37 percent used marijuana and of those only 6.5 percent were heavy users. After 21 months of the practice, only 12 percent continued to use marijuana and of those most were light users; only one individual was a heavy user. The decrease in abuse of LSD was even more marked. Before starting the practice of transcendental meditation, 48 percent of the subjects had used LSD, and of these subjects about 14 percent were heavy users. In the 3 months following the start of the practice of meditation, 11 percent of the subjects took LSD while after 21 months of the practice only 3 percent took LSD. The increase in the number of non-users after starting the practice of meditation was similar for the other drugs: non-users of the other hallucinogens after 21 months of the practice rose from 61 to 96 percent; for the narcotics, from 83 to 99 percent; for the amphetamines, from 70 to 99 percent; and for the barbiturates, from 83 to 99 percent.[117]

As the researchers point out, these correlations are not proof of causation. "Involvement in other kinds of self-improvement activities may also lead to decreased drug abuse. The motivation to start meditation may have influenced the subjects to stop drug abuse. The subjects in the present study may have spontaneously stopped, continued, or increased taking drugs independently of transcendental meditation."[118]

Despite these necessary caveats, the results are striking, especially in an area in which, as the study delicately points out, "Existing programs for the alleviation of [non-narcotic] drug abuse usually involve education as to the dangers of the effects of drugs and sometimes provide personal counseling or psychiatric care. The efficiency of these programs has yet to be established.[119] (Staff Paper 6, by Dr. Andrew Weil, deals with meditation and other nonchemical means of achieving altered stages of consciousness.)

CONCLUSION

Few solid conclusions emerge from this morass of conflicting information. It is clear that methadone is a helpful treatment modality, but just how helpful is not yet known. It is equally clear that its almost inevitable expansion will create new problems, some of them predictable and some of them totally unexpected. Not much can be said about the other treatment modalities and concepts. Those who favor them have not yet proved their case, but neither have those who are skeptical. On the whole, it seems probable that they will turn out to have only marginal effectiveness as drug-treatment methods, although they may have possibilities as a part of the more general human-potential movement. The basic problem is that we lack any solid theory or understanding of the nature and causes of addiction. As researchers have repeatedly pointed out, for most drug users the drugs are functional and adaptive mechanisms. Society cannot make long-term progress toward developing more effective treatment mechanisms without grasping and accepting this fact. At present, however, we have little choice but to proceed empirically.

NOTES

1. Alfred Lindesmith, *The Addict and the Law* (New York: Vintage ed., 1967), pp. 105–6, 124. (Hereafter cited as Lindesmith.)

2. Charles Terry and Mildred Pellens, *The Opium Problem* (Bureau of Social Hygiene, 1928), p. 627. (Hereafter cited as Terry and Pellens.)

3. *Ibid.*, pp. 137–65.

4. Troy Duster, *The Legislation of Morality* (New York: Free Press, 1970), p. 15.

5. Terry and Pellens, pp. 30–32. These authors are skeptical and believe that physicians would have reported only addicts under curative treatment.

6. Rufus King, *The Drug Hang-up–America's Fifty Year Folly* (in press), MS. pp. 76–77.

7. Terry and Pellens, p. 866.

8. King, *op. cit.*, note 6, MS. p. 57.

9. Norman Zinberg and John Robertson, *Drugs and the Public* (in press), MS. p. 40.

10. Lindesmith, pp. 99–134. For a brief review of relevant population estimates, see Arthur D. Little, Inc., *Drug Abuse and Law Enforcement* (A Report to the President's Commission on Law Enforcement and Administration of Justice: 1967), "Appendix C: History of the U.S. Addict Population." This report argues that "what is apparent is not the constancy of the addict and his habit, but rather that the addict deserts his habit quite easily" (pp. C–4 and C–5). It points to sources showing a decline from about 246,000 in 1890 to 100,000 in 1926. These sources are criticized in the cited portion of Lindesmith.

11. Frances Gearing, "Methadone Maintenance Treatment Program: Progress Report of Evaluation Through March 31, 1970" (mimeograph, 1970), p. 11. (Hereafter cited as Gearing, 1970.)

12. The studies are summarized in John O'Donnell, *The Relapse Rate in Narcotic Addiction: A Critique of Follow-up Studies* (New York State, Narcotic Addiction Control Commission Reprints, 1968) (originally published in 1965).

13. William Martin, Statement in *Narcotics Research, Rehabilitation, and Treatment,* Hearings before the Select Committee on Crime, House of Representatives, 92d Cong., 1st sess., April 26–28 and June 2–4, 23, 1971 (GPO,

1971), Part 2, pp. 437–38. (A number of statements at these hearings are cited hereafter. They are footnoted as *Hrgs.*

14. These summary statements are drawn from a large number of published sources and interviews. Some of them are discussed at greater length later in the paper, particularly in the methadone section. For development and discussion of psychological characteristics, see Isador Chein, Donald Gerard, Robert Lee, and Eva Rosenfeld, *The Road to H* (New York: Basic Books, 1964), a book that equals *The Opium Problem* as a classic in the field.

15. David Smith, George Gay, and Barry Ramer, "Adolescent Heroin Abuse in San Francisco," *Proceedings Third National Conference on Methadone Treatment, November 14–16, 1970* (GPO, 1971), pp. 89, 90. (These proceedings are hereafter cited as *Third Meth. Conf.*)

16. Howard Jones, *Hrgs.*, p. 588.

17. George Gay, Alan Matzger, William Bathurst, and David Smith, "Short-Term Heroin Detoxification on an Outpatient Basis," *International Journal of the Addictions*, VI, No. 2 (June, 1971), 241, 259–60.

18. Kramer, *Hrgs.*, p. 668.

19. U.S. Comptroller General, *Limited Use of Federal Programs to Commit Narcotic Addicts for Treatment and Rehabilitation* (September 20, 1971), p. 6; Jonathan Cole, "Report on the Treatment of Drug Addiction," in President's Commission on Law Enforcement and Administration of Justice, *Task Force Reports: Narcotics and Drug Abuse* (GPO, 1967), pp. 135, 140–41.

20. O'Donnell, *op. cit.*, n. 12.

21. These are reviewed in Cole, *op. cit.*, note 19, pp. 135–36.

22. Duster, *op. cit.*, note 4, p. 134. The description and statistics that follow are taken from Duster and from John Kramer, Richard Bass, and John Berechochea, "Civil Commitment for Addicts: The California Program," *American Journal of Psychiatry*, CXXV (1968), 816.

23. Kramer, *Hrgs.*, p. 654.

24. Compare the descriptions of the two programs in National Institute of Mental Health, National Clearinghouse for Mental Health Information, *Directory of Narcotic Addiction Treatment Agencies in the United States, 1968–69* (GPO, 1970), pp. 5–6. (Hereafter cited as *NIMH Directory.*)

25. Jones, *Hrgs.*, pp. 565, 584. The budget estimate is calculated from the budget numbers given. It is not a statement of the Commissioner.

26. For a thoughtful critique based on observation of five centers, see Community Service Society of New York, Committee on Youth and Correction, *Observation on Five Residential Facilities of the Narcotic Addiction Control Commission* (1971), pp. 89–101.

27. *New York Times*, October 4, 1970. See, also, the statement of the Health Policy Advisory Center:

The program promises to return the addict to a useful life "through extended periods of treatment in a controlled environment followed by supervision in an after-care program." The emphasis is on "controlled." The addict receives about as much rehabilitation as the criminal prisoner with about as much result—the recidivist rate for addicts is much higher than for criminals. Moreover the rehabilitation centers are run like prisons. There are guards, most of whom receive training for prison work—one guard for every two inmates, recalcitrant addicts are beaten and placed in isolation on reduced diets; inmates are sexually abused; there is no separation of the young from the old. The few rehabilitation programs that do exist are staffed by instructors and therapists who have received little or no training. For the 5,000 or so inmates in the 14 separate institutions there are only 4 psychiatrists, 16 psychologists, and 78 teachers and vocational instructors. The prison-like atmosphere has caused a large percentage of the addicts to try to escape. [Health Policy Advisory Council, Health/PAC *Bulletin*, June, 1970, pp. 16–17.]

28. Carl Chambers, *Hrgs.*, p. 566.

29. U.S. Comptroller General, *op. cit.*, note 19, pp. 12–17.

30. Information furnished by the Bureau of Prisons.

31. The information on 1969 was furnished by NIMH. The 1971 information is from Bertram Brown, *Hrgs.*, p. 470.

32. Brown, *Hrgs.*, p. 433.

33. U.S. Bureau of Prisons, "Narcotic Addict Rehabilitation Act: Progress Report" (mimeograph), February 22, 1971.

34. These are difficult numbers to pin down. According to the *NIMH Directory* (p. 144), 40 programs listed themselves as therapeutic communities as of about 1968. It is not clear how stringent the standards for inclusion were, however, and this may include some programs that are essentially outpatient abstinence with group work. At the other end, it misses some of the newer therapeutic communities.

The population figure is also an educated guess. Most TC's are in New York, and knowledgeable sources estimate that the Phoenix Houses (the city's TC program) had about 1,000 residents and private TC's about 1,400 in 1970. Synanon had about 1,400 residents (*NIMH Directory*, p. 32). These places account for the largest number of TC residents, but there are many others with 10 to 100 residents scattered throughout the country. The estimate of 5,000 residents is probably an upper limit.

35. A description of four of the New York City projects is given in Community Service Society of New York, Committee on Youth and Corrections, *The Long Road Back from a Living Death: A Study of Four Voluntary Treatment and Rehabilitation Programs for New York City's Narcotics Addicts* (Part I) (1967).

36. Kramer, *Hrgs.*, p. 667.

37. *Ibid.*

38. This study was given to us on a no-attribution basis.

39. *NIMH Directory, passim.* For a detailed description of two projects, see Community Service Society of New York, Committee on Youth and Corrections, *Lifeline to Tomorrow: A Study of Voluntary Treatment Programs for Narcotic Addicts* (Part II) (1969).

40. Robert DuPont, *Hrgs.,* p. 144.

41. D.C. Department of Corrections, "Performance of Corrections Referrals Under Three Narcotic-Addiction Treatment Modalities" (Research Report No. 42: mimeograph, July, 1971).

42. Friends of Psychiatric Research, Inc., *Uniform Evaluation of Programs to Combat Narcotic Addiction* (Baltimore, 1970).

43. *Op. cit.,* note 39, pp. 93–94.

44. The data that follow are from S. B. Sells and Deena Watson, "A Spectrum of Approaches in Methadone Treatment: Relation to Program Evaluation," *Third Meth. Conf.,* p. 17.

45. Vincent Dole, "Planning for the Treatment of 25,000 Heroin Addicts," *Third Meth. Conf.,* p. 111.

46. *NIMH Directory,* p. 144; Second National Methadone Maintenance Conference, New York, October 26–27, 1969, published in the *International Journal of the Addictions,* V, No. 3 (September, 1970) (hereafter cited as *Second Meth. Conf.); Third Meth. Conf.*

47. Charles Edwards, *Hrgs.,* p. 395.

48. Elmer Gardner, *Hrgs.,* p. 397; Brown, *Hrgs.,* p. 440.

49. Avram Goldstein, "Blind Controlled Dosage Comparisons with Methadone in Two Hundred Patients," *Third Meth. Conf.* (hereafter cited as Goldstein, 1970); Ray Trussell, "Treatment of Narcotics Addicts in New York," *Second Meth. Conf.,* pp. 347, 352; Lynwood Holton, *Hrgs.,* pp. 600–601. Governor Holton's statement is particularly interesting because it makes budget estimates within the context of a comprehensive state treatment program.

50. Gearing Report 1970 and "Successes and Failures in Methadone Maintenance Treatment of Heroin Addiction in New York City," *Third Meth. Conf.,* p. 2.

51. Goldstein 1970, p. 31.

52. DuPont, *Hrgs.,* p. 173.

53. See, e.g., Gordon Stewart, "A Survey of Patients Attending Different Clinics in New Orleans," *Third Meth. Conf.,* p. 27.

54. The information on MMTP is drawn, except where otherwise indicated, from three sources; the Gearing Report, 1970; the 1969 edition of the same report; and the paper presented at the methadone conference, cited in note 50.

55. Carl Chamber and Dean Babst, "Characteristics Predicting Long-Term Retention in a Methodone Maintenance Program," *Third Meth. Conf.,* p. 140.

56. Herman Joseph and Vincent Dole, "Methadone Patients on Probation and Parole" (mimeograph) (New York: Rockefeller University Press, 1970), p. 9.

57. Chambers and Babst, *op. cit.,* note 67.

58. Joseph and Dole, *op. cit.,* note 56.

59. The Second National Methadone Maintenance Conference had reports

from New York, Chicago, Minneapolis, St. Louis, Baltimore, New Haven, Vancouver, New Orleans, and Miami. The Third National Methadone Treatment Conference had reports from New York, Brooklyn, Chicago, New Orleans, Santa Clara, Philadelphia, Vancouver, Baltimore, Denver, and Washington as well as from Sweden.

60. Henry Brill, "Methadone Maintenance: A Problem in Delivery of Service," *Journal of the American Medical Association,* CCXV, No. 7 (February 15, 1971), 1148–50.

61. Goldstein 1970, p. 37.

62. The incidence of hepatitis among addicts has been described as "unbelievable." Some experts think the sale of blood by these addicts is creating a major public-health problem. See Stewart, *op. cit.,* note 53.

63. For a more detailed discussion, see Staff Paper 1.

64. Vincent Dole and Marie Nyswander, "Methadone Maintenance and Its Implication for Theories of Narcotic Addiction," in Abraham Wikler, ed., *The Addictive States* (Baltimore, Md.: Williams & Wilkins Co., 1968), p. 359, postulates an inherent neurological vulnerability. But, at the Second National Methadone Maintenance Conference, Dr. Dole was asked: "Apart from any psychological factors or emotional factors, is there a metabolic irregularity which causes a craving for drugs in the first place or does the metabolic irregularity come after the use of drugs or both?" His response was: "This is a very important question for which I have no adequate answer. I can only guess. My opinion is that a heavy exposure to heroin induces the metabolic changes. According to this theory, the abnormal drug craving in man, like the induced drug seeking behavior in animals, is a result of exposure to narcotic drugs and not the original cause of the addiction." *Second Meth. Conf.,* pp. 359, 370.

65. Dr. Dole seems to lean toward the idea that the metabolic change is permanent. He has stated: "I believe one has to reckon with the fact that heroin hunger is probably a symptom of a pharmacological imprint that may last for a man's life." Vincent Dole, "Research on Methadone Maintenance Treatment," *Second Meth. Conf.,* pp. 359, 370.

66. See, e.g., Avram Goldstein, "Blind Dosage Comparisons and Other Studies in a Large Methadone Program" (paper presented at the National Heroin Symposium, June 20, 1971, pp. 12–13; to be published in the *Journal of Psychedelic Drugs*). (Hereafter cited as Goldstein 1971.)

67. William Martin, "Pathophysiology of Narcotic Addiction: Possible Roles of Protracted Abstinence in Relapse" (unpublished paper, 1970), pp. 6–7, and private communications.

68. Abraham Wikler, "Interaction of Physical Dependence and Classical and Operant Conditioning in the Genesis of Relapse," in Wikler, ed., *The Addictive States, op. cit.,* note 76. The views of Wikler and Martin can be merged into one coherent psycho-physical theory. See Max Fink, "Narcotic Antagonists in Opiate Dependence," *Science,* CLXIX (September 4, 1970), 1005.

69. The maturation hypothesis was first proposed by Charles Winick in "Maturing Out of Narcotic Addiction," *Bulletin on Narcotics,* XIV, No. 1 (1962). Since then a number of researchers have looked at particular groups of addicts to determine whether they do, in fact, mature out. The one-third figure is based on a number of these works as well as on interviews.

70. See Cole, *op. cit.,* note 19.

71. Goldstein 1970.

72. Jerome Jaffe, "Methadone Maintenance: Variation in Outcome Criteria as a Function of Dose," *Third Meth. Conf.,* p. 37.

73. William Weiland and Arthur Moffett, "Results of Low Dosage Methadone Treatment," *Third Meth. Conf.,* p. 48. See also Hugh Williams, "Low and High Methadone Maintenance in the Out-patient Treatment of the Hard Core Heroin Addict," *Second Meth. Conf.,* p. 439.

74. Goldstein 1970, p. 24.

75. See, e.g., Gearing Report 1970, pp. 8–9.

76. Stewart, *op. cit.,* note 64.

77. Goldstein 1970.

78. Goldstein 1971, pp. 2–3.

79. Gearing Report 1971.

80. Gearing, *op. cit.,* note 50.

81. For a general review of ambulatory induction, see the material from the different cities contained in *Second Meth. Conf.* and *Third Meth. Conf.*

82. Dole, *op. cit.,* note 65, pp. 364, 370, 386.

83. Jerome Jaffe, "Further Experience with Methadone in the Treatment of Narcotics Users," *Second Meth. Conf.,* pp. 375, 383–84, 386.

84. Goldstein 1971, pp. 13–14.

85. Goldstein 1971, pp. 14–15.

86. *Ibid.,* p. 14. William Vandervort, "Treatment of Drug Abuse in Adolescents," *Third Meth. Conf.,* p. 87.

87. William Martin, "Commentary on the Second National Conference on Methadone Treatment," *Second Meth. Conf.,* p. 545.

88. Quoted in Joseph and Dole, *op. cit.,* note 56, pp. 14–15.

89. See Gerald Davidson, *Hrgs.,* pp. 326–27.

90. See material in *Second Meth. Conf.* and *Third Meth. Conf.,* which includes several papers on possible psychopathology. See also John Kramer, "Methadone Maintenance for Opiate Dependence," *California Medicine,* CXIII, No. 6 (December, 1970), 6, 9.

91. Kramer, *Hrgs.,* pp. 668–69.

92. Goldstein 1970, p. 35.

93. John Langrod, "Secondary Drug Use Among Heroin Users," *International Journal of the Addictions,* V, No. 4 (December, 1970), 611.

94. Ivan Bennett, "Development of a Newly Formulated Tablet for Methadone Maintenance Programs," *Third Meth. Conf.,* p. 143.

95. This statement was made by Dr. Goldstein at the Third Methadone Conference. It was not included in the printed version.

96. See the papers presented at the Second and Third Methadone Conferences. Many of them are directed specifically at side effects. This section summarizes what seems to be the general experience of the programs.

97. Edwards, *Hrgs.*, pp. 393–430; *Washington Post*, November 2, 1971. For a discussion of some of the problems, see "Oral Methadone Maintenance Techniques in the Management of Morphine-type Dependence"; Combined Statement of the Council on Mental Health and Its Committee on Alcoholism and Drug Dependence, American Medical Association; and the Committee on Problems of Drug Dependence, National Research Council, March 16, 1971.

98. Jaffe, *Hrgs.*, p. 210.

99. Brown, *Hrgs.*, p. 455.

100. Stewart, *op. cit.*, note 53; Goldstein 1971.

101. The antagonists were introduced as an experimental addiction treatment modality in 1965. Max Fink, "Narcotic Antagonists in Opiate Dependence," *Science*, CLXIX (September 4, 1970), 1005. For a review of the pharmacology, see Jerome Jaffe, "Narcotic Analgesics," in Louis Goodman and Alfred Gilman, *The Pharmacological Basis of Therapeutics*, 4th ed., (New York: Macmillan, 1970), pp. 237, 264–71.

102. City of New York, Health Services Administration, *Narcotics Antagonists Research Program: The Current State of Knowledge of Drug Antagonists for Heroin Addiction* (mimeographed staff paper: 1971), p. 7. (Hereafter cited as HSA.) We have found that this is the best source written in a form comprehensible to laymen.

103. Martin, *Hrgs.*, pp. 435–36.

104. HSA, pp. 3, 8–9. HSA said that the consensus of researchers is that it would take three to five years for a long-lasting antagonist or long-lasting depot vehicle to be ready for use, and, in any event, there is no guarantee of success. Other people we have talked to are skeptical about the feasibility of the whole idea, and raise both pharmacological and social objections.

105. Fink, *op. cit.*, note 101, says that, since 1968, 40 per cent of more than 450 adult male addicts have remained in cyclazocine treatment.

106. Martin, *Hrgs.*, p. 435.

107. *Ibid.*, p. 436.

108. Treatment for an opioid overdose consists of immediate administration of an antagonist to prevent death from respiratory depression. See Jerome Jaffe, *op. cit.*, note 101, pp. 237, 268. The treatment of barbiturate poisoning is considerably more complicated and requires more elaborate medical facilities. See Seth Sharpless, "Hypnotics and Sedatives: 1. The Barbiturates," in Goodman and Gilman, pp. 97, 117–18.

109. There are variations, of course. The user who has taken an excess of hallucinogen or cannabinol is not dangerous. He requires support but rarely restraint. The user who has taken too much methamphetamine may have paranoid delusions, and considerably more caution is indicated.

110. Side effects are not always encountered, but those that are, are

"many, varied, and can be quite severe." They usually occur only with continued use, however. See Charles Solow, "Drug Therapy of Mental Illness: Tranquilizers and Other Depressant Drugs," in Richard Rech and Kenneth Moore, eds., *An Introduction to Psychopharmacology* (New York: Raven Press, 1970), pp. 289, 299–301.

111. Chlorpromazine, although a powerful tranquilizer, is not a drug of abuse. See Staff Paper 1.

112. David Smith and Donald Wesson, "Phenobarbital Technique for Treatment of Barbiturate Dependence," *Archives of General Psychiatry,* XXIV (January, 1971), 56–57.

113. Herbert Benson and R. K. Wallace, "Decreased Drug Abuse with Transcendental Meditation: A Study of 1,862 Subjects," in *Hrgs.,* pp. 682, 684.

114. Smith, Gay, and Ramer, *op. cit.,* note 15.

115. William McGlothlin, "Policies Concerning Hallucinogenic Drugs," in Hudson Institute, *Policy Concerning Drug Abuse in New York State,* II (Hudson Institute, 1970), 27, 31–32.

116. See John Kramer, "An Introduction to Amphetamine Abuse," *Journal of Psychedelic Drugs,* II, No. 2 (1969), 1, 13. Dr. Kramer, commenting on treatment, states that ". . . abstinence is probably the most important therapeutic device, and that may be difficult to attain. Many users who attempt abstinence find it difficult because of the fatigue which results, extreme at first, gradually diminishing, but persistent, perhaps for months."

117. Benson and Wallace, *op. cit.,* note 113, pp. 683–84.

118. *Ibid.,* p. 685.

119. *Ibid.,* p. 682.

The Economics of Heroin

by John F. Holahan, with the assistance of Paul A. Henningsen

Production • Policy Options: What Can Be Done • Distribution • Consumption • Conclusion

This paper applies economic analysis to the heroin market and to the effect of alternative government policies on this market. The principal concern is supply, but some discussion of demand is included because the effects of public policy on the supply of drugs cannot be adequately analyzed without some knowledge of the effect on demand of changes in price, risk, and availability. The analysis must be considered tentative. Accurate information on the economic aspects of all drugs of abuse is scarce, that which exists is frequently unreliable, and conclusions are often suspect. This paper is no exception.

Much of the data used were taken from two studies: (1) *The World Opium Situation* (October, 1970), by the Bureau of Narcotics and Dangerous Drugs (BNDD) Intelligence Staff; and (2) *Economics of Heroin Distribution* (1970), by Mark Moore. While these papers contain the most extensive economic research available in this area, the information is not unimpeachable. This is not because of deficiencies in the studies—which are excellent —but because of the inherent difficulty of gathering accurate information on illegal enterprises or consumers of illegal commodities.

The BNDD staff paper is the result of an extensive survey of opium production and consumption throughout the world. The paper provides considerably more data, in terms of both quantity and quality, than are available from the United Nations or from other publications. Unfortunately, it is not possible to verify this information through other sources, nor does it appear that it will be possible to do so in the near future.

The Moore paper provides a microeconomic analysis of the heroin distribution system, as well as considerable interview data on daily expenditures of addicts and sources of funds. The data are not derived from sufficiently large samples to allow precise estimates, but they do indicate rough orders of magnitude. Other data derived from interviews with BNDD staff members or U.N. publications are subject to the same general weaknesses.

PRODUCTION

SOURCES OF SUPPLY

The production and distribution of opiate narcotics at the international level are complex and little-understood matters. The crisis of heroin addiction that has afflicted the United States in recent years has obscured the fact that the growing of opium is an age-old, legal occupation in many areas of the world. Heroin addicts in the United States consume only a very small amount of the total quantity of opiates produced worldwide. The Bureau of Narcotics and Dangerous Drugs estimates that 10,000 to 12,000 pounds of heroin are sufficient to supply the entire addict population in the United States for one year.[1] Since, as is generally acknowledged, ten pounds of opium are required to manufacture one pound of heroin, only 100,000 to 120,000 pounds of opium are needed for illicit heroin use in the United States— about 2 per cent of the estimated world production.[2]

Of the opium used by the U.S. heroin market, 80 per cent

comes from Turkey, 15 per cent from Mexico, and 5 per cent from the Far East.[3] These are not precise figures, however, but assumptions rather generally derived from heroin seizures and knowledge of the international illicit drug-import routes.[4] Moreover, several recent developments may change the sources of supply for the U.S. market. On June 30, 1971, President Cevdet Sunay of Turkey decreed that all poppy cultivation and opium production in that country will be forbidden beginning in the fall of 1972. Until that time, licit opium production will be limited to only four provinces and strictly policed. How well this policy will be enforced, and what ultimate effect it will have on heroin use in the United States, cannot as yet be determined. However, already there has been considerable speculation that the Far East supplies a greater amount than was thought previously. The tighter controls now being imposed by Turkey and the increased contacts between the U.S. and Southeast Asia caused by the Indo-China War have shifted the sources of supply somewhat.

Raw opium itself is produced from the poppy plant (*papaver somniferum*—the sleep-bearing poppy), which consists of a thin main stalk, three to four feet tall, with several egg-shaped pods on top. Between June and July, the poppy blooms, and, 10 days later, when the blossoms lose their petals, the pods are ready for the opium resin to be extracted. Incisions are made in the pods, and a milky fluid oozes out. At the end of the day, this substance is scraped off the pods by hand. It later hardens into a brown gum and is pressed into cakes of raw opium. The amount of opium produced from a poppy crop will increase if this process is repeated once again, as in Turkey, or several times, as in India, but the morphine content will be reduced with each lancing.[5]

Many factors affect the opium yield per acre—the quality of the soil, the temperature, rainfall, the quality of the seed, irrigation, fertilization, and crop rotation. Intensive cultivation and a great deal of labor are required to produce opium, particularly during harvest, when the pods must be incised and the raw opium collected by hand, but labor is also needed during the growing season to thin the poppy plants. It is estimated that between 175 and 250 man-hours of labor are required to produce 1 kilo of opium.[6] Because of this labor-intensive production process, poppies tend to be raised only where labor is abundant and relatively inexpensive; but there seems no clear reason, given a different set of relative prices for labor and capital, that a more capital-intensive process could not be employed.

Most poppy cultivation occurs in a zone stretching from central Turkey through Iran, Afghanistan, Pakistan, India, Burma, Laos, Thailand, and southern China, with the greatest concentration in India and Southeast Asia. Poppy cultivation is legal in India, Turkey, the U.S.S.R., and Iran. Turkish licit poppy acreage was reported to be 29,600 acres in 1970.[7] According to U.N. figures, India has at least 86,500 acres planted.[8] Iran, which abolished the production of opium from 1956 to 1968, planned 29,600 acres of poppy cultivation for 1970. In addition, roughly 30,000–32,000 acres each are believed to be planted in the Soviet Union, Afghanistan, and Pakistan, and negligible amounts of licit opium are produced in Yugoslavia and Japan.[9]

According to figures reported to the United Nations by producing countries, the total licit world production of opium is 1,060–1,085 metric tons, or approximately 40–45 per cent of the total produced. India is by far the world's largest licit producer of opium, with a reported 750 metric tons in 1968. Turkey and the U.S.S.R. each contribute 115–120 metric tons of licit production. An estimate of 75–100 metric tons was made for Communist China, based on expected medicinal needs for its population. The estimated totals for licit and illicit production are presented in Table 4–1.

Licit opium is used primarily in the manufacture of medicinal opiates. Legal morphine production currently amounts to approximately 150 metric tons per year—a substantial rise from around 85 metric tons per year in the mid-1950's. This growth is due chiefly to the rising demand for codeine, but a small portion of the licit opium is used for opium-maintenance programs in India, Pakistan, and Iran.

The world's illicit production of opium is estimated at 1,250–1,400 metric tons annually.[10] The principal concentration of illicit production is in the Burma-Laos-Thailand region, which

TABLE 4–1
ESTIMATED WORLD OPIUM PRODUCTION[a]
(In metric tons)

Producing country	Licit production	Illicit production	Total production
India	750	175–200	925–950
Turkey	120	100	220
U.S.S.R.	115	—	115
Yugoslavia	negl.	—	negl.
Pakistan	negl.	175–200	175–200
Japan	negl.	—	negl.
China[b]	75–100	Unknown	75–100
Afghanistan	—	100–125	100–125
Burma	—	400	400
Thailand	—	200	200
Laos	—	100–150	100–150
Mexico	—	5–10	5–10
Other[c]	—	5–10	5–10
TOTALS:	1,060–1,085	1,260–1,395	2,320–2,480

[a] As reported by licit exporting countries to the United Nations, except Communist China.

[b] Based on medicinal needs for population.

[c] Mainly North Africa and the Near East.

SOURCE: BNDD Intelligence Staff, *The World Opium Situation,* unpublished paper, October, 1970, p. 10.

produces an estimated 700–750 tons. The Afghanistan-Pakistan area produces another 250–300 tons of illicit opium, and the illicit output of Turkey is estimated at 100 tons. Illicit cultivation of the plant also occurs in parts of Mexico, South America, and North Africa, although the amounts produced there are negligible. While some illegal acreage is planted in Turkey, most of the illicit opium there is diverted from the yield on legal acreage. On the other hand, all the opium produced in Afghanistan, Burma, Laos, and Thailand and part of the outputs of India and Pakistan are derived from illegal acreage. About 40 metric tons of illicit Turkish production was thought to enter Iran in 1970; the remainder is exported to Western Europe and the United States.

The Southeast Asian countries consume most of their own opium, but some is shipped to Hong Kong for use there and for distribution throughout the Far East. A small amount, perhaps one or two metric tons, is shipped to the United States, although this figure has probably risen recently. India also consumes the major part of its illicit production; and, although some of the Afghanistan-Pakistan production is consumed internally, approximately 200 metric tons is thought to enter Iran. Iran is the largest consumer of illicit opium in the world, with an estimated 350,000 opium and heroin users. In 1969, Iran began controlled production of opium in order to maintain its own addicts.

YIELDS, MARKET PRICES, AND INCOMES

Income from poppy cultivation is affected by the opium yield obtained, the morphine content of the raw opium, and the current licit and illicit market prices. The reported yields per acre in 1969 for four countries are presented in Table 4–2, but, since these are government figures provided by the local farmers, both yields and acreage are probably understated. This is undoubtedly the case for the crop yields in Turkey and Pakistan. Turkish yields are closer to 13.4–14.2 pounds per acre, with the non-reported amount diverted to illicit traders.[11] Opium yields are estimated at 8.6–28.6 pounds per acre in Southeast Asia[12] (probably closer to the lower figure[13]), and the Soviet Union reports yields of 27.5–32 pounds per acre.[14]

Prices for opium vary with quality. The morphine content of Turkish opium, reportedly the highest in the world, varies from 9 to 13 per cent, while in other producing countries the morphine

TABLE 4–2
OPIUM PRODUCTION IN SELECTED COUNTRIES, 1969

Country	Acres	Opium harvest (lbs.)	Yield (lbs. per acre)
India	86,571	1,914,140	22
Iran	2,498	17,147	6
Pakistan	2,856	17,108	6
Turkey	31,940	257,887	8

SOURCE: "Statistics on Narcotic Drugs for 1969," International Narcotics Control Board (New York: United Nations, 1970), p. viii. Data are given in hectares in the original table. One hectare=2.471 acres. In the transformation into acres, figures have been rounded off to the nearest whole numbers.

content varies from 4 to 12 per cent. Prices to farmers for raw opium are presented in Table 4–3. Because of its quality, the prices for Turkish opium are the highest, with the exception of the Iranian price, which is supported by the government in order to discourage diversion to illicit traders. The licit prices are determined by the world market price: the price at which the national opium monopolies can sell to pharmaceutical companies. In Turkey, the illicit price varies with the yield of the current year's harvest, the season, enforcement efforts, and the demand for Turkish opium from other countries, particularly Iran. The illicit price in Iran is extremely high because of the strict enforcement of laws against illicit trading.

TABLE 4–3
PRICES TO FARMER FOR RAW OPIUM

Producing country	U.S. $ per kilogram	
	Licit	Illicit
Turkey	$11	$25
Pakistan	10	12–15
India	10	—
Burma/Laos	—	12
Iran	50–60*	300–400

* Iranian government support price, set to discourage illicit trading.

SOURCE: BNDD Intelligence Staff, *The World Opium Situation,* unpublished paper, p. 7.

The absolute income per farm from opium cultivation is greatest in Turkey, but the percentage of total farm income accounted for by opium increases as one moves eastward. In the late 1960's, there were an estimated 70,000 farms producing opium in Turkey. If 120 tons are sold by these farms at the licit price of $11 per kilo (1 kilo = 2.2046 pounds) and 100 tons on the illicit market at $25 per kilo, the gross income from opium amounts to $3,820,000, or $55 per farm. This amounts to roughly 5–10 per cent of farm income in Turkey. In India, roughly 200,000 farms earn $70–75 from poppy cultivation, or 15–20 per cent of average total income per farm. Since the income figures include income-in-kind (food, clothing produced on farm), the income from opium provides an even higher percentage of cash income than we have indicated. Opium is probably the principal source of farm income in Burma, Laos, and Thailand; cultivation is said to be concentrated in areas controlled by guerrilla insurgents, who transport much of the output to Hong Kong and use the proceeds for arms purchases.[15]

Licit production of opium is of minor importance even in India and Turkey. India earned roughly $6–7 million for exports of 530 metric tons in 1968, compared with total export earnings of $2 billion. Indian farmers earned approximately $7.7 million on production of 700 metric tons. Turkish exports of 120 metric tons yield approximately $1.7 million, less than 0.3 per cent of total exports. Turkish production is also very small in relation to national income of $9 billion. On the other hand, opium sales are undoubtedly of great economic importance to the producing regions of Burma, Laos, and Thailand.

POLICY OPTIONS: WHAT CAN BE DONE

Policies designed to attack the heroin problem at the source of supply devolve into two basic alternatives: (1) the purchase of entire opium crops, or (2) direct controls on production. Each of these proposals has problems difficult to surmount at present.

PRE-EMPTIVE BUYING

The first alternative would be for the United States to purchase the total output of opium from those countries that supply the heroin entering its borders. The administrative simplicity of this proposal makes it appear deceptively attractive. In time, however, pre-emptive buying would necessarily involve purchases of both licit and illicit production in all countries where opium is currently grown. The U.S. offer price would have to be raised above the maximum price illicit traders are willing to pay; otherwise, the farmer would have an incentive to sell to the higher bidder. If the offer price is less than the illicit price, leakages into the illicit market would probably result, and the policy would therefore have little effect on the supply of opiates sent to the United States, especially since the amount is so small relative to total world production. And, seemingly, the illicit trader would be willing to increase his offer price substantially, because, given the large markups at each stage of the distribution system, the price of raw opium has relatively little effect on the ultimate retail price in the United States (see Table 4–4). (For example, if the current price to the farmer for 10 kilos of illicit opium is $250, and the retail street price for 1 kilo of heroin is $264,900, then raising the farm price 100 per cent would raise the retail price only .09 per cent.)

A pre-emptive buying policy would become very costly, because opium producers would have a clear incentive to increase their outputs, and other farmers would have a similar incentive to begin substituting opium for other crops. Eugene Rossides, Assistant Secretary of the Treasury for Enforcement and Operations, has gone on record as strongly opposing any concept of pre-emptive buying. He told a congressional committee that "it would simply stimulate production and it would take away the responsibility of each nation to handle the problem as part of the international community."[16]

Moreover, without strict administrative controls, this policy would not only increase production in all countries currently producing opium but might induce other countries whose climate is suitable to begin production in the hope of sharing in the windfall.

If this policy were directed at only one source of supply, such as Turkey, it would not prevent traders from obtaining illicit supplies in other producing countries. The 100,000–120,000 pounds of opium used by the U.S. market could be grown in an area of, at most, 11.2–23.2 square miles and thus could easily be absorbed in another producing region.[17] In fact, some experts believe that 35 pounds of opium could be produced on a single acre of land if a capital-intensive process were employed under controlled circumstances. If this proved true generally, only 4.5–5.4 square miles would be needed to supply the entire U.S. market. Consequently, a pre-emptive buying policy, in the long run, could result in a change of location for the source of U.S. supply with little or no effect on the addiction problem.

Pre-emptive buying within an individual country might prove

effective in dealing with an internal addiction problem if coupled with strict limitations on acreage and illicit importation. Iran, for example, has discouraged export to illicit markets in other countries by purchasing its entire internal opium crop at a very high price, restricting production to certain designated areas, and strictly enforcing its laws against illicit markets. The legal opium purchased by the government is used by the state-run addict-maintenance program, in which 50,000 individuals are registered. The potential expense is one problem with the high-support-price approach. If nearly all Iran's 300,000–400,000 users and addicts entered the program, the cost would rise dramatically. Furthermore, even with severe penalties against smuggling and illicit trading, Iran still experiences difficulty in trying to prevent the importation of opiates. Some success has been reported in eliminating illicit supplies from Turkey, but imports from Afghanistan and Pakistan have not been halted. The mid-1970 price in Iran for Afghani opium was well below the licit price, despite intensive law-enforcement efforts. It seems that the heavily armed mountain tribes operating out of both Afghanistan and Pakistan have not as yet been deterred by either the border authorities or the death penalty on smuggling. On the other hand, the price of illicit Turkish opium in 1970 was as high as $400 per kilo in Tehran—six to seven times the government support price.

As the Iranian example shows, the success of a pre-emptive buying policy, even if accompanied by administrative controls, depends on whether government can effectively exert its will over the producing regions. In fact, most of the world's opium supply is produced in areas where little political control exists. Administrative controls themselves are difficult to enforce, as we shall see. Therefore, because of the size of the world market relative to U.S. heroin consumption, the high elasticity of supply, and the difficulty of control, it is unlikely that a policy of pre-emptive buying could be successful.

DIRECT CONTROLS

The application of administrative controls alone is the other basic alternative to reduce opium supplies. This involves restricting the acreage on which opium can be grown and maintaining a low official price. A low official price may reduce the illicit price, at least in the short run, and thereby discourage illegal planting and crop diversion. Certainly, taken by itself, a low official price will not induce new production. But the most salient feature of direct controls is increasing the risks of illicit trading and consequently reducing the profitability.

Practically, however, continuous enforcement of direct controls is both difficult and costly, and the necessary resources available to most producing countries are quite limited. Especially in countries with weak central governments, controls present severe administrative problems. All countries with an illicit trade lack adequate numbers of both trained law-enforcement personnel and motor vehicles. Given the low wages in public-service jobs and the large profits in the opium trade, corruption of government and police officials is a widespread problem in most countries and is likely to continue. The bribes that illegal importers are willing and able to pay are considerably higher than the amounts officials are currently accepting for inaction or nonenforcement of the law. Widespread social acceptance of opium use in many rural areas of Pakistan, Afghanistan, India, Burma, Laos, and Thailand is another difficulty that makes enforcement of controls for the benefit of an outside country appear especially burdensome. In Turkey, where there is reportedly little opium use, controls have been extremely unpopular because of both the loss of an important source of farm income and the rising anti-American sentiment. While limitations on local financial resources could presumably be eased by American aid, the administrative and political difficulties severely limit the possibility of successful controls.

If, however, the desire and resources to do so were present, controls could probably be applied successfully in certain individual countries. Communist China and Iran successfully eliminated production in the 1950's. Turkey has restricted legal acreage of poppy cultivation to 29,652 acres from 103,782 acres in 1960. In the process, illegal production may have been somewhat reduced, because illicit Turkish opium is believed to come principally from larger than declared yields on legal acreage.[18] Turkish officials seem committed to their pledge to enforce a ban on all poppy cultivation by the fall of 1972. The chances of this policy's success will be discussed later.

The major problem in curtailing opium production is that most of the world's supply is produced in areas where no national control exists. The lack of control is virtually complete in the producing regions of Burma, Laos, and Thailand. Areas that are largely controlled by tribal groups are responsible for opium production and distribution in Pakistan and Afghanistan. Therefore, it seems likely that attempts to control or abolish opium production in Turkey would have little effect, as illicit traders turned to these areas for supplies. Indeed, the recent changes in Turkey do not seem to have caused any decrease in total U.S. imports of illegal opiates.

Still another difficulty is that of restricting opium production in one country when neighboring countries do not, or cannot, restrict production. After twelve years of prohibition, Iran returned to limited production, because its addicts were purchasing illicit opium from Turkey, Pakistan, and Afghanistan.

Even in Turkey and India, control systems have failed to halt the cultivation of illicit opium. Turkish farmers make written declarations to the government of their licensed acreage and expected kilogram yields, selling the surplus to the illicit market. In 1969, for example, Turkish officials collected 116 tons of licit opium from poppies in eleven provinces. But in 1970, when nine provinces were allowed to produce, only 60 tons were turned in. Presumably diversion accounts for some of the difference. Some illicit production in Turkey has occurred from unlicensed acreage, but this is relatively easy to discover if sufficient efforts are made, since the poppies have a long growing season and are easy to detect, especially from the air. In India, on the other hand, the illicit opium output is produced principally on unlicensed acreage.

Direct controls might be more effective if they were combined with crop substitution, subsidies for production of other goods, or direct payments for not growing poppies. But crop substitution is unlikely to be successful, since it is difficult, if not impossible, to find crops that yield as high a return per unit of land as opium. For example, attempts to substitute a high-yielding Mexican wheat in Pakistan failed because the crop provided a return per acre roughly half that of opium, assuming opium is sold at official prices.[19]

In Turkey, there has been a sound agricultural reason that crop substitution is difficult. Apart from low-income-producing grains, the poppy is the only autumn-sown crop and is not easily replaceable by the higher-yielding spring crops, such as cotton, maize, sugar beets, tobacco, or melons. The opium produced is important to the small farmer, not only because of the amount of income gained, but also because it is harvested before the grain and therefore provides expense money for the main harvest. Furthermore, the harvest of opium occurs in a period when the farmer has little else to do and can spend his time on the lancing of the poppies and collection of the opium.

Subsidies for production of alternative crops would certainly be required if the substitute crops provided less income than opium. The cost of producing a unit of a substitute crop would be reduced by a subsidy, and the transfer payment from the government would allow the grower to increase production and, in the process, bid resources, land, and labor away from other crops, including opium. Because these inputs would become more expensive, the cost per unit of producing opium would increase.

However, if demand for opium in this particular national black market is relatively insensitive to changes in price, opium production would be little reduced, and little reduction in farmer income would result. A higher subsidy would be necessary to raise the relative return on the alternative crop. If the demand for opium varies with price,[20] perhaps because of the availability of opium from other sources or synthetic opiates, then the subsidy would probably reduce much of the country's production.

Clearly, subsidies for output of other goods could be set high enough so that the output of opium in a given country could be greatly reduced. This may come, however, only at great expense to the government or to the United States, if the latter sponsors the program. The same types of administrative problems that exist in the crop-purchase proposal are repeated here.

Basically, it may be difficult to determine how much of the production of the subsidized crop is actually land diverted from opium.

Similar administrative problems would result if governments made payments to producers for not growing opium, since it would be difficult to determine how many farmers who do not grow opium now would demand payment. In 1972, when Turkey's complete prohibition on poppy cultivation goes into effect, the government plans to pay farmers on the basis of the value on the international market of their whole opium crop sold the previous year to state officials. But, if only those who were originally "licensed" to produce are given payments, and no payments go to those who planted illegal acreage, there is no incentive for these growers to cease producing opium, nor is there an incentive for nongrowers to resist the urge to produce. Furthermore, to be effective, payments must exceed the return on output sold illegally. Since the illicit price of opium is extremely low relative to the retail price of heroin in the United States, it could rise greatly without much effect on the final price to the addict. Therefore, payments would have to be extremely high to be effective and would make the program very costly. Thus, it also seems unlikely that a policy of direct controls on opium production, even if combined with crop substitution, subsidies for production of other goods, or direct payments for not growing opium, could be completely successful.

General economic development in poppy-growing areas may eventually reduce the relative profitability of this crop. The usual process is for technological innovations in agriculture to increase the productivity of farms to the point where large surpluses of labor develop. Migration of labor to the cities occurs because of the availability of employment and public services. As industrial development increases the demand for labor, real wages rise, and capital-intensive production processes become more desirable. If no capital-intensive method of cultivating opium can be found, then the return on poppy falls relative to other goods and opium cultivation is greatly reduced. Clearly, this ignores changes in the demand for opium; moreover, it is, at best, a long-run solution. This situation may eventually develop in Turkey but is not likely for a very long time in the East.

DISTRIBUTION

Several books and articles have described the system by which opium is transformed into heroin and imported into the United States. They are all in substantial agreement, possibly because the primary source of information on the subject is the Bureau of Narcotics and Dangerous Drugs.

In the case of Turkish opium, growers either withhold part of their output or plant illegal acreage. Small-scale entrepreneurs gather opium from the farms in relatively small quantities and deliver it to syndicates in or near Istanbul. At this point, the opium is transformed into morphine, which cuts the volume by 90 per cent. This process formerly took place in Syria, but, as relations between Syria and Turkey have deteriorated in recent years, border controls have been tightened and the morphine labs moved to the Istanbul area. From Istanbul, the morphine is transported overland through Bulgaria and Yugoslavia or by ship to its destination in southern France, where covert laboratories refine the morphine into heroin. (One theory is that some of the heroin labs are located in trucks and are thus mobile and difficult to detect.) Once refined, the heroin is smuggled to the United States through New York, Montreal, or some other large port. According to some sources, shipments are also being sent to the U.S. via South America through a Southern port.

MARKET STRUCTURE

The best available outline of the domestic heroin distribution system, at least for New York City, was developed by Mark Moore of the Hudson Institute,[21] who obtained much of his information, in turn, from the Bureau of Narcotics and Dangerous Drugs. It has been further developed by John Casey and Edward Preble.[22]

Moore suggests that heroin passes through six levels of distribution: the importer, the kilo-connection, the connection, the weight dealer, the street dealer, and, finally, the juggler or pusher. Table 4–4 shows the outline of the system and includes estimates of the prices and value added to the heroin at each level. Before reviewing the operation of the specific segments of the system, it

TABLE 4–4

I.	Wholesale value of "kilo" of heroin at first sale=	5,000
	Maximum retail value of "kilo" (assumed 80% pure) =	400,000*
	*Maximum retail value= ($5.00/bag)	1 "kilo"
	(.8 kg. pure/"kilo")	$(10 \times 10^{-6}$ pure/bag)
II.	Importer pays	5,000
	sells to kilo connection @ $15,000/kilo=	15,000
	value added	10,000 or 200%
	kilo connection pays	15,000
	cuts 1:1	
	sells 2 kilos to connections @ $20,000=	40,000
	value added	25,000 or 167%
	2[a] connections pay	40,000
	cut 1:1	
	sell 2 kilos to weight dealer @ $700/ounce	
	$\times$ 35.3 ounces=	98,800
	24,700	
	value added	58,800 or 147%
	4 weight dealers pay	98,800
	cut 1:1	
	sell 2 kilos @ $600/ounce	
	$\times$ 38 "short"[b] ounces	182,400
	22,800	
	value added	83,600 or 84%
	8.5[c] street dealers pay	182,400
	cut 1:½	
	consume 25% or .38 kilos[d]	
	sell 75% or 1.12 kilos @ 22,900/kilo=	219,300
	50% to jugglers (.75)	
	25% to consumers (.38)	
	value added	36,900
		+ 25% consumption
	6.4 jugglers pay	146,200
	no cuts	
	consume ⅓	
	sell ⅔ @ 30,900=	130,600
	value added	− 15,600
		+ 33% consumed

[a] A simplifying assumption on this chart is that all levels of distribution deal in quantities of one kilo. This helps us keep track of the dilution process independent of the price increases. At each level, a unit of heroin is diluted with quinine, milk, sugar, mannite, or other adulterants, which makes it possible for two units to be sold to the next level. Thus, whenever a kilo is "cut" 1:1, there will be two kilo lot dealers at the next level for every one at the previous level. The total "value added" at each level includes sales by all kilo lot dealers who can be supplied at that level by the one kilo of 80 per

is important to discuss the over-all market structure of the business. The key questions here are: How tight is vertical organization? How competitive is the system at the various levels? How much increase in risk would be required to make it unprofitable for large operators to stay in business?

For many years, conventional wisdom held that the heroin business was monopolized by organized crime, perhaps by the Mafia. BNDD now seems to believe, probably as a result of recent arrests of South Americans at relatively high levels, that 10 or 12

---

cent pure that we started with. Thus, the total sale at each level is the product of the dollar value of a kilo lot sale (cut and sold) and the number of kilo lot dealers. For example, each connection, assumed to be dealing in kilo lots, sells two kilos for $24,700 after cutting and marking up the price. Because two connections dealing in kilo lots can be supplied by the original kilo (80 per cent pure), the total sales at this level = (two connections) (two kilos sold by each) ($24,700—the new price of an adulterated kilo). The assumption will not be made when we estimate the number of dealers at each distribution level.

b There is much evidence that "short" ounces frequently appear in the marketing system and that this is an accepted practice—within ambiguous limits. It is likely, however, that it is most prevalent at the last stage before the heroin gets to the street. This is the last opportunity for some significant market power to be exploited and also a difficult place to weigh carefully the amount of heroin purchased. About 3 short ounces are added to account for some extra profit at this level. This represents less than a 10% reduction in the quantity of material supplied as an "ounce." These few short ounces were also necessary to get the kilo of heroin divided into 80,000 bags to be consistent with our estimate of 10 milligrams/bag, 80 per cent original kilo, and the simple dilution process described. It would be possible to devise a more complete dilution process that yielded the 80,000 bags with 10 milligrams/bag without "short ounces," but it is more realistic to keep the dilution process simple (since complex weighing would be a significant technological problem for the distribution system) and admit the presence of "short ounces" (which is a well-known phenomenon).

c The extra .5 street dealers is derived from the weight dealer's adding 3 extra ounces. The total ounces supplied by weight dealers from the original kilo are 4×2×38=304 ounces. If we stick to our assumption of one kilo lot deals, then there must be 304 ounce/35.3 ounces/kilo, or about 8.5 street dealers in business.

d Consumption estimates here imply that out of 12.75 kilos of heroin available after last dilution, street dealers consume about 3.23 kilos (.38×8.5), or about 25 per cent, and jugglers consume 2.8 kilos (⅓×6.4), or about 22 per cent. Together they consume 6.03, or 47 per cent, of heroin. This is consistent with the estimate of 46.5 per cent of heroin consumed by those in trade.

SOURCE: Mark Moore, *Policy Concerning Drug Abuse in New York State, Vol. III: Economics of Heroin Distribution* (Croton-on-Hudson, N.Y.: The Hudson Institute, 1970), pp. 69–71.

large wholesalers with varying degrees of connection to organized crime now control the distribution process in the United States.

It seems clear that many economic principles operating in society at large must also apply to illegal enterprises,[23] since the business of supply and distribution of illicit drugs is presumably subject to the same general economic laws, and responds to the same general set of incentives, as prevail in more open industries. There are, of course, some crucial differences caused by the fact of illegality and also by the moral problems associated with dealing in many of these drugs—for example, the need to minimize the risk of detection of the origin of the distribution system.

The Hudson monograph argues that the objective of the industry is to maximize profits within the constraint of the risk of arrest and imprisonment, and that this objective is most likely to be attained if the industry is organized into several small distribution units separated vertically from one another, if higher levels in the system are monopolized, and if lower levels are competitive with some elements of market power (monopolistic competition). The small distribution units in the heroin industry are separated from one another by restricting information at one level about the identity and activities of other levels. Risks are limited by close supervision and discipline of employees, thus reducing the probability of information leaks, and by the fact that penetration of one level will not result in penetration of another. The primary disadvantage of small, separate distribution units is their inability to adjust to large changes in demand; suppliers end up with either excessive or deficient inventories.

Moore argues that a monopoly could most efficiently perform the functions required of the high levels in the distribution network. The top levels in the system must: (1) restrict the total supply of heroin to maintain high market prices, (2) regularly and reliably supply an amount of heroin fairly close to the realized demand, (3) manipulate supply conditions above them with a minimum of explicit planning and negotiation, and (4) adjust to errors in supply with a minimum of negotiation and activity. A centralized organization would be more effective in handling each of these problems. A monopolist can restrict the total supply, allowing high prices throughout the system. In addition, he is in a position to have an efficient ordering policy, thus successfully accommodating uneven deliveries and lead time. Agents can be coerced into holding inventories or resupplied when short of heroin. Tight control can be maintained over the circulation of information. Finally, a monopolist can maintain a monopoly position in relation to producers, thus reducing lead times, unevenness, and quality deterioration.

In contrast, a competitive market would be less likely to ensure a smooth, restricted supply, adjusting to errors in a discreet, efficient manner. In a more competitive situation, it is more difficult to pool shipments or parcel out uneven deliveries of heroin. With many suppliers at the top, there are more transactions, more explicit negotiations, more occasions of short supply or large inventories, more information circulating freely—and thus a greater probability of arrest. A monopoly, therefore, is logically the most efficient type of organizational structure at high levels.

But a successful monopoly requires the existence of some type of leverage or barrier to entry, such as (1) special knowledge unavailable to others, (2) total control over some vital raw material, or (3) total control over the market as to make the cost of entry prohibitive, especially if entry requires a large fixed investment. It is doubtful that any of these considerations applies to the heroin traffic. The knowledge required to refine opium into heroin is certainly not difficult to acquire. It is also doubtful that the knowledge of methods of conducting illegal activities—such as smuggling—is so limited as to allow any firm to maintain a monopoly. There are no substantial fixed costs other than the investment in an information system, needed to offset the high level of risk in the trade. However, the difficulty, and thus the cost, of developing such an information network may be a formidable barrier to entry.

Trusted personal relationships with Turkish or French syndicates may have put some organizations in a monopoly position for Turkish opium. However, it would be in the interest of the Turkish or French firms to sell to as many importers as possible, forcing them to bid against each other and thus raise the price of heroin. A firm desiring to enter the business should, therefore, be able to establish the necessary connections.

It is possible, of course, that the suppliers are not profit maximizers; they may not wish to accept increased risks for the sake of increased profits. Instead, after establishing an acceptably low level of risk, they may seek to maximize profits within this constraint. Such an approach would sacrifice many of the benefits of competition among buyers because of the need to limit the number of people who know the supplier's identity. (This factor also operates as a barrier to entry at other high levels of the distribution system.) If the barriers to entry in the market for Turkish opium are too great, however, a potential importer could go to Hong Kong, Bangkok, Karachi, or Saigon.

Finally, as noted, trying to erect a barrier to entry by attempting to control the raw material does not seem feasible. The U.S. market relative to total world production is simply too small to prevent other supplies from becoming available. Also, the retail product is homogeneous and easily divisible, making it difficult to hoard.

However, for an illegal business, there are additional techniques of monopolization. Violence is the most likely method of securing market control; illegal operators can readily hire agents or firms willing to kill quietly and efficiently. If a heroin-distribution monopoly became established early and acquired both a large organization and a sophisticated information system, it could make it extremely dangerous for a rival to compete. First of all, it might have the key advantage of knowing who is trying to enter the business before its own prior presence can be discovered. Since rivals would find it difficult to purchase a comparable intelligence service secretly, this acts as an important barrier to entry. Another way of enforcing monopoly of an illegal product is to control the use of legal force—corrupting police officials to serve one's own ends. An effective use of corrupt police would be to have one's rivals eliminated via arrest; sufficient arrests would satisfy the public and allow the police to refrain from attacking the monopoly itself. It is in the interest of the police, in turn, to eliminate competition, protecting the source of their payoff money while appearing to be effective law enforcers. The symbiosis between criminal enterprise and elements in law enforcement is well known and has occupied many investigatory commissions without being eliminated.[24]

A firm could also obtain police cooperation without police corruption. If one organization has better intelligence than any other, and better intelligence than the police, it could simply inform the police of the competing ring and possibly provide the evidence necessary to break it up.

The BNDD believes that 10 or 12 large wholesale operations exist in the United States today. Thus, the potential barriers to entry have apparently not been strong enough to allow any one firm to enforce a monopoly. The system has probably developed into an oligopoly or cartel, with each firm maintaining a type of monopoly control of firms below it in the lower distribution levels. It is not clear what agreements, if any, exist among these firms with respect to prices or market areas, but the risk of detection may limit the mobility of distributors between top-level suppliers, thus allowing firms at the top to maintain vertically integrated supply systems.

At lower levels in the system, there are many competitive suppliers, strict monopoly being impossible because of the difficulty of disciplining customers. At these levels, most customers are addicts who are highly motivated to maintain relations with as many suppliers as possible. Low-level suppliers are arrested much more frequently than those in higher levels, because they deal more often and more openly. Thus, relationships between consumers and suppliers are constantly breaking up and beginning again. Furthermore, addicts are always trying to break into the lower levels of the system, and, given the small amount of trust, skill, and capital needed, personnel and organizations change rapidly.

Nevertheless, some elements of monolopy control remain. Information is often unavailable to consumers, thus restricting the number of markets in which they can buy. Also, addicts find it useful to restrict their purchases to dealers who consistently provide a high-quality product and who give them lower prices as loyal and trusted clients. Thus, limited information and product differentiation maintain elements of monopoly advantage even for suppliers at low levels.

Costs and Profits

Existing analysis of the economics of each segment of the heroin industry is fragmentary because of the nature of the business. The best available analysis is again that of Moore, and most of the comments in this section are derived from his model of the system.

For the importer and kilo-connection at the higher levels of the distribution system, the operating costs—principally wages and inventory finance costs—are estimated to be a much greater percentage of value added than at lower levels (50–55 per cent versus 30 per cent). Importers need skilled employees for the smuggling process and periodically require large amounts of capital to finance transactions with producers and processors. Kilo-connections have relatively large wage costs because of the elaborate organization needed for exchanges and maintaining inventories as well as disciplining lower-level suppliers. Financing costs are also high at this level because of the need to store inventories for uncertain periods of time.

Operating and finance costs are more moderate for connections. Although they need to employ agents to develop new markets, discipline customers, dilute heroin, and make deliveries, there is a much faster turnover of inventories at this level. The rate of turnover minimizes financing, but connections may be forced to accept it from sources higher in the organization. Weight dealers, street dealers, and jugglers are, for the most part, self-employed; inventories are turned over quickly, and individuals at these levels rarely have financing problems.

In contrast to operating costs, expenditures for bribes as a per cent of value added appear to increase as one moves from high to low levels (2 per cent versus 5 per cent). At the importer and kilo-connection levels, well-placed bribes can secure considerable immunities at relatively low costs. Expenses for bribery increase at the connection level, because they are more vulnerable to arrest, engaging in a relatively more visible activity. They must also frequently make payments to other criminal organizations for "protection." Weight dealers, street dealers, and jugglers become even more vulnerable to extortion and will also have to pay rather large bribes (as a per cent of value added) to law-enforcement agencies.

Profits are great at each level of the distribution network but decrease as a per cent of value added at lower levels of distribution. Gross profits include (1) a financial return equal to what could be made in the firm's next best alternative line of business (its opportunity cost), (2) a return to compensate for the risk of arrest and incarceration, and (3) a return to monopoly power.

The kilo-connection at the top level of distribution is probably the single most powerful component in the system. At this level, gross profits are high and are maintained by a large degree of monopoly power. Economic theory suggests that the firm's profits must be at least as high as the return from other attractive illegal opportunities, such as loansharking or gambling. While risk—the probability of arrest—is relatively low, the combination of monopoly power and high opportunity costs makes profits at this level high. For the importer, profits are probably less than those of kilo-connections. His risks are low, because, being high on the ladder, he is difficulty to identify. Opportunity costs are low, because, with the substantial investment in building his information network, an importer can make more money dealing in heroin than he could make elsewhere. Some monopoly power exists because the personal-relations network operates as a barrier to entry, but this is probably limited by the encouragement by kilo-connections of free-lance importers.

Gross profits of connections are less than those of the two upper levels. The restricted access to information about operations allows some degree of monopolization, but risks become greater as visibility increases and the police become more successful at arrest and conviction. At this level, opportunity costs are low because of the large investment in personal relations, which are not valuable unless the connection is engaged in the heroin trade. Connections can accept lower profits, and still find the business more profitable than alternatives.

The remaining levels are characterized by relatively high risk and low opportunity costs. All three levels of operation are relatively visible, have relatively high arrest rates, and thus require adequate compensation for risks incurred. On the other hand, opportunity costs are low because few operators on this level have the skills required in other types of enterprise. At the weight-dealer level, a small degree of monopoly is maintained, because access to information is limited. At the street-dealer and juggler levels, monopoly profits are minimal.

Analyzing operating costs and profits at each stage of heroin distribution carries important implications for law-enforcement policy. In summary, if a firm's costs are high, and it has little monopoly power or attractive income-producing alternatives, it may be quite easy to increase the risk enough so that the firm leaves the industry. If these conditions do not hold—if profits are high and protected by monopoly, or if few good alternative profit opportunities exist—the firm might well absorb the cost of the increased risk. These factors largely determine the outcome of possible law-enforcement strategies.

EFFECTS OF POLICE PRESSURE

Increased police pressure on the distribution system can clearly increase the risks and operating costs of those involved. Evidence does not show, however, that any one firm is large enough or monopolistic enough so that its destruction or neutralization would have an important impact on the total distribution system and thus on heroin use at the street level. During the last few years, the arrest of even major distributors and traffickers has had no significant impact on the price or availability of heroin. On the international level, for instance, in the first six months of 1971, BNDD participated in the arrest of 113 major traffickers outside the United States, seizing large quantities of drugs in the process. Federal officials face an almost impossible task of trying to stop the smuggling of drugs at the border. About 250 million people enter the country every year. Approximately 65 million cars and trucks, 306,000 planes, and 157,000 ships entered in 1970.[25] If this were not enough, customs officials state that, on an average-size ship arriving at the Port of New York, there are 30,000 places where heroin can be hidden. Domestically, the situation is not much different. A study of the undercover unit of the New York City police narcotics division revealed that, in 1970, agents made 7,266 buys of narcotics that resulted in 4,007 arrests. However, only 4.97 pounds of highly adulterated heroin were seized in these actions, at a total cost of $91,197, and with no appreciable effect on heroin distribution citywide.

In such a situation, law enforcement must rely on the indirect effects of general deterrence rather than on direct disruption. But it is far from clear how firms operating in the field regard a successful attack on another firm. Possibly, such an attack will cause them to reassess their own risks and assume that they are in greater danger than they believed before. On the other hand, it may be that existing firms will simply assume that the destroyed operation was incompetent or lacking in security and see no need to reassess their own risk.

To the extent that police are successful in increasing a distributor's probability of arrest, one would expect the chain to lengthen as each supplier attempts to deal with fewer buyers and places more distance between himself and the street. Suppliers would invest more time and absorb greater operating costs in designing more complex delivery systems to better conceal their activities. The risk involved in holding inventories would cause suppliers to hold less in reserve, thus increasing the time and complications involved in arranging purchases and sales. However, police pressure might also increase a monopoly's hold on the system. A monopoly can absorb the increased risks more easily and is also likely to be better protected. Markets might become even more centralized. Because of higher costs and lack of competition, prices could be expected to rise.

For all these reasons, it seems clear that law enforcement can raise the price of heroin. The effects of higher prices, and thus the ultimate impact of law enforcement, are uncertain. They depend heavily on how total demand reacts to the changes.

One hypothesis is that demand is inelastic, that an addict is dependent on heroin and will try to maintain his level of consumption regardless of price. If this is so, then law-enforcement policy will have little effect. The added costs of greater risks will be shifted to consumers, and the revenues of the industry will increase. So will the social costs of the activities addicts engage in to support the habit. (A logical question is why firms are not already maximizing profits—that is, if prices and revenues could be raised before the increased cost was incurred, why did this not, in fact, take place? This may be due to concern with public reaction. Higher heroin prices cause higher crime rates, which increase the public's demand for strong policy measures against the heroin traffic. Therefore, firms may attempt to maximize profits, given the constraint of maintaining a low level of risk. This calls for keeping prices low enough so that the crime needed to support it remains "tolerable." Competition might also play a part.)

A second theory is that demand is elastic, that a price rise does cause a disproportionate decrease in consumption. If so, then the suppliers would have to absorb the increased cost of higher risks or raise the price and accept a decline in total revenues.

While it is commonly believed that the addictive nature of heroin causes the demand for it to be inelastic, it might, in fact, be elastic, for two reasons: First, the development of methadone during the past few years has created a low-cost alternative for addicts that did not exist before. Secondly, over the last thirty years there has been a substantial long-term rise in the price of heroin relative to the price of other consumer goods. This may have produced a situation in which most addicts are maintaining their habit at the highest price level they are able to support. If the price increased further, these addicts would have no choice except to decrease the quantity of heroin used, because they would be unable to raise their income enough to meet the new cost.

If the demand is elastic, a law-enforcement policy could be effective. If the price of heroin increased and methadone was necessarily substituted, the social costs of addiction, including crime, would decrease. If addicts chose to adapt by using less heroin for the same cost, however, the crime costs would not be decreased. It could be argued, on the other hand, that increasing the cost of being an addict hastens the time when the addict voluntarily leaves the addicted life.

The firm attempting to maximize profits, subject to the constraint of maintaining a low level of risk, may choose to absorb the risk as increased operating costs rather than attempt to shift it to the consumers. This, of course, results in a lower rate of return and reduces the attractiveness of heroin distribution. In the heroin business, the gross profits of a firm (revenues minus operating costs) must be at least equal to the return the firm could earn in an alternative investment (its opportunity cost).

Profits that exceed opportunity costs can be considered a return to a monopoly position or compensation for risk. Gross profits must exceed opportunity costs by at least enough to compensate the firm for the risks it undertakes. If gross profits, less opportunity costs, exceed the compensation required for risk, the firm will stay in the business. Alternatively, if gross profits, less opportunity costs, are less than the return required for undertaking risk, the firm will not be willing to absorb the risk and will leave the industry.

Risk for an illegal firm can be viewed as equal to the probability of punishment, as the firm perceives it, times the cost of certain punishment to that firm. The cost of certain punishment is equal to the amount the firm would be willing to pay to avoid it.[26]

The probability of punishment can be affected by public policy and by the firm's own actions, because it depends on the probability of being apprehended and successfully prosecuted. Changes in the criminal-justice system are essential if high-level distributors are going to be put out of business. These include more sophisticated training of police personnel, higher salaries to lessen the temptation of bribes, and higher budgets for purchasing information. In reality, law-enforcement agencies have been unable to raise the level of risk anywhere near what would be required to make this criminal enterprise unprofitable.

The cost of the expected punishment to the illegal operation can also be influenced by changes in judicial procedures and increases of sentences. Currently, many defendants in narcotics cases forfeit bail, become fugitives, and, if apprehended, are more likely to be tried for violating the conditions of bail than for the original charge. If convicted, this means a lesser sentence. The economic cost in such a case—the amount the offender would pay to avoid detection—should be equal to the amount of bail, plus the probability of being arrested while at large, times the penalty for jumping bail. This cost would be increased if a change in public policy raised the amount of bail or the penalty for violating its conditions.[27]

On the other hand, the probability of punishment can be reduced if the illegal operation spends more on bribes and devising elaborate, less conspicuous pickup and delivery systems. If increased amounts are spent to reduce risks, however, the illegal firms reduce their gross profits at the same time. A firm will expend these sums if in doing so it can keep its gross profits (minus opportunity costs) above the cost of escaping imprisonment. If it is impossible, through further spending, to reduce the expected risk below gross profits, less opportunity costs, firms will leave the business. Alternatively, firms could limit sales to trusted buyers, thereby reducing revenues and gross profits but also reducing the chances of getting caught.

According to Moore's analysis of the distribution hierarchy, gross profits are considerable at every level. However, for the kilo-connection, high-yielding alternatives are the greatest, and it is possible that monopoly at this level could be broken. BNDD appears to believe that the monopoly has already been broken, and that the industry is now operating as an oligopoly with ten or twelve firms. But, conceivably, an oligopoly or cartel could develop techniques for supplying the total market as efficiently as a centralized organization. If satisfactory agreements can be reached, the amount of explicit communication necessary to guarantee avoidance of frequent shortages or surpluses would be minimal. However, the market becomes more unstable with a cartel, because there is always an incentive for one firm to increase its sales at the expense of another. If one firm does try to improve its position, the others are likely to follow. If all try to do so, oversupply develops, attempts to expand the market increase, prices decline, and profits fall. In the process, higher levels of the distribution system become more visible to the authorities, and the probability of punishment increases. A kilo-connection may then find one of his high-yielding alternative opportunities more attractive and leave heroin distribution. Thus, there is always some incentive for the police to attempt to infiltrate the network at higher levels. Arrests made at this level reverberate through the system, making arrests easier at all levels.

It is far from clear, however, that such a public policy is altogether sound. While it could have a high payoff in terms of seizures of heroin and arrests, it would lead to considerable market expansion and increased heroin availability. The elimination of monopoly would permit the entrance of new firms; a competitively organized industry will always provide more goods at lower prices than will a monopoly. Market expansion would occur if lower prices increase the demand for heroin, and, in fact, this may be occurring. Two very large seizures by BNDD in May and June of 1970 reportedly had no effect on price. No panics occurred following the seizures, as one would expect, and the short-term trend over the year was one of declining prices.

Theoretically, the best allocation of police power is at the levels of the distribution hierarchy, where the incremental gains from their actions (in terms of reduced social costs) are equal to the incremental costs of the enforcement efforts. This clearly requires employment of more resources at some levels than at others. While the payoff from attempts to infiltrate higher levels may be large, this policy is also very expensive. And, again, it is possible that such a policy would lead to a larger, less organized trade. Use of police resources at lower levels has less potential for large payoffs but is less costly. It is much easier to interrupt the heroin traffic at the retail level, because firms engage in more transactions, concealment is more difficult, and information is more available.

On the other hand, risks must be increased considerably before it becomes no longer profitable for low-level operators to remain in the industry, because their opportunity costs are low—i.e., they probably could not earn nearly so much doing something else. Police are continually eliminating these low-level operators through arrest, but, given the high profit potential, others still find it worthwhile to enter the business because of their low opportunity costs, mistaken perceptions of the probability of punishment, or the low value placed on being incarcerated for a given period. In addition, most street dealers and pushers are themselves addicts. Being in the business keeps them near the source of supply, giving them an income sufficient to finance their own consumption and enabling them to buy their own drugs wholesale.

Clearly, if heroin demand becomes relatively elastic at some point as prices rise, the police could eventually be successful in eliminating the industry. However, to accomplish this, it is probable that society would have to allocate an extraordinary amount of law-enforcement resources. Society might prefer to reduce the industry to the "optimum" size, where the costs imposed by heroin use are just equal to the additional cost required to reduce it further.

CONSUMPTION

The consumption of heroin imposes costs on the rest of the community, because most purchases are financed through criminal acts such as theft. Because of these involuntary redistributions of existing wealth, the community spends resources to prevent crime and to apprehend, try, punish, and rehabilitate criminals. This includes private expenditures on locks, alarms, lights, and security guards and public expenditures on police, courts, and correctional systems. To the extent that these human and material resources would be employed elsewhere in the absence of heroin addiction, they are properly counted as costs of addiction. Social costs also include the medical expenses and foregone productivity of individuals injured in crimes and the lost productivity, medical expenses, and premature deaths of addicts. Finally, one must also include the fear and anxiety, avoidance of normal activity, disruption of community life, and use of less efficient and more expensive modes of transportation that are unquantifiable but nonetheless very real costs of crime and drug addiction. This section examines the direct cost of heroin consumption and estimates the amount of crime required to finance it.

The most elementary question in determining the direct costs of heroin consumption is the total cost of the heroin consumed— that is, how much money do addicts need to support their addiction? But this calculation depends on several unknowns: the number of addicts, the average number of days per year heroin is consumed, and the average cost of heroin per day, with an adjustment for the amount of heroin "earned" from profits on sales to other addicts.[28] This information is essential for determining the magnitude of the problem and the benefits from any investments designed to control or reduce it.

THE ADDICT POPULATION

The actual number of heroin addicts in the United States is unknown and probably can never be determined precisely with present techniques of estimation. Addicts become known to officials only through death, arrest, or participation in treatment programs. It is difficult to estimate the size of the addict population from the number of deaths or arrests, because each of these figures depends on other variables as well as sum totals. For example, the ratio of addict deaths to addict population will vary not only with the number of addicts but also with the probability that a decedent will be medically identified as an addict. Similarly, the frequency of addict deaths from overdose will vary with sudden changes in the concentration of pure heroin in the local supply. The ratio of addict arrests to number of addicts can vary with the intensity of police efforts in certain areas. The ratio of addicts in treatment to total addicts can vary with the addicts' perception of the value of treatment or the short-term availability of heroin.

Because of these difficulties, most estimates of the addict population are mere guesses. However, there are two methods that may ultimately prove useful, although both have pronounced weaknesses at present. One is the "Baden" formula, developed in New York City by Dr. Michael Baden of the Medical Examiner's Office, and frequently applied elsewhere. New York is unique in having a register of local heroin addicts as reported by medical and police sources. The formula was computed by comparing the number of addicts on the registry to the number of overdose deaths and the number of deaths among persons named on the register.[29] Baden found that 50 per cent of the heroin addicts who die are on the Narcotic Addict Register. On this basis, he estimated that the total addict population numbers about twice the registry total. In 1968, for example, the New York Register had 42,500 addicts listed; it was therefore concluded that the total addict population was approximately 85,000.

This method has several problems, of which its originators were well aware and are quick to acknowledge. They were seeking a way of making a quick estimate of the total population that would be more adequate than the register alone without incurring expenses for research time. (It is ironic that Dr. Baden is sometimes castigated for defects that he was the first to point out.) First, it is assumed that addicts who are on the register have the same probability of dying as those who are not. If registered addicts are heavier users and thus more susceptible to disease, such as malnutrition and hepatitis, they would have a higher probability of dying. On the other hand, if addicts not on the register are less experienced users they may be more likely to die of overdose. Either, both, or neither hypothesis could be correct, and it is impossible to determine the net effect.

Secondly, since the register is cumulative over a five-year period, some on the list will no longer be addicts because of successful treatment, abstinence, or incarceration. To the extent that this is the case, the estimate will exceed the actual total by twice the size of the error in the register.

Third, the probability that an addict is listed on the register is, in part, a function of his age and length of addiction. A thirty-year-old addicted for ten years is more likely to be listed than an eighteen-year-old addicted for one year. A sophisticated application of the technique requires at least an age breakdown, and possibly other distinctions as well. Baden himself works with such distinctions, but others who use the method often do not. Serious difficulties develop when officials attempt to use the Baden formula in other cities or at other points in time. Statistical analysis of one set of circumstances is rarely transferable to different situations. In other words, heroin addicts in different places, for whatever reasons, probably do not die at the same rate. Furthermore, differences in diagnostic method change the probability of a decedent's being identified as an addict. For example, in Washington, D.C., during the eighteen months preceding July, 1970, diagnostic drug screens were performed on only 6.3 per cent of all autopsied deaths; during the last six months of 1970, drug screens were performed on 51 per cent of all autopsied deaths.[30] This frequency can also vary between cities, and a small variance, when using Baden's formula, would change the estimated population greatly, because the number of addicts who die in any given year is likely to be only 1–2 per cent of the total register.[31] And New York has by far the best register of any city.

The Bureau of Narcotics and Dangerous Drugs has developed

a somewhat similar approach in estimating the total addict population. It multiplies the number of known users who could be rearrested by the ratio of total heroin arrests to the number of known users included in these arrests.[32] On the basis of this method, BNDD unofficially estimates that there are at present 315,000 addicts nationally.

This method also has several problems. First, known addicts are voluntarily reported to BNDD by local police departments. Reporting practices can vary considerably with locality, as can intensity of enforcement efforts.

Secondly, the probability of any addict's being arrested in period 2 is assumed to be the same regardless of whether he had been arrested in period 1. This hypothesis is unproved. It may be that addicts already known to the police are heavy users and commit more crimes or are under greater surveillance. Therefore, the probability of their rearrest would be greater, and the estimate of the total addict population would be less than the actual. On the other hand, if the addicts unknown to the police are younger, and therefore more recently addicted, the probability of their arrest may be higher, because younger addicts tend to commit riskier crimes, such as robbery. In this case, the estimate would be too large.[33]

Thirdly, it is difficult to determine the number of addicts reported in period 1 who remain active users and are therefore eligible for arrest during period 2. Statistical adjustments must be made for the probability that a known user will be in jail during period 2, will die, will become abstinent spontaneously, or will be in a treatment program. BNDD has thus far adjusted satisfactorily only for the probability that an addict will be in jail.

Some of the problems involved in these adjustments are shown by the difficulty of estimating the probability of death. BNDD made its adjustments on the average probability that any individual over twenty-five will survive to the next year. But the mortality rate for addicts is undoubtedly higher than that of other individuals of the same age. On the other hand, there may not be many addicts over forty, and thus the mortality rate as originally calculated was biased upward by calculating an average probability for all individuals over twenty-five. Without knowing the true mortality rate, it is difficult to make the proper adjustments to the estimates.

Some addicts do mature out of addiction as they age, but the number is not known. Even active addicts may have weeks or months of abstinence, but again no numbers are available. Work on these problems is going on, and the results will probably reduce the estimate below the present 315,000. However, since reports from various urban areas indicate that the number of addicts is still increasing, we will use alternative estimates of 250,000 and 350,000 for the total addict population.

Some officials make a "best guess" estimate and then attempt to test the reasonableness of the figure by comparing it with the total population. For example, the Narcotic Treatment Agency in Washington, D.C., has a population of 95 per cent black, 85 per cent male, and 85 per cent between the ages of fifteen and thirty-four. Assuming that the addict population not in treatment has the same characteristics, one can make an estimate of the penetration of addiction into the total population with these characteristics. If there are 15,000 addicts in Washington, 10,296 are black males between the ages of fifteen and thirty-four. According to 1970 Census data, there are a total of 83,158 black males between fifteen and thirty-four in Washington, D.C. Thus, 12.1 per cent of this population is addicted under the assumption of 15,000 addicts, and 8.2 per cent is addicted under the assumption of 10,000 addicts. The problem with these projections is that 8.2 per cent and 12.1 per cent seem equally "reasonable." If an estimate approached 25 per cent or 30 per cent of a given population, one would suspect exaggeration. Penetration projections appear to have little value except as very rough assessments.

DAILY EXPENDITURES FOR HEROIN

Addicts vary in the amounts of heroin they consume per day and the per cent of time spent actively using the drug. Some addicts can afford to increase their habits as their tolerance to the drug grows; others cannot. There is also great variance in vulnerability to arrest and incarceration as well as in the frequency of "vacations" from addiction in hospitals or treatment facilities. These periods of treatment also serve to reduce the size of the habit for a time after release. The Hudson Institute study, using interviews with ex-addicts and police, developed a breakdown of the addict population of New York City.[34] From their data, presented in Table 4–5, one can estimate that an average addict is an active user 70 per cent of the time, or 255 days per year per addict.

TABLE 4–5
USE OF HEROIN BY ADDICT CLASS

Class	Size of class	Bags per day on street	Pure heroin per day on street per person	% of year on street	Pure heroin per year per class	% yearly heroin con- sumed
Joy poppers	7,000	.4	4 mg	100	10.2 K	1.3
Small-habit apprentices	14,000	2.0	20 mg	80	81.8 K	8.8
Medium-habit hustlers	16,100	5.0	50 mg	60	176.3 K	19.0
Large-habit hustlers	8,400	9.0	90 mg	55	151.8 K	16.4
Large-habit dealers	7,700	18.0	180 mg	70	354.0 K	38.2
Small-habit dependents	6,300	2.0	20 mg	80	36.8 K	4.0
Women	10,500	5.0	50 mg	60	115.0 K	12.4
TOTALS:	70,000				925.9 K	100.0

Note: This table may contain inaccuracies due to memory error or inaccurate sample size.

SOURCES: Mark Moore, *Policy Concerning Drug Abuse in New York State, Vol. III: Economics of Heroin Distribution* (Croton-on-Hudson, N.Y.: The Hudson Institute, 1970), p. 66.

The frequently quoted estimates of the daily costs of supporting an addiction are often exaggerated. Many are derived from interviews with addicts who regard large habits as status symbols and commonly overstate the level of their own use. In general, the amounts of heroin consumed by addicts vary widely, and reports of these amounts are unreliable. To say that an addict has a $50 habit does not mean that he will spend this sum day after day. Ideally, an addict would like to use as much heroin as he needs to "get high." In fact, however, the increasing difficulty of obtaining the necessary money to pay for increasing dosages imposes an upper limit on most addicts' habits. But if an addict cannot consistently obtain large enough dosages of heroin to get high, he can use smaller amounts without feeling acute withdrawal symptoms. In effect, the habit size of a long-time heavy user is often not at the level of euphoria but only at a level sufficient to suppress withdrawal or to keep the withdrawal mild. Moreover, while there are many addicts with expensive habits, there are also many addicts in the early stages of dependence whose habit requires only $10–15 per day. These factors should be kept in mind when interpreting any estimates of the total cost of addiction.

The price, and quality, of heroin needed by an addict determine his cost per day. Retail prices were obtained by BNDD for December, 1970, for several U.S. cities, and are listed in Table 4–6. The considerable variation in price is probably due to differences in local supply and demand, risks taken by suppliers, and, probably, nonrandom buying procedures. The unweighted average price—except in Chicago, where it is extraordinarily high for unknown reasons—is about $0.55 per milligram.

The average quantity used per day is probably about 55 milligrams of pure heroin.[35] At $0.55 per milligram, this results in daily expenditures of approximately $30 per day for the average addict, representing the amount paid on the street by the addict who buys solely for his own consumption. Some earn their heroin through services rendered as a distributor of heroin—i.e., pusher; thus, the price paid by the ultimate consumer includes the payment for that service. Heroin "earned" in pushing, therefore, means that fewer addicts have to steal from the community, or that some percentage of the addict population supports the rest by theft, prostitution, or legitimate work. The Hudson Institute study estimated that 45 per cent of the heroin consumed is used by those involved in its distribution and profit from its sale. If other factors remain the same, the total social cost of heroin addiction will be less if the percentage of consumed heroin "earned" from pushing is increased.

A rough estimate of the annual cost of heroin purchases can be made using the information presented in the preceding pages. The assumptions are that (1) addicts spend 70 per cent of the

TABLE 4–6
RETAIL PRICES FOR HEROIN AS OF DECEMBER 30, 1970

City	Price per milligram
Boston	$ .53–.84
New York	.31–.67
Philadelphia	.58–1.00
Washington, D.C.	.33
Miami	.60–.90
Chicago	2.34
New Orleans	.57–.63
Dallas	.70–1.05
Houston	.33
Seattle	.16–.29
Los Angeles	.42–.63

SOURCE: BNDD.

year using heroin, (2) 45 per cent of all heroin is earned through pushing, (3) the addict population nationally is estimated at 250,000, and (4) the average cost per day per addict is $30. If these assumptions are reasonably correct, heroin purchases in the United States cost approximately $1,053,937,500 annually. If the addict population is, in fact, 350,000, the annual cost of heroin purchases would rise to $1,475,512,500.

From Table 4–4, using the estimate of the total cost of a kilo of heroin originating from data on the supply side, we can derive a check on the estimate from the demand for heroin. The cost of a kilo of 80 per cent pure heroin is computed as follows:

25% consumed by street dealers	$ 45,600
25% sold to consumers by street dealers	73,100
50% consumed or sold to consumers by jugglers	146,200
TOTAL	$264,900

The cost of a kilo of 100 per cent pure heroin, if sold on the street, would be 25 per cent higher after dilution—$331,125. This figure, divided into the estimate of total annual addict expenditures for heroin ($1,475,512,500), yields an estimated 4,456 kilos of pure heroin in the United States per year, equivalent to 9,984 pounds of pure heroin, or 99,840 pounds of opium. This is approximately the BNDD estimate for total U.S. imports.

SOURCES OF FUNDS FOR HEROIN PURCHASES

The high cost of heroin requires most addicts to resort to crime to finance their habits. Estimates of the various sources of funds for the support of heroin addiction can be made with data obtained by the Hudson Institute from ex-addicts in New York City. As discussed previously, approximately 45 per cent of the heroin consumed by the addict population is obtained by selling heroin. This does not mean that 45 per cent of all addicts are pushers but that 45 per cent of the heroin used by addicts is obtained in exchange for services rendered in the distribution network. The remainder of the addict population finance their own habits and those of pushers by various means, including robbery, burglary, shoplifting, prostitution, and legitimate work. Most addicts employ a combination of means, legal or otherwise, in their constant quest to obtain funds.[36] The breakdown of sources of funds presented in Table 4–7 was developed from the Hudson material.[37] These figures represent the funds used to purchase the 55 per cent of heroin consumed that is not financed by rendering services in the distribution network.

It is assumed that shoplifting, burglary, and larceny yield real property, and that pickpocketing, robbery, and confidence games yield cash. Therefore, the total property stolen in these crimes can be roughly divided into 80 per cent real property and 20 per cent cash.[38] It is assumed that real property is fenced at one-third its value, so that an addict must steal, on the average, property worth $2.60 to obtain $1.00 with which to finance his habit.[39]

TABLE 4–7
ESTIMATES OF SOURCES OF FUNDS

Shoplifting	22.6%
Burglary	19.0
Pickpocketing	5.4
Larceny	7.5
Robbery	3.3
Confidence games	4.6
Prostitution	30.8
Welfare	3.0
Other, legal sources	3.9
TOTAL	100.0%

The data needed to estimate the funds obtained through property crime, prostitution, and legal sources used for heroin purchases can be summarized as follows:

Number of addicts (N)	250,000; 350,000
Per cent of year in active use (T)	70
Average daily expenditure (X)	$30
Per cent of heroin earned through pushing (d)	45
Proportion of funds obtained through property crime (a)	.62
Reciprocal of fencing discount (average) (f)	2.6
Proportion of funds obtained through prostitution (b)	.31
Proportion of funds obtained through legitimate sources (w)	.07

The estimates of funds obtained from each of the three alternative sources of funds are presented in Table 4–8. Clearly, any of these data could be biased in either direction and thus limit the usefulness of the estimates derived from them.

TABLE 4–8

ESTIMATES OF FUNDS OBTAINED BY ADDICTS ANNUALLY FROM PROPERTY CRIME, PROSTITUTION, AND LEGITIMATE SOURCES[40]

	N = 250,000	N = 350,000
Property crime (net income)	$ 653,441,250	$ 914,817,750
Cost to victims	1,698,947,250	2,379,426,150
Prostitution	326,720,625	457,408,875
Legal activity	73,775,625	103,285,875

CONCLUSION

The economics of heroin distribution has been examined for whatever assistance such analysis may bring to future policy considerations. Can heroin use be curbed? Can it be eliminated? What are the most efficient methods of attacking the problem?

In the marketing of any product, there are two sides to a transaction—supply and demand. Our examination has shown that public policies dealing with the production of opium and the domestic distribution of heroin—the supply side—will never be completely successful in eliminating heroin use in the United States and the consequent street crime. Indeed, past reliance on law-enforcement measures has accompanied an epidemic growth of the heroin-addict population. It is ironic that our national policy, by resorting almost exclusively to criminal sanctions to eliminate addiction, has bred a thriving illegal market that can be sustained only by criminal activity.

Two factors primarily impede public policy designed to suppress the supply of heroin. First, the amount of opium needed to supply the demand for heroin in the United States is only a minute portion of total world production. It is probably impossible to curb all opium production, licit and illicit, everywhere in the world. Secondly, the profits earned in domestic distribution are so great that it is unlikely the risks can be raised high enough to force dealers out of business. As one former distributor has stated: "If you put me away, somebody else is going to stand in my spot."[41]

Clearly, more effort and greater resources must be spent to curb the demand for heroin. For example, more addicts must be treated and rehabilitated. Education to prevent drug abuse must be expanded and made more meaningful. Finally, the environmental factors that breed and sustain addiction must be more successfully attacked. John Ingersoll, Director of the Bureau of Narcotics and Dangerous Drugs, has stated before a congressional committee that law enforcement

> . . . is the first-aid agency of society. It is not the curative, not the doctor, and it doesn't eliminate causes of these problems. Our society has gotten itself into an unfortunate state of affairs regarding drugs because it has assumed that by passing laws and enforcing them, the problem will go away.
>
> So it seems to me that while you can expect law-enforcement agencies to do the first-aid work, if you want a cure, then we have got to go back to the basic causes and find out what can be done from that end. We have to look to improved and increased rehabilitation programs. We have to find out more about drugs and why people use them, knowing of the debilitating consequences.[42]

No policy, of course, will be successful if it addresses only a part of the problem. There appears to be, for instance, a causal relationship between strict law enforcement and the number of addicts in treatment programs. If the probability of arrest is increased, more addicts are induced to enter treatment. Conversely, if more hard-core addicts enter treatment programs, pushers must seek out new, less reliable clientele; they become more visible and thus more vulnerable to arrest. Development of an effective policy combining efforts to suppress supply and inhibit demand for heroin necessarily involves close scrutiny of the economic system and the relative benefits and costs of various alternatives. In choosing between policy alternatives, cost-benefit analyses can illuminate the probable reduction in the social costs of addiction to be derived from one policy as compared with another. In choosing between policy alternatives, cash benefit analyses can show that the probable reduction in the social costs of addiction to be derived from one policy will exceed the reduction to be derived from another. If our public monies are to be spent efficiently, it is imperative that such choices be illuminated by full-scale studies of this nature.

NOTES

1. BNDD Staff. Interviews, November, 1971. This assessment is based on two other estimates: the total number of addicts in the United States, and the quantity of pure heroin consumed by each addict per day. The accuracy of these estimates will be analyzed later. But just one year ago, BNDD believed that only 5,000–6,000 lbs. of imported heroin was sufficient to supply the U.S. market. The current estimate should be interpreted accordingly; the actual total is probably somewhat less than 10,000 lbs.

2. BNDD Intelligence Staff, *The World Opium Situation* (unpublished paper), October, 1970, p. 13 (hereafter cited as *WOS*). This assumes that the illicit production estimates are accurate.

3. *Ibid.*, p. 16.

4. Select Committee on Crime, *Hearings into Narcotics Research, Rehabilitation and Treatment,* U.S. House of Representatives, 92d Cong., 1st sess., Serial 92–1, 1971, p. 358.

5. *WOS.*

6. *WOS.*

7. *WOS*, p. 4.

8. International Narcotics Control Board, "Statistics on Narcotics Drugs for 1967." International Narcotics Control Board (New York: United Nations, 1970), p. viii.

9. *WOS*, p. 5. This publication is the chief source of the data in this section.

10. It is extremely difficult to estimate illicit production and consumption. Except for Turkey, illicit production estimates were made on the basis of domestic consumption. Some allowance for exports is included but is probably subject to error. The BNDD staff considers the estimates to be accurate within a confidence interval of 20 per cent.

11. BNDD Staff, interview, March, 1971. Indian opium is often adulterated with seed, leaves, and other foreign matter. Indian yields are also higher because of additional lancing.

12. United Nations Survey Team, "The Hill Tribes of Thailand and the Place of Opium in Their Social Economic Setting," *Bulletin of Narcotics,* XX, No. 3 (July–September, 1968).

13. *WOS,* p. 7.

14. G. Shulzin, "Cultivation of the Opium Poppy and the Oil Poppy in the Soviet Union," *Bulletin of Narcotics,* XXI, No. 4 (October–December, 1969).

15. BNDD Staff, interview, March, 1971.

16. Select Committee on Crime, *op. cit.,* note 4, p. 68.

17. These figures are approximate. In fact, the necessary land area could be considerably less, depending on the number of total addicts and the opium yield per acre. The 11.2–23.2 square-mile estimate is obtained from the data in Table 4–2. For example, if the yield per acre is assumed to be 8.07 lbs. (the approximate reported yield in Turkey), then the area required to produce 100,000 and 120,000 lbs. of opium is approximately 19.4 square miles and 23.2 square miles, respectively. (If 1 acre yields 8.07 lbs., then 12,391.5 acres will yield 100,000 lbs. This acreage is approximately 19.4 square miles.) On the other hand, if the true Turkish yield, as suspected, is approximately 14 lbs. per acre, then the area required to produce 100,000 and 120,000 lbs. is approximately 11.2 and 13.4 square miles, respectively.

18. *WOS,* p. 32.

19. *WOS,* p. 8.

20. If demand is price-elastic, the percentage reduction in quantity sold exceeds the percentage increase in price, thus reducing farm revenues.

21. Mark Moore, *Policy Concerning Drug Abuse in New York State, Vol. III: Economics of Heroin Distribution* (Croton-on-Hudson, N.Y.: Hudson Institute, 1979), pp. 67–73.

22. John Casey and Edward Preble, "Taking Care of Business: The Heroin User's Life on the Street," *International Journal of the Addictions,* IV, No. 1 (March, 1967), 12.

23. T. S. Schelling, "Economics and Criminal Enterprise," *The Public Interest,* No. 7 (Spring, 1967), 61–78.

24. *Ibid.*

25. Select Committee, *op. cit.,* p. 3.

26. $R = pV$, where R is the cost of risk to the firm, p is the probability of punishment as perceived by the firm, and V is the value, or cost, of the expected punishment to the firm.

27. Select Committee on Crime, *Hearings into Crime in America: Heroin Importation, Distribution, Packaging and Distribution,* U.S. House of Representatives, 91st Cong., 1970, pp. 52–91.

28. The annual cost of heroin consumption can be stated by this equation:
$$C_H = 365 \, [N \, (1-d) \, TX], \text{ where}$$

C_H = net annual expenditures for heroin;

N = number of heroin addicts;

d = the percentage of all heroin consumed by the addict population, which is obtained for services rendered in the distribution network—i.e., pushing;

T = average percentage of the year heroin is consumed by addicts; and

X = average cost of drugs per day to the addict population.

29. Baden's formula is:

$$\hat{N} = D \cdot \frac{n}{d}, \text{where}$$

$\hat{N}$ = estimated total addict population;

D = total number of deaths of addicts in given year;

n = number of addicts on Narcotic Register in given year;

d = number of deaths of addicts on Narcotic Register in given year; and

N = actual total addict population.

30. Robert J. DuPont, "Profile of a Heroin Addiction Epidemic," in Select Committee on Crime, *op. cit.*, pp. 4, 167.

31. For example, the derived $\frac{n}{d}$ in Baden's formula for New York City has been used to estimate the number of addicts in Washington, D.C. The equation becomes:

$$\hat{N} = \frac{n}{d} \cdot D, \text{where}$$

$\hat{N}$ = estimated total addict population in D.C.;

n = number of addicts on New York City Narcotics Register;

d = number of deaths of addicts on New York City Narcotics Register in given year; and

D = total number of addict deaths in Washington, D.C.; and

N = actual total addict population in Washington, D.C.

The problem here is that differences in capabilities for identifying narcotics overdose deaths can make $\frac{n}{d}$ vary among cities. If $\frac{n}{d}$ in DC $> \frac{n}{d}$ in New York City, then $\hat{N} < N$; alternatively, if $\frac{n}{d}$ in D.C. $< \frac{n}{d}$ in New York City, then $\hat{N} > N$. Clearly, similar problems arise with efforts to use $\frac{n}{d}$ for time period 1 to estimate the addict population in period 2 with the total number of deaths in period 2.

32. BNDD Staff. Interviews. Included are only those important features of the method necessary for clear description. Their equation is:

$$\hat{T} = N \cdot \frac{t}{n}, \text{where}$$

$\hat{T}$ = the estimated total addict population in period 2;

N = the number registered with BNDD in period 1, who could be arrested in period 2;

t = the total number who are arrested in period 2;

n = the number registered with BNDD in period 1, who are arrested in period 2; and

T = the actual number of addicts in period 2.

Once it is known how many addicts have been arrested in period 2 (t), and what the number of these previously registered with BNDD in period 1 (n) is, then N can be used to estimate T.

33. As discussed in the text, the BNDD method assumes $\frac{n}{N} = \frac{t}{T}$. But, if m is the number of addicts arrested in 2 who were not arrested in 1, and if M is the total number of addicts not registered with BNDD in period 1, then $\frac{n}{N} = \frac{m}{M}$ must hold for the method to yield true estimates. If $\frac{n}{N} > \frac{m}{M}$ then $\hat{T} < T$; similarly, if $\frac{n}{N} < \frac{m}{M}$ then $T > T$.

If $\frac{n}{N} = \frac{m}{M}$ a particularly useful feature of this method would be the fact that new entrants in the current period do not bias the estimate of the total population.

34. Moore, *op. cit.*, note 21, p. 66. These estimates were made on the basis of a relatively small number of interviews and should not be interpreted strictly. However, this table provides the best available information on these aspects of addict behavior.

35. This estimate, while lower than several others, may still be too high. First, the Hudson Institute average of 55 milligrams includes an estimate that large-habit dealers (11 per cent of the total user population) use 180 milligrams per day. While heroin dealers might have the income to maintain such a large habit, it seems unlikely that they could be active entrepreneurs and at the same time use such quantities of the drug. The Hudson estimate was also derived from interviews with addicts, who reportedly exaggerate estimates of use. So, too, there may be less than 10 mg. of pure heroin per bag.

36. The amount of funds obtained from each of three alternative sources of funds (property crime, prostitution, legal sources) can be estimated with the following equation:

$$C = 365 \left[(1-d) \, NTX \, (af + b + w) \right]$$

where d, N, T, and X have the same meaning as in the equation in footnote 28.

C = the gross amount of funds obtained annually from various sources for heroin purchases;

a = the proportion of funds spent on heroin that comes from property crime;

b = the proportion of funds spent on heroin that comes from prostitution;

c = the proportion of funds spent on heroin that comes from legitimate sources—i.e., work, public assistance, family, or friends;

f = the factor by which the amount stolen must exceed the amount yielded by a property crime. (A stolen good must be transferred from the thief to a fence to a final consumer. The thief receives only a fraction of the market value of the good. To obtain a given target yield, an addict can be expected to steal a given amount, depending on the fencing discount, and the proportion of value stolen that is property and not cash.)

The amount of money annually spent by addicts for heroin can be estimated with the equation in footnote 26.

The cost to victims of property crime committed by addicts can be estimated by this equation:

$$C_v = 365 \left[(1-d) \text{ NTX (af)} \right]$$

where C_v = cost to victims of property crime.

37. These estimates are also weakened by the interview technique employed and thus should not be considered a precise reflection of addict behavior.

38. The value of property stolen cannot be counted totally when the costs to society are added. Some percentage of the value of goods stolen accrues as a type of subsidy to people who, knowingly or unknowingly, purchase stolen goods because the price they pay is significantly below the market price. This factor reduces the cost of crime to all society by the value of real property stolen multiplied by the reduced resale value (the fencing discount).

However, in ascertaining how large an adjustment to make, it is difficult to compare the utility of gains to the purchaser with the utility of the losses to the victim—is it greater, less, or the same? In addition, from the point of view of the community, the loss to the victim may be given more weight than the gain to the ultimate consumer. The item may, in fact, lose "value" because it is a stolen good. Objectively, although a stolen television set may still operate as well as before, the purchaser may feel that it is worth less than the market value because of the risk of holding a stolen good.

39. $\dfrac{.80}{1/3} + .20 \ (\$1) = \$2.60$

40. The net annual addict income from property crime can be estimated by the following equation:

$$PC = 365 \left[(1-d) \text{ NTXa} \right]$$

where d, N, T, and X have the same meaning as in footnote 28 and

PC = net annual addict income from property crime.

The cost to the victims of the stolen property is determined by multiplying the net addict income from property crimes by the reciprocal of the average fencing discount.

41. Select Committee on Crime, *op. cit.*, note 27, p. 238.

42. *Ibid.*, note 4, p. 367.

Federal Expenditures on Drug-Abuse Control

by Peter B. Goldberg and James V. DeLong

Availability of Information • Total Federal Expenditures • Federal Activities

AVAILABILITY OF INFORMATION

Comprehensive, reliable information on federal expenditures on drug-abuse programs is difficult to obtain. No detailed program budget describing the allocation of federal resources in this area has ever been made public or possibly even compiled. Although both the Office of Management and Budget and the Council on Executive Reorganization have made efforts to put together information, the results have been closely held. The figures used in this paper are based on budget requests and amendments, accounts of congressional hearings and other documents issued by the government, and interviews with government officials.

The accuracy of this information is sometimes suspect. Government cost accounting has never been known for its rigor, and, since drug abuse is now receiving high-priority attention at the highest levels of government, there is an incentive for agencies to find a drug-abuse rationale for programs that may have only a peripheral relationship to the field.

There are also technical problems. The Law Enforcement Assistance Administration, the Department of Housing and Urban Development, and the Social and Rehabilitation Service of HEW all award block grants to states and cities. (Block grants are funds that can be used for any specific projects chosen by the recipients within a given area of activity.) It is only after the close of the fiscal year that the portion of these funds spent for drug abuse can be determined. For these programs there is no information on fiscal 1972 at the present time.

On June 17, 1971, President Nixon announced a new drug-abuse program, including a supplemental budget request of $155,-655,000 for fiscal 1972. Shortly thereafter, the President stipulated that there was to be a 5 per cent, across-the-board reduction in government personnel as part of the anti-inflation effort. Some federal agencies are still unsure which of these directives will take precedence.

There are obvious differences among budget requests, congressional authorizations, appropriations, and actual expenditures; however, these distinctions are not made consistently in this report. Generally, appropriations are used for fiscal 1970 and 1971 and budget requests are used for fiscal 1972, but some amounts are agency allocations within larger appropriations. Usually, the figures are fairly close to the actual amounts that were or will be spent for the activities in each year. However, in some areas, such as research, expenditures may lag somewhat behind appropriations.

Some agencies, such as the Department of Defense and the Internal Revenue Service, have specific funding allocations for drug-abuse activities in fiscal 1972, but did not have such allocations in fiscal 1971.

Because of these problems, some of the figures given here represent judgment and estimate rather than certain fact.

TOTAL FEDERAL EXPENDITURES

Table 5–1 shows federal expenditures for fiscal years 1970, 1971, and 1972 broken down by agencies. Table 5–2 shows the same expenditures broken down by functional categories. Table

5–3 shows the requested budget for fiscal 1972 before and after the President's supplement request.

As the tables indicate, the government will spend about $417,-601,000 on drug-abuse activities in fiscal 1972, almost double the amount spent in fiscal 1971. Several agencies that could not provide a breakdown of funds spent in fiscal 1971 could do so for fiscal 1972. To avoid undue exaggeration of the increase, we have made rough estimates of the fiscal 1971 totals.

Table 5–4 compares the project estimate of the fiscal 1972

TABLE 5–1
FEDERAL EXPENDITURES, BY AGENCY (in $000)

	Fiscal 1970	Fiscal 1971	Fiscal 1972
Department of Justice			
Bureau of Narcotics and Dangerous Drugs	27,772	42,737	66,689
Law Enforcement Assistance Administration	12,945	44,582	44,582[b]
Bureau of Prisons	1,000[a]	1,000[a]	2,775
Department of Treasury			
Bureau of Customs	9,200	13,400	40,465
Internal Revenue Service	2,000[a]	2,500[a]	7,500
Department of HEW			
National Institute of Mental Health	38,833	64,487	140,007
Office of Education	0	6,000	13,000
Social and Rehabilitation Service	1,614	2,315	3,493
Office of Economic Opportunity	4,000	12,709	18,000
Veterans Administration	0	330	17,000
Department of Defense	1,000[a]	5,000[a]	34,225
Department of Labor	0	0	510
National Commission on Marijuana	0	250	1,000
Department of Transportation	0	200	250
Department of Agriculture	0	0	2,100
Department of State—AID	2,000[a]	4,000[a]	10,000[a]
Department of Housing and Urban Development	1,500[a]	13,005	13,005[b]
Special Action Office	0	0	3,000
TOTAL	101,864	212,515	417,601

[a] Project estimate.
[b] We have assumed that block-grant awards for fiscal 1972 will be equal to those made in fiscal 1971.

TABLE 5–2
FEDERAL EXPENDITURES, BY FUNCTION (in $000)

	Fiscal 1970	Fiscal 1971	Fiscal 1972
Enforcement			
Bureau of Narcotics and Dangerous Drugs	26,228	40,139	61,971
Bureau of Customs	9,200	13,400	40,465
Law Enforcement Assistance Administration	3,339	5,886	5,886[b]
Internal Revenue Service	2,000[a]	2,500[a]	7,500
Department of State—AID	2,000[a]	4,000[a]	10,000[a]
TOTAL	42,767	65,925	125,822
Treatment and rehabilitation			
National Institute of Mental Health	20,295	42,445	99,798
Office of Economic Opportunity	4,000	12,709	17,580
Social and Rehabilitation Service	1,453	1,915	3,093
Department of Defense	500[a]	2,500[a]	30,000[a]
Veterans Administration	0	330	16,750
Bureau of Prisons	1,000[a]	1,000[a]	2,775
Law Enforcement Assistance Administration	5,530	16,600	16,600[b]
Department of Labor	0	0	200
Department of Housing and Urban Development	750[a]	9,343	9,343[b]
TOTAL	33,528	86,842	196,139
Research			
National Institute of Mental Health	15,175	17,379	30,738
Bureau of Narcotics and Dangerous Drugs	838	1,383	3,467
Law Enforcement Assistance Administration	938	1,893	1,893[b]
Social and Rehabilitation Service	161	400	400
Department of Agriculture	0	0	2,100
Department of Transportation	0	200	250
National Commission on Marijuana	0	250	1,000
Veterans Administration	0	0	250
Department of Defense	0[a]	0[a]	2,000[a]
Department of Labor	0	0	120
TOTAL	17,112	21,505	42,218
Education, prevention, and training			
National Institute of Mental Health	3,363	4,663	9,471
Office of Education	0	6,000	13,000
Bureau of Narcotics and Dangerous Drugs	706	1,215	1,251

TABLE 5–2 (*Continued*)
FEDERAL EXPENDITURES, BY FUNCTION (in $000)

	Fiscal 1970	Fiscal 1971	Fiscal 1972
Department of Defense	500[a]	2,500[a]	2,225[a]
Law Enforcement Assistance Administration	3,138	20,203	20,203[b]
Department of Labor	0	0	190
Office of Economic Opportunity	0	0	420
Department of Housing and Urban Development	750	3,662	3,662[b]
TOTAL	8,457	38,243	50,422
Special Action Office	0	0	3,000
GRAND TOTAL	101,864	212,515	417,601

[a] Project estimate.
[b] We have assumed that block-grant awards for fiscal 1972 will be equal to those made in fiscal 1971.

TABLE 5–3
FISCAL 1972 SUPPLEMENTAL BUDGET, BY FUNCTION (in $000)

	Supplemental budget	Total fiscal 1972
Enforcement		
Bureau of Narcotics and Dangerous Drugs	7,600	61,971
Bureau of Customs	15,000	40,465
Law Enforcement Assistance Administration	0	5,886[b]
Internal Revenue Service	7,500	7,500
Department of State—AID	0	10,000[a]
TOTAL	30,100	125,822
Treatment and rehabilitation		
National Institute of Mental Health	51,000	99,798
Office of Economic Opportunity	0	17,580
Social and Rehabilitation Service	0	3,093
Department of Defense	30,000[a]	30,000[a]
Veterans Administration	14,100	16,750[b]
Bureau of Prisons	0	2,775
Law Enforcement Assistance Administration	0	16,600[b]
Department of Labor	0	200
Department of Housing and Urban Development	0	9,343[b]
TOTAL	95,100	196,139
Research		
National Institute of Mental Health	12,000	30,738
Bureau of Narcotics and Dangerous Drugs	2,000	3,467
Law Enforcement Assistance Administration	0	1,893[b]
Social and Rehabilitation Service	0	400
Department of Agriculture	2,100	2,100

TABLE 5–3 (*Continued*)
FISCAL 1972 SUPPLEMENTAL BUDGET, BY FUNCTION (in $000)

	Supplemental budget	Total fiscal 1972
Department of Transportation	0	250
National Commission on Marijuana	0	1,000
Veterans Administration	0	250
Department of Defense	2,000[a]	2,000[a]
Department of Labor	0	120
TOTAL	18,100	42,218
Education, prevention, and training		
National Institute of Mental Health	4,000	9,471
Office of Education	0	13,000
Bureau of Narcotics and Dangerous Drugs	0	1,251
Department of Defense	2,225[a]	2,225[a]
Law Enforcement Assistance Administration	0	20,203[b]
Department of Labor	0	190
Office of Economic Opportunity	0	420
Department of Housing and Urban Development	0	3,662[b]
TOTAL	6,225	50,422
Special Action Office	3,000	3,000
GRAND TOTAL	152,525	417,601

[a] Project estimate.
[b] We have assumed that block-grant awards for fiscal 1972 will be equal to those made in fiscal 1971.

TABLE 5–4
PROJECT *versus* GOVERNMENT ESTIMATES OF FEDERAL EXPENDITURES IN FISCAL 1972

	Project estimates	Government estimates
Enforcement	125,822	107,100
Treatment and rehabilitation	196,139	197,000
Education, prevention, and training	42,218	29,200
Research	50,422	34,600
Community planning projects	0	2,000
Special Action Office	3,000	0
TOTAL	417,601	369,900

budget with the latest available official government estimates.[1] The Project's figures are higher. The difference can be attributed to a number of factors, but probably the most influential is that the data for our estimate were compiled in September and October, 1971, rather than in June, and thus the agencies had more time in which to survey their activities. This seems especially important for the Law Enforcement Assistance Administration.

FEDERAL ACTIVITIES

LAW ENFORCEMENT

Four federal agencies have law-enforcement responsibilities: the Bureau of Narcotics and Dangerous Drugs (BNDD) and the Law Enforcement Assistance Administration (LEAA) in the Department of Justice; and the Bureau of Customs and the Internal Revenue Service (IRS) in the Treasury Department. In fiscal 1972, these agencies will spend $115,822,000 enforcing laws against the illegal importation, manufacture, distribution, and possession of narcotics and dangerous drugs.

As the product of a 1968 merger between the Treasury Department's Federal Bureau of Narcotics and the Department of Health, Education and Welfare's Bureau of Drug Abuse Control, BNDD has the widest mandate. It is primarily responsible for most of the federal government's national and international police operations. BNDD also works with state and local officials on cases of major importance to the total illegal-distribution system.

During fiscal 1972, BNDD will receive $66,689,000.[2] This will represent a doubling of its appropriations in two years. Personnel has increased almost as rapidly—from 1,465 in fiscal 1970 to 2,319 in fiscal 1971 to 2,718 in fiscal 1972. The number of actual agents has also increased from 884 in 1970 to 1,437 in 1971.[3] (Data for fiscal 1972 are not available.) Over 90 per cent of BNDD's money, or $61,971,000, will be spent on law-enforcement activities in 1972.[4]

BNDD's principal predecessor, the Federal Bureau of Narcotics, was often accused of overconcentrating its efforts against users and street dealers of narcotics and not being seriously concerned with the higher levels of distribution. In 1970, BNDD claimed that it had reversed this policy and was concentrating its efforts on the higher levels of the marketing structure. Appearing before a House Appropriations subcommittee in March, 1970, Director John Ingersoll stated:

The new operational plan is a systematic approach to developing prosecutable cases and obtaining convictions on specifically identifiable individuals and groups who are responsible for most of the illicit drug traffic in this country.

The shift in emphasis of federal narcotic and dangerous drug law enforcement from the addict, abuser, and small time street peddler to the important illicit traffickers and illegal supply sources will undoubtedly result in fewer total arrests. But those made should have a greater impact on the supply of narcotics and drugs available for distribution to the consumers in this country than a larger number of less significant arrests.[5]

Statistics on BNDD's output confirm this shift in policy to some extent. One would expect that such a change would result in fewer arrests per agent because of the increased investigatory work required. Table 5–5 shows that this appears to be the case.

Consistent with this shift in priorities, BNDD has begun analyzing the distribution systems for the various drugs and identifying organizations and individuals involved. The agency claims that so far it has identified nine principal and 129 secondary international drug-distribution systems and has immobilized 870 of the 2,150 individuals identified as having major importance in them.[6]

For several years, there has been a conflict between BNDD and the Bureau of Customs over operations in foreign countries. In February, 1970, President Nixon declared that BNDD would be the accredited agency "in dealing with foreign law-enforcement officials on narcotics questions."[7] This announcement apparently resolved the dispute.

During the last two years, there has been a major expansion of BNDD's foreign operations. The Bureau had 13 foreign offices in fiscal 1969, 16 in 1970, and 28 in 1971. During these three years, the number of agents assigned to foreign posts rose from 26 to 27 to 61[8] Of the 50 new agents requested in the original 1972 budget, 15 will be assigned to foreign offices, and new offices will be opened in South America and the Far East.[9] From President Nixon's supplemental budget request, $1 million will be allocated to BNDD for international training and technical-assistance activities.[10]

One of the chronic difficulties of law enforcement in the drug

TABLE 5–5
BNDD OUTPUT MEASURES

	Fiscal 1969	Fiscal 1970	Fiscal 1971
Drugs removed from the domestic market			
Heroin (lbs.)	140	427	226
Cocaine (lbs.)	73	197	427
Marijuana (lbs.)	8,825	17,401	12,723
Hashish (lbs.)	N.A.	N.A.	1,054
Hallucinogens (dosage units)	N.A.	7,127,742	3,697,737
Depressants (dosage units)	N.A.	2,339,590	319,006
Stimulants (dosage units)	N.A.	7,196,481	10,319,923
Arrests—BNDD-caused			
BNDD, direct	2,265	1,600	2,212
BNDD, foreign, cooperative	214	207	281
BNDD, state and local, cooperative	1,713	900	2,247
TOTAL	4,192	2,707	4,740
Arrests per agent			
Number BNDD agents in the field	644	757	1,236
Average arrests per agent	6.5	3.6	3.8

SOURCE: BNDD Fact Sheet.

field is corruption, and the old Federal Bureau of Narcotics had a substantial problem. In the words of Attorney-General John Mitchell:

> There was considerable lack of integrity on the part of many of the agents of predecessor organizations. . . . Some of them have been indicted. Others have had administrative procedures instituted against them, and a lot of them have left. I believe that it is being overcome.[11]

However, because there is so much money in the drug trade, internal corruption will undoubtedly continue to be a problem. Indeed, the pursuit of higher-level (and richer) traffickers will increase the stakes and the temptations. So far, BNDD has not been involved in any major scandals—a considerable accomplishment.

The Bureau of Customs is responsible for the prevention of smuggling. In fiscal 1972, the Customs budget for antidrug activities will be $40.5 million, $15 million of which will come from the supplemental budget request.[12] Customs officials state that they will actually spend about $52 million in this area during fiscal 1972. This estimate is based on a performance-measurement system that uses random time-sample analysis to determine the allocation of effort of Customs personnel. Based on this same measurement system, Customs estimates that $31,600,000 was actually spent on antidrug activities during fiscal 1971.[13] The results of Customs activity, as measured by the quantity of material seized and the number of arrests made, is shown in Table 5–6.

For all categories except dangerous drugs, the quantity of material seized in fiscal 1971 exceeded that of the previous year, with heroin and cocaine showing the most dramatic increases. Customs officials say that about 5 per cent of their seizures are made as a result of tips and 95 per cent as a result of "cold searches"—situations in which suspicions were based on conduct at the time of entry rather than on advance information.[14]

The Law Enforcement Assistance Administration (LEAA) was created in June, 1968, under Title I of the Omnibus Crime Control and Safe Streets Act. Its stated purpose is to offer "large scale financial and technical aid to strengthen criminal justice at every level throughout the nation."[15] LEAA is thus a major link between federal funds and technical expertise and state and local narcotics-law enforcement. The major types of financial aid to states and cities are as follows:

TABLE 5–6
RESULTS OF CUSTOMS ACTIVITY

	Number of seizures		Lbs. confiscated	
	Fiscal 1970	Fiscal 1971	Fiscal 1970	Fiscal 1971
Heroin	203	503	45.00	937.11
Opium	42	141	20.61	38.19
Cocaine	88	176	107.86	360.42
Marijuana	4,115	5,969	104,303.86	177,388.44
Hashish	646	1,335	3,121.37	3,162.76
Dangerous drugs	1,080	1,509	12,271,023[a]	6,310,060[a]
Number of arrests	7,340			7,810

[a] 5-gram units.

1. Planning grants—allocated to states according to population for the creation of statewide, comprehensive law-enforcement improvement plans.
2. Block-action grants—allocated to states according to population to carry out specific improvement plans.
3. Discretionary action grants—awarded at LEAA's discretion for anticrime programs, with emphasis on special aid to cities.

Some information on drug-abuse expenditures is available for the block-grant and discretionary-grant programs. Some of the planning funds are undoubtedly spent in this area as well, but the amount is not obtainable.

Block-grant funds awarded to state governments are normally spent in accordance with the comprehensive law-enforcement-improvement plans formulated by the recipient. The amount allocated to drug-law enforcement in part reflects the judgment of the states as to the severity of their drug-abuse problems. The discretionary-grant program represents LEAA's own allocation of resources to antidrug activities. The agency emphasizes attempts to improve upon interjurisdictional law-enforcement techniques, particularly in metropolitan areas where city-suburban cooperation is important. To some extent, it seems to try to fill a gap left by BNDD, as that agency now focuses increasing attention on national drug-trafficking systems rather than on smaller local groups.

In fiscal 1971, the states allocated $3,172,879 of block-grant funds to 26 programs designed to improve law-enforcement techniques and efforts, and LEAA used $2,713,206 of its discretionary funds.[16] Information on the funding levels for LEAA-financed, drug-abuse programs during 1972 will not be available until after the close of the fiscal year, since the grantees of the block grants do not have to file detailed reports until then. LEAA has not, apparently, analyzed the comprehensive plans to provide any prediction. Nor has the agency yet finalized its own plans for the discretionary-grant program. (In the tables we have presented, it is assumed that LEAA-financed, antidrug expenditures will remain constant in 1972.)

The Internal Revenue Service has long had a more general law-enforcement role, in that tax laws are frequently used against organized crime and other special offenders. Undoubtedly, the IRS has spent money on investigations and prosecutions related to drug abuse in the past. However, the $7,500,000 proposed for IRS in President Nixon's supplemental budget represents the first funds clearly earmarked for this purpose. The money is to be used to hire 541 new auditors and investigators and to pay the incidental expenses of their investigations.[17] (The 5 per cent reduction in government personnel has thrown this plan into uncertainty.)

Other federal agencies are involved in law enforcement to a limited extent, as described below.

The President's supplemental budget contained the first specifically identifiable funds for drug-abuse-related activities in the Department of Defense. It is not yet possible to determine the proportion of these funds that will be used for enforcement purposes, but it will probably be small. The Department already has its own enforcement system for violators. (The tables in this chapter do not include any estimate for Department of Defense law enforcement.)

During fiscal 1971, the Department of Agriculture conducted an experimental marijuana-eradication program in eleven Midwest counties. The cost of this project ($55,000) was assumed by BNDD. It has not been determined whether this program will be expanded or dropped in fiscal 1972, or, if it is continued, which agency will fund the program.

The federal government is also placing considerable emphasis on foreign crop eradication. In fiscal 1970, the Agency for International Development (AID) gave $1 million to Mexico to buy three light planes, five helicopters, remote sensing equipment, and chemicals and other eradication equipment. Similar grants totaling $627,000 were made in 1961 and 1965, without apparent effect.[18] It is not clear whether additional sums have been spent since, but it seems probable.

Similar emphasis is placed upon persuading Turkish farmers to substitute other crops for opium. According to government officials, both loans and grants tied to this purpose have been made, and BNDD has stated that in 1970 AID had $3 million to spend on it.[19]

In 1971, major U.S.–Turkey agreements were made, whereby Turkey would phase out opium production over the ensuing years.[20] No monetary *quid pro quo* has been publicly announced, but presumably it is substantial. More recently, on September 28, 1971, the State Department signed a U.S.–Thailand Memorandum of Understanding that will make U.S. aid available to Thailand for the purpose of controlling drug traffic in that country.[21] Again, no funding level has been announced.

The United Nations has established a Fund for Drug Control, supported by voluntary contributions from governments and individuals. Before the Fund came into being, the United States pledged an initial contribution of $2 million.[22] Presumably, this has been paid, but it is not clear which agency paid it or whether it is an annual contribution. In the tables, it is allocated to State–AID for fiscal 1971 contributions to international organizations. It has not been annualized.

It is difficult to know how to handle these assistance funds. To carry them at zero is clearly an error, but any specific number is a guess. A recent newspaper report stated that the total cost of the program in Turkey would be $35 million over four years, and that the United States would pay $20 million of it.[23] Project staff believe it likely that the United States will also absorb at least part of the other $15 million in some form, and that cost over-runs are always possible. Given all the uncertainties, we have estimated State–AID expenditures at $10 million per year, starting in fiscal 1972. This is probably a little conservative.

TREATMENT AND REHABILITATION

The principal federal agency concerned with treatment and rehabilitation is the National Institute of Mental Health (NIMH) within HEW, which operates four types of drug-treatment programs.[24] For three of these programs—Community Assistance, NARA inpatient, and NARA aftercare—funding levels are known: they were $42,445,000 for fiscal 1971 and will be $99,798,000 for fiscal 1972. Under the fourth program, the Community Mental Health Centers Act, drug users are only one of a number of categories of people treated, and an accurate calculation of expenditures cannot be made.

The Community Assistance Program has expanded dramatically in recent years. From a budget of $3.1 million in fiscal 1970 and $21.3 million in fiscal 1971, it has grown to $76.8 million under the revised fiscal 1972 budget. In his supplemental budget request, President Nixon asked for $67 million more for NIMH than was contained in the original budget; of this, $49.8 million will be channeled into the Community Assistance Program.

The increased emphasis on the Community Assistance Program reflects NIMH's belief that it is most effective and efficient to treat addicts in their home communities rather than in a central, isolated facility. Treatment is not confined to any one method. Different centers use different approaches or combinations of approaches. The modality chosen for any particular center is the result of the community's suggestion and NIMH's ratification.

During fiscal 1971, 13,258 patients were admitted to the 23 operational centers. NIMH estimates that about 10,000 remained enrolled. At the very end of fiscal 1971, 22 additional centers were funded; these did not accommodate any patients during that year but will add substantially to the total capacity in fiscal 1972. As funding more than triples in fiscal 1972, it is reasonable to expect even more increases in the number of operational centers and enrolled patients.

Under the Narcotic Addict Rehabilitation Act of 1966 (NARA), NIMH operates both inpatient and aftercare civil-commitment facilities. Originally, there were two central inpatient facilities, one at Lexington, Kentucky, and the other at Fort Worth, Texas. These facilities were generally underused, and now, consistent with the emphasis on community treatment, NIMH has dissociated from Fort Worth and is in the process of opening a series of smaller, geographically dispersed incare service facilities. The central facility at Lexington will remain operational and will serve patients for whom no local facilities are available. At present, about 700 people are in the inpatient phase of civil commitment. The second phase of civil commitment is community aftercare on an outpatient basis. NIMH has contracted for these services with 144 different community programs. These units are generally small. Together, they serve a population of about 1,250. The treatment at each of these centers is determined by NIMH personnel.

Under the Community Mental Health Centers Act, NIMH is funding some 450 centers designed to treat people with basic psychological problems. Many of these centers handle drug-abuse treatment under this general mandate. Information is not available on the number of drug users served by these centers or the amount of money involved. (No estimate is made in the tables.)

The Social and Rehabilitation Service (SRS) of HEW also funds rehabilitation programs through grants to state vocational-rehabilitation agencies. In fiscal 1971, an estimated $1,915,000 was spent for 1,000 "rehabilitations," and, in fiscal 1972, SRS expects to spend $3,093,000 for 1,600 "rehabilitations." The criterion for rehabilitation is the ability to secure and maintain employment.[25]

Because of the increased focus on drug-use in the military, the Veterans Administration is accelerating its drug-rehabilitation program. In fiscal 1971, the VA inaugurated its first five drug-abuse treatment units. Originally, the VA had planned to open 13 more centers in fiscal 1972 and another 14 in fiscal 1973. However, the President's supplemental budget request included $14.1 million to enable the VA to open all 27 new units this year.[26] Each of these units will be located in a VA hospital and will accommodate approximately 15 inpatients. The primary treatment modality will be methadone maintenance, with patients inducted for four to six weeks in the hospital and then continued on an outpatient basis. VA officials say that they expect to treat about 6,000 patients under this program during fiscal 1972.

As of July 1, 1971, the Office of Economic Opportunity (OEO) had 20 active grants budgeted at $12.3 million.[27] OEO concentrates its treatment and rehabilitation activities on programs for young drug users and assistance to community groups. OEO-funded treatment modalities range from therapeutic communities to methadone maintenance. Some of the projects also include an education component, but it is not possible to extract the amount of money spent by OEO for this purpose. For fiscal 1972, OEO has requested $18 million for drug-abuse-related expenditures. The neighborhood health-center concept would receive increased attention under this plan, according to OEO.

Some Model Cities funds from the Department of Housing and

Urban Development have been used to operate drug-treatment and rehabilitation centers. Because the funding mechanism is the block grant, the only information available from HUD is on fiscal 1971 expenditures—no accurate estimate can be made for fiscal 1972. The majority of these treatment and rehabilitation programs are directed toward young users. Services at the different centers range from outpatient counseling to comprehensive inpatient care. In fiscal 1971, there were 21 treatment and rehabilitation programs run in 13 states, the District of Columbia, Puerto Rico, and the Virgin Islands at a total cost to HUD of $9,343,000.

The Job Corps, part of the Department of Labor, will spend $200,000 in fiscal 1972 on three drug-demonstration projects. "The purpose of the . . . projects is to develop effective program models for man-power training programs to prevent and control drug misuse by disadvantaged adolescents."[28]

Total LEAA expenditures for treatment and rehabilitation in 1971 amounted to just over $16.6 million. LEAA estimates that it allocated over $4.5 million of its own fiscal 1971 discretionary funds to treatment and rehabilitation programs, and the states spent $12.1 million of the block-action grants for similar purposes.

LEAA officials say that the funding rationale is the relationship between drugs and crime. The medical and psychological needs of addicts must be treated to eliminate their criminal acts. These treatment and rehabilitation programs contain a strong crime-prevention component, most observable in the treatment and rehabilitation centers run for predelinquent addicts. Treatment varies from the use of antagonist drugs to therapeutic communities, and many of the centers offer both inpatient and outpatient clinical care.

The Bureau of Prisons runs two similar treatment and rehabilitation programs. First, under Title II of the Narcotics Addict Rehabilitation Act (NARA), inpatient and aftercare treatment are provided. The budget for fiscal 1972 is $2,118,924. The program has the capacity to treat 600 inpatients for an average of 18 months apiece. The actual population in treatment, as of August, 1971, was about 375.[29]

The Bureau of Prisons does not dispense any maintenance drugs. Rehabilitation programs center on educational and vocational training, individual, group, and family counseling, and "milieu therapy." The Bureau also runs a "para-NARA" program, which serves drug-dependent persons who, for one reason or another, do not qualify under NARA Title II. This program, operationally similar to NARA, will be budgeted at $655,955 in fiscal 1972, and the five centers will eventually treat a total population of 250. Four of the centers are now operational, and 104 people are enrolled. The fifth center is about to inaugurate operations with an initial population of 39. These figures are exclusive of the Fort Worth facility, which the Bureau of Prisons has just recently taken over from NIMH. It is expected that this facility will increase NARA and para-NARA capacity by only 200. The additional budgetary allotment required was not available.

The President's supplemental budget request included the first large-scale identifiable funds for Department of Defense drug-abuse activities. The total request for the department was $34,255,000, but a functional breakdown of this budget is not available. The Army will receive $19,699,000, the Navy $3,231,000, and the Air Force $11,295,000. Of the Army's funds, $18.2 million will be channeled into a new program—the Alcohol and Drug Abuse Prevention and Control Program. The objectives are defined as follows:

- Prevention of alcohol and drug abuse
- Identificaton of drug abusers
- Detoxification of drug abusers
- Rehabilitation of drug abusers, either short term in Army facilities or long term under the Veterans Administration
- Suppression of illegal drug distribution
- Collection of statistics and dissemination of information

How much money is to be allocated for each objective is not known, but it is likely that the primary emphasis will be on treatment and rehabilitation. The Navy and the Air Force will establish similar programs, funded, respectively, at $2.8 million and $11.1 million. The remainder of the DOD funds will probably be used for research.[30]

RESEARCH

The National Institute of Mental Health is the principal vehicle for government research on drug abuse. As concern about the problem has mounted, so has the NIMH drug-research budget. The growth curve is shown in Table 5–7, prepared for the House Select Committee on Crime by the director of NIMH. Probably the most important of the "other divisions" mentioned in the table is psychopharmacology, which is concerned primarily with the use of drugs in the treatment of mental illness.

The supplemental budget presented by the President in June, 1971, increased the total amount for drug-abuse research in fiscal 1972 to $30.7 million. The allocation of this amount is not known.

TABLE 5–7
NIMH DRUG-RESEARCH BUDGET, 1968–72 (in $000)

	1968	1969	1970	1971 estimate	1972 estimate
1. Research grants:					
DNADA	$ 2,506	$ 2,614	$ 3,650	$ 5,600	$ 6,549
Other divisions	9,523[a]	10,131[a]	9,800[a]	9,800[a]	9,828[a]
2. Contracts (marihuana study)	466	600	956	1,138	1,495
3. Intramural research (addiction research center) Lexington, Ky.	770	752	769	841	866
4. Other dir operations (operating costs within Division of Narcotic Addiction and Drug Abuse)	187	200	396	408	415
Total Institute drug-abuse research activities	13,452	14,297	15,571	17,787	19,153

[a] Represents those NIMH research grants which are not funded by the Division of Narcotics Addiction and Drug Abuse; they include projects which are directly relevant to drug-abuse research and some which are indirectly related. For example, they include projects which deal with drug research methodology, drug synthesis, the mechanisms of action in drugs, metabolic effects, and psychological effects. Even research on drugs which are not abused often produces basic new knowledge which is useful in drug-abuse research.

SOURCE: U.S. Congress, *op. cit.*, note 20, Statement of Director Bertram Brown, Director of NIMH, p. 472.

NIMH research covers a variety of drugs, including marijuana and the opiates, amphetamines, barbiturates, and hallucinogens. In fiscal 1970, the only year for which we have figures, the distribution was as follows:

Drugs	$ in millions
Barbiturates	5.3
Opiates	3.8
Amphetamines	2.8
Marijuana	2.3
Hallucinogens	1.8
Other	.3
TOTAL	16.3

This total is higher than the total shown in Table 5–7, which notes only $15.6 million for 1970. Probably the material presented to Congress is correct, and the information in the breakdown by drugs represents preliminary estimates.

Drug research draws on the disciplines of chemistry, pharmacology, sociology, psychology, psychiatry, and epidemiology, alone or in combination. There are no breakdowns by discipline, but NIMH does have a basic categorization of the areas within which it makes grants and contracts:

1. Systematic, controlled evaluation of currently promising treatment-program techniques

2. Development of treatment agents/devices for use in the treatment of drug dependence

3. Clinical studies of the effects of treatment drugs and abuse drugs

4. Surveys and instrument development to determine incidence, prevalence, and patterns of drug abuse:

    a. among students

    b. among other groups (hippies, psychiatric patients, etc.)

    c. New York City Narcotic Addict Register

5. Psycho-sociological studies of drug abuse and the abuser to determine the motivation for use, environmental influences, effects

on personality, characteristics of drug-using subculture, etc.

  6. Legal aspects of controlled drugs to explore alternative types of legal control systems

  7. Genetic studies to determine effects of drugs on chromosomes and offspring:

    a. marijuana
    b. LSD
    c. amphetamines and barbiturates

  8. Use of animal models for studies of abuse potential of drugs

  9. Exploration of mechanisms of action of drugs on the brain at the biochemical, neurophysiological, and behavioral levels:

    a. opiates
    b. marijuana
    c. amphetamines and barbiturates
    d. LSD

  10. Improved chemical methods for systematic and reliable detection of drug abuse

  11. Chemical studies of plant alkaloids to determine presence of hallucinogenic properties; to determine geographic origin of opium

  12. Development of methods/preparation of natural and synthetic marijuana

  13. Development of materials/methods for campaign on prevention and education of drug abuse

  14. Training

  15. Fellowships and scientist development awards.[31]

Many of these categories include only a small number of projects.

The Addiction Research Center (ARC) in Lexington, Kentucky, budgeted at about $0.8 million per year, is NIMH's major facility for intramural drug research. It has two major functions —the investigation of the addiction potential of various drugs before they reach commercial channels, and the development of antagonists to opiates. Basic research into the nature of drug action, abuse, and dependence is not a primary function, although ARC has some highly respected researchers who have done distinguished work in these areas.[32]

In the last two years, there has been a major push to do

research on marijuana. The total expenditure has gone from $1.5 million in fiscal 1969 to $2.8 million in fiscal 1971. Fiscal 1972 data are not available. Much of the past expenditure ($1.1 million in fiscal 1971) is done on contract, a procedure "utilized by the NIMH when it is important that the government define precisely what needs to be done, how it shall be done, and what the product will be." Between 1968 and 1972, NIMH did not use contracts for research in any area of drug abuse except marijuana.[33]

The Social and Rehabilitation Service, also a part of the Department of Health, Education and Welfare, plans to allocate approximately $400,000 for research in fiscal 1972. The bulk of this money will be used to investigate techniques by which the vocational and social services performed by this agency may be better utilized to facilitate therapeutic programs designed for young drug abusers.[34]

The National Commission on Marijuana and Drug Abuse was officially established on March 22, 1971, for a two-year period. It has a dual purpose: First, it is currently analyzing the marijuana situation and will, in March, 1972, recommend any desirable modifications of public policy. During its second year, the Commission will explore some of the broader aspects of drug usage under a mandate to investigate the causes of drug abuse. The budget for fiscal 1972 is estimated to be about $1 million, allocated entirely to general expenses and research.

The President's supplemental budget allocated $2.1 million to the Agricultural Research Service of the Department of Agriculture. The money will be used to develop techniques to detect and destroy illicitly grown narcotic-producing plants without causing adverse ecological effects.[35] Two other federal agencies, LEAA and BNDD—both within the Justice Department—conduct research programs, primarily to improve law-enforcement techniques.

LEAA research funds come from the block-action grant and discretionary-grant programs discussed above and from programs conducted by LEAA's National Institute of Law Enforcement and Criminal Justice (NILECJ).[36] During the past two fiscal years, the funding levels for research and education were as follows:

	Fiscal 1970		Fiscal 1971	
	Number of programs	Amount	Number of programs	Amount
Block-action grants	21	$485,922	15	$1,349,952
Discretionary grant	7	305,662	1	99,250
NILECJ	2	146,731	8	443,808
TOTAL	30	938,315	24	1,893,070

Figures for fiscal 1972 are not yet available. The discretionary-grants program has not been finalized, and most states have not yet submitted their plans for the fiscal 1972 block-action grants. In the tables, we assume that the funding will remain the same as in fiscal 1971.

LEAA-funded research has emphasized two project areas: investigation of possible relationships between drug use and aggressive behavior and crime, and evaluations of LEAA-funded, community-based treatment and rehabilitation projects. It can be expected that LEAA research programs will retain this thrust in fiscal 1972.

BNDD research is limited to projects directly related to law enforcement, such as the abuse potential of particular drugs or the market characteristics of the drug-distribution system. In fiscal 1971, BNDD had a research staff of 20 and a total research budget of $1,383,000. For fiscal 1972, BNDD originally asked for a research budget of $1,467,000; the increase, however, would have covered only the cost of annualization of positions, and would not have resulted in any additional activities.[37] The President's supplemental budget allocated an additional $2 million to BNDD "for development and implementation of new technology for detection, surveillance, communications and automatic data processing as tools in the enforcement of drug laws."[38]

Other federal agencies are conducting research into nonlaw-enforcement aspects of drug abuse. For the most part, however, the following programs are limited in scope and peripheral to the central goals and purposes of the agency involved.

The Job Corps has budgeted $120,000 for a national drug survey of 16 Job Corps centers in fiscal 1972, to obtain information about knowledge, attitudes, and patterns of drug use among different subcultural groups of Job Corps enrollees.[39]

The Department of Transportation has been conducting research on the effects of drugs on drivers and driving. DOT says that in fiscal 1972 it will spend an estimated $250,000 on the following studies:

- Incidence of drugs in people admitted to a university clinic after auto accidents
- Investigation of a sample of 1,000 fatally injured drivers for drugs
- Incidence of drugs in drivers who are not involved in accidents
- Simulation studies of drug effects
- A study of the driving record of heroin addicts before and after addiction and while on methadone

In fiscal 1972, the Veterans Administration plans to spend $250,000 for a general research program concerned primarily with the biological and behavioral aspects of drug addiction and to be conducted in Veterans Administration hospitals.[40]

The Food and Drug Administration (FDA) is investing a limited amount of funds in drug-abuse-related research. A budget breakdown is not available, but the agency estimates that these projects will consume four and a half man-years of time in fiscal 1972. Two of FDA's most important activities in this area are reviewing methadone-treatment programs for medical soundness and reviewing proposals to market methadone as a proven rather than an experimental drug.

Finally, part of the Department of Defense's supplemental budget will be used for research activities. The Army will get $1.5 million for research, development, testing, and evaluation in fiscal 1972; the Navy and Air Force will be given lesser amounts.[41] Information on specific projects is not yet available.

EDUCATION, PREVENTION, AND TRAINING

It is not always possible to distinguish sharply between this category and other categories. For example, funds for BNDD programs to educate local law-enforcement officers are included under law enforcement; treatment and rehabilitation programs undoubtedly include some money for training the agencies' own workers; and the line between prevention and enforcement is not always clear. Programs in this section include the following types of activity:

- Efforts to alert the general public to the drug-abuse problem and to explain its scope and significance
- Efforts to reach actual or potential drug abusers and to explain the effects and dangers of drug abuse
- Programs to train education workers
- NIMH programs to train rehabilitation workers (because of the scope of NIMH rehabilitation programs, the training activities are sufficiently large to warrant separation)
- Information services for persons interested in the drug field

In fiscal 1971, the Office of Education (OE) budgeted approximately $6 million for drug-education programs. Of this, $2 million was allocated to state departments of education to train educational personnel. The other major OE endeavors in fiscal 1971 were 26 community programs, 11 drug-education projects initiated by local school districts, and 20 college-based pilot programs initiated and operated by students primarily for fellow students but sometimes with a community-outreach component.[42]

For fiscal 1972, the Office of Education originally requested a budget of $6 million to continue existing programs.[43] As a result of a supplemental request, however, OE will receive $13 million for drug-abuse-related programs. The major new undertaking will be a training program called "Help Communities Help Themselves": Eight regional centers will be inaugurated to train community people on how to develop and maintain community-education and information programs; in the first year, OE hopes to train about 2,500 people. This project will cost about $6.5 million.

For fiscal 1972, NIMH has budgeted $2,571,000 for public-information services, a nominal increase over the fiscal 1971 amount of $2,563,000. Part of this money will be used by the National Clearinghouse for Drug Abuse Information, which answers general inquiries for information by sending out NIMH brochures and fact books. More specific requests are answered by information specialists, who send out reprints of published articles. The Clearinghouse has also developed a fairly comprehensive standard bibliography as well as a computerized information system that lists, indexes, and abstracts published articles in the field and conducts searches in response to individual requests.

The NIMH and the Department of Defense and Justice are co-sponsoring a special advertising campaign designed to counteract peer pressure to use drugs. This campaign, in the second of three years, has an annual cost of $150,000 equally divided between the sponsors.

In fiscal 1972, NIMH will spend $6.9 million on training, compared with $2.1 million budgeted in fiscal 1971. Part of this increase will be absorbed by the expansion of a program to develop educational materials and to train lawyers, ministers, and others who spend part of their time working with drug-dependent persons.[44]

The Office of Economic Opportunity has awarded a $420,000 grant for fiscal 1972 for the inauguration of a National Training Institute in Washington, D.C., to provide six months of intensive training for former addicts working on local projects, with follow-up training, if necessary.[45]

In fiscal 1971, $3,066,000 of HUD's Model Cities funds were used for 37 programs in the area of education, prevention, or training. Within this broad category, the states have programmed many diverse projects. Some have used their funds to develop curricula for drug-education programs in the schools; others have funded workshops for teachers and counselors; still others have directed their efforts toward the general community. At least one program has been run for law-enforcement officers.

The Job Corps, within the Department of Labor, will spend $40,000 in fiscal 1972 to develop, collect, and distribute educational material deemed appropriate and relevant to the Job Corps population.[46] This project will also help Job Corps staffs improve their understanding of the problems of drugs and drug abusers.

BNDD also operates a public-education campaign. In fiscal 1971, this division was staffed by 26 people at a cost of $1,215,000. The education division responds to requests from the general public for information on the drug problem and preventive programs. This division also provides materials and films upon request and arranges for speakers for national, state, and regional programs. In fiscal 1971, BNDD personnel made 1,500 speeches to an estimated audience of 150,000. They also made 191 radio and television appearances. These figures represent significant declines from the preceding year, apparently the result of a policy decision to place highest priority on addressing groups of people capable of establishing ongoing drug-prevention programs rather than the public at large. In fiscal 1972, this division will again consist of 26 people but at a cost of $1,251,000. This budget increase, however, will cover only annualization of positions.[47]

LEAA estimates that approximately $20.2 million of its fiscal 1971 funds were spent on education, prevention, and training, more than was spent in any other drug-abuse category. The major objective of LEAA's program is "to provide students and adults with the knowledge necessary to make intelligent decisions concerning the personal use of addicting or habituating drugs and other harmful substances." LEAA has developed the concept of a "concerned community" that must be made aware of the nature and magnitude of the problem before it can respond. The agency stresses four programs:

1. Coordination of local and state public education and information programs to attain maximum participation and efficiency
2. Implementation of health-information programs in every school at the earliest feasible grade level
3. Development of educational programs, seminars, and workshops designed to provide accurate information for adults
4. Predelinquent counseling services through the use of neighborhood information centers.[48]

The funding level of these programs in fiscal 1972 is not yet known.

THE SPECIAL ACTION OFFICE

In his special message to the Congress on June 17, 1971, the President proposed the temporary establishment of a Special Action Office of Drug Abuse Prevention accountable directly to the President. Pending congressional approval, the President, through an executive order, instituted the position of Special Consultant for Narcotics and Dangerous Drugs to fulfill, to the extent legally possible, the duties of the proposed Special Action Office. Under this revised organizational plan, it would become the responsibility of the Special Action Office to coordinate and direct all the drug-abuse activities of the various federal agencies, with the exception of those dealing with the problems of law enforcement.[49] The President has requested $3 million in fiscal 1972 for the staff and administrative costs of the Special Action Office.[50]

NOTES

1. Latest White House estimate as reported in the *National Journal,* July 3, 1971, p. 1417.

2. House of Representatives Document No. 92–133, *Amendment to Budget Fiscal Year 1972, Drug Abuse Problem,* June 21, 1971, p. 4 (hereafter H.R. 92–133).

3. U.S. Congress, *Hearings on Appropriations,* House of Representatives, 92d Cong., 1st sess., 1971 (hereafter *App. Hrgs. 1971*), Justice, Pt. 1, p. 333; H.R. 92–133; U.S. Department of Justice, Bureau of Narcotics and Dangerous Drugs, *Fact Sheets,* unpublished, 1971 (hereafter BNDD Fact Sheets).

4. This figure is arrived at by subtracting BNDD appropriations for research and for education, prevention, and training from the total requested budget.

5. U.S., Congress, *Hearings on Appropriations,* House of Representatives, 91st Cong., 2d sess., 1970 (hereafter *App. Hrgs. 1970*), Justice, Pt. 1, pp. 987–88.

6. *App. Hrgs. 1971,* Justice, Pt. 1, p. 868.

7. *National Journal,* July 3, 1971, p. 1422.

8. These figures come from the BNDD Fact Sheets. At the House Appropriations Hearings in March, 1971, however, the agency stated that total staff of foreign offices had risen from 34 to 70 in 1970. BNDD Fact Sheets; *App. Hrgs. 1971,* Justice, Pt. 1, pp. 848, 868.

9. *App. Hrgs. 1971,* Justice, Pt. 1, p. 848.

10. H.R. 92–133, p. 4.

11. *App. Hrgs. 1970,* Justice, Pt. 1, p. 220.

12. Information supplied by the Bureau of Customs.

13. *Ibid.*

14. *App. Hrgs. 1970,* Treasury, Pt. 2, p. 583.

15. Department of Justice, Law Enforcement Assistance Administration, *A Program for a Safer, More Just America,* p. 3.

16. Information supplied by LEAA.

17. H.R. 92–133, p. 5.

18. *App. Hrgs. 1970,* Foreign Assistance and Related Agencies, Pt. 2, p. 11. Mexico's total legitimate exports are about $1.1 billion, and the marijuana trade may be worth an additional $100 million in foreign exchange. Some experts have estimated that 500 kilograms of marijuana per day go from Mexico to the United States. This comes to about 400,000 pounds per year. An average price of $25 per pound F.O.B. Mexican border does not seem unreasonable, based on many sources of information. The exact figures depend, of course, on one's estimate of marijuana use and average price. A case can be made for almost any figure between $70 million and $120 million.

19. *App. Hrgs. 1970,* Foreign Assistance and Related Agencies, Pt. 2, p. 11; John Ingersoll, "New Horizons of Narcotic and Dangerous Drug Enforcement," Speech at the Law Enforcement Executive Conference, Williamsburg, Virginia, July 22, 1970, p. 8.

20. U.S., Congress, House of Representatives, Select Committee on Crime, *Narcotics Research, Rehabilitation and Treatment,* Hearings, 92d Cong., 1st sess., 1971, pp. 70–73.

21. U.S., Department of State, *U.S.–Thai Memorandum of Understanding,* September 28, 1971.

22. *App. Hrgs. 1971,* Justice, Pt. 1, p. 372.

23. *Washington Evening Star,* November 4, 1971.

24. NIMH's Division of Administration Management and Financial Management provided much of the information in this section.

25. Information supplied by SRS.

26. Veterans Administration, Alcohol and Drug Dependence Service, *Progress Report,* August 19, 1971, p. 1.

27. Office of Economic Opportunity, *Drug Rehabilitation Projects Status Report,* July 1, 1971.

28. U.S., Department of Labor, *Job Corps Drug Task Force Projects,* 1971, p. 1.

29. Information supplied by the Bureau of Prisons.

30. H.R. 92–133, p. 3.

31. National Institute of Mental Health, Center for Studies of Narcotic and Drug Abuse, Memorandum, *Program Development Goals with Grants and Contract Supported Active During FY 1969,* August 13, 1969.

32. *App. Hrgs. 1970,* U.S., Department of Health, Education and Welfare, Pt. 1, pp. 448–50.

33. U.S. Congress, *op. cit.*, note 20, pp. 474, 476–77.

34. Information supplied by SRS.

35. H.R. 92–133.

36. Information on LEAA supplied by LEAA.

37. *App. Hrgs. 1971,* Justice, Pt. 1, p. 845.

38. H.R. 92–133, p. 4.

39. U.S., Department of Labor, *Job Corps Drug Task Force Projects,* memorandum, August 31, 1971, p. 1.

40. Veterans Administration, Alcohol and Drug Dependence Service, *Progress Report,* August 19, 1971, p. 3.

41. H.R. 92–133, p. 3.

42. *Congressional Record,* July 26, 1971, p. E8287.

43. *App. Hrgs. 1971,* Office of Education and Related Agencies, Pt. 1, pp. 975–76, and information supplied by the Office of Education.

44. Information supplied by NIMH.

45. Office of Economic Opportunity, *Drug Rehabilitation Projects Status Report,* July 1, 1971, p. 3.

46. U.S., Department of Labor, *Job Corps Drug Task Force Projects,* p. 1.

47. *App. Hrgs. 1971,* Justice, Pt. 1, p. 845; *App. Hrgs. 1970,* Justice, Pt. 1, pp. 924, 979, 998.

48. Information supplied by LEAA.

49. See *Message from the President to the Congress of the United States,* June 17, 1971.

50. H.R. 92–133, p. 3.

Altered States of Consciousness

by Andrew T. Weil, M.D.

The Pharmacology of Consciousness-Altering Drugs •
Altered States of Consciousness, Drugs, and Society

THE PHARMACOLOGY OF CONSCIOUSNESS-ALTERING DRUGS

The single most important fact to emerge from research on consciousness-altering drugs in this century is that individual responses to them result from set and setting as much as from the drug itself. Occasionally particular combinations of set and setting completely reverse the "pharmacological action" of a drug as described in a text on pharmacology. For example, with proper suggestion and in a restful setting, amphetamines can produce sedation. Drug, set, and setting, therefore, appear to be interdependent in shaping drug responses; no one factor seems vastly more determining than any other.

This principle is logical enough. No physiological event takes place without a corresponding event in the central nervous system. Therefore, every "bodily" response is actually a psychosomatic response. In the case of medical drugs like digitalis and atropine, no one is very much interested in the psychic component of response, so that we have come to think of these substances as producing constant physiological responses (although there is still enough variation from patient to patient to make their clinical administration a ticklish business). In the case of "psychoactive" drugs like heroin and LSD, the psychic component of response becomes the focus of attention; but, because we do not understand it according to present models of consciousness, we try in vain to make these drugs, too, fit our simplistic conceptions of pharmacology. How nice it would be if we could derive a method of predicting an individual's response to a psychoactive drug from purely pharmacological considerations. But we cannot do so.

Two upsetting conclusions follow from this line of reasoning: First, it is impossible to talk meaningfully about the effects of psychoactive drugs, except by reference to their effects on specific individuals on specific occasions; and secondly, pharmacology is not a useful approach to understanding the effects of these drugs either on individuals or on society. A pharmacologist, of course, would disagree with me, but his view of things would be as biased in its own way as that of the law-enforcement officer who favors continued efforts to stop people from using drugs by means of the criminal law. Most of what is written about LSD and heroin in pharmacology texts is meaningless in this sense: It says nothing about what will happen to you if you take LSD at eight o'clock tonight; gives you no power to help me if I come to you for assistance in breaking a heroin habit; and is quite irrelevant to any considerations of what the United States ought to do about the continuing increase in negative use of these drugs.

What we need is a new science of consciousness, based on subjective experience rather than on objective physiology. The materialistic psychology that has dominated Western thought about consciousness is no longer adequate to the task of explaining the mind in terms that are useful to us. (An especially galling aspect of the drug problem for the medical profession is that psychologically ignorant users of drugs appear to have more practical information about their effects than doctors have.) I predict that, from an experiential viewpoint, many unifying principles of drug states will become visible. In the pharmacological model, there is some unity; for example, alcohol, barbiturates, and minor tranquilizers are grouped together as sedative-hypnotics—a useful grouping, because it alerts us to the danger that drugs like chlordiazepoxide (Librium) and meprobamate (Equanil) produce a dependence resembling dependence on alcohol. But pharmacology offers no clue why the psychological changes of a marijuana high have much in common with those of an LSD trip, or why heroin users may be able to satisfy their need for a certain experience by inhaling nitrous oxide, a general anesthetic.

In the following pages, I will review briefly what is known and what is not known about the major pharmacological classes of psychoactive drugs—briefly, because, in view of the limited usefulness of this scheme of classification, it is not worth discussing, except at the most general level.

SEDATIVE-HYPNOTICS

Alcohol and the barbiturates are associated with stubborn forms of drug dependence, marked by relatively constant, dose-related physiological changes, some of which become irreversible over time. These changes include tolerance (probably the clinical correlate of the induction of degradative enzymes in the liver) and withdrawal (a syndrome that persists until metabolism readjusts to its predrug state). Unlike narcotics, alcohol and barbiturates cause life-threatening reactions when they are withdrawn from addicted persons. Chronic use of sedative-hypnotics is associated with structural damage to the nervous system; this association is stronger than for any of the other classes of drugs discussed below. Alcoholism is particularly associated with chronic liver disease, possibly because alcohol is directly toxic to liver cells. Barbiturates are often implicated in accidental self-poisonings, because tolerance to the lethal dose does not develop as fast as tolerance to the hypnotic dose. The minor tranquilizers have been promoted as anti-anxiety agents, but they behave just like mild sedative-hypnotics.

Most persons use sedative-hypnotics to reduce anxiety by substituting a "high" state of consciousness that permits sleep, relaxation, or the mild disinhibition valued in certain social encounters.

These drugs are associated with dependence because (1) they do not affect the source of anxiety; (2) the development of tolerance encourages more and more frequent use; (3) their use in our culture is strongly linked to destructive (especially self-destructive) behavior patterns; and (4) people in our society do not know how to make use of altered states of consciousness.

The pharmacological model of these drugs offers no hope of cure or prevention of dependence on sedative-hypnotics. It can, however, offer treatment of acute toxic episodes and withdrawal reactions. It seems unlikely that elucidation of the exact metabolic derangements underlying dependence will open the way to any pharmacological means of intervening in the course of the disease.

Nothing important is known about the action of these drugs on the mind. Since their major action is depression of neurological activity in the central nervous system, it has been assumed that the "paradoxical stimulation" observed with low doses (the high that precedes the stupor of alcohol intoxication) is the result of inhibition of inhibitory brain centers (which are conveniently postulated to respond to lower doses). However, some researchers have suggested that low doses may have direct excitatory action on nerve cells. That this kind of debate should still be going on in 1970 suggests how far we are from understanding conscious experience in physiological terms. (If alcohol intoxication were looked at by an experiential science of consciousness, it might turn out that the high is not causally related to the drug, which might be a pure depressant, after all.)

It is ironic that we have chosen our one sanctioned intoxicant from this class of drugs. In no other class is pharmacological action (in this case, on liver and nerve-cell metabolism) so clearly related to long-range physiological deterioration.

NARCOTICS

Like sedative-hypnotics, narcotics are central depressants that produce stubborn dependence. Unlike sedative-hypnotics, they are not directly associated with long-range physiological damage or life-threatening withdrawal reactions. Tolerance to narcotics develops faster than tolerance to sedative-hypnotics; hence, visible dependence develops faster. Because narcotics are illegal, their use is much more bound up with antisocial, negative, and, often, self-destructive behavior.

"Addiction" to and "withdrawal" from narcotics have become stereotypes in the public mind, but reality does not often conform to these conceptions. Far from being a physiological constant, dependent on dose and frequency of administration of a drug, the physical craving for narcotics is very much a matter of set and setting. Some individuals, when they find tolerance appearing, work out a method of spacing injections of heroin so that they never become really "hooked," even though they use the drug regularly for years. (The number of such persons is unknown but may be greater than the number of hooked addicts; they often lead stable lives and may never come to the attention of groups concerned with narcotics.) Other people seem not to be able to handle the development of tolerance and quickly go on to experience strong physiological dependence. Similarly, withdrawal reactions from narcotics are strongly shaped by non-pharmacological factors. In a supportive setting with strong positive suggestion, a heroin addict can undergo comfortable withdrawal with no medication other than aspirin.

Narcotics do not affect the primary reception of pain or other sensory stimuli; rather, they alter secondary perception. A person in pain, given morphine, might say, "The pain is still there, but it doesn't bother me." In other words, the pain is perceived through an altered state of consciousness. Pharmacological research on narcotics has been unproductive. In the first place, no real success has been achieved in separating the analgesic and addicting properties of this class of compounds. Secondly, the metabolic changes accompanying narcotics dependence are beyond our present understanding; even if they were understood, there is no reason to think our difficulties with addiction would be any fewer. Thirdly, no purely pharmacological method of controlling addiction has come along.

The problems associated with heroin (death from overdose; hepatitis; crime; mental and physical deterioration) appear to have no causal relationship to the pharmacological action of the drug. Rather, they correlate better with features of the social context in which heroin exists in our country. In fact, the discrepancy between pharmacology and experience is best illustrated by phenomena accompanying dependence on drugs of this class.

AMPHETAMINES AND RELATED DRUGS

Drugs that stimulate the central and sympathetic nervous systems include the amphetamines (a chemical class), several drugs that are chemically but not pharmacologically distinct from the amphetamines (like methylphenidate—Ritalin; and phenmetrazine—Preludin), and cocaine. These drugs cause the release of norepinephrine from adrenergic nerve endings. Tolerance to them develops very quickly, but withdrawal from them, although sometimes a psychological ordeal, has few physiological accompaniments in contrast to withdrawal from sedative-hypnotics or narcotics.

Little is known about the neurological consequences of chronic, heavy use of amphetamines. Speed freaks who take enormous doses of amphetamines intravenously develop a paranoid psychosis that looks suspiciously organic and may be correlated with depletion of the body's stores of norepinephrine. (It may just as well be correlated with the prolonged wakefulness induced by these drugs.) To date, there is no firm evidence of actual neurological deterioration resulting from any of these drugs, including cocaine. Although low doses do not change eating behavior in most people (contrary to the claims of pharmaceutical-industry advertising), very high doses do shut off the hypothalamic hunger center and can result in severe malnutrition. The high incidence of hepatitis among amphetamine users has led to speculation that the drug may be directly toxic to liver cells. (If this hepatitis is, indeed, chemical, it may also be due to a common contaminant of black-market methadrine.)

Until recently, amphetamine dependence was considered less serious than narcotic dependence, because it was "less physiological." In fact, however, amphetamine dependence is *more* serious, because it is inherently less stable. When a person begins to use a tolerance-producing drug, he must soon face the problem of trying to stabilize his use in order to keep his life from being disrupted. More than any other class of drugs, the amphetamines foil a user's attempt to reach equilibrium with his habit, because they induce such powerful and unrelenting tolerance. Consequently, users develop erratic patterns of use, such as "spree shooting" and alternation with barbiturates and, eventually, with heroin. The high correlation of amphetamine use with impulsive and violent behavior is consistent with this pharmacological instability.

Abusive oral use of diet pills may be associated with serious psychological problems but is not accompanied by the physical changes associated with intravenous use.

HALLUCINOGENS

Hallucinogens stimulate the central and sympathetic nervous systems (some are simple derivatives of amphetamine) but, in addition, induce perceptual changes and the kinds of mental states associated with trance, mystic rapture, and psychosis. Except for the visual hallucinations (in particular, the ever-changing, geometric patterns seen on surfaces), most of these effects are common in altered states of consciousness unrelated to drugs. The hallucinogens differ from one another only in duration of action and in relative prominence of stimulant versus psychic effects. Pharmacological research tells us little more about them than about the amphetamines; it offers no satisfactory explanation for the effects of hallucinogens on consciousness. No one takes these drugs frequently enough to get into pharmacological trouble with them. (Tolerance is so rapid that regular consumption is impractical; you can't stay high on LSD for too long at one stretch.) Therefore, the pharmacological body of data is quite irrelevant to our understanding of the difficulties people get into with hallucinogens. Also, there is no indication that use of these drugs is associated with physical damage of any kind, in either short- or long-term use.

Most bad trips on hallucinogens are nonpharmacological panic reactions. Others are nonspecific toxic psychoses—overdose reactions that disappear when the drug wears off.

MARIJUANA

Marijuana differs from the hallucinogens in two ways: It does not cause hallucinations, and it is not a stimulant. In fact, marijuana has virtually no significant pharmacological actions, which probably accounts for its popularity. It provides a high with minimal physiological accompaniment, so that people who are anxious about it can easily pretend to themselves that they have done nothing to their bodies or minds. For the same reason, it is useless to study marijuana in the pharmacological laboratory, because there is no physiological handle on the phenomenon under consideration.

Except for the possibility of lung disease related to chronic inhalation of the drug, there is no evidence that marijuana is physically harmful in short- or long-term usage. No other drug is like marijuana in having so few physiological effects. For this reason, it seems wise to think of marijuana as a class unto itself, no more closely related to the hallucinogens than to the sedative-hypnotics. Its unique chemical structure is consistent with this idea.

Toxins, General Anesthetics, and Special Substances

Persons who enjoy the altered state of consciousness called delirium (actually, a nonspecific response of the brain to a toxin) will occasionally induce it by inhaling volatile solvents and petroleum distillates such as glue. Repeated use of deliriants appears to be correlated with structural damage to the central nervous system. In addition, petroleum distillates are frequently toxic to the liver, especially when taken with alcohol. Delirium is characterized by confusion, disorientation, and hallucination; it is sometimes called "acute brain syndrome" or "toxic psychosis," and it can also occur in response to overdoses of any of the classes of drugs mentioned above, including marijuana.

General anesthesia is an altered state of consciousness induced by a heterogenous class of chemicals, some of which (ether and nitrous oxide) are occasionally taken for nonmedical purposes. It is instructive to reflect that no satisfactory theory has been proposed thus far to explain general anesthesia in pharmacological or neurophysiological terms, even though millions of persons have been put into this state under close observation. Because the psychic phenomena of general anesthesia can be reproduced nonchemically (by hypnosis, for example), it is tempting to speculate that this altered state of consciousness, too, would be better understood from the point of view of subjective experience rather than from the point of view of objective pharmacology.

Drug users who are deprived of their usual drugs sometimes resort to special substances like nutmeg and morning-glory seeds to get high. Many natural products of very diverse pharmacology have been so employed, and it seems likely that set and setting determine whether they produce pleasant altered states of consciousness, sickness, or, indeed, no effects at all.

ALTERED STATES OF CONSCIOUSNESS, DRUGS, AND SOCIETY

The general thesis of this paper is that drug experience can be understood only if it is viewed as an altered state of consciousness rather than as a pharmacological event. A subthesis is that this approach will make it possible for society to reduce significantly the problems now associated with the use of psychoactive drugs.

All of us experience occasional states of consciousness different from our ordinary waking state. Obviously, sleep is such a state. Less obviously, perhaps, are daydreaming and movie watching unusual modes of awareness. Other distinct varieties of conscious states are trance, hypnosis, psychosis, general anesthesia, delirium, meditation, and mystic rapture. In our country, until recently, there has been no serious investigation of altered states of consciousness as such, because most Western scientists who study the mind regard consciousness as annoyingly nonmaterial and, therefore, inaccessible to direct investigation. Their research has focused on the objective correlates of consciousness instead of on consciousness itself. In the East, on the other hand, where nonmateriality is not seen as a bar to direct investigation, much thought has been devoted to altered states of consciousness, and a science of consciousness based on subjective experience has developed.

It would make sense to study all forms of nonordinary consciousness together, because they seem to have much in common. For example, trance, whether spontaneous or induced by a hypnotist, is in many ways simply an extension of the daydreaming state in which a person's awareness is focused and directed inward rather than outward. Except for its voluntary and purposeful nature, meditation is not easily distinguishable from trance. Zen masters warn their meditating students to ignore *makyo*—sensory distortions that often take the form of visions seen by mystics in rapturous states or hallucinations similar to those of schizophrenics. And, curiously, the state of being high on drugs shares many characteristics with these other forms of altered consciousness, regardless of what drug induces the high.

It is my contention that the desire to alter consciousness is an innate psychological drive arising out of the neurological structure of the human brain. Strong evidence for this idea comes from observations of very young children, who regularly use techniques of consciousness alteration on themselves and one another when they think no adults are watching them. These methods include whirling until vertigo and collapse ensue, hyperventilating and then having another child squeeze one's chest to produce unconsciousness, and being choked around the neck to cause fainting. Such practices appear to be universal, irrespective of culture, and present at ages when social conditioning is unlikely to be an important influence (for example, in two- and three-year-olds). Psychiatrists have paid little attention to these common activities of children. Freud, who did note them, called them "sexual equivalents"—which they may be, although that formulation is not very useful for our purposes.

As children grow older, they soon learn that experiences of the same sort may be had chemically—for instance, by inhaling the fumes of volatile solvents found around the house. General anesthesia is another chemically induced altered state of consciousness that many children are exposed to in their early years. (The current drug-using generation was extensively tonsillectomized, by the way.) Until a few years ago, most children in our society who wanted to continue indulging in these states were content to use alcohol, the one intoxicant we make available legally. (Incidentally, there are some good reasons that alcohol may not be a wise choice for sole legal intoxicant—apart from its devastating medical effects.) Now, large numbers of young people are seeking chemical alterations of consciousness through a variety of illegal and medically disapproved drugs. It is possible to see this change as primarily a reaction to other social upheavals—and, certainly, much has been written about the social causes of drug use. It may be more useful, however, to consider what many drug users themselves say: They choose illegal drugs over alcohol in order to get better highs. There is no question that social factors influence the forms of drug use in a society, or that changes in patterns of use of intoxicants go along with major cultural upheavals, but we must remember that every culture throughout history has made use of chemicals to alter consciousness.* Instead of looking for explanations of drug taking in a foreign war or in domestic tension, therefore, perhaps we should pay more careful attention to how we allow people to satisfy chemically their innate drive to experience other states of awareness.

Most societies, like our own, are uncomfortable about having people go off into trances, mystic raptures, and hallucinatory intoxications. Indeed, the reason we have laws against possession of drugs in the first place is to discourage people from getting high. But innate, neuropsychological drives cannot be banned by legislation. They will be satisfied at any cost. And the cost in our country is very great, for, by trying to deny young people these important experiences, we maximize the probability that they will obtain them in negative ways—that is, in ways harmful to themselves and to society.

Why are altered states of consciousness important? Primarily because they seem to be doorways to the next stages of evolutionary development of the human nervous system. We commonly assume that a major division of our nervous system (the autonomic system) is involuntary—beyond our conscious control —and that this leaves us open to many kinds of illnesses we can do nothing about (for example, cardiovascular diseases). Yet, hypnotized subjects often show an astonishing degree of autonomic control, to the extent of developing authentic blisters when touched with cold objects represented to them as being red hot. And Yogis frequently demonstrate voluntary control of heart action and blood flow that astonishes physicians; they themselves

---

* Except the Eskimos, who had to wait for the white man to bring them alcohol, since they could not grow anything.

ascribe their successes to regular periods of meditative effort, asserting that there is no limit to what consciousness can effect through the "involuntary" nervous system. In addition, creative genius has long been observed to correlate well with psychosis, and much of the world's highest religious and philosophic thought has come out of altered states of consciousness.

At the very least, altered states of consciousness appear to have potential for strongly positive psychic development. Most Americans do not get the chance to exploit this potential, because their society gives them no support. The prevailing attitude toward psychosis is representative. We define this experience as a disease, compel people who have it to adopt the role of sick, disabled patients, and then ply them with special kinds of sedatives that we call "antipsychotic agents" but that simply make it hard for them to think and to express their altered state of consciousness in ways disturbing to the staffs of psychiatric hospitals. The individual learns from early childhood to be guilty about, or afraid of, episodes of nonordinary awareness and is forced to pursue antisocial behavior patterns if he wants to continue having such episodes. Negative drug taking has become a popular form of this kind of behavior.

I implied earlier that alcohol may not fulfill the need for alteration of consciousness as well as other drugs. Like all psychoactive drugs, it does induce a high with positive potential. (A vast body of prose, poetry, and song from all ages testifies to this "good side" of alcohol.) The trouble, however, is that an alcohol high is difficult to control; in drinking, one slips easily into the dose range where the effects become unpleasant (nausea, dizziness, uncoordination) and interfere with mental activity. Marijuana, on the other hand, maintains a "useful" high over an extremely wide dose range and allows a remarkable degree of control over the experience. But, as with other drugs, set and setting determine the effects of marijuana by interacting with the drug's pharmacological action. Unfortunately, current social factors create strongly negative sets and settings, thus increasing the likelihood that users will be drawn into the negative side of consciousness alteration instead of being encouraged to explore its positive potential.

By focusing our attention on drugs rather than on the states of consciousness people seek in them, we develop notions that lead to unwise behavior. Users who think that highs come from joints and pills rather than from their own nervous systems get into trouble when the joints and pills no longer work so well (a universal experience among regular consumers of all drugs): Their drug use becomes increasingly neurotic—more and more frequent and compulsive with less and less reward. In fact, this misconception is the initial step in the development of drug dependence, regardless of whether the drug is marijuana or heroin, whether it produces physiological dependence or not. And dependence cannot be broken until the misconception is straightened out, even though the physiological need is terminated. (Hence the failure of methadone to cure addicts of being addicts.) By contrast, a user who realizes that he has been using the drug merely as a trigger or excuse for having an experience that is a natural and potentially valuable element of human consciousness comes to see that the drugged state is not exactly synonymous with the experience he wants. He begins to look for ways to isolate the desired aspect of the chemically induced state and often finds that some form of meditation will satisfy his desire to get high more effectively. One sees a great many experienced drug takers give up drugs for meditation, but one does not see any meditators give up meditation for drugs. This observation has led some drug educators to hope that young people can be encouraged to abandon drugs in favor of systems like the transcendental meditation of Maharishi Mahesh.

Society labors under the same delusions as dependent users. It thinks that problems come from drugs rather than from people. Therefore, it tries to stop people from using drugs or to make drugs disappear rather than to educate people about the "right" use of drugs. No drug is inherently good or evil; all have potential for positive use, as much as for negative use. The point is not to deny people the experience of chemically altered consciousness but to show them how to have it in forms that are not harmful to themselves or to society. And the way to do that is to recognize the simple truth that the experience comes from the mind, not from the drug. (Once you have learned from a drug what being high really is, you can begin to reproduce such state without the drug; all persons who accomplish this feat testify that the non-pharmacological high is superior.) Ironically, society's efforts to stop drug abuse are the very factors causing drug abuse. There really is no Drug Problem at all, rather a Drug-Problem Problem. And it will continue growing until we admit that drugs have a positive potential that can be realized.

Many non-Western societies have experimented with this alternative. The primitive Indian tribes of the Amazon basin, for example, make free use of drugs but have no problems of abuse. That is, although these groups use a multitude of hallucinogenic barks, seeds, and leaves, no one takes the drugs to express hostility toward society, to drop out of the social process, to rebel against his parents or teachers, or to hurt himself. These Indians admit that their world contains substances that alter consciousness; they do not try to make them go away or to prevent their use. They accept the fact that people, especially children, seek out altered states of consciousness. And, rather than attempt to deny their children experiences they know to be important, they allow them to have them under the guidance of experts in such matters, usually the tribal shamans. Recognizing that drugs have potential for harm, the shaman surrounds their use with ritual and conveys the rationale of this ritual to his charges. Furthermore, the states of consciousness induced by drugs in these remote areas are used for positive ends, and are not just lapsed into out of boredom or frustration. Some drugs are used only by shamans, for communing with the spirit world or for diagnosing illness; others are used by adolescents in coming-of-age rites; still others are consumed by the whole tribe as recreational intoxicants on special occasions.

I am not suggesting that we return to a primitive life in the jungle, but I do think we have much to learn from these Amazonian peoples. One reason we are so locked into wrong ways of thinking about drugs is that no one can see a goal worth working for, only problems to work against. The Indian model is an ideal —not something to be substituted overnight for our present situation, but something to be kept in mind as the direction to move toward. Let me list the three chief features of this ideal system as proposals for our own society:

1. *Recognition of the importance of altered states of consciousness and the existence of a normal drive to experience them.* There is a considerable lack of enlightenment in scientific circles concerning the nature of consciousness, in both its ordinary and its nonordinary forms, and there would doubtless be resistance from the professional community to these propositions. But, because consciousness is, above all, a matter of inner experience, most laymen are quite willing to accept these ideas. Many adults have simply forgotten their childhood experiences with altered states of consciousness and recall them vividly as soon as they try to. Therefore, I think the possibilities for re-education are good.

As thinking about drugs moves in this direction, society will become less and less inclined to try to frustrate the human need for periods of altered awareness, so that the role of the criminal law in this area should diminish. At the same time, there may be a culmination of the present efforts of younger scientists to bring the study of altered states of consciousness into the "respectable" disciplines and institutions. A very great body of information exists on these states; it simply needs collecting and arranging, so that we can begin to correlate it with what we know objectively about the nervous system.

2. *Provision for the experience of altered states of consciousness in growing children.* Rather than drive children to seek out these states surreptitiously, we must aim to do as the Indians do: let children learn by experience under the watchful guidance of an elder. "Drug education" in the United States means thinly disguised attempts to scare children away from drugs. True education would let those who wanted to explore consciousness do so without guilt and with adult support and supervision. Such explorations should include drug experience, because drugs are legitimate tools for altering awareness. Because they have a potential for negative use, they cannot be used wantonly but must be used in certain prescribed ways, at certain times, and for certain purposes. Thus, we must develop a "ritual" for drug experience analogous to the Indian tribal rituals. We will also need analogs of the shamans—persons who, by virtue of their own experience with altered states of consciousness, are qualified to supervise the education of the young.

3. *Incorporation of the experience into society for positive ends.* It is not enough that we come to tolerate alterations of consciousness. We must put them to use for the good of individuals and society. We have come to think of drug experience as an escape from reality; but, if it is so in our society, we have made it so. People who can openly and purposefully spend time away from ordinary consciousness seem superior when they function in ordinary consciousness. They are healthier, both physically and mentally; they lead more productive lives; and they can become numerous enough to constitute a great natural resource in any society. In addition, they may be utilizing their nervous systems to their fullest potential—a goal most of us are far from reaching.

To these three aims, I would add a fourth, not derived from the Indian pattern:

4. *Encouragement of individuals to satisfy their needs for altered consciousness by means that do not require external tools.* Any tools used to alter consciousness—not just drugs—tend to cause dependence, because they delude people into believing that the experience comes from them rather than involuntarily from within the mind. To guard against this tendency, therefore, we must educate people and not try to do away with the tools. Our goal should be to train people to live safely in a world where there are things with potential for both harm and good, to show them that inimical forces can be changed into friendly ones. To do this, we should not try to shield young people from things that may harm them; they must learn by experience. Perhaps it is possible to convince adolescents that meditation is better than drugs as an approach to altered consciousness, but they will not believe it unless they have been through drug experience and seen its limitations for themselves.

I will conclude by affirming my belief that this system is a real possibility and not a hopeless, unattainable ideal. As such, it is well worth working toward. The first step need be nothing more than to stop what we are now doing to prevent us from reaching the goal. And that is nearly everything we are doing in the name of combating drug abuse.

Narcotics Addiction and Control in Great Britain

by Edgar May

Background • The Clinics • Law Enforcement • Research • The Statistics • Results • Personal Observations

After a decade of spiraling narcotics addiction in England, the trend was reversed in 1970.

The British narcotics problem admittedly is minor when compared with that of the United States. England had never counted more than 3,000 narcotics addicts; estimates in the United States range from 150,000 to 250,000. However, while American drug experts warn of a continuously growing number of addicts, Britain's Home Office recently reported a drop of almost 8 per cent, the first since the drug problem became a serious national concern.

The slowdown had already begun in 1969, when the annual increase of addicts was held to a trickle, one year after the government tightened its narcotics policies by limiting the prescribing of heroin to staff physicians of government-run drug clinics. Previously, any general physician was permitted to prescribe heroin. Until the clinic system had been operating for a year, the number of narcotics addicts in England doubled every -sixteen months. The reversal of this trend has been accompanied by a significant drop in new addicts. In 1968, a total of 1,476 previously unknown cases were reported. In 1969, the figure was 1,030, and by 1970 it had dropped to 711.

These encouraging figures, however, concern only a part of the British drug-abuse problem, albeit the toughest and the one over which there is the most public concern. But addicts and abusers of amphetamines and barbiturates are not included in this count. Furthermore, there is a far greater and increasing army of marijuana and hashish users, for which there is no accurate tally.

But, while the latest statistics may give the English drug scene a more optimistic appearance than it deserves, the bizarre anecdotes that have been published in both the English and American press may have colored the past picture with more despair than is justified.

In the twitching kaleidoscope that is Picadilly Circus, the scene is as harsh and distorted as the electric letters that flash their spasmodic messages from high about the throng. The pallid young addicts, staggering out of doorways to panhandle enough for a fix, casting furtive glances at passersby while pills or other drugs are exchanged . . . a jab of a needle in the toilet of the Underground . . . a hypodermic protruding between the toes of a grimy, infected foot . . . a spurt of fresh blood on a soiled shirt . . . a young girl collapsing in a doorway after taking a barbiturate injection. It's all there and more.

These scenes may have become part of the tourist attractions of London's Times Square, but they don't reflect accurately the addiction problem in England. Although it is risky to offer findings in the complex and often-disputed field of drug addiction, some basic trends are clear:

- Heroin addiction is no longer the major "hard" drug problem in England. The rising tide of new heroin addicts has been stopped and, in fact, has significantly receded. The quantity of

heroin prescribed in government clinics continues to decline.
- Methadone is the most frequently used drug in England today and is replacing heroin. But the drop in heroin is not fully matched by the rise in methadone. New addicts tend to be addicted to methadone rather than heroin, but the number of newcomers addicted to anything is smaller than in previous years.
- Methadone maintenance generally is not practiced in England as it is in the United States, in that far more English addicts inject methadone than take it orally.
- British hard-drug users often are polyaddicts, injecting a variety of drugs, obtained both legally and illegally. The most recent craze is the injection of barbiturates, a particularly damaging habit that has raised the concerns of all those working in the British drug field.
- Although the backbone of the English drug program is the government-sponsored clinic, where addicts obtain free drugs, the phrase "British clinic system" is misleading. There is very little system to the clinics beyond the fact that they all prescribe narcotics. Clinics vary widely in services offered, treatment approach, staff, and facilities. Nevertheless, the clinics are credited widely with curbing the heroin problem, while the degree of their contribution to the problem of methadone addiction is debated. Furthermore, clinics are considered to have had an impact on improving the total hard-drug picture, but evidence for this generally is subjective rather than objective and statistical.
- Although there is some black-market activity in all drugs, it appears to be on neither a major nor a very professional scale. No one interviewed claimed that there was a vast, hidden opiate-addict population supplying itself from the black market.
- No one in England saw any correlation between drug addiction and a rise in crime.
- Finally, the commonly held view in the United States that heroin addiction automatically turns the user into a completely antisocial, unproductive misfit is simply not shared in

England. Many English addicts hold regular jobs. Estimates
of employment of all known addicts range from 40 to 50
per cent.

But perhaps to find the most glaring difference between the
two countries, you have to go back to the hurlyburly of Picadilly
Circus. There, in a locked cabinet on a medicine shelf at Boots
the Chemist, which attracts a disproportionate number of addicts
because it is open all night, you can find heroin tablets in small
bottles. A printed-in-red retail price list says:

Heroin   100 tablets   18 S.

At the 1970 rate of exchange, this is $2.16. On New York's
streets, the retail price for the same amount of heroin can run as
high as $1,000.

BACKGROUND

Unlike the United States, England has consistently treated drug
addiction as a medical problem. Even while moving toward more
restrictive policies in the drug-abuse field, the nation has never
wavered from this medical point of view. "The addict should be
regarded as a sick person, he should be treated as such and not
as a criminal, provided that he does not resort to criminal acts,"[1]
said the Brain Committee, which formulated the first significant
changes in the country's drug laws seven years ago.

Hard-drug abuse in England, also unlike the United States,
became a problem only in the last ten years or so, as Table 7–1
clearly indicates. In 1954, the first year nationwide heroin statistics were available, there were only 54 identified heroin addicts.
The majority of the 335 known drug addicts that year, a total of
179, were addicted to morphine, and most were women. Also, the
majority of these addicts had become addicted after receiving a
narcotic to relieve pain related to a lengthy illness. Among the few
nontherapeutic addicts, a high proportion were doctors and
nurses who had experimented with narcotics and subsequently
became hooked.

Today, of course, the numbers, the reasons for addiction, and the average addict age (see Table 7–2) have all changed. For example, only 2 per cent of the reported addicts in 1968 were classified as therapeutic. Among heroin addicts that year, 32 per cent were under twenty years of age. Men outnumbered women by more than 3 to 1.

TABLE 7–1
NUMBER OF KNOWN ADDICTS, SEX, AND DRUGS USED

Year	Number of known Addicts	Sex		Drugs used*				
		M	F	Heroin	Meth-adone	Mor-phine	Co-caine	Peth-idine
1945	367	144	223					
1950	306	158	148					
1955	335	159	176	54	21	179	6	64
1960	437	195	242	94	68	177	52	98
1961	470	223	247	132	59	168	84	105
1962	532	262	270	175	54	157	112	112
1963	635	339	296	237	55	172	171	107
1964	753	409	344	342	61	162	211	128
1965	927	558	369	521	72	160	311	102
1966	1,349	886	463	899	156	178	443	131
1967	1,729	1,262	467	1,299	243	158	462	112
1968	2,782	2,161	621	2,240	486	198	564	120
1969	2,881	2,295	586	1,417	1,687	345	311	128
1970	2,661	2,071	590	914	1,820	346	198	122

* Alone or in combination with other drugs.

SOURCE: Drugs Branch, Home Office.

England differs from the United States again in that its addicts today are not as a rule from disadvantaged families, are not members of minority groups, and do not "turn on" to blot out the economic dispair of the ghetto. "On the contrary," says Dr. David V. Hawks, a key staff member of the Addiction Research Unit of London's Institute of Psychiatry; "those notified in the 1960's were often construed as 'middle class dropouts' whose addiction, far from being explicable in terms of some material disadvantage, appears to have been motivated by the deliberate rejection of middle-class norms and opportunities."

TABLE 7–2
AGES OF ADDICTS KNOWN TO THE HOME OFFICE

	1959	1960	1961	1962	1963	1964	1965	1966	1967	1968	1969	1970
Under 20												
All drugs	—	1	2	3	17	40	145	329	395	764	637	405
Heroin*	—	1	2	3	17	40	134	317	381	709	598	365
20–34												
All drugs	50	62	94	132	184	257	347	558	906	1,530	1,789	1,813
Heroin	35	52	87	126	162	219	319	479	827	1,390	1,709	1,705
35–49												
All drugs	92	91	95	107	128	138	134	162	142	146	174	158
Heroin	7	14	19	24	38	61	52	83	66	78	101	95
50 and over												
All drugs	278	267	272	274	298	311	291	286	279	260	241	253
Heroin	26	27	24	22	20	22	16	20	24	20	46	50
Age unknown												
All drugs	34	16	7	16	8	7	10	14	7	82	40	32
Heroin									1	43	26	18

* Beginning with 1969, this figure includes addicts to heroin and/or methadone.

SOURCE: Drugs Branch, Home Office.

This does not mean that the poor have escaped heroin addiction. They have not. But they aren't—by any count—in the majority.

The basic guidelines for Britain's drug-abuse policy were established in 1926, a dozen years after America passed the Harrison Act, which set the stage for the U.S. addict-criminal doctrine. A committee chaired by Sir Humphrey Rolleston, a prominent English physician, turned the problem over to doctors and steered it away from the police. The Rolleston committee said that doctors should be allowed to prescribe narcotics to wean patients off these drugs, to relieve pain after a prolonged cure had failed, and in cases where small doses enabled otherwise helpless patients to perform useful tasks and lead relatively normal lives.

The Rolleston Committee's findings were the basis of British drug policy for almost forty years. They were reaffirmed in general in 1961 by the Interdepartmental Committee on Drug Addiction, chaired by Sir Russell Brain. However, the addiction statistics began to move upward, the Brain Committee was reconvened, and a second report was issued on July 31, 1965. It recommended the first significant restrictions on the prescribing of heroin and cocaine.

The report succinctly stated the motivation and fears behind England's drug policies and their sharp differences with those of the United States:

We have borne in mind the dilemma which faces the authorities responsible for the control of dangerous drugs in this country. If there is insufficient control it may lead to the spread of addiction— as is happening at present. If, on the other hand, the restrictions are so severe as to prevent or seriously discourage the addict from obtaining any supplies from legitimate sources, [they] may lead to the development of an organized illicit traffic. The absence hitherto of such an organized illicit traffic has been attributed largely to the fact that an addict has been able to obtain supplies of drugs legally. But this facility has now been abused, with the result that addiction has increased.

The Brain Committee recommended the following changes:

1. "All addicts to dangerous drugs should be notified to a central authority." (This authority later became the Chief Medical Officer of the Home Office.)

2. "To treat addicts a number of special treatment centers should be established, especially in the London area."

3. "There should be powers for compulsory detention of addicts in these centers." (This recommendation later was rejected by the Minister of Health.)

4. "The prescribing of heroin and cocaine to addicts should be limited to doctors on the staff of these treatment centers."

5. "It should be a statutory offence for other doctors to prescribe heroin and cocaine to an addict."

The government accepted these recommendations and incorporated them in the Dangerous Drugs Act of 1967. In February, 1968, the compulsory notification of addicts went into effect. By April of that year, heroin and cocaine prescribing was restricted to doctors in the newly created treatment centers.[2]

During the almost three years that passed between the committee's report and the effective date of its recommendations, hard-drug addiction soared. From 1964, the latest year for which a full year's statistics were available to the committee, to 1967, heroin addicts alone increased fourfold, from 342 to 1,299. A year later, the heroin-addict figure reached 2,240.

The committee's concern that "insufficient control may lead to the spread of addiction" was more than confirmed. Although it is unjust to blame the British medical profession alone for the sharp rise in addiction, the fact is that general over-prescribing and the activities of a few medical charlatans fueled the craving for heroin.

Some addicts were receiving prescriptions from general practitioners for as much as 20 or more grains of heroin a day (1,200 milligrams). Very few addicts used that amount themselves (a dosage, incidentally, that would kill almost any American adult). Most beneficiaries of overprescribing doctors sold their surplus and, of course, addicted others. What is surprising is that the Disciplinary Committee of the General Medical Council, the policing arm of the British medical profession, permitted this situation to continue as long at it did.

The problem of overprescribing doctors, with strong hints that their conduct was ethically questionable, was discussed in print as early as 1965 in the public report of the Brain Committee:

> From the evidence before us we have been led to the conclusion that the major source of supply has been the activity of a very few doctors who have prescribed excessively for addicts. Thus we were informed that in 1962 one doctor alone prescribed almost 600,000 tablets (6 million milligrams or 6 kilos) of heroin for addicts.[3] The same doctor, on one occasion, prescribed 900 tablets (9,000 milligrams) of heroin to one addict and three days later prescribed for the same patient another 600 tablets (6,000 milligrams) "to replace pills lost in an accident." Two doctors each issued a single prescription for 1,000 tablets (10,000 milligrams).

Overprescribing was so extensive during the years after the Brain Committee report and before the opening of the clinics that pure, British-manufactured heroin was readily and relatively inexpensively available on the black market, where imported, illicit heroin was virtually unknown. While prices for all consumer products rose during this period, black-market heroin—the overprescribed surplus—held the line against inflation and stayed at one pound sterling a grain. This meant that, for $2.40 a day, an addict could support a heroin habit. (Today, incidentally, British-manufactured heroin is both relatively scarce and expensive on the black market, with a sixfold increase to six pounds, or $14.40 a grain.)

One psychiatrist, reviewing the years immediately preceding the opening of the clinics, felt that general practitioners were overprescribing to such an extent that, for every two addicts receiving prescriptions, at least one other was maintaining his habit from these supplies. Another psychiatrist believed that about a third of the reported addicts were not *bona fide* addicts at all but were merely sometime heroin users who conned doctors into issuing regular prescriptions that they would then sell.

But a few doctors clearly had not been sweet-talked by addicts into writing too-generous prescriptions. They had purposely turned the narcotics problem into a lucrative enterprise with the simple stroke of a pen. They wrote prescriptions for pay—at a going rate of one pound to two pounds per script. These were the junkie doctors whose names can be found in almost every London clinic's case records.

One of them, a dermatologist with a passion for gambling, ended his prescribing days issuing orders from a taxi parked in front of the Baker Street Tube Station. He was nabbed on a technicality—failing to keep proper narcotics records—spent a short period in jail, and finally had his license to practice revoked by the General Medical Council after numerous complaints of his activities from druggists and Home Office officials. Another was reported to have issued prescriptions to 140 addicts with a daily average of 6 to 8 grains at the height of his narcotics enterprise. He is also without a medical license today. He went to jail for conspiracy to commit murder.

While no one knowledgeable about the English drug scene will say that the nation would not have had a hard-drug problem had it not been for overprescribing doctors and outright charlatans, there is consensus that overgenerous prescriptions, whatever the doctor's motivation, helped significantly to create the chaotic drug scene that the government clinic program was expected to remedy.

THE CLINICS

In 1970, a monthly average of 1,154 drug addicts obtained government-paid-for heroin and/or methadone and a little cocaine from clinics scattered throughout England and Wales. Recently, the clinic figures have remained relatively stable, fluctuating by fewer than 100 addicts every month. The number of new addicts registered with clinics dropped from a monthly average of 66 to 41 in 1971. (See Table 7–3.)

Nevertheless, it is risky to conclude that this relative stability in clinic enrollment reflects containment of drug addiction in England. Some clinics appear to have set a quota of addicts and simply do not accept, or cannot accept, more because of staff or

TABLE 7–3
SUMMARY OF MONTHLY RETURNS FROM HOSPITAL BOARDS

	Number of new outpatients during month		Number of outpatients at end of month	
	London	*All clinics*	*London*	*All clinics*
1969				
January	65	91	895	1,115
February	46	74	894	1,130
March	56	83	904	1,130
April	46	64	927	1,159
May	47	78	934	1,171
June	48	70	936	1,170
July	47	58	964	1,180
August	30	49	924	1,136
September	40	66	914	1,159
October	48	73	922	1,179
November	32	53	898	1,145
December	32	40	903	1,146
1970				
January	36	53	891	1,133
February	32	36	909	1,157
March	27	40	927	1,160
April	34	45	947	1,171
May	25	35	963	1,191
June	20	31	966	1,133
July	37	47	986	1,149
August	27	46	992	1,159
September	27	45	982	1,160
October	28	44	985	1,162
November	29	41	962	1,142
December	15	27	956	1,131

SOURCE: Department of Health and Social Security.

facility limitations. The slow reduction in new addicts, however, is a hopeful sign.

There are 14 clinics in London, which has four fifths of the country's addicts. Elsewhere, an addict may obtain drugs at 13 special facilities or at some 42 hospital outpatient departments These are prepared to service an occasional addict as part of their regular outpatient program.

The special clinics vary in every conceivable way—in type of facility, size of patient load, size of staff, treatment approach, and prescribing philosophy. There is no central authority over the clinics to provide specific guidelines for staffing or determine treatment or prescribing policies. Because of this, it is a mistake to refer to the English "drug clinic system." There is no common "system" beyond the fact that addicts may obtain heroin and methadone from government-supported clinics.

Each clinic director is doing "his own thing," based on his own particular approach to drug addiction. He works with the facility, staff, and budget he was able to get from his own hospital and Regional Hospital Board, the governing body that supervises medical care for a given area.

These various approaches have not been evaluated comparatively for cost or effectiveness. The addicts, however, are usually in agreement about which are the "best" clinics in a less than scientific rating system, which might be called the "Santa Claus" scale. It ranks candidates on their drug-prescribing generosity.

The lack of central direction is the result not of careless management but rather of design. Americans often have the impression that the British National Health Service is a monolith that dictates everything from aspirin dispensing to appendix removing, but the fact is that the government's Ministry of Health has approached physicians both within and outside of the National Health Service with the circumspection of an impresario dealing with a diva.

After the government accepted most of the second Brain Committee recommendations and prepared the necessary legislation to implement them, the Department of Health and Social Security issued a memorandum to Regional Hospital Boards and hospital governing groups.[4] The Ministry directed its memo particularly at mental hospitals and psychiatric departments of general hospitals. As a result, today the clinic directors are psychiatrists, most of whom follow a general psychiatric practice in addition to their interests in the drug field.

The Health Department memorandum included a list of the known addicts in each Regional Hospital area. Since most addicts were in the London area, it asked city hospitals with psychiatric departments to plan for drug clinics. At the same time, the Health Department asked hospitals to set up inpatient beds for withdrawal treatment and to assess addicts who would obtain their drugs as outpatients for the required dosage. Today most clinics have such beds available to them. Significantly, the "how" of operating clinics was not described.

The decision to supply an addict with drugs and whether to seek to substitute other drugs, the assessment of dosage, and the method of supply rest with the clinician. It is to be expected, however, that where possible, the dosage will be determined by assessment during inpatient observation and that this will usually be offered, though continued treatment cannot be made conditional on acceptance. [This in-hospital assessment is rarely done today, and it is clear that most clinic directors reject this Health Department "expectation."] The organization of services will depend on the method of supplying drugs that is adopted by clinicians. It is, however, desirable in any area that there should be a fairly uniform approach; otherwise, the organization of services and the sharing of the load will be obstructed because addicts will gravitate to those clinics where they think drugs are easiest to get. While direct administration of drugs by the medical staff of the treatment center is not excluded, supply by the hospital or by retail prescription is likely to be more generally practicable.

The clinics have certain statistical reporting obligations, both to the Health Department and the Home Office. There is an exchange of views and information among clinic directors and other medical staff members at periodic meetings called by the Health Department. A department official told me that these meetings generally are held every two months, but the records show that such sessions are usually held on an irregular basis. Minutes of the meetings indicate that not all clinics are represented at every meeting and not every clinic director attends regularly.

FACILITIES

The differences between clinics is apparent from inspection of their physical facilities. In the naval-base city of Portsmouth, the clinic is in a large general hospital tucked behind a door marked "Dental Waiting Room." In East London, the center is in its own building on the grounds of a mental hospital. In the Denmark Hill area, it is part of the hospital's general outpatient department.

If you visit St. Giles Clinic in the Church of England Community Center, you are reminded of an Alec Guinness movie. Dr. James H. Willis, a young psychiatrist, holds court resplendent in a white medical coat, seated behind a large wooden table in a room marked "Lecture Hall." He is flanked by two pianos and a bass fiddle. Above and behind his head, a brass plaque reads: "The trustees of St. Giles Center gratefully acknowledge the generous support given by the Rotary Club of Camberwell."

It is doubtful that the Rotarians would rush to support the effort now going on in the lecture hall. It is lack of such support that has prevented Dr. Willis from using a new $192,000 building specifically constructed for his drug clinic by the two hospitals and the Regional Hospital Board sponsoring it. The building, which includes eight single rooms for inpatient assessment, stood empty for more than a year after it was completed. Public protest —exploited by local politicians—forced the hospital to rescind its decision to bring young addicts into the middle-class neighborhood of St. Giles.

In his churchly retreat, Dr. Willis has no facilities even for basic medical examinations, and patients leave urine specimens in the center's men's room.

STAFFING

A most basic difference among clinics is in the kind and size of staff that operate them. One of the most significant contrasts is between St. Clement and Lambeth Hospital Clinics. The staffing patterns are as follows:

LAMBETH (96 active patients)

Doctors:
> 1 3½ days a week
> 1 2½ days a week
> 1 1½ days a week

Social worker:
> 1 2½ days a week

Nurse:
> 1 full time

Secretary:
> 1

ST. CLEMENT (71 active patients)

Doctors:
   1 full time
   1 1½ days a week
   1 psychiatric intern 1½ days a week
Social workers:
   2 full time
Nurses:
   10 full time
Secretary:
   1

The nurses at St. Clement function like social workers: they counsel patients and make home calls both to patients and to their families, relatives, or close friends.

The Lambeth Clinic, run by Dr. Thomas H. Bewley, a well-known author of medical articles on the English drug scene, is far closer to the English clinic prototype.

The besieged Dr. Willis at St. Giles, incidentally, was even worse off when it came to staffing. With 75 active patients and 64 inactive patients, the clinic included three doctors, two full time and another one-third time. Although there were two slots for social workers, both were temporarily empty. Dr. Willis has no nursing help. His only other assistance comes from a secretary and a hospital porter, who acts as factotum around his piano-flanked emporium.

St. Clement, in terms of staff time for the addict, is clearly exceptional. It was originally intended as a day hospital where an addict would come for the entire day, returning to his home only at night. The original staffing pattern was retained when the clinic was turned into what can be described more accurately as a day center that addicts of the clinic may or may not attend. There is a ping-pong table, art classes, and a "fixing room" where addicts can inject themselves. Individual- and group-therapy sessions also are held in the day center.

Among all London clinics, the amount of social-work time provided to addicts varies from 475 hours per week (St. Clement) to none, according to a questionnaire filled out by the clinics themselves.

Because of the difference in staff time between St. Clement and Lambeth, the addict's relationship to these clinics is vastly different. At St. Clement, each social worker and nurse has about ten cases. They know each addict by his first name, and the easy, relaxed relationship that comes with familiarity is evident. One addict, for example, came in to show his nurse pictures of his recent wedding and to thank her for her congratulatory telegram.

At Lambeth, the lone social worker, who provides twenty hours a week, has a caseload of 30 addicts out of the 96 active with the clinic. Of the 30, she estimated that she has what she called "a deep relationship" with a half dozen. "They get a good half hour a week."

Of the clinic's work, she said: "We're containing it, regularizing it a bit; but, we're not treating it. I think I do first aid a lot."

At St. Clement, staff members were slightly, but not much, more encouraging. Not only did this clinic represent the most concentrated staff effort with addicts, but its patients resemble American ghetto addicts more closely than any other London group.

St. Clement is a 128-bed mental hospital in East London, an area that in terms of income and class—but not color—can be compared to New York's Harlem or Bedford-Stuyvesant. The addiction clinic of St. Clement serves patients from the surrounding neighborhoods, the bleak row houses that bring to mind a Charles Dickens novel. Eighty per cent of St. Clement's addiction-clinic customers are East End boys; the other 20 per cent come from the far more affluent middle- and upper-class West End.

While an estimated 10 per cent of the East End population is colored (i.e., Negro, Indian, Pakistani), only one of the clinic's 100 patients is half-Negro. This appears to reflect accurately the fact that in England few "colored" are involved with narcotic drugs.

The clinic is located on the hospital grounds in a separate pre-fab building constructed especially for this use at a cost of 14,000 pounds, or $33,600. The annual operating cost for salaries and drugs is estimated by its director to be about the same amount.

Psychiatrist John Denham is both clinic director and head of the St. Clement Hospital. Much of the day-to-day operation of the clinic fell on Dr. Margaret Tripp, the full-time psychiatrist who served at the clinic from the summer of 1968, when it opened, to 1971.

Neither Dr. Denham nor Dr. Tripp makes any grand claims for the clinic, even though they, and it, have received considerable publicity in U.S. media (*Look* magazine, various television and radio networks). Dr. Denham has a thick file of letters in response to this publicity requesting permission to visit and interview him. He does not trade on this notoriety.

As is true of virtually all other clinics, St. Clement's heroin dispensing is dropping monthly—from 214 grams in March, 1969, to 73 grams in May, 1970. Methadone, both ampoules for injection and oral, has increased at St. Clement, but not in proportion to the drop in heroin. Dr. Denham attributes this heroin reduction to the use of methadone, to more conservative prescribing, and to greater expertise among clinic doctors. He readily admits to the confusion that apparently hit every clinic in the opening period of 1968. "A drug addict presented himself and said he needed six grains of heroin a day. We knew he could do with two, but that he would settle for four. It was as haphazard as that."

The same kind of candor is evident in a paper published by Dr. P. H. Connell, another of the early pioneers in drug-addiction control in England.[5] Reporting on 107 narcotics users attending a London clinic between March, 1968, and February, 1969, Dr. Connell acknowledged that some of these patients had become addicted to drugs by the clinic.

REGISTRATION

How do you begin obtaining free drugs?

Some of the addicts interviewed are convinced it is getting harder to get on the rolls. Some say that, for a new addict to get on, he has to buy black-market narcotics for a while and then show wicked withdrawal symptoms.

Doctors discount the severity of these statements but acknowledge that they are getting more conservative. Interclinic monthly heroin and methadone prescription quantities are distributed among the clinics, and this may have developed a touch of competition to stay in the range of low prescribers. At St. Clement, for example, a monthly graph is kept showing its standing against the all-London average.

Doctors agree that identifying an addict and prescribing the correct quantity of drugs is the toughest part of their jobs. They use words like "haggling" and "bargaining" sessions to describe the difficulties of deciding how much an addict should receive.

The Health Department's suggestion of in-hospital assessment before prescribing to addicts generally is not part of the procedures of the London clinics. An occasional applicant may be sent for observation for several days, but this is the exception and not the rule.

In Portsmouth, however, Dr. Ian Christie will not accept a new patient unless he agrees to three days of hospitalization to determine the kind and size of his habit, or, for that matter, if indeed he has one.

In London, addicts arriving at a clinic for the first time, or to reapply, usually are given at least two interviews. The first may be with a nurse or social worker and the second with a clinic psychiatrist. After acceptance, addicts generally report once every week to their psychiatrist or social worker. Some are requested to come in several times a week, while others, who may be more stable, are permitted to report every two weeks.

Before acceptance, one, and sometimes several, urine tests are scheduled, usually two or more days apart. Drug-positive urine tests play a key role in the decision-making process.

Urine tests, incidentally, are not regularly scheduled for every addict after he has been accepted by a clinic. Their frequency varies from clinic to clinic. At St. Giles, Dr. Willis formerly demanded only sporadic urine tests. Now, however, every patient gives a sample at each clinic visit. In other clinics, it appears that tests are made when there is some suspicion of other than clinic-prescribed drug use.

A key step in the preacceptance interview procedure is the completion of a form outlining the addict's biography, his drug history, and his physical characteristics. This is sent to the Home

Office, where it is compared with the master list of registered addicts. The procedure helps to identify previously unknown addicts and to prevent duplicate registering at two or more clinics.

Have addicts succeeded in getting on the rolls of two different clinics? Yes, but how many or how often is difficult to document. At St. Clement, Dr. Denham does not remember a case where the Home Office check produced duplicate registration. However, he does recall an incident indicating that the problem is real. Not long after the clinic opened, a boy, while stoned, told his fellow addicts that he was obtaining drugs from two clinics. This came to the attention of the staff, and a nurse was sent to the clinic closest to St. Clement. Seven addicts were identified as St. Clement boys and five others confessed to duplicate registration. At the time, this represented 12 per cent of the St. Clement caseload.

"Did that surprise you?" I asked Dr. Denham.

"At the time, it annoyed me."

Dr. Connell, in his study of 107 drug users, also found that four had been attending other clinics, where they requested help without, of course, acknowledging the duplication.

From observation, it appeared that a seasoned addict with a long Home Office or clinic record, or both, had much less difficulty in re-registering at a clinic than a previous "unknown." Dr. Bewley permitted me to sit in on a series of interviews with addicts applying to the Lambeth clinic. All had been previously interviewed by the clinic's part-time psychiatrists, who also sat in on these second interviews.

My notes for this session are as follows:

1. Male, out of prison since May 1. Was with Lambeth a year ago, had received 200 mg. daily of heroin and methadone; long criminal record, most recent possession of burglar tools, *cannabis*; told to return for urine test. Dr. Bewley indicated he probably will be re-registered with 20 mg. methadone a day as starter.

2. Male, long criminal record, now under three-year suspended sentence; long drug history, longest period off drugs was six weeks; told to come back for urine test. Dr. Bewley indicated he probably will be put on clinic rolls.

3. Male, 23, in and out of series of building industry jobs; said he started with drugs at 16, shooting heroin and methadone at 20; said now buying six ampoules of methadone a day on black market at $1.20 per ampoule or $7.20 for day's supply; no criminal record; first urine test showed methadone; told to come back after weekend for another urine test. Bewley estimated there was a 50-50 chance he would not be back. If he comes and test is positive, he probably will be accepted.

Dr. Connell, in his study of the previously cited 107 drug users at a London Clinic, found a large dropout rate between urine tests. "Refusal to prescribe at first attendance, whilst awaiting results of urinalysis, led to a high incidence of failed reattendance. Thus 92 per cent prescribed heroin reattended, whilst only 35 per cent prescribed no drugs returned." This was true, even though 22 out of 36 who had been given no drugs had positive urine tests.

This led Dr. Connell to conclude: "In view of the essential need for accurate diagnosis, it seems inescapable that a prescribing method of management should not be adopted until firm evidence of daily use is obtained by, say, three consecutive positive urines collected on different days and over a period of ten days or more to take into account the fact that methadone is excreted more slowly than morphine."

4. Female, 23, no previous history with clinic; arrested four times, shoplifting, abuse of floor walker; said she was taking 130 mg. heroin daily obtained from black market. She was turned down.

The psychiatrist who first interviewed the girl acknowledged, as did Dr. Bewley, that much of this decision-making process is guesswork. Will this girl now go out and steal enough merchandise to fuel what may be a drug habit? Will she overshoot herself to convince Lambeth or another clinic that she really is addicted? No one could answer these questions.

DRUG DISPENSING

None of the London addicts receives his drugs from the medical staff in the clinics. Rather, a prescription is mailed directly to the druggist of the addict's choice. Only on rare occasions does the addict receive a prescription personally—for example, if it is clear that the post office cannot deliver it in time to fill an immediate need.

Each prescription form is filled out by the clinic physician, generally for a week's supply. Prescription blanks are kept under lock and key, for there is a black-market price on blank National Health Service prescription forms.

Although a week's order may be on one prescription, the addict must collect his supplies from the druggist daily. On Saturday, he generally receives two days' supply because of Sunday closing. Black-market prices for drugs, incidentally, are highest on Sundays, because of weekend demands by occasional users and addicts who have shot up their two-day supply on Saturday.

Drugstores are monitored periodically by the police. However, these reviews generally are confined to the larger distributors of drugs. The Scotland Yard Drug Squad has four detectives specifically assigned to inspecting drugstores.

Drugstores keep detailed records of both incoming and outgoing drugs. I examined this procedure in Boots Picadilly, the all-night drugstore in London's famed square. Dangerous drugs are kept in a special locked cabinet. Each prescription is double-checked and, of course, recorded. One pharmacist will make up the order and initial the package, which is checked by a second pharmacist. This particular store served 36 addicts daily at the time of this review.

Retail prices are standardized. Heroin is a bargain compared with the various forms of methadone. The 1970 retail prices were as follows:

Heroin	100 tablets	(10 mg. each)	1000 mg.	$2.16
Methadone	100 ampoules	(10 mg. each)	1000 mg.	7.50
Methadone linctus (syrup)	5 bottles	(200 mg. each)	1000 mg.	7.80

Since addicts come under National Health Service coverage, the drugs are free except for a small—25 cents—weekly service charge. Disposable needles and syringes are provided directly to addicts by some clinics or are supplied by the drugstore.

I was able to locate only two clinics in England that provide drugs administered directly by the staff. These are in Southampton and Portsmouth. I visited the Portsmouth clinic, directed by Dr. Ian Christie, in St. James Hospital. Because of the small number of patients, significant conclusions cannot be drawn from the in-clinic, drug-administering approach at this hospital. Seven addicts, six receiving methadone and one heroin, come to the clinic twice a day for their injections. These are given by hospital nurses in early-morning and late-afternoon sessions in the hospital's dental department. Injections are given in the deltoid muscle. The methadone addicts I interviewed said that they do not get a "flash" from the methadone intramuscular injection as they did from heroin when they administered it intravenously themselves in preclinic days.

Although all addicts mentioned the inconvenience of coming twice a day to the hospital—which is not centrally located—only one complained vociferously about it. He said he had to take a cab from work daily in order not to miss his second injection, at the 5:15 afternoon clinic. His employer was unaware of his addiction and, he said, probably would fire him if he found out.

In addition to the twice-daily clinic patients, Dr. Christie has four others receiving methadone linctus which he provides via prescription and two heroin addicts—a husband and wife with a long history of addiction—who also receive prescriptions and administer the drug themselves. "This probably was a mistake," Christie said.

None of those receiving any drug is provided with any rehabilitation services. "If they chose drugs, they get drugs," Dr. Christie said.

He gives each addict alternatives: hospital in-patient withdrawal ("Everyone who has tried that method has relapsed"); in-hospital assessment with subsequent in-clinic daily drug taking; and, finally, entry into a therapeutic community, called the Alpha Unit.

PRESCRIPTION TRENDS

Since the clinics began operating in 1968, the quantity of heroin used by English addicts has been greatly reduced. In the clinics, the monthly total grams of heroin have dropped from 2,177 in January, 1969, to 1,131 in December, 1970 (see Table 7–4).

Furthermore, while in 1968 the vast majority of English addicts were taking heroin, today the majority are taking methadone— alone or in combination with heroin. Whatever the opiate, the daily amount each addict takes is generally significantly less than the preclinic daily quantity.

Statistics show that only 10 per cent, or 140, of all known addicts receiving opiates were receiving heroin alone on December 31, 1970. However, this may be somewhat misleading, not only because the reporting procedure may be less than perfect, but because prescribing physicians frequently change both the quantity and the kind of drug prescribed.

It is important to remember that methadone in England most frequently is provided for intravenous injection (as is heroin), and not for oral consumption, as is common in the United States. More than twice as much methadone is prescribed for injection as orally. Most important, injected methadone has a good "rush" —oral methadone does not.

Most clinics have adopted the policy of moving from heroin to methadone. Often, this is done gradually by giving a combination of heroin and methadone for a certain period and then shifting to methadone only. Finally, an attempt is made to shift to oral or linctus methadone. Psychiatrists agree that the hardest task— beyond total drug abstention—is to convince the addict to give up the needle.

This prescribing trend is reflected in the individual clinics. Here are some samples:

- Lambeth—8 on heroin alone, 12 on methadone and heroin, 76 on methadone alone
- St. Clement—36 on methadone and heroin, 35 on methadone
- St. Giles—54 on heroin or methadone and heroin, 11 on methadone for injection, 10 on methadone oral
- Charing Cross—2 on heroin, 10 on methadone and heroin, 45 on methadone for injection, 33 on methadone oral

- Portsmouth—3 on heroin only, 6 on methadone for injection, 4 on methadone oral

The shift from heroin to methadone is further indicated by the fact that clinics today infrequently interview a new heroin addict. The head nurse of the largest London clinic, Charing Cross, could not recall the last time a new heroin addict had been interviewed; all the new cases were methadone addicts. In Portsmouth, Dr. Christie said, no one addicted to heroin had applied for help in the previous year; all the newcomers were methadone addicts.

METHADONE MAINTENANCE

Directors of government clinics do not practice the Dole-Nyswander methadone-maintenance technique, emphasizing blocking the effect of heroin. Significantly, four clinic directors expressed doubts about the effectiveness of the blocking method. Dr. Christie, for example, believes that methadone blocks heroin in American addicts because they are accustomed to receive low and diluted doses of the latter drug. "When an addict takes only four or five $5 bags a day, which don't contain more than 20 milligrams of heroin, then it works." The others agreed that an addict who takes large doses of heroin daily cannot be blocked with methadone.

However, a private London clinic, run by Dr. Peter A. L. Chapple, has experimented with the methadone-maintenance approach known in the United States. This is the National Addiction and Research Institute, which has at least as many active patients as the biggest government clinic. Dr. Chapple prescribes only oral methadone. He is not licensed to prescribe heroin in his clinic, and he is opposed to prescribing methadone for injection because it perpetuates the needle cult. In 1969, he prescribed oral methadone to 106 patients, 70 per cent of whom were receiving blocking dosages (between 100 and 200 milligrams a day). There are no scientific data available indicating whether these addicts actually were blocked from the effect of heroin. Recently, however, Dr. Chapple said that he has been trying to

TABLE 7–4

QUANTITIES OF HEROIN AND METHADONE PRESCRIBED TO
HEROIN ADDICTS ATTENDING LONDON OUT-PATIENT CLINICS

| | Heroin (grams) | Methadone* (grams) | |
		Ampoules	Other preparations
1969			
January	2,177		
February	1,792		
March	1,743		
April	1,632		
May	1,549		
June	1,470		
July	1,490		
August	1,398		
September	1,263	820	221
October	1,306	861	220
November	1,250	850	209
December	1,323	810	231
1970			
January	1,300	764	214
February	1,226	691	192
March	1,362	827	248
April	1,377	833	283
May	1,162	847	240
June	1,169	891	248
July	1,152	920	247
August	1,168	889	240
September	1,109	923	222
October	1,099	920	237
November	1,045	930	227
December	1,131	931	251

*Interclinic statistics kept only since September, 1969.

SOURCE: Department of Health and Social Security.

reduce the dosages of oral methadone. "It probably was a mistake to go as high as 200 milligrams a day," he added. The maximum is now 100 milligrams a day, while younger addicts are more likely to be around the 30-milligram-per-day level. Dr. Chapple said he has shifted from giving a blocking dose because there is less heroin around. He said he wanted to satisfy the drug hunger and not necessarily to block heroin.

He acknowledged that it is very difficult to work with younger addicts using oral methadone, largely because of their delinquent and erratic behavior. Last year, a young addict died as a result of taking barbiturates while also taking oral methadone. (Dr. Connell, in his examination of 107 addicts at a government clinic, also recorded an oral-methadone overdose death. This involved an addict on 100 milligrams a day who obtained the next day's supply shortly after midnight and drank both within hours of each other.)

If England's drug doctors do not subscribe to methadone maintenance, why have they shifted so dramatically to methadone from heroin?

First, the very creation of the clinic approach was prompted by what England viewed as a growing heroin epidemic. There was public and political pressure to halt the rise in heroin addicts. The monthly distribution of a dossier showing the amounts of heroin prescribed by each clinic made it clear to each clinic director where he stood among his peers in this respect and undoubtedly created pressure to bring the quantity down.

Secondly, there is general agreement among clinic physicians that methadone has a longer-lasting effect than heroin. Thus, the addict needs fewer injections a day.

Thirdly, methadone for injection is considered somewhat more sterile than heroin, since it comes in liquid form, so that the addict merely transfers the ampoule content directly into his syringe. With heroin, he mixes a 10-milligram pill with water, usually unsterile and sometimes from a tap or even a toilet bowl, to dissolve the pill before injecting.

Finally, methadone for injection is viewed by a number of doctors as the bridge to oral methadone. Breaking the needle cult is considered an important success step in the drug-treatment program in England.

Unfortunately, addict performances on heroin, methadone for injection, and oral methadone have received no detailed scientific comparison in England. Furthermore—surprisingly, to an outsider—methadone continues to be available outside of the drug clinics. There is nothing to prevent general practitioners from prescribing it. A few, in fact, do. (Scotland Yard Drug Squad detectives, who monitor drugstores, say that about six London doctors prescribe methadone on a regular basis.) Ironically, the second Brain Committee foresaw the possibility that a substitute drug might become potentially as dangerous as heroin. When the committee urged and achieved prescribing restrictions on heroin, it said: "If, in future, circumstances should change, and other drugs of addiction should take the place now occupied by heroin and cocaine, it would be necessary promptly to amend the 'restricted' list accordingly." A number of leading professionals have urged that methadone be placed on the "restricted" list, but this has not been done.

The clinic shift from heroin to methadone, plus the absence of prescribing prohibitions on general practitioners, undoubtedly had led to a new methadone-addiction problem. The key issue is how big a problem it is. The over-all clinic drug-dispensing statistics indicate strongly that considerably lower quantities of combined heroin and methadone are being prescribed today than the largely heroin-only prescriptions at the beginning of the clinic era, but exactly how much lower is impossible to show, since methadone statistics were not reported until September, 1969.

However, it appears that there has not been a simple switch from a heroin to a methadone problem. Doctors interviewed are concerned about rising methadone cases but do not suggest that they are replacing heroin cases on a one-for-one basis. That is, the methadone increase is moving at a considerably slower pace than the sharp drop in heroin addiction, although no one can document the relative rates of change.

The police, however, are less inclined to make distinctions. In a 1970 report, Scotland Yard said:

There has been a transference of addiction in as much as the treatment centers have succeeded in reducing the amount of heroin prescribed to addicts, thereby reducing the availability of this drug on the "illicit market." But, in so doing, they have increased the prescribing of methadone to counterbalance this reduction; consequently, there is now far more methadone available on the "illicit market."

DRUGS OUTSIDE THE CLINICS

How many other drugs do addicts take to supplement those prescribed by the clinics?

While evidence in this area is both fragmentary and some-times disputed, there is agreement that English addicts often sup-plement the clinic-prescribed drug diet, with a wide assortment of chemicals that affect both the mind and the body. These in-clude black-market methadone or heroin, amphetamines, bar-biturates, tranquilizers, and marijuana, or, for that matter, a smattering of all of them. In short, the addict in England more often than not is a polydrug taker.

The most significant evidence comes from a wide-ranging study conducted by two staff members of the Addiction Research Insti-tute. Between March and November, 1969, they interviewed in depth 111 heroin users attending the London clinics, representing about 10 per cent of all clinic patients in England.[6] The results showed that only a small proportion of English addicts can be considered "stable" in their drug-taking habits.

Several clinic directors expressed reservations about the study, claiming that it did not represent a true cross-section of their population since it included only active heroin addicts. At the time of the interviews, they said, many of their patients, particu-larly the more promising ones, had already been weaned off heroin and onto methadone only. The study, however, did include 91 (of the 111) who were receiving heroin in combination with methadone.

Eighty-four per cent reported to interviewers that in the month prior to the interview they had used drugs other than those prescribed for them by the clinics. Among these other drugs, the largest number reported using barbiturates and tran-quilizers (75 per cent), which, in the majority of cases, were prescribed by private physicians. This is an important indication that extracurricular drug taking did not necessarily mean adding larger doses of illegally obtained narcotics.

The range of drugs used is demonstrated in Table 7–5. These statistics show that the one additional drug all 111 heroin addicts had used was marijuana or hashish (*cannabis*).

An interesting sidelight brought out during the interviews was that 37 per cent had on occasion sold, lent, or exchanged at least some of the drugs the clinics prescribed for them. In addition, the study confirmed the worst fears of physicians about the

TABLE 7–5
OTHER DRUGS USED BY HEROIN ADDICTS

	In last month				Ever used	
	Prescribed		Used			
	Num- ber	Per cent	Num- ber	Per cent	Num- ber	Per cent
Methadone	91	82	95	86	107	97
Other opiates, (e.g., morphine, opium, pethidine)	0	0	25	22		
Amphetamine, amphetamine/ barbiturate mixtures, and other stimulants	14	13	49	44	109	98
Sedatives and hypnotics	51	46	83	75	103	95
Tranquilizers	5	4	19	17	90	81
Cocaine	14	13	32	29	104	94
Cannabis	0	0	68	61	111	100
Psychedelics	0	0	13	12	72	65

unsterile procedures that are an important risk when addicts administer drugs to themselves. The report speaks best for itself:

All subjects were using heroin by injection. In the week prior to interview 28 (25%) subjects had injected themselves at home only, a further 17 (15%) had injected themselves at their clinic or at a day center as well as at their home, 46 (41%) had injected themselves at some time during the week in a public toilet as well as at home, clinic, or day center, and 20 (18%) had injected themselves in a "public place"—e.g., shop doorways, in the street, or in telephone kiosks—in addition to any of the above places. Sixty-two (56%) had injected themselves whilst other addicts were present and also injecting themselves.

The majority of subjects (101, 91%) used a disposable syringe for their injections and of these 67 (66%) regularly used their syringes more than once. Seventy-two subjects (68%) did not clean their arms prior to injection.

Although the most frequent method for preparing an injection was to dissolve heroin in sterile water, 54 (49%) had at some time during the week used ordinary unboiled tap water, and 12 (11%) had used water from a lavatory basin. Nine subjects reported sharing a syringe with another addict during the week.

If injection practices are defined as sterile when normal medical procedure is followed (i.e., using a new disposable syringe for each injection or using an adequately sterilized glass syringe, not sharing a syringe, cleaning the arm prior to injection, and making up the injection with sterile water) then in the total sample, 12 subjects (11%) are using sterile injection practices. In the week prior to interview all others had engaged in some non-sterile practice.

This kind of unsterile drug taking often led to medical complications. Thirty-nine per cent had been in hospitals for treatment of septicaemia, hepatitis, abscesses, or overdose. Of all addicts interviewed, 40 per cent reported hepatitis and overdose and 46 per cent reported abscesses treated both in and outside of hospitals.

Although this report indicated no particular trend in polydrug taking, since the clinics began doctors have seen definite increases in two drugs: methylamphetamine (speed) and barbiturates. In 1968, methylamphetamine was injected by addicts with such frequency that authorities asked its manufacturers to agree to withdraw it from the retail market and restrict its distribution to hospital pharmacies. Within weeks of its disappearance from retail drugstores it disappeared among the addict population.

Misuse of barbiturates by addicts became an acute problem in 1969. Some physicians, however, feel that it has slowed somewhat since the last part of 1970. Addicts inject barbiturates even though they are not manufactured, so that they will dissolve completely in water. The undissolved particles result in collapsed veins and serious abscesses on addicts' arms and legs. Addicts I've interviewed said that they resorted to barbiturates when they couldn't get enough heroin or methadone from the clinics. This, like all addict testimonials, is open to question.

The degree of barbiturate abuse—particularly by injection—is another aspect of the English drug scene that is left largely to conjecture. A study in 1969 of a small sample of heroin addicts —again conducted by a team from the Addiction Research Unit—showed that among this sample the problem was huge.[7] Sixty-five heroin addicts were interviewed in May, June, and July of 1969, and 80 per cent were found to have injected barbiturates. Almost all of them—62 of the 65—had taken barbiturates either by injection or orally. Of course, some had used the drug only to help induce sleep. However, 65 per cent acknowledged they had taken it for no medical reason and only for "kicks."

A few addicts will take barbiturates with them to the clinics, although they may have obtained them from a general practitioner or bought them illicitly. I observed an especially bizarre scene in one of the clinics.

There were two chairs in the room, a steel sink, a length of rubber hose to use as a tourniquet, some cotton, and a supply of paper towels. The walls and the chairs were stained with dried blood; in general, the physical appearance of the room was far from the kind of antiseptic clinic presented by the likes of Drs. Kildare and Ben Casey. The characters on this stage were two young addicts, both unsteady on their feet from drugs taken earlier. One took a syringe from his pocket, washed it out with tap water from the sink, pulled a folded piece of paper from another pocket, removed a barbiturate capsule, broke it in half over the syringe, and emptied its contents into the tube.

Once the white powder was in the syringe, he added tap water, shook the contents vigorously for several seconds, and handed the syringe to his friend. Since his arms and ankles were marked with sores, however, it took several minutes to locate a usable vein. Finally, he settled on a spot about eight inches below the knee. (The other addict, incidentally, shortly afterwards injected himself in the sole of his foot.)

A third addict, more stable, helped the first boy out of the clinic by steadying him with an arm around his shoulders. But once outside the clinic, the boy sagged and collapsed on the grass. A few addicts nearby helped to drag the boy out of the sun to a tree, where they sat him up against its trunk.

I was not alone in observing this sequence; a clinic psychiatrist watched the entire scene with me. No effort was made to assist, dissuade, or reprimand the addicts. We were both spectators, like a couple of medical students watching surgical techniques from behind a glass partition.

LAW ENFORCEMENT

Although the English have consistently viewed drug addiction as a medical problem, this does not mean that the police have been dismissed from the drug scene. Possession, selling, and importing most dangerous drugs are against the law.

An addict can go to a government clinic and, after convincing doctors of his addiction, obtain free heroin, but this does not mean that anyone can walk around London with a pocketful of "horse" or any other opiate. Possession of heroin, methadone, and similar dangerous drugs is illegal without a prescription. In the case of heroin, the only source of such a prescription is a government clinic.

Marijuana and hashish are illegal, period. There are no prescriptions given for these drugs and no medical "cover" exists to protect the owner of them. In England, they are clearly the number-one illegal drug, and their use continues to rise along with the arrest statistics of those who are caught with them. From 1968 to 1970, the number of *cannabis* offenses more than doubled—from 3,071 to 7,520. In 1970, *cannibis* seizures amounted to 1¼ tons.

Unlike the United States, Britain has no national police agency for drugs. For that matter, if there is no equivalent to the U.S. Bureau of Narcotics and Dangerous Drugs, neither is there one for the Federal Bureau of Investigation. Scotland Yard is essentially a London agency, and, when a Scotland Yard man is found looking for clues on some fog-shrouded English moor (usually in a paperback detective thriller), he is there on loan from London. In short, there is no national police force.

Drug squads have been created largely because of need or, sometimes, because of the personal interest of an individual police officer. These squads have no nationwide resources available to them either from an enforcement or from a training point of view. Drug-squad members, including the higher-echelon officers in charge of them, are largely self-educated about drugs. Even Scotland Yard's Drug Squad is likely to have a director today who next month or next year may be shifted to a completely different area of police work.

However, this does not mean that expertise has not built up. There is no better example of expertise constructed largely out of self-developed personal interest than Detective Sergeant Alan Russell, who heads the drug squad in Portsmouth. If a national police drug force ever should be established, as some are urging, Sergeant Russell should have a prominent role in it on the basis of his record in Portsmouth.

Russell has an excellent, and unpublicized, working relationship with Dr. Christie of the Portsmouth drug clinic: Christie doesn't squeal on addicts and Russell doesn't give away police plans, but it is clear from the way the two men speak of each other that each has developed a warm respect for the other's approach to addiction. The addicts appear to respect Russell as well. When the residents of Alpha Unit, the therapeutic community directed by Dr. Christie, decided to hold an open house, they invited Russell, even though he had arrested a number of them on past occasions.

Because of the Christie-Russell liaison—and addicts corroborate it—there is virtually no black market in heroin or methadone in the Portsmouth area. In 1969, Russell's squad arrested two persons for possessing heroin, and this involved only minute traces found in a syringe. During the entire year, there were 12 to 15 methadone-possession arrests.

Russell, however, regards opiate addiction as only a small part of his concern. "Dependence on opiate drugs is only the tip of the iceberg," he says. "You have millions of people in this country who are dependent on barbiturates and amphetamines."

In the greater Portsmouth area, with a population of about 500,000, he estimates that there are as many as 1,500 users of marijuana, barbiturates, and amphetamines, some of whom may dabble with all of these drugs. This estimate is in marked contrast to the very low numbers of hard-drug addicts—14 in the clinic and 17 in the Alpha Unit therapeutic community.

Possibly in part because of his respect for Dr. Christie, Portsmouth's chief drug police officer has a very positive attitude toward the clinics. "Make no mistake about it—and some people tend to forget it—a few years ago this country had a serious heroin problem."

In London, there is considerable criticism of the clinics among members of Scotland Yard's Drug Squad, although not a single police officer whom I interviewed was willing to scrap the clinics. Several officers thought that some clinic doctors were still being conned by addicts into issuing larger prescriptions than required. However, all the officers agreed that overprescribing had been reduced drastically since preclinic days.

As an example that the problem has not been eliminated entirely, they cite a case in 1969: A member of the squad searched the apartment of a longtime addict who had been receiving drugs from one of the central London clinics before his death. The search uncovered a horde of heroin—900 tablets or 9,000 milligrams, worth more than $2,100 on the British black market and easily three times as much on the U.S. market. Although there was no evidence that the addict had been selling from this cache, the police felt strongly that it corroborated their overprescribing charge.

Furthermore, police are annoyed that there is no limit on the amount an addict with a clinic prescription may carry. Recently, they stopped an addict with 40 grains (2,400 milligrams) of heroin. He told officers he had been reducing his prescribed quantity, and no arrest was possible, even though the police strongly doubted his story.

Yet, such dramatic anecdotes are the exception. A review of squad arrest records shows that, from the beginning of June to September 7, 1970 (the date of the interview), there hadn't been a single heroin arrest and only two methadone-possession arrests. (These were not the only London drug arrests; for, although the squad is the only police unit concerned solely with drugs, other London policemen make drug arrests in the course of their regular activities.)

Some members of the drug squad frankly admit that they would be in trouble if heroin were completely outlawed. None is campaigning for such a move. One top drug-squad officer, a critic of the present clinic approach ("They sustain addiction . . . there is no place in England where a drug addict can be cured") is not interested in abolishing them, either. He would like to see all drugs administered by the clinics in the clinics. Instead of fourteen separate clinics in London, he would like four open on a twenty-four-hour-a-day, seven-day-a-week basis.

Scotland Yard detectives acknowledge that the clinics have reduced not only the quantity of heroin prescribed but the amount available on the black market. Cocaine, they say, has also been reduced dramatically. Like their colleagues in Portsmouth, however, they are often more concerned about the other drugs that are available on the black market.

The lead drug, of course, is marijuana. They claim that large-scale trafficking is mainly carried on by England's new immigrant population, primarily the Pakistanis. Marijuana comes into England frequently by parcel post directly from the producing countries. Students also bring it in from such well-known drug centers as Morocco.

LSD most often comes from the United States, even though in 1969 English police raided and closed down at least two illicit laboratories producing LSD for both local consumption and export.

There appears to be little organized importation of heroin. What there is generally comes from Hong Kong and is imported by Chinese sailors and distributed by inhabitants of the small Chinese community in London. Addicts generally are not fond of Chinese heroin because of its uncertain strength and, since it comes in powder form, the necessity to heat it in a spoon—in the U.S. mode—before mixing it for injection.

Police acknowledge that one can buy a variety of illicit drugs in the network of side streets in and around Picadilly Circus and in some other areas of London where youth congregate, often in or around the late-night clubs. However, these illicit business enterprises are small and unorganized, particularly in the hard-drug line.

Black-market prices in 1970, according to the addicts and confirmed by clinic physicians and police, are as follows:

Heroin (British-manufactured)	$14.40 a grain (60 mg.)
Heroin (Chinese)	$3.60 a packet (30-60 mg.)
Methadone	$7.20-$12.80 a grain (60 mg.)
Barbiturates	25 cents a capsule

There is no evidence anywhere that large numbers of hard-drug users are supplying themselves from this black market. Furthermore, there is no evidence at all that heroin manufactured in

France—the principal source of supply for U.S. addicts—is being smuggled into England. The market just isn't big enough to make such an enterprise profitable.

Scotland Yard does keep track of international and particularly European illicit-drug activity. Its principal source for this information is not Interpol but the European office of the U.S. Bureau of Narcotics and Dangerous Drugs. The drug-squad detectives express a great deal of respect for their American colleagues and are quick to admit that, if they need information or have a common problem, they will call Paris rather than Interpol. Often, they say, an American narcotics agent will arrive on the next plane.

In 1970, the BNDD for the first time assigned a permanent man to the embassy in London, as part of its over-all European expansion of manpower. A London slot was created because of the LSD traffic from the United States to England and the marijuana and hashish flow from England to the United States.

John T. Cusack, the BNDD's European regional director, is not enthusiastic about the English clinic approach. Of all police officers interviewed, he was the most strongly negative about the clinic program. "The clinics are not going to work giving away heroin. They are going to sustain and create some addicts," he said.

He had three principal objections: "[1] It fools society. It kids all of us that it's doing a job when it isn't doing a job. [2] The addicts will take what they can get from the clinics and then they will get some more from the outside. [3] The clinics flirt with a conflict of the Hypocratic oath of the medical profession. They sustain a medical-psychiatric sickness." (This argument is also made by some British physicians, like Dr. Ian James, a British prison psychiatrist.)

Cusack, however, is not a throw-them-all-in-jail police officer. He wants medical treatment for addicts and believes that governments don't spend anywhere near what they should on hospital care for addicts. "I feel so strongly about it that I'd like to sweep up all the addicts off the New York streets and put them into hospitals. It's incredible to me to leave addicts on the street. It's a big, expensive job to bring them in, but we don't let our mental patients run loose, do we?"

If Cusack strongly disagrees with the English clinic philosophy, his London police colleagues sharply differ with their American counterparts over one vital aspect of the drug problem: the connection between crime and addiction. *No one in England—from the toughest London detective to the most liberal-prescribing clinic physician—suggested to me that narcotics addiction increases criminal behavior.* This does not mean, of course, that drug addicts are crime-free. On the contrary, a significant number of addicts engage in criminal behavior, and some criminals are addicts. But in England there is no cause-and-effect relationship.

Scotland Yard says it in writing. In a 1970 report, its drug expert wrote: "There is no concrete evidence to connect any particular criminal activity with those dependent on the 'hard' drugs (e.g., heroin) but without doubt, the increasing demand for the amphetamine-type drugs leads to thefts from chemists' premises, hospitals, and, in a smaller degree, to thefts of prescription forms."

Study after study documents the fact that sticking a needle into his arm doesn't propel a man into the robber and burglar fraternity. More likely, he will have been initiated long before. What these studies do show is that addicts often have a whole series of antisocial "hang-ups," of which addiction is just one more on the lengthy list.

In the previously cited 1970 study of 111 heroin addicts attending London clinics, 51 per cent reported a conviction for a non-drug offense *before* their first use of heroin.[8] Thrity-six per cent reported such a conviction since using heroin.

A 1967 study of 50 addict-criminals in London prisons again indicates that a track record in court and prison often is established before track marks on the subject's arms.[9] Brixton Prison psychiatrist Ian James found that 22 addicts had a history of juvenile-court conviction and 16 had adult-court convictions prior to heroin addiction. In all, "Three quarters had a history of court convictions *predating* their addiction to narcotics, and there was usually a story of personal and social maladjustment dating from adolescence (educational dropout, employment instability, sociopathic conduct, etc.)."

Ten of the subjects had been convicted only since they became addicted, but only two were in prison for their very first conviction. Dr. James found, too, that, if one discounts drug convictions, fewer convictions for crimes were recorded *after* addiction than before.

Although it is risky to draw conclusions about United States addicts based on English findings, one young American doctor did suggest that what was true about preaddiction delinquency in Britain may be even more valid in the United States. Dr. Michael Paris, formerly on the staff of the Federal Hospital for Addict Rehabilitation at Lexington, Kentucky, worked with Dr. Bewley in 1970 in his London clinics. Asked to compare U.S. and British addicts, he said that the Americans he saw at Lexington had had at least twice as much antisocial behavior in their early teens as the London addicts.

In the first study of heroin users in a provincial town, investigators found a reduction rather than an increase in crime after addiction began. Twenty of 37 heroin users had been convicted of breaking the law.[10]

> The crimes not involving drugs were generally petty in nature, such as stealing two pints of milk, minor shopliftng, and taking and driving away a motor vehicle. Of the ten people who had been convicted of nondrug offenses, three had committed them before using any drugs at all, and seven between first trying drugs and first trying heroin. There was only one person who was convicted of a nondrug offense after heroin use began, and this person had already been convicted of such a crime before the onset of heroin use.

These findings prompted investigators to suggest further research:

> Many of our subjects were in full-time employment or were full-time students; most were still living at home with their parents, a high proportion of whom knew of their heroin use. Although there were instances of nondrug crime before heroin use began, there was only one such conviction (a second offense) afterwards. Whether drug use is for some people an "alternative" to other types of delinquent behavior is a question which suggests itself for investigation and remains open, but it is clear that our sample in no way constitutes a drifting criminal subculture.

RESEARCH

Until 1967, research in drug addiction in England depended on the personal interest of a physician. A handful of doctors wrote papers based on their personal experiences with addicts. Public awareness of the problem still was slight, and concern and knowledge among doctors in general were not much greater. Funds for research simply were not available.

Today, the veterans of the predrug-crisis era continue to produce papers for both national and international medical publications, but they have been joined not only by individual newcomers but by a government-supported research project as well.

The Addiction Research Unit is a kind of scientific conglomerate that investigates three of man's major vices—drinking, smoking, and drug addiction. The unit, a part of the Department of Psychiatry of London University's Institute of Psychiatry, began in 1964 as an alcoholism research group. In 1967, after the Brain Committee report was translated into legislation and public concern heightened with the catapulting addiction statistics, political pressure prompted the Health Department to provide funds for drug-addiction research. Drug investigations were added to the unit's agenda, and sufficient funds were supplied to construct a separate building on the grounds of Maudsley Hospital. Research on smoking was added in 1969.

Each area of investigation has a separate staff and coordinator, with the largest number in the drug-addiction field. Dr. Griffith Edwards, whose earlier interest was in alcoholism, is director of the entire unit, and Dr. David V. Hawks, a psychologist, is coordinator of the eleven-man (and woman) Drug Research Group.

Another organization, the Institute for the Study of Drug Dependence, a privately financed group, does no clinical research, although it is looking for funds to finance both clinical and other investigations. The Institute, with Sir Harry Greenfield as board chairman, is directed by a retired foreign-service officer with a personal interest in addiction. In the two years since it began, this struggling enterprise—financed by small foundation grants—has carved out a useful function as an information clearinghouse. It is the one place in England where a researcher can find extensive, indexed, and easily available material on the English drug scene as well as numerous items involving other countries.

Until now, the national Department of Health has done no specific drug-addiction research of its own. In 1970, a joint committee of the Health Department and the Home Office was created primarily to try to straighten out the sometimes confused drug statistics. It recommended establishment of a Drugs Research Group to be staffed by both agencies. While no specific research program was proposed, the committee suggested the following areas of investigation:

1. Developing a typology of heroin users.
2. Measuring the effectiveness of different forms of treatment in the existing clinics.
3. Comparing the effectiveness of compulsory treatment (in prison) with voluntary treatment in hospitals.

More important, perhaps, was the committee's recommendation that statistical information be compiled on all persons addicted to *any* dangerous drug in England and Wales. The Department of Health is now building such a data bank, which already includes a total of 2,400 names, with the basic information obtained when an addict applies to a clinic or is hospitalized. Other government statistical records to be tapped include:

1. Dates and causes of death from the General Register office.
2. Admissions and length of stay in psychiatric hospitals from the Department of Health and Social Security records.
3. Details of employment histories, sickness and unemployment payments from the Department of Health and Social Security's Mental Health Inquiry Records.
4. Criminal records and prison statistics from the Home Office Statistical Division.

This will be a vital resource for investigators and will open numerous research opportunities into drug addiction in England.

THE STATISTICS

How accurate are the drug statistics in England today?

It is difficult to generalize. Some statistics are clearly more solid than others. A number of persons interviewed expressed skepticism about the validity of one or more sets of statistics. Included among the skeptics was a Department of Health official who works with the drug numbers.

The problem with the statistics is that reporting depends on individual physicians and clinic personnel whose information is not channeled through a system of cross-checks. The new Health Department data bank should help to improve the accuracy of some of these statistics.

Among the numerical data available, the clinic figures reporting quantities of drugs prescribed appear to be least open to significant error. Apart from an occasional bookkeeping mistake, these statistics should accurately reflect the downward trend of heroin use and the rise in methadone.

The monthly clinic-attendance figures should stand up. However, the number of new addicts that clinics report every month may be a somewhat soft statistical area, because clinics may vary in their definition of a new addict.

The clinic figures for the percentage of addicts employed could be on the high side, since "employment" depends on the individual's definition, and the accuracy of the addict's statements is questionable. The data bank, which will include employment records based on social-security information, should provide a cross-check for these claims.

The vital Home Office figures on addicts have to be separated into addicts reported any time during the year and addicts known to be receiving drugs at the end of the year.

The figures for the total year tend to be accepted as reasonably correct by those interviewed, with the general acknowledgment that obviously not every addict in England is known to the Home Office. However, no one suggested that the number of "unknowns" is as large as the numbers listed. Opiate addiction, under the English drug approach, is difficult to conceal if it is taking place on any significant scale. The highest estimate for unreported opiate use was 25 per cent, but this guesstimate included occasional users as well as addicts.

The Home Office figures for 1968 may be unusually high because inauguration of the clinics may well have flushed out previously unknown addicts. As a result, the tiny increase in the total 1969 figures may not accurately reflect the degree of change. Not until the end of 1970 did England have a firm statistical basis for concluding that the narcotic-addiction spiral of the 1960's had been halted.

RESULTS

There is a shortage of hard statistical data about the success or failure of Britain's drug approach, either before or after the clinic program was begun. Most available evaluations were done prior to the inauguration of the clinic program. These do not generate applause.

For example, in 1968, a study of 1,271 heroin addicts who became known to the Home Office between 1947 and 1966 showed that 70 per cent were still taking opiates in 1966.[11] Of the nontakers, some 293 addicts—64 per cent—were in prison, hospital, or other institutions, and 89 were dead, the majority as a result of overdose, suicide, or sepsis.

The death rate among English addicts has been very high—according to the Bewley study, twice as high as among U.S. addicts. However, this study was conducted prior to the clinic program, when British addicts were receiving huge amounts of heroin prescribed by general practitioners. The death rate among addicts included in this review was 28 times greater than the rate for the equivalent age group in the general population.

Studies of withdrawal treatment in hospitals are not more encouraging. In one follow-up of 23 hospital admissions, 12 relapsed within a week, five within a month, and three within two months. Only three were still avoiding narcotics three months after discharge.[12]

Like their American brethren, the English today have no file folder marked "cures"; there is no computer printout on clinic performance that supports either the critics or the defenders of the program.

There is, however, a cautious thread of optimism that runs through conversations with clinic directors and also a surprising degree of candor in identifying areas of shortcoming and outright failure. Furthermore, these subjective evaluations by different directors generally make nearly identical points of both promise and disappointment. Finally, they are echoed by those who have no particular vested interest in the clinics.

Dr. Margaret Tripp, a doctor at St. Clement with no previous experience with drug addicts, frankly admits that her charges conned her in the beginning. Two years later she said: "I think we are controlling legal heroin. Much to my surprise, we have stabilized the addicts—they're not dead, and they are better. They are more stable than before; their drug use has gone down, they work longer, and they are less of a nuisance to everybody."

Dr. Tripp chooses her words very carefully: "Three or four of the [present] cases are reasonably off drugs."

Dr. Willis, at St. Giles, also avoids words like "success" and "cure." He also cites the drop in heroin and agrees that the rise of addiction has slowed. "It's been possible to mount a general tidying-up operation. They are more stable now than they were a year ago. Their general appearance is better. They are not asking for more drugs, and they are not claiming as much drug loss [in order to obtain replacements] as they did before."

Dr. Connell, who is among the handful of English drug-treatment veterans, a consultant to the national Health Department and director of the Maudsley Hospital drug clinic, summed it up this way:

I'm pleased that the frightening curve of heroin addiction has leveled off. I'm disturbed that methadone and barbiturates have risen. In terms of containing the heroin problem, they [the clinics] are successful. They have provided some treatment services where none have existed. All of the terrible prognostications of American workers in the drug field have been unfounded. But [Dr. Connell added] in terms of research they are a failure.

Similar sentiments are voiced by those who are being asked to evaluate their own work.

Even the most hardened policeman—as we noted in the law-
enforcement section—is not prepared to suggest that England
should scrap the clinics. Despite the grumbling about doctors who
are either too softhearted—in the eyes of the police—or simply
conned by addicts, the interviewer is left with the distinct impression that even law-enforcement officers believe that the hard-drug
picture has improved somewhat.

Among druggists, there also is cautious optimism for the clinic
approach. For example, Jerry Young, chief chemist at Boots Picadilly, says flatly:

> I'm very pleased with the clinic system. I'd even be more pleased
> if they'd take the whole thing in their hands [administer drugs
> directly in the clinics]. We see more stability in the addicts. They
> don't come in making exorbitant demands on our service and our
> time. The genuine addicts are less of a nuisance. On the whole, they
> look physically better. They respond better.

Asked for some tangible proof of his assessment, Mr. Young
said that, prior to the spring of 1968, when the clinics began, he
had to call the police on the average of twice a week to control
an unruly addict in his pharmacy. Now, he said, he can't remember a recent call for police assistance with a clinic addict. Occasionally, he asks police help with a forged prescription or when
someone under the influence of barbiturates makes a disturbance.

Mr. Young's analysis, like those of the physicians who send
him prescriptions, is subjective. However, there are at least a few
statistical indications—developed since the clinic program began
—that tend to support these assumptions. To find them, you have
to go to an institution dealing with a considerably larger clientele
than drug addicts.

Brixton Prison, with its incongruous flower-filled inner court-
yard, is to London what the Tombs is to New York. It is a re-
mand prison, where all London-area male prisoners are brought
while awaiting trial. There are 12,000 "receptions" there annually.

Brixton, in 1970, had on its staff the one man who may have
seen more English drug addicts personally than any other individual. Dr. Ian James, the prison psychiatrist, has a long interest

in drug addiction. His small prison office is lined with maps showing the routes by which drugs come to England, the location of addict arrests in London, the location of clinics, the arrests of those who are off drugs—all appropriately marked in clusters of multicolored pins.

In 1969, Dr. James saw 223 drug addicts who were at Brixton for both drug and other offenses. They represented about 10 per cent of all heroin addicts reported to the Home Office during the year. Significantly, Dr. James said it was rarely that he saw an addict unknown to the Home Office.

Dr. James in the past has been a vocal opponent of the clinic program. His opposition was based largely on medical ethics.

Nobody prescribes two bottles of gin a day with duly enriched Vitamin B for alcoholics. The doctor knows that the addict will use an unsanitary procedure to satisfy his habits. He will take unsterile pills [heroin tablets], hold them in his sweaty hand, and put them in a syringe which he pulls from his grimy pocket. What kind of medicine is that?

But Dr. James's own statistics are softening his anticlinic stand to the point where he said: "I think the clinics are succeeding, but on the wrong premises."

Dr. James's accounting may not give overwhelming proof to the statement that the clinics are having a positive impact, but it does add some significant bone behind the subjective flesh of cautious optimism.

In 1970, a third fewer drug addicts were admitted to Brixton than during the previous year. Almost three-fourths of all addicts received at Brixton in 1970 were attending a drug-addiction clinic prior to their arrest. In 1968, only three-fifths of the drug addicts were clinic-registered.

These statistics not only buttress the cautious optimism of English drug experts but also cast doubt on any contention that there is a large addict population unknown to the Home Office or to the clinics. If such an "unknown" addict pool in fact existed, sustaining itself from the high-priced black market, a significant number of its members surely would appear periodically inside the steel gates of Brixton.

There are other substantive indications that the narcotics situation is improving. At three London centers, the number of addicts holding jobs almost doubled in two years. In these same clinics, a series of urine tests given a year apart showed that, while many addicts still were taking more and different drugs than those prescribed, such misuse had been reduced.[13] In yet another survey, there were fewer arrests a year after addicts had been with a clinic than before.

But what does all this mean for the United States? What relevance does it have to America's ever-increasing narcotics problem? In the past, almost all visiting American drug experts have said flatly: None.[14] The two countries, they said, are just too different. Not only do some key narcotics laws point in opposite directions, but the two societies' traditions, youth culture, and race problems are so disparate that what works in the row houses of London could not possibly work in the walk-ups of New York.

A young researcher at the Addiction Research Unit may well have given an explosive jolt to such blanket dismissals. Jim Zacune, a social psychologist, in 1970 examined in detail the performance of Canadian addicts in their native land and after they emigrated to England. His study is significant to the U.S.-Britain narcotics-policy argument, since Canada's approach to opiate addiction is largely patterned after ours.

Zacune traced and interviewed 25 of the 91 Canadian addicts who are known to have come to England in the 1960's. The rest of the émigrés could not be located or had either died or been deported. For those he was able to interview, Zacune compared work records, prison records, and crime records in the two countries. He diplomatically says that his findings should not be used to condemn one country's addiction approach while praising another's, and cautions that his sample may have included the most stable of the Canadians who packed up their syringes for England. But his findings are nevertheless startling:

- At home, the Canadians spent 25 per cent of their addicted years, a combined total of 141 years and 2 months, in jail; in England, less than 2 per cent, a combined total of 2 years and 5 months.

- At home, they compiled 182 offenses; in England, 27.
- At home, in the high addict-crime category of theft, which included robbery and burglary, they committed 88; in England, 8.

Not only did they commit far fewer crimes, but, while in England, many of them were crime-free. In Canada, 16 of the 25 had committed five or more crimes, with one of them recording more than 20 separate offenses. In Britain, none committed more than four offenses and nearly half (12) were never charged with any unlawful behavior.

Despite the fact that the Canadians consumed far more daily heroin than the London average, many of them became job holders and led fairly normal lives while in England. Their living accommodations were far more stable. In Canada, only five had a constant residence for more than three years; in England, ten had lived at their present address for two or more years, eight for one to two years, and five for less than one year. Two were in the hospital at the time of the survey.

The employment record showed the most dramatic difference between the two countries. In Canada, only one addict claimed to have worked steadily while addicted. In England, the majority (13) worked full-time, and four worked part-time. Six had held the same job for at least three years. Seven had semiskilled or skilled manual jobs, two were office workers, one in sales, and one worked as a croupier. One was a full-time housewife and one a student. "For once we could work and live like humans," the addicts said. The interviews contained again and again this and other personal and pragmatic assessments. "There is less trouble from the police . . . we don't constantly have to be paranoid . . . there is less pressure . . . there is no need to steal."

This study may encompass too small and special a group of addicts to permit definitive conclusions. But, together with the other fragmentary evidence, it suggests that the English approach is an alternative not to be dismissed summarily, as it is in a widely distributed U.S. Government pamphlet, which claims that "The British system is considered a failure and has been modified to meet the increasing problem of addiction."[15]

PERSONAL OBSERVATIONS

For the American visitor, the most pervasive impression of the English drug scene comes in the form of a question:

Why has the United States, decade after decade, continuously viewed narcotics addiction as largely a criminal, instead of a medical, problem?

With all its imperfections and inconsistencies, the British approach to drug addiction convinced me that the United States will never make significant headway with the drug problem until it shifts the emphasis from the criminal to the medical. Until this national policy is changed, American addicts will continue to be an ostracized subculture—morally exiled and often barred from the very medical and social-work help they need so desperately, but physically very much present in the criminal countdown of the larger society, which has had to lock itself behind doors for the luxury of guarding an unworkable dogma.

Until this national policy is changed, the black market will continue to flourish no matter how many more narcotics agents are enlisted, and daily will help to infect others, because of the astronomical profits to be made.

Based on my research in England, I believe that the United States should experiment with both a methadone- and a heroin-maintenance program under more controlled and restrictive conditions than generally prevail in Britain today.

I believe that England provides significant research opportunities about the effects of different opiates, which could fill the knowledge void that is plaguing the addiction field in so many countries. For example, what is the precise difference between the effects of heroin and of injected and oral methadone? What are the differences in work performance, antisocial behavior, and life-styles among addicts who use heroin and injectable and oral methadone? Because heroin addicts can be observed in England under relatively controlled circumstances, a whole series of comparative clinical and sociological studies are possible.

No simple "yes" or "no" answer can be given to the question: "Is the British approach to addiction a success or a failure?" The question itself may not be valid in a field that has so much difficulty with the word "success." A more accurate question may be: Is the British approach to addiction helpful or harmful? Even then, the answer may only be "Yes, but . . ."

Can the British and American approaches to addiction legitimately be compared? The study of Canadian addicts' performance in England certainly suggests that such comparisons no longer can be dismissed out of hand. In England, at least, comparisons are made. Everywhere I went, opinion on this was uniform. On my final day in London, a Home Office official, whose knowledge of drug addiction has brought him an international reputation, summed it up:

"We don't want to force our system on you, but for God's sake don't bring your system over here."

1. The Second Report of the Interdepartmental Committee on Drug Addiction (Brain Committee), para. 22, July 31, 1965.

2. There are about 500 British physicians licensed to prescribe heroin and cocaine to addicts. This is a far larger figure than the actual number of physicians working within the drug clinics. However, a special license to prescribe these drugs has become part of the British medical profession's kitbag of status symbols. The Home Office is hopeful of reducing this figure.

3. That is enough heroin to support over 800 American addicts with a $20-a-day habit for an entire year.

4. National Health Service, The Treatment and Supervision of Heroin Addiction, memorandum issued March 7, 1967.

5. Ramon Gardner and P. H. Connell, "One Year's Experience in a Drug-Dependence Clinic," *The Lancet* (1970), pp. 455–58.

6. G. V. Stimson and A. C. Agborne, *A Survey of a Representative Sample of Addicts Prescribed Heroin at London Clinics,* Addiction Research Unit, 1970.

7. Martin Mitcheson *et al.,* "Sedative Abuse by Heroin Addicts," *The Lancet* (March 21, 1970), pp. 606–7.

8. *Op. cit.,* p. 370.

9. I. Pierce James, "Delinquency and Heroin Addiction in Britain," *British Journal of Criminology* (April, 1969).

10. Kosviner *et al.,* "Heroin Use in a Provincial Town," *The Lancet* (1968), i, pp. 1189–92.

11. Bewley, ben-Arie, James, "Survey of Heroin Addicts Known to the Home Office," *British Medical Journal* (1968), 1, pp. 727–30.

12. Zacune, Mitcheson, and Malone, "Heroin Use in a Provincial Town—One Year Later," *International Journal of the Addictions* (1969), IV, 557–70.

13. Bewley, James, and Mahon, "Effectiveness of Prescribing Clinics for

Narcotic Addicts in the United Kingdom," 1968–70. A paper, presented at the International Symposium on Drug Abuse, University of Michigan, Ann Arbor, on November 9, 1970, evaluating the efficacy of such clinics.

14. Among the few exceptions was Professor Alfred R. Lindesmith of Indiana University, who has concerned himself with the drug problem for more than thirty-five years. He was a defender of the British view of addicts as sick people long before England moved to the clinic approach. Because of these views, Professor Lindesmith has been one of the academic *bêtes noirs* of the old U.S. Bureau of Narcotics, predecessor to the present BNDD, as well as to the drug professionals who in the past shared its addicts-are-criminals view.

15. A Federal Source Book: *Answers to the Most Frequently Asked Questions About Drug Abuse* (Government Printing Office, 1970), p. 25.

THE CONTRIBUTORS

Patricia M. Wald is a graduate of the Yale Law School. She has served as a member of the District of Columbia Crime Commission; as a consultant to the President's Commission on Law Enforcement and the Administration of Justice, the National Advisory Commission on Civil Disorders, and the National Commission on the Causes and Prevention of Violence; and as a staff attorney for Neighborhood Legal Services and for the Center for Law and Social Policy. Since January 1, 1972, she has been a member of the Board of Trustees of the Ford Foundation.

Peter Barton Hutt is a graduate of Exeter Academy, Yale University, and the Harvard Law School. At the time of the study, he was a partner in the Washington law firm of Covington & Burling, and at present he is General Council of the Food and Drug Administration. He is a member of the National Academy of Sciences' Institute of Medicine and has been deeply involved in medical and governmental projects involving alcoholism and drug abuse.

James V. DeLong is also a graduate of the Harvard Law School. He has been a litigation attorney, a Special Assistant in the Department of Housing and Urban Development, and a Senior Staff Member of the Program Evaluation Staff of the U.S. Bureau of the Budget. He now works for the Drug Abuse Council.

Peter A. Wilson, a graduate of Princeton University, is finishing his dissertation in political science at the University of Chicago. He is also a consultant to the Rand Corporation.

John F. Holahan holds a doctorate in economics from Georgetown University. He is now at the Urban Institute working on health-economics problems.

Annette Abrams is a graduate of Howard University. She has been a Staff Assistant to a Midwestern senator and a member of the Staff of the National Coordinating Council on Drug Education. She now works for the Drug Abuse Council.

Peter B. Goldberg is a graduate of the State University of New York at Albany and is finishing the requirements for a graduate degree in urban planning at George Washington University. He now works for the Drug Abuse Council.

Paul A. Henningsen, a former legislative assistant and press secretary to a Midwestern congressman, has also been involved in the promotion of minority business development. He now works for the Drug Abuse Council.

Dr. Andrew T. Weil is a graduate of Harvard Medical School. He is a co-author of some of the first clinical studies of marijuana done in this country in modern times and of a recent book on drugs. At present, he is engaged in a study of drug use among Indians in South America.

Edgar May holds a degree in journalism from Northwestern University. He has been a reporter for several newspapers and has won numerous journalistic awards, including the Pulitzer Prize. From 1964 to 1968 he was with the Office of Economic Opportunity, first as Special Assistant to the Director and then as Director of the Office of Inspection. Subsequently he was Special Adviser to the United States Ambassador to France. He is now a free-lance journalist based in Paris.